Henri Lefebvre

Henri Lefebvre

Key Writings

Edited by
STUART ELDEN, ELIZABETH LEBAS
and
ELEONORE KOFMAN

continuum
NEW YORK • LONDON

This work is published with the support of the French Ministry of Culture – Centre national du livre.
This book is supported by the French Ministry for Foreign Affairs, as part of the Burgess programme
headed for the French Embassy In London by the Institut Français du Royaume-Uni.

Liberté • Égalité • Fraternité
RÉPUBLIQUE FRANÇAISE

CONTINUUM
The Tower Building, 11 York Road, London SE1 7NX
370 Lexington Avenue, New York, NY 10017-6503

First published 2003

Editorial Material © Stuart Elden, Elizabeth Lebas and Eleonore Kofman
Original Extracts © Publishers
English Language Translations © Continuum
'Unity of Doctrine', English Language Translation © John Sturrock
'The Worldwide Experience', Engish Language Translaton © Norbert Guterman
'The Style of the Commune', English Language Translation © Elizabeth Lebas
'The Worldwide Experience', English Language Translation © Elizabeth Lebas

All rights reserved. No part of this publication may be reproduced or
transmitted in any form or by any means, electronic or mechanical,
including photocopying, recording or any information storage or retrieval
system, without prior permission in writing from the publishers.

British Library Cataloguing-in-Publication Data
A catalogue record for this book is available from the British Library.

ISBN 0-8264-6645-1 (hardback)
　　　0-8264-6646-x (paperback)

Typeset by Aarontype Limited, Easton, Bristol
Printed and bound in Great Britain by MPG Books Ltd, Bodmin, Cornwall

Contents

Acknowledgements	vii
Introduction: Coming to Terms with Lefebvre – Stuart Elden and Elizabeth Lebas	xi

Marxism and Philosophy
Introduction – Stuart Elden	3
Retrospections (from *L'Existentialisme*, 1946)	6
Unity of the Doctrine (from *Dialectical Materialism*, 1939)	14
Prolegomenas (from *Métaphilosophie*, 1965)	22
Marxian Thought and Sociology (from *The Sociology of Marx*, 1966)	31
Beyond Structuralism (from *Au-delà du structuralisme*, 1971)	37
Hegel, Marx, Nietzsche (from *Hegel, Marx, Nietzsche ou le royaume des ombres*, 1975)	42
Triads and Dyads (from *La Présence et l'absence*, 1980)	50
Twelve Theses on Logic and Dialectic (from *Logique formelle, logique dialectique*, 3rd edn, 1982)	57
State (from *Le Retour de la dialectique*, 1986)	61
Becoming and the Historical (from *Le Retour de la dialectique*, 1986)	65

The Critique of Everyday Life
Introduction – Elizabeth Lebas	69
Mystification: Notes for a Critique of Everyday Life (Henri Lefebvre and Norbert Guterman, *Avant Poste*, 2 [1933])	71
Elucidations (from *Critique de la vie quotidienne II: Fondements d'une sociologie de la quotidienneté*, 1961)	84
The Social Text (from *Critique de la vie quotidienne II: Fondements d'une sociologie de la quotidienneté*, 1961)	88
The End of Modernity? (from *Critique de la vie quotidienne III: De la modernité au modernisme (Pour une métaphilosophie du quotidien)*, 1981)	93
On Vulgarity (from *Critique de la vie quotidienne III: De la modernité au modernisme (Pour une métaphilosophie du quotidien)*, 1981)	96

Myths in Everyday Life (from *Cahiers Internationaux de Sociologie*, XXXIII (1962))   100

The Country and the City
Introduction – Eleonore Kofman   109
Perspectives on Rural Sociology (from *Cahiers Internationaux de Sociologie*, XIV (1953))   111
Preface to the Study of the Habitat of the 'Pavillon' (from *L'Habitat Pavillonnaire*, 1966)   121
Levels and Dimensions (from *La Révolution urbaine*, 1970)   136
The Other Parises (from *Espaces et Sociétés*, 13/14 (1974–5)   151

History, Time and Space
Introduction – Stuart Elden   163
The Inventory (from *La Somme et le reste*, 1959)   166
Time and History (from *La Fin de l'histoire*, 1970)   177
The Style of the Commune (from *La Proclamation de la commune*, 1965)   188
The Rhythmanalytical Project (Henri Lefebvre and Catherine Régulier, *Communications*, 41 (1985))   190
The Worldwide Experience (from *De l'Etat*, Vol IV, 1978)   199
Preface to the New Edition (from *La Production de l'espace*, 3rd edn, 1986)   206

Politics
Introduction – Elizabeth Lebas   217
Nation and Culture (from Norbert Guterman and Henri Lefebvre, *La Conscience mystifiée*, 1936)   220
Between Yourself and You (from Norbert Guterman and Henri Lefebvre, *La Conscience mystifiée*, 1936)   229
Being a Communist (from *La Somme et le reste*, 1959)   231
From the Social Pact to the Contract of Citizenship (from *Du Contrat de citoyenneté*, 1990)   238
Some Questions About Asking Questions (from *M: Marxisme, Mensuel, Mouvement*, 7 (Janvier 1987))   255

Notes   258
Index   278

Acknowledgements

The full sources of the extracts are as follows:

MARXISM AND PHILOSOPHY

'Retrospections', *L'Existentialisme* (Paris: Éditions Sagittaire, 1946), pp. 55–66; new edn (Paris: Anthropos, 2001), pp. 40–50; 'Unity of the Doctrine', *Dialectical Materialism*, tr. John Sturrock (London: Jonathan Cape, 1968), pp. 100–13; 'Prolegomenas', *Métaphilosophie: Prolégomènes* (Paris: Les Éditions de Minuit, 1965), pp. 7–19; new edn (Paris: Syllepse, 2000), pp. 23–32; 'Marxian Thought and Sociology', *The Sociology of Marx*, tr. Norbert Guterman (Harmondsworth: Penguin, 1968), pp. 14–24; 'Beyond Structuralism', *Au-delà du structuralisme* (Paris: Anthropos, 1971), pp. 20–5; 'Hegel, Marx, Nietzsche', *Hegel, Marx, Nietzsche ou le royaume des ombres* (Paris: Casterman, 1975), pp. 9–12, 46–52; 'Triads and Dyads', *La Présence et l'absence* (Paris: Casterman, 1980), pp. 143, 225–31; 'Twelve Theses on Logic and Dialectic', *Logique formelle, logique dialectique*, 3e edn (Paris: Terraines Éditions Sociales, 1982), pp. 3–8; 'State', *Le Retour de la dialectique* (Paris: Éditions Sociales, 1986), pp. 17–21; 'Becoming and the Historical', *Le Retour de la dialectique* (Paris: Éditions Sociales, 1986), pp. 40–2.

EVERYDAY LIFE

'Mystification: Notes for a Critique of Everyday Life', Henri Lefebvre and Norbert Guterman, *Avant Poste*, 2 (1933), pp. 91–107; 'Elucidations', *Critique de la vie quotidienne II: Fondements d'une sociologie de la quotidienneté* (Paris: L'Arche, 1961), pp. 74–8; 'The Social Text', *Critique de la vie quotidienne II: Fondements d'une sociologie de la quotidienneté* (Paris: L'Arche, 1961), pp. 306–12; 'The End of Modernity?', *Critique de la vie quotidienne III: De la modernité au modernisme (Pour une métaphilosophie du quotidienne)* (Paris: L'Arche, 1981), pp. 50–2; 'On Vulgarity', *Critique de la vie quotidienne III: De la modernité au modernisme (Pour une métaphilosophie du quotidienne)* (Paris: L'Arche, 1981), pp. 74–8; 'Myths in Everyday Life', *Cahiers Internationaux de Sociologie* (vol. XXXIII; Paris, PUF, 1962).

THE COUNTRY AND THE CITY

'Perspectives on Rural Sociology', *Cahiers Internationaux de Sociologie*, XIV (1953), pp. 22–40; repr. in *Du Rural à l'urbain*, 3ᵉ édn (Paris: Anthropos, 2001), pp. 63–78; 'Préface' in Henri Raymond, Marie-Geneviève Raymond, Nicole Haumont and M. Coornaert, *L'Habitat pavillonnaire* (Paris: Éditions du C.R.U., 1966), pp. 3–13, 14–23; repr. as 'Introduction à l'étude de l'habitat pavillonnaire' in *Du Rural à l'urbain*, 3ᵉ édn (Paris: Anthropos, 2001), pp. 159–70, 171–80; 'Levels and Dimensions', *La Révolution urbaine* (Paris: Gallimard, 1970), pp. 105–10, 113–38; 'The Other Parises', *Espaces et Sociétés*, 13/14 (Octobre 1974–Janvier 1975), pp. 185–90, 192.

HISTORY, TIME AND SPACE

'The Inventory', *La Somme et le reste* (Paris: Méridiens Klincksieck, 1989 [1959]), pp. 642–55; 'The End of History', *La Fin de l'histoire* (Paris: Éditions de Minuit, 1970), pp. 190–1, 195–6, 200–2, 205–6, 211–13, 215–16, 225–9; 2ᵉ édn (Paris: Anthropos, 2001), pp. 162–3, 167–8, 172–4, 176–7, 182–3, 185–6, 193–7; 'The Style of the Commune', *La Proclamation de la commune: 26 mars 1871* (Paris: Gallimard, 1965), pp. 20–3; 'The Rhythmanalytical Project, Henri Lefebvre and Catherine Régulier, *Communications*, 41 (1985), pp. 191–9; 'The Worldwide Experience', *De l'Etat Vol. IV: les contradictions de l'état moderne* (Paris: Collection 10/18, Union Générale d'Éditions, 1978), pp. 413–22, 435–41; 'Preface to the New Edition', *La Production de l'espace*, 3ᵉ édn (Paris: Anthropos, 1986), pp. i–xii; repr. in *La Production de l'espace*, 4ᵉ édn (Paris: Anthropos, 2000), pp. xvii–xxviii.

POLITICS

'Nation and Culture', Norbert Guterman and Henri Lefebvre, *La Conscience mystifiée* (Paris: Syllepse, 1999 [1936]), pp. 81–91; 'Between Yourself and You', Norbert Guterman and Henri Lefebvre, *La Conscience mystifiée* (Paris: Syllepse, 1999 [1936]), pp. 145–6; 'Being a Communist', *La Somme et le reste* (Paris: Méridiens Klincksieck, 1989 [1959]), pp. 683–92; 'From the Social Pact to the Contract of Citizenship', *Du Contrat de citoyenneté* (Paris: Syllepse, 1990), pp. 17–37; 'Some Questions About Asking Questions', *M: Marxisme, Mensuel, Mouvement*, 7 (Janvier 1987), pp. 54.

The publishers and editors have made all possible efforts to trace copyright holders for the pieces included here. In the event that any have been overlooked, the publishers would welcome being informed, and will make full acknowledgement in the next edition.

The editors wish to express their deep gratitude to Imogen Forster, who made the translations of the majority of the selections. Although we have carefully edited and revised these, in order to provide terminological and stylistic consistency, and therefore take full responsibility for them, we are indebted to her. We are also extremely grateful to Tristan Palmer, our editor at Continuum, for his patience and assistance, and to our colleagues and friends who have helped with some of the more arcane footnote problems.

The editors and publishers have made every effort to contact all copyright holders of material excerpted in this book. The publishers will be happy to correct any omissions in further editions.

Introduction:
Coming to Terms with Lefebvre

What does it mean to come to terms with a thinker? How do we understand the way in which their works interrelate, comprehend the influences on their thought and make a judgement about the validity and applicability of their ideas? What does it mean to reappropriate a thinker, to move them into a different context in time and space, to read them in another language? How does their thought travel; how can their ideas be deployed in new situations; what is living and dead in their thought? For Lefebvre, these questions seem particularly important. While books with titles such as *The New Nietzsche*, *The New Spinoza* and *The New Bergson* appear, it would be hard to imagine one entitled *The New Lefebvre*. Although this book appears twelve years after his death and two years after his centenary, Lefebvre is still a thinker who is known in a very narrow way in the English speaking world, who remains to be discovered, rather than rediscovered.

Henri Lefebvre, who was born in 1901 and died a few days after his ninetieth birthday,[1] had a life which spans almost the whole of the twentieth century, and is therefore both near to us and far away. There are aspects of his work which are well known, more which are unfamiliar, and much which remains hidden from view. Though he anticipated contemporary concerns such as cybernetics, globalization, marginality, the demise of rational urban planning and new forms of citizenship, his first published works date from 1924 – the year of Lenin's death – and discuss issues such as André Gide, Dadaism and Ramon Fernandez.[2] While many of his early writings are almost impossible to find today – more than one book was destroyed either during the Nazi invasion of France or by French Communist Party (PCF) censors – his last book appeared in 1992.[3] Indeed, the entirety of his writings have yet to be catalogued and published.

Only a small proportion of Lefebvre's writings are available in English translation. There was a brief flurry of interest in the late 1960s and early 1970s, when four of his books were translated: *Dialectical Materialism*, *The Sociology of Marx*, *The Explosion: Marxism and the French Upheaval* and *Everyday Life in the Modern World*.[4] In 1976 a truncated version of his *The Survival of Capitalism* was published, but this was the last of his books to appear for fifteen years.[5] These presented *a* view of Lefebvre's work, but one that was narrowly confined. Then, just months after his life came to an end, the first volume of the *Critique of Everyday Life* series and *The Production of Space* became available.[6] Interest in Lefebvre sharpened at this point, with appropriations and commentary in a range of fields, particularly in those disciplines largely bereft of Marxist analyses in the 1980s and early 1990s, such as geography, architecture and cultural studies.

In 1995 *Introduction to Modernity* was translated, and this was followed the next year by a collection of some of his work on urbanism in *Writings on Cities*.[7] Although Michael Trebitsch's introduction to *Critique of Everyday Life* and David Harvey's afterword to *The Production of Space* had been significant contributions to the literature on Lefebvre, the introduction to *Writings on Cities* was instrumental in bringing a wider range of Lefebvre's concerns to an English audience. *Writings on Cities* included the full text of *Le Droit à la ville* [*Right to the City*], as well as excerpts from *Espace et politique* [*Space and Politics*], *Elements de rythmanalyse* [*Elements of Rhythmanalysis*] and some interviews and shorter pieces. The editors of that last volume have contributed their selections to this current collection. A number of other books of Lefebvre's are due to appear in translation in the next few years, including volumes two and three of *Critique of Everyday Life*, *La Révolution urbaine* [*The Urban Revolution*] and *Rhythmanalysis*.[8] Even so, over 50 books will not be translated.

Key Writings seeks to contribute to the ongoing project of coming to terms with Lefebvre by showing the range of his work both in terms of subject matter and the date of publication, and its aim is one of complementing, broadening and problematizing dominant English language perceptions of his work. To subsume Lefebvre within any disciplinary boundary is inherently problematic. To portray him as a philosopher, a sociologist, a historian or a political activist would not only fail to do him justice, in terms of the range of topics he discussed, inspired or indeed initiated, but would also allude to a disciplinary categorization which he vigorously repudiated. There is only one category he would have accepted – Marxist – and all that this implies; that is, being a philosopher, sociologist, historian and foremost, politically *engagé*.[9] Nevertheless, his work, in close to 70 books and numerous articles, ranged widely across the social sciences and humanities, and has inspired activists and academics across an equally broad scope.

PRESENCE AND ABSENCE

In attempting to address the gaps in the English reception of Lefebvre's work, this current volume is more likely to reveal them. It seeks not only to demonstrate the range of Lefebvre's concerns but also the different ways he expressed them: sometimes as scholar, sometimes as political intellectual, sometimes as colleague and mentor and even sometimes as companion.[10] In particular it seeks to show how Lefebvre can and should be taken seriously as a philosopher, and particularly as a Marxist philosopher. By philosopher we do not mean simply work done within a philosophy department, but perhaps something closer to the notion of a thinker. The first section of this collection therefore stresses the importance of conceptual and theoretical work, and demonstrates how these writings impact on the more practical analyses, whilst in turn being shaped by this work and reformulated in new ways. One of our aims is to show that Lefebvre is a much more serious thinker than he is generally given credit for.

Another central aim is to show what a political thinker he was. Again this does not mean Lefebvre was what might now be called a political scientist, although some of his work might be categorized in that way, and it is immediately apparent that he had a sound grasp of classical political theory. Rather, as a member of the PCF for almost 30 years, and in some ways even more of a Marxist when he left, Lefebvre was always politically active and aware. A range of the writings chosen reflect these concerns. Along the way other interests are developed. For example, we show how his work on urban issues was complemented by a long-standing interest in rural affairs; and how his influential theorization of space was partnered and indeed often generated by a thinking through of issues around time and history.

Although we have tried to demonstrate the range of Lefebvre's concerns, there have been inevitable losses or, perhaps rather, absences. The most obvious of these is that we have included nothing from the work he did, principally in the late 1940s and 1950s, on key figures within the French intellectual tradition – from writers such as Rabelais and Musset to thinkers such as Descartes and Pascal.[11] One of the reasons Lefebvre worked on such individuals was that he was restricted by the PCF from writing on more explicitly political or philosophical topics, and so he moved to a less obviously contentious area of study. At a time when science in the Soviet Union and the PCF was dominated with the dispute over Lysenko's genetic theories, Lefebvre's claims about logic, dialectics and science were dangerously heretical.[12] Indeed, a book entitled *Méthodologie des sciences* [*Methodology of Sciences*] was printed and then censured on the order of the party. It has recently been published for the first time in France.[13] In this intellectual atmosphere Lefebvre used his studies of seemingly safer writers as a surrogate for other concerns, with long passages of intellectual history, meditations on the historical materialist approach and other more political or philosophical issues.[14] On the other hand it is worth noting that Lefebvre was also the official intellectual of the PCF at this time, mobilized in 1946 to critique existentialism's challenge to Marxism, and here playing a central role in a broader project of appropriating classical authors, that is, French cultural capital, for Marxist purposes.

It would therefore not be true to say that Lefebvre wrote nothing about political or philosophical issues during the period 1947–58 – but more accurate to say that he wrote about them 'in disguise'. The books on literary figures such as Diderot or Rabelais are extremely political; they are both ways of thinking through what historical materialism is, and exercises in putting that into practice. If we put these books in chronological order, we would have a wide-ranging intellectual history of France between the fifteenth and eighteenth centuries. Equally these books anticipate themes developed in other contexts. For example, the book on Rabelais discusses the notion of the *fête*, the festival, which is also important in his studies of May 1968 and the 1871 Paris Commune, as well as more generally in the work on everyday life.[15] The books on Pascal and Descartes are also extremely philosophical – and there are some interesting discussions on issues of spatiality which prefigure the later work of the 1970s.[16]

RECEIVING LEFEBVRE

Assessing the extent of renewal of interest in Lefebvre's thought and work in France, the English-speaking world and elsewhere (Lefebvre's thought has been influential in Germany for example, and he is translated in several other languages), is an important consideration. Assessing the relevance of this reception is another. As was noted above, in the late 1960s and early 1970s there were a number of English translations, but under quite different conditions than those of today: more overtly politicized, less conservative, not yet influenced by postmodernist thinking. Moreover, at this time, although Lefebvre was less officially and more belatedly honoured than his intellectual peers, who included Foucault, Althusser and Lacan, like them, he carried heavy institutional and professional responsibilities and responded to the attentions of the popular and academic media.[17] It is worth noting – though it should be obvious – that French writers who are famous in the Anglophone world are not always considered the same way in their home territory. Foucault, for example, although English language interest has been constant since his first publications, slipped somewhat off the agenda in France until relatively recently.[18]

In short, in the earlier period of interest in the Anglophone world Lefebvre was still alive, and continuing to take both responsibility and control over the assessment of the relevance of his work and thinking. This was effectively integral to his notion of metaphilosophy and was a deep tribute to both classical philosophy and Jansenism – as can be illustrated by his extraordinary text *La Somme et le reste* [*The Sum and the Remainder*] of which two extracts are included in this collection. It is in this book – testament, disputation, elucidation and confession, published shortly after his departure from the PCF in 1958 – that can be found both the conceptual and political means of assessing the relevance of thought and practice for a society, its history and its everyday life, as well as the origins of Lefebvre's own myth-making of himself.

The mythmaking has developed since his death. Indeed, it could be argued that Lefebvre's vitality, perhaps more than his Marxism, is what has appealed to and influenced the present generation of largely English-speaking and male academics. Lefebvre is no longer alive to challenge and be challenged. Reliance, if not overreliance, on Rémi Hess's biography, a somewhat romanticized and muscular account written with Lefebvre's cognizance, may be partly responsible for this.[19] The outcome has tended to be a projected and largely male English-speaking discourse that can tell us almost as much about the crisis underlying the masculine appropriation of ideas and British and American academic identity, as it can about Lefebvre's thought itself. This may of course also be related to the disciplines which English publication of the second wave of translations have addressed themselves to – urban geography, planning and architecture – disciplines not abundantly furnished with female practitioners and scholars. Yet the response to Lefebvre's writings, whether or not in translation, by academics of other disciplines, particularly cultural studies, has shown a different articulation and gendering.[20]

This collection attempts to redirect the reader towards a more critical and heterodox reading of Lefebvre's works. This is appropriate because demolishing myths was one of Lefebvre's first intellectual projects. At the same time, it suggests, particularly in the section on 'The Critique of Everyday Life', that for Lefebvre, women were not only the objects of love and struggle, as indeed they were, but ultimately, the subjects of revolution. For Lefebvre, the future was feminine.

In the past few years Lefebvre has undergone something of a renaissance in France. Hess, the biographer mentioned above, and a former student of Lefebvre, is largely responsible for the current republication of many of his works, some out of print for decades. The publishing houses Anthropos and Syllepse have recently reissued *Métaphilosophie* [*Metaphilosophy*], *La Conscience mystifiée* [*The Mystified Conscience*], *Rabelais*, *L'Existentialisme* [*Existentialism*], *La Production de l'espace*, *Espace et politique*, *Du Rural à l'urbain* [*From the Rural to the Urban*], *La Fin de l'histoire* [*The End of History*], *L'Irruption de Nanterre au sommet* [*The Eruption from Nanterre to the Summit*], *Contribution à l'esthétique* [*Contribution to Aesthetics*], and *La Survie du capitalisme*. As already mentioned, the previously unpublished *Méthodologie des sciences* has also recently been made available. In the near future, Lefebvre's 1939 book *Nietzsche* is due to be reissued. This will be an especially important event. It was a book published by the PCF house press *Éditions Sociales Internationales* and was one of the books seized and burnt by the occupying German forces the following year. To accompany these republications there have been two recent symposia on Lefebvre in Paris, which Hess has also been centrally involved in.[21]

It is notable that in France, while there is an interest in Lefebvre's writings on the urban, everyday life, and space, greater attention is paid to his writings on citizenship, *mondialisation*, capitalism and the state. English language work in these areas has been much sparser. Many other areas of Lefebvre's life and work remain relatively unexplored. *La Somme et le reste* remains largely unknown, despite its insights into politics, philosophy and his own life. Although Lefebvre was a central figure in the PCF for many years, the teacher of Jean Baudrillard and Daniel Cohn-Bendit, a colleague of the Situationists, friendly with surrealists and Dadaists, and cited by Nicos Poulantzas, Jean-Paul Sartre and others, his links to other thinkers are generally neglected in the literature. Despite his interest in the state, Lefebvre is rarely linked into the Miliband-Poulantzas debates within 1970s Marxism. Lefebvre is both close to and distant from Marcuse's work. Less immediately apparent comparisons between Lefebvre, Deleuze, Foucault and Bourdieu present interesting avenues of future research. As we have already hinted, despite the age of some of his works, he acts almost as a prehistorian of contemporary developments, with his insights into technology, globalization, popular protest and post-ideological politics open to all manner of possible uses. We should also note that Lefebvre's thought can remind us that thinking is also 'the lived' and not a substitute for it.

THE PRESENT WORK

One way this collection differs from *Writings on Cities* is the editorial team that has worked on it. Elizabeth Lebas is the common link between the two projects, with her coeditor on *Writings on Cities*, Eleonore Kofman, working with the team on the 'The Country and the City' section. Lebas's other interests are in visual culture and landscape history, and with Kofman she has also written on the relationship between Lefebvre and the Situationist Constant Nieuwenhuys.[22] They have been joined by Stuart Elden, author of a book on Heidegger, Foucault and the relation between space and history, for this collection.[23] Elden is currently writing a book on Lefebvre for Continuum, and has also written some other shorter pieces about him.[24] There has been a division of labour for this project. Apart from the individually named texts, Stuart Elden took the lead on terminological issues and the editor's footnotes, while Elizabeth Lebas supervised the overall translation.

Translating writers is always difficult, and we will not satisfy everyone with the choices we have made. We have, as far as possible, tried to preserve Lefebvre's very personal style of writing. This was a peculiar mixture of neologisms, semantic rigour and plays on words, written in a very disjointed way, with elliptical comments, asides, digressions and inelegancies. His prose was not therefore the most elegant – and neither are the new translations of texts included here. Some existing translations have attempted to smooth over these rough edges: we have preferred to let Lefebvre speak in English as he may have spoken it – and in this endeavour have transgressed some current translation practices. These are entirely our responsibility and not that of our translator, Imogen Forster. There are naturally often moments where English is inadequate to convey Lefebvre's meaning – the wordplay, the subtlety of vocabulary, the neologisms – but by and large Lefebvre presents less problems than other French writers of the twentieth century. In a few instances we have added footnotes to explain a difficult turn of phrase or term; more often we have added a French word or two in brackets.

Editors' footnotes have been added more frequently to explain some of Lefebvre's comments or allusions, to provide English references for quotations, or to give biographical notes on some of the figures to which he refers. Like many writers of his generation, Lefebvre was more than a little sloppy in referencing his work. Whilst we have tried to complete his references, provide English versions where available, and in some cases give a reference where he gave none, this has not always been possible. We hope readers will forgive the few we have been unable to locate. (We should note that the references Lefebvre gives in parentheses in the text have generally been relegated to footnotes.) For the biographical material we have erred on the side of completeness. Many will no doubt find some of these surplus to requirements; but it is difficult to know where to draw the line, and we hope that we have not missed a note where one would have been helpful.[25] Not infrequently, Lefebvre's allusions are shrouded in mystery – referring to people by surname alone in texts pre-World War II for example. At times, educated guesses had to be employed. Lefebvre's own notes are unmarked; editors' notes, or additions to Lefebvre's notes, are marked.

MODE D'EMPLOI – WAYS TO USE THIS BOOK

In editing this book we have chosen to foreground Lefebvre's work on Marxism and Philosophy, before moving onto the more concrete concerns for which he is better known in the English-speaking world, but this is not necessarily the only way to read the book. We believe that there are a number of possible ways into the material presented here, and it should almost go without saying that those we now list are far from exhaustive.

The most obvious, perhaps, is to start with the explicitly theoretical work at the beginning, and then move on to areas of particular concern. By giving precedence to Lefebvre's work on Marxism and philosophy, we hope to provide readers with new means of reading and rereading Lefebvre's more topical works and also to show how concepts travel over time in his thinking. For example, the themes of alienation and consciousness are present almost from the outset and will occupy the centre of his work on everyday life, as will absence and presence. However, later writings in turn illuminate earlier ones – or reveal how Lefebvre often recycled his own work, or more precisely, repositioned recycled work. The themes of time, style and adulthood as myth are cases in point.

Alternatively a reader could start with texts in an area with which they are already familiar. Those who know the first volume of the *Critique of Everyday Life* or *Everyday Life in the Modern World* will find a very early piece on 'Mystification' which sets out many of the ideas explored in later pieces, as well as excerpts from Volumes Two and Three. Those who have an interest in *The Production of Space* will benefit from the first English translation of a preface Lefebvre wrote for later editions, which sets out some self-criticisms and notes areas that he neglected; it is also supplemented by texts on the rural and the urban that prefigure the theoretical summary. In many of these pieces theoretical ideas are developed – the regressive/progressive model for combining sociology and history in 'Contributions to Rural Sociology', the theory of moments in 'The Imaginary', the notion of *dépérissement* (overcoming) and many others.

In the various sections of this book are pieces that we believe complement each other. A reader who began with the Preface to *The Production of Space* could move on to look at Lefebvre's work on history from around the same time, and then from there to the works on the urban and rural, which combine elements of both approaches, back to everyday life, and finally back to philosophy and Marxism. The political texts of the final section are complemented by the section on the 'State' from the 'Marxism and Philosophy' section; the work on 'The End of History' is more theoretically analysed in 'Becoming and the Historical', also in the 'Marxism and Philosophy' section. There are numerous other possibilities. We should note that our organization of texts is thematic rather than chronological, although we have provided a date for the publication of each piece to avoid misunderstandings. Whilst some of his work on a particular theme was also of a particular time – for example the work on the urban in the 1960s and 70s – most of his concerns crossed over the decades of his life. Juxtaposing texts from different times in thematic sections shows the breadth of his concerns and the interconnections between different periods of his life. Of course, given the dating provided, a reader could conceivably read the sections in chronological order.

Our intention, therefore, is that this is not simply a book to be read from the first to the last page, but a range of books in one; that it is a book which complements *Writings on Cities* and other existing translations, rather than replaces them; and that it needs, indeed asks, to be read in a range of ways. Of course, as we noted above, it is not a full guide. The volume of Lefebvre's writing mitigates against such an intention. In that respect it is an outline, a map, a set of directions. If the disposition of texts in this collection has a central aim, it is to encourage the reader to approach lesser known material in order to understand afresh hitherto familiar work. It hopes to offer possibilities for deviations, or as Lefebvre and his former Situationist comrades would have called them, *détournements*. It is our hope that *Key Writings* will introduce a wide range of Lefebvre's topics, whilst simultaneously being an opening toward further study and translation of this writer who, despite writing most of his works in quite different historical and cultural contexts, still has a great deal to say to contemporary concerns.

Stuart Elden and Elizabeth Lebas

Marxism and Philosophy

Introduction

This opening section deals with Lefebvre's writings on philosophy and his interpretation of Marxism. As these concerns are immanent throughout his work, it will deal with the more explicit and theoretical formulations. As well as situating Lefebvre as a philosopher and political theorist, it also sets the tone for many of the later sections of the book, contextualizing his work on everyday life, space, time and history.

Lefebvre's most important influences were Hegel, Marx and Nietzsche – on whom he wrote extensively – but he was also constantly engaged and in debate with the work of Heidegger. Other thinkers of interest included Freud, Lenin and Mao. He was also critical of contemporary interpretations of Marx (notably those of Althusser and Lukács) and with aspects of contemporary thought in general – Foucault, Sartre, Merleau-Ponty, Lévi-Strauss and others. Some of this critical work was at the behest of the Parti Communiste Français for whom he played the role of party intellectual.

Little of Lefebvre's writing in this area has previously been available in English, and the bulk of this section therefore contains newly translated material. Two selections are made of material already in English – from *Dialectical Materialism* and *The Sociology of Marx*. These books are long out of print. As will be seen from the extracts, their importance justifies their inclusion.

The selection of texts is designed to demonstrate the range of Lefebvre's concerns, and to show how he situated himself in relation to other thinkers and patterns of thought. Together they serve a variety of purposes.

First, they make clear how Lefebvre read Marx. Lefebvre was opposed to both the Sartrean and the Althusserian readings of Marx. Instead of privileging the early, 'humanist' Marx, or the later, 'scientific', Marx, Lefebvre read Marx as a thinker who developed and modified his ideas over time, whilst remaining within a common problematic. It is a reading of Marx in a dialectical relation with himself, subsuming early ideas in new contexts. Lefebvre reads Marx as a theorist of alienation *and* production, as a dialectician, moving toward a science of history. He is opposed to reductive, dogmatic readings (a challenge that is directed particularly at Stalin), and argues for the centrality of idealism to Marx's thought. This is especially shown in the extracts from *Dialectical Materialism* and *The Sociology of Marx*.

Second, the selections show how this reading of Marx is at once Hegelian and against Hegel. More broadly they show how Lefebvre was able to appropriate some ideas from Hegel into his wider thought. Third, they show how Lefebvre is similarly indebted to and critical of Nietzsche and Heidegger. These purposes are shown in the extracts from *Dialectical Materialism* and *The Sociology of Marx*, but also in the sections from *Hegel, Marx, Nietzsche ou le royaume des ombres*, and *L'Existentialisme*.

The fourth purpose is to show how Lefebvre engaged with philosophical movements of his time – the examples here being existentialism and structuralism. The relevant selections are from the books *L'Existentialisme* and *Au-delà du structuralisme*. In the pages preceding the extract from *L'Existentialisme*, Lefebvre recounts how in 1924 he had been involved with the publication of *Le Manifeste de «Philosophies»* and that this had anticipated many of the ideas of existentialism. He puts these ideas down to 'juvenile presumptions' and suggests that reading Marx led him out of this. He openly wonders what Sartre's excuse is. In the selection from *Au-delà du structuralisme* several earlier themes are reprised: notably the critique of idealism and dogmatism, the role of Hegel in understanding Marx, and the importance of the dialectic and history.

Fifth, a number of the extracts demonstrate how he developed his own philosophical and theoretical positions. This is particularly shown in the extracts from works such as *Métaphilosophie* and *La Présence et l'absence*. In the former, Lefebvre outlines his understanding of, and the relation between, several key concepts including time, space, politics, production, everydayness and technology. The extracts from *Le Retour de la dialectique* similarly illuminate the central terms of state and history as well as drawing a distinction between *la politique* (the political) and *le politique* (politics). This distinction separates the thinking of the political from political action. With his favourite thinkers it enables him to turn their thought to political purposes other than those they favoured, initiated or influenced (the Prussian state for Hegel, Stalinism for Marx, Hitler and Nazism for Nietzsche). This extract should be read in conjunction with the selections from *Hegel, Marx, Nietzsche*. The selections chosen from *La Présence et l'absence* provide insight into Lefebvre's understanding of representation, dialectics and his use of triads instead of opposed binary pairs. There are never simply two terms: 'there are always Three: There is always the Other'.[1] The importance of dialectical thinking is also central to the last selection of this section, from the preface to the Third Edition of *Logique formelle, logique dialectique*. Originally written in 1947, this book demonstrates the grasp of the dialectic that Sartre described as 'beyond reproach'.[2] In the Third Edition preface Lefebvre underlies the centrality of this understanding to his career, showing how struggle in logic and dialectic is, at the theoretical level, a higher form of 'classic' struggles in thought and society.

Finally, through all the above purposes, this section aims to illuminate the work selected for the other sections. As he suggests in *Hegel, Marx, Nietzsche*, he broadens his 'critical analysis while still striving to keep it concrete'.[3] This relation of theoretical interests to practical concerns is at the very heart of Lefebvre's work. The range of issues he was concerned with theoretically is paralleled by the wide number of areas in which he did more practical analyses. Lefebvre's Marxism and philosophy are indispensable in understanding these other concerns.

Stuart Elden

Retrospections

(from *L'Existentialisme* (Paris: Éditions Sagittaire, 1946), pp. 55–66; new edn (Paris: Anthropos, 2001), pp. 40–50)

11. Let's go back to 1928. Our little existentialist coterie had a certain cohesion, at least on the face of it. Since we had to earn a living, we tried out several business ventures, including an improbable project to manufacture ornaments.

In fact, one of us, the capitalist, was supporting a good many of our little gang – what could be more natural? In all religions, the priests, those who devote themselves to the contemplation of a higher truth, live at the expense of the faithful. Spiritualism degenerated into parasitism, and in the ranks of finance capitalism, no less, something to which, of course, we declared ourselves opposed, and which made us suffer, too.

Did our friend and patron graciously maintain us free of charge? I'm not suggesting anything improbable in saying that secret, perhaps unconscious calculations (the secret of his 'existence') lay behind his undoubted generosity. He asked for payment, not in cash, but in 'spiritual' commodities, ideas, glory, influences. He had more or less consciously adopted the principle of earning 'spiritual' interest from his dough. Those he supported had to work, write, produce, with him, as a member of his staff.

Now, during that period of transition and despondency, I had stopped working. I had destroyed the manuscript of the books I had previously written (the *Déclaration des droits de l'Esprit*). I felt I was at a dead end. I had exhausted my subject-matter and it wasn't replenishing itself. I had nothing left to say – that wasn't so surprising. Others, greater than me, had fallen silent. I didn't even try to cover up this spiritual 'emptiness' with poetical declamations or romantic stories. I allowed myself to live a little. Some friends began to hint that I was a cynic. One day, two of them, whom I shall identify later as A and B, came to see me. They began to lay charges against me, and their arguments seemed both undeniably well-founded and at the same time profoundly false in a way that I sensed without being able to explain. They neither understood nor wished to understand the situation. They found outrageous the fact (which seemed very simple to me) that I wasn't writing any more. It was a dreadful day; they gave me my notice. I was excluded, drummed out of the group. In the space of an hour, I found myself out in the street, with my family, virtually incapable of earning a proper living, except in ways that at the time seemed akin to prostitution: journalism, writing, teaching. I was reduced to bare 'existence'. Yes, it was dreadful, and they were revolting. Their business interests excited them greatly; towards me, their 'friend', their consciences were boundlessly clear. They were untroubled, justified. I was faced with two just men and two judges. They liked to think of themselves ultimately as realists, but could only conceive of realism as cruelty. They had a field day, browbeating the weak and vulnerable man who appeared before them. As far as the friendship of wise or 'spiritual' men, or of philosophers, was concerned, their wisdom, 'Spirit' and philosophy were neither here nor there.

I became (of my own free will, O champions of liberty) a manual worker, then a taxi driver. And that really was a laugh!

A huge volume could not contain the adventures and misadventures of this existentialist philosopher-taxi driver. The Paris underworld unfolded before him in all its sleazy variety and he began to discover the secrets of its brothels, knocking-shops and gambling dens, dance halls (for white and coloured), fancy hotels and greasy spoons, shady dealers, high and low-class pederasts, bookmakers, armed robbers and police squads. I plumbed some of the smelly depths of 'existence' and what I dragged up would have sent the neo-existentialists of the Café Flore[1] into transports of delight. But to what purpose? I want to remember only my contact with an infinitely more precious and more moving reality: the life of the people of Paris.

A serious accident – a stroke of luck – got me out of this situation (for years I couldn't get into a car without shaking and trembling). Norbert Guterman, who had always supported me, pleaded my cause. *La Revue Marxiste* was being launched, edited by Norbert under the name Mesnil. I was taken onto the publisher's staff.

Just at that moment, the adventure of the philosophers was ending in a huge scandal, one of the strangest tragi-farcical affairs of that era. Reduced to its simplest, the scenario consists of a dialogue between the two protagonists, A and B.

A. Philosopher, poet, man of action – or at least believing himself as such. He has an undeniable verbal power, but words hide things from him. Because he's poor, wealth fascinates him, and he loathes it. When he talks in his eloquent way about money, rich folk who are not absolute bastards start to feel ashamed and get their wallets out. At twenty-six, he thinks he's reached the pinnacle of realism; he's going to make the Revolution a big production, using advertisements, propaganda, newspapers, publishing houses, journals, colleges, universities and all kinds of other organizations. He has a maxim: 'It takes money to beat money.' As a result, he gets carried away by a professional gambler (a crook) and on the assurance of an infallible martingale system, goes off to Monte Carlo and loses the considerable sums confided to him for his revolutionary projects, on roulette.[2]

B. The Hamlet of decadent capitalism. Not a bad man, actually quite good; not stupid, in fact, rather intelligent. A bit heavy, a bit stiff, a bit solemn. And above all, rich. Very rich. Too rich. He first came begging for – 'a little bit of existence, if you please?' – and his money gave him importance in our little circle of philosophers. He's caught in a terrible dilemma: 'If I'm rich, I only exist through my money, if I'm poor, I'm nothing, nothing at all!' So he wants to give, but not in return for nothing. He wants existence, pure friendship, love, glory, power – everything – in exchange for his money. He thinks he is generous. Candidates come forward. He takes fright. He wants to take it back, get a grip on himself. Only 'A' has total confidence in him; together they will change the world. While 'A' (playing roulette with his approval), loses the dough, he suffers, suffers dreadfully. Then he recovers, he's cured of the illness: youth.

Round these two protagonists is a little crowd of friends, relatives, panic stricken women, sidekicks, hangers-on, parasites and buffoons.

Thus end, in 1929, the adventures of the 'old style' existentialist philosophers.

To the precise degree that they had an 'authentic' intention, they were fated to be confronted with the real world. And the moment they collided with the 'world', the real 'object', their philosophy bursts like a soap bubble against the corner of a wall.

12. This story has a primary purpose: to show, using a very narrow but specific case, the relation of ideas to their social conditions at a time of 'growing awareness'. All the elements of the problem are quite clearly revealed in their reciprocal relationships: the role of the social structure and its movement, the role of events and individuals, the function of words and existing ideological formations.

13. Subsequently, these adventures, somewhat pathetic in themselves, would give a foretaste of 'new style' existentialism.

It would face the same problems; it faced them already:

a) *The problem of faith and choice.* Discussions between Christian and atheist existentialists already show the impossibility of finding, in the name of existentialism, a direction and meaning in existence. The old questions come up again: Mind or Nature? Thought or Matter? God or not-God? Since an existentialist cannot choose rationally, he must resign himself to choosing arbitrarily. Hence the doctrine of Liberty, the equivalent of the old fideism.[3]

Present-day existentialism says, in essence, 'If I'm free, it's because I start by being nothing, before becoming something. First I exist, but I am uneasy, anxious; I seek myself; I have no fixed nature; then I choose myself, I make myself, in the course of an adventure that forces me to recognize in others the same indeterminacy, the same freedom'.[4]

You don't have to be a professional philosopher to recognize here the position of the 1924 manifesto: the same cult of adventure, of the 'other', of the 'possible' that is not determined in advance. It is not hard to recognize the same contradiction: the simultaneous postulation of 'commitment' and total 'open-mindedness'. In 1945, as in 1924, existentialism foregrounds the speculative problem of freedom and offers two conceptions of Freedom: to be nothing (while able to become everything) and to be anything at all (after an arbitrary 'adventure'). These two propositions are equally false, but existentialism masks the contradiction by endlessly oscillating between the two; it tells those who are nothing, 'Freely become something! Choose, make yourself an essence!' To those who are already prisoners of 'something', it says, 'Free yourselves! Go back to consciousness, to existence, pure and simple.' The existentialists of 1924 staked and lost the best years of their youth on this gamble, this sterile adventure. . . .

This contradiction was not specific to philosophers; we also find it among men of letters. The 'open-mindedness' of M. Gide[5] and his characters, and their fleeting 'commitments', is heightened in existentialism, reaching a general indeterminacy, a dreary, flabby mixture that passes for the reality of human existence.

In fact, its connection with previous experiments and proven failures means that existentialism is already out of date. It is a post-war doctrine, but of the First World War.

M. Henri Mougin is thus perfectly correct when he writes, of M. Sartre's existentialist novels, that to him they 'seem like a literary celebration of the pre-war years' (pre-1939). He continues, 'the young characters are taken from Cocteau',[6] apart from one who is 'a repeat of (Gide's) Lafcadio',[7] and so on and so forth. These literary ghosts also mark the 'inability of the French novel of today' to portray human beings.[8]

A doctrine of the inter-war years that should now be out of fashion, it is precisely now that existentialism is enjoying success and gaining a large public following. This is not hard to understand. But in fact, and in a more profound sense, 1946 is not like the years 1920–5. History has moved on. Power relations have changed. Worldwide capitalism is incapable of rebuilding itself and some peoples are no longer prisoners of the precepts of reactionary nationalism. Ever larger sections of the population have an increased awareness of the situation.

Nevertheless, as far as appearances go, in the moral and psychological climate of the decadent classes, the middle class, or intellectuals in thrall to abstract, reactionary thinking, 1946 does resemble those other post-war years – but in an uglier, more desperate version. It seems to many that we're falling back into our old ways, or worse, that we can't even find the old ways, and are falling into the abyss. So that young people who come from those social classes, or are the prisoners of an abstract culture that does not allow them to think about the times they are living in, feel abandoned. They search for themselves and are a problem to themselves without positive or objective givens, a strictly individual problem: a problem of consciousness starting from a *tabula rasa*. They are nothing but question and emptiness; they search for themselves in a state of anxiety and each of them comes to recognize in his companions the same anxiety and empty freedom: that of being everything and nothing.

These abandoned creatures quite naturally become existentialists.

And that all the more easily since existentialism benefits in its own way from the new situation and the progress of history. The settings, ambiences and embellishments, the bourgeois aesthetics and morality that perverted consciousness, have collapsed. Furthermore, anarchism has been wiped out in France on the political level, but not in people's minds or mores. This is how existential philosophy, which extends traditional-style anarchism in such a way that it is seen purely from the perspective of *individual* consciousness, can disguise itself as humanism and announce that the existentialist 'wishes to lose nothing of his times.' It thus provides the anxious, without compromising them much, with a very comfortable position: they can be interested in their times, talk for ever about commitment, have the impression of being committed, while being able endlessly to draw back and endlessly return to the freedom of being 'open-minded'.

This piece of sophistry sticks out a mile for anyone who is not looking for a sophism with which to justify himself. A sensibility and consciousness inclined towards anarchism have camouflaged themselves as a formula that passes for new and that disguises them as a (theoretical and speculative) 'interest' in 'the world' and 'the human', while in fact making it possible to evade the problems of the 'world' and 'the human' – not to mention their solutions!

What shall we be? What should we want? What must we do?[9] The existentialist cannot give an answer, because all answers, even the lack of an answer, are to him equally acceptable. Under the pretext of describing his search for himself and going down the good old roads of freedom,[10] he merely recounts all the depravity, disgust, failure and disappointment encountered in the course of their private 'adventures' by these unhappy people in thrall to their own nothingness.

Escapism, and not even into dream or the ideal, but into scornful contemplation of one's self and of the 'world' in which one plays at engaging and disengaging oneself, alternately, one by the other.

Since all this is absurd, M. Camus proves the most reasonable of the existentialists when he states, in *The Myth of Sisyphus,* that the world is absurd and everyone has the right to be an 'absurd human being' and to do whatever he pleases without the slightest constraint of logic, morality, truth or error. And that's the way M. Camus sums up his thinking in his prefatory aphorism: 'There is but one truly serious philosophical problem and that is suicide.'[11] But he proves his right to the absurd, and this aphorism enables him, precisely, not to commit suicide and to do a whole lot of things – journalism and so on. M. Camus is playing; he is playing at distancing himself from existence, through the notion of suicide, in order then to further commit himself, briefly, to one or more little 'adventures'.

Isn't an existentialist someone who plays with existence? Who does not exist very much?

Existentialism presents itself as a theory of freedom, and therefore of choice. The tragedy of existence would supposedly be the tragedy of choice. Freedom could be thought to 'exist' as the need to choose, a ceaseless, perpetual necessity. But what would a man who every morning chose between fascism and anti-fascism represent? Such a case might be quaint and interesting, but in what way would this man be superior to one who had chosen, once and for all, the fight against fascism, or who had not even had to choose? And isn't that a typical example of the false problem, the speculative metaphysical problem?

In fact, considered as a living individual, the existentialist will probably *stop short of choice*. His belief system, which permits him everything, also allows him not to choose, knowing that he has to choose. And so he ensconces himself in a comfortable indeterminacy, as is the case with M. Sartre's fictional characters (so unromantic, so untragic, so trivial and ephemeral, such talkers), especially the central figure in *The Roads to Freedom,* the philosopher Mathieu. More still, the existentialist may go beyond choice; he chooses – or rather he has chosen and knows he has chosen – for reasons that are neither philosophical nor existentialist. For example, in everyday life or in his contacts with people who act in the world. So, discovering with hindsight the reasons or justifications for his alleged 'choice' (which proves to be external necessity, the most external of all necessities) he has in fact left existentialism behind. To become what? A Catholic, a Protestant, a fascist, a communist, a grocer or a pimp, depending on the most external of circumstances.

Isn't that just what happened during the existentialist experiment of 1923–9?

It is also true that the problem can be avoided by a piece of trickery. That's more or less what M. Sartre, the crafty fellow, does. His book, *Being and Nothingness*, opens with a 'description of consciousness', pure and simple. His study of the German School (Husserl, Heidegger) instilled this method in him and he presents it as a method absolute in itself. But the description of consciousness does away with the traditional opposition of subject and object. (The 1924 Manifesto was explicitly clear on this point.) If consciousness is consciousness of the world, the object, the other – then the world, the object and the other are implied and enveloped in consciousness. The description of consciousness is both necessary and sufficient to reach them. And this is why the supposed 'realism' and 'materialism' of existential philosophy in fact amount to the most absolute idealism. Whether one says, 'consciousness exists as consciousness of the object', or, 'the object is a datum of consciousness', the result is *in fact* the same, even though *theoretically* speaking, consciousness represents, in the second formulation, a closed self, and in the first, a self open to the world. In both cases, it is understood that one arrives at the object *through consciousness,* and not through the concept, through objective reason, through science. A description, an inventory of consciousness, should suffice. And there is a ban on talking about the object 'in itself'. Thus M. Sartre has launched into a vast description of the world and of human beings; along the way he throws out the Hegelian dialectic (which implies the opposition of subject and object and a dialectical movement that is deeper than consciousness) because it is conceptual and external to directly experienced existence.[12] At the same time, he also rejects the 'scientific viewpoint [*le regard scientifique*]' and its 'attempt to de-humanise the world' (p. 142).[13] Further on, M. Sartre introduces some very different ideas that are quite incompatible with a simple 'description of consciousness': the notions of the 'in itself' and the 'for itself'. This is what enables him to sketch the outlines of a dialectic of man. 'It is as if the "in itself" and the "for itself" appeared in a state of disintegration in comparison with an ideal synthesis.'[14] M. Sartre thus ushers in a form of humanism, a metaphysics, a system of morality. His book ends on this positive promise, and is nothing but this promise; it has no meaning, no value, apart from that.

But the 'in itself' and the 'for itself' are concepts, and the 'in itself', in particular, only makes sense in terms of an objective, historical dialectic, defying direct description. The 'in itself' cannot be arrived at except through a concept or an idea. M. Sartre has therefore reintroduced in the course of his book a philosophical element that wasn't there at the beginning – in order to deal with the difficulties that spring from his 'phenomenological ontology', difficulties that M. Merleau-Ponty saw clearly and points out in *Les Temps Modernes.* 'We are not saying that [the] paradox of consciousness and action is entirely elucidated in *L'Etre et le néant.* ... It is clear that the author ... is reserving for elsewhere a study of that "realization" of nothingness in being which is action', etc., etc.[15]

Yes, M. Sartre deals with the future. But (and this is serious) he introduces new ideas without explicitly alerting the reader in advance. One needs an attentive critical eye to perceive the change from one position to another. This means one of two things: either M. Sartre has not noticed this change, and is not a philosopher, or he has noticed it but not thought it worth mentioning; since honesty is, as far as I know, still part of the philosopher's mentality (and intellectual rigour is certainly the best feature of that mentality), M. Sartre no longer deserves the name philosopher. Despite – because of – his facility and virtuosity, he is only a philosopher in the eyes of men of letters, and a man of letters only in the eyes of philosophers.

Something even more serious. The objective dialectic that begins to take shape and form towards the end of *L'Etre et le néant*, brings M. Sartre strangely close to Marxist humanism and *dialectical materialism,* but it only brings him closer! On the theoretical, as on the political level, he flirts with solving problems, comes as near as his wish not to compromise himself, not truly to commit himself, will allow him; he approaches a solution, with the idea of supplanting it. He manoeuvres. He makes use of the situation. He snatches in passing those who are trying to find a solution and would be able to do so. He knows this. He is a man of this period of transition, and wishes transition would stop with himself. And it is this that makes the 'Sartre Case' (relatively) serious. But none of this is new. And here again, the study of 'old style' existentialism and surrealism throws a certain amount of light on transition and periods of transition.

Existentialism, therefore, to the extent that it is not the work of professional sophists, comes up against the problem of choice – the problem of science and objective knowledge – the problem of action.

This is to say that – to the extent that it will be or will do something, and will not amount to nothing but café chit-chat, affectation and literary fashion at a time of transition – 'new style' existentialism is bound to go down the same road, follow the same trajectory as that of an earlier post-war era. Existentialists will come to a sad end, or they will break with existentialism and 'overcome' themselves. There's no question of sparing them the ordeals and failures that will hit hardest the most loyal and most rigorous among them. This is intended as a warning, and can be no more than that. May these pages help some people to avoid errors that, at an individual level, are always liable to be irreparable, and may they also merit some indulgence!

Unity of the Doctrine

(from *Dialectical Materialism*, tr. John Sturrock (London: Jonathan Cape, 1968 [1939]), pp. 100–13)

The recent publication of the 1844 *Manuscript* and *The German Ideology* has thrown a new light on the formation and objectives of Marxian thought.

The texts in question did not reveal Marx's humanism, which was already known from *The Holy Family*, *The Jewish Question* and the *Critique of Hegel's Philosophy of Right*, but they do show how the development of his ideas – his economic theory – did not destroy his concrete humanism but made it richer and explicit.

Dialectical materialism was formed and developed dialectically. Marxian thought began from Hegel's logic and first of all denied this logic in the name of materialism, that is, of a consequent empiricism. The discovery of the natural (material) man of flesh and blood was the first moment of this development. It seemed incompatible with Hegel's Idea and with his absolute method, which constructs its own abstract object. And yet this humanism went further than the materialism of the eighteenth century, which had been based on the early results of the natural sciences; it implied Hegel's theory of alienation and gave alienation a decisive scope, attributing to it both a good and a bad side and determining it as a creative process. In the 1844 *Manuscript*, the theory of alienation is still closer to Hegelian rationalism than to Feuerbach's naturalism. However, it demands that speculative philosophy be transcended, in the name of action and practice; practice is seen as both a beginning and an end, as the origin of all thought and the source of every solution, as a fundamental relation of the living man to Nature and to his own nature. The critical investigation into economics (whose importance Engels was the first to notice) then comes to be naturally integrated with humanism, as being an analysis of the social practice, that is, of men's concrete relations with each other and with Nature. The most pressing human problems are determined as economic problems, calling for practical, that is, for political solutions, politics being the supreme instance of the social practice, the only means of acting consciously on social relations.

As this humanism becomes more profound it next reveals the dialectical elements it had contained: a dialectic of historical contradictions and the economic categories, a dialectic of 'reification' or alienation. Historical materialism, inasmuch as it is a science of economics, integrates the dialectical method with itself and, raised thereby to a higher level, appears as an application of the general method – the scientific dialectic – to a specific field. After having been denied by Marx, the dialectic joins up again with a more profound materialism; it has itself been freed from its momentary and congealed form: Hegelianism. It has ceased to be the absolute method, independent of the object, and has become the scientific method of exploration and exposition of the object. It discovers its truth by being united with the actual content.

In other words:

(a) The materialist dialectic accords the primacy explicitly to the content. The primacy of the content over the form is, however, only one definition of materialism. Materialism asserts essentially that Being (discovered and experienced as content, without our aspiring to define it *a priori* and exhaust it) determines thought.

(b) The materialist dialectic is an analysis of the movement of this content, and a reconstruction of the total movement. It is thus a method of analysis for each degree and for each concrete totality – for each original historical situation. At the same time it is a synthetic method that sets itself the task of comprehending the total movement. It does not lead to axioms, constancies or permanencies, or to mere analogies, but to laws of development.

(c) Thus understood, the dialectical method therefore constructs the historical and sociological object, while locating and determining its specific objectivity. A brute objectivity of history would be inaccessible, transcendent to the individual mind, the concept and discourse. It would be overwhelming and inexorable in character; allowing itself to be described indefinitely, but without our being able to glimpse any explanatory analysis or effectiveness in it. Conversely, without an object and without objectivity there is no science; every historical or sociological theory that sets out to be a science must establish the reality of its object and define the method that enables it to approach this object. Dialectical materialism satisfies this double requirement of the scientific mind. It establishes the economic objectivity without hypostatizing it; it locates the objective reality of history but straight away transcends it, as being a reality independent of men. It thus introduces living men – actions, self-interest, aims, unselfishness, events and chances – into the texture and intelligible structure of the Becoming. It analyses a totality that is coherent yet many-sided and dramatic.

Is not dialectical materialism therefore both a science and a philosophy, a causal analysis and a worldview, a form of knowledge and an attitude to life, a becoming aware of the given world and a will to transform this world, without any one of these characteristics excluding the other?

The movement and inner content of Hegel's dialectic, between rationalism and idealism, that is, are taken up again in dialectical materialism, which, in one sense, is more Hegelian than Hegelianism. A plurality of different and perhaps even incompatible meanings of the dialectic survived in the speculative dialectic. The dialectic as a method of analysis of the content excluded the dialectic as an a priori construct, and these two meanings did not fit in very well with the theory of alienation. By positing a total, a priori object – absolute knowledge, the system – Hegel went against the content, against the Becoming, against living subjectivity and negativity. Dialectical materialism restores the inner unity of dialectical thought. It dissolves the static determinations attributed by Hegel to the Idea, to knowledge, to religion and to the State. It rejects any speculative construct, any metaphysical synthesis. Thus the different meanings of the dialectic become not only compatible but complementary. The dialectical method epitomizes the investigation of the historical development; it is the highest consciousness which living man can have of his own formation, development and vital content. Categories and concepts are elaborations of the actual content, abbreviations of the infinite mass of particularities of concrete existence. The method is thus the expression of the Becoming in general and of the universal laws of all development. In themselves these laws are abstract, but they can be found in specific forms in all concrete contents. The method begins from the logical sequence of fundamental categories, a sequence by virtue of which we can recover the Becoming, of which they are the abridged expression. This method permits the analysis of particularities and specific situations, of the original concrete contents in the various spheres. It becomes the method that will guide the transformation of a world in which the form (economic, social, political or ideological) is not adequate to the content (to man's actual and potential power over Nature and his own artefacts) but enters into contradiction with it.

The Third Term is therefore the practical solution to the problems posed by life, to the conflicts and contradictions to which the praxis gives birth and which are experienced practically. The transcending is located within the movement of action, not in the pure time-scale of the philosophical mind. Wherever there is a conflict there may – but it is not inevitable – appear a solution which transforms the opposed terms and puts an end to the conflict by transcending them. It is up to the analysis to determine this solution, up to experience to release it, and up to action to realize it. Sometimes there is no solution: no social group was capable of putting an end to the economico-political contradictions of the Roman world in its decadence.

The relation between the contradictories ceases therefore to be a static one, defined logically and then found again in things – or negated in the name of a transcendent absolute. It becomes a living relation, experienced in existence. Several of Hegel's illustrations of the reciprocal determination of contradictories (*summum jus, summa injuria* – the way East is also the way West, etc.) become insufficient. The opposed terms are energies, or acts. The unity of the contradictories is not only an interpenetration of concepts, an internal scission, it is also a struggle, a dramatic relation between energies which are only by virtue of one another and cannot exist except one against the other. Thus Master and Slave or, if one prefers, the different species of animals. This struggle is a tragic relation, in which the contradictories are produced and support one another mutually, until either one of them triumphs and they are transcended or else they destroy each other. Taken in all its objectivity, the contradiction is fluid, and the logical relation is only its abstract expression. The transcending is action and life, the victory of one of the two forces, which overcomes the other by transforming it, transforming itself and raising the content to a higher level.

The problem of man – or, more precisely, the problem of modern society, of the 'social mystery' and its transcending – is central for dialectical materialism, which has appeared in this society at its appointed hour, as a scientific expression of its reality, its multiform contradictions and the potentialities it contains.

However, in order to elucidate modern industrial society, the analysis must go back to older societies. These it determines in their relation to the concrete totality as given today, inasmuch as they are original totalities that have been transcended, that is, in the only historical reality that we can conceive of or determine. In the past this analysis finds, under specific forms, certain relations (such as that between Master and Slave for example, which Marx called 'the exploitation of man by man') or else typical modes of thought or social existence, such as Fetishism. Dialectical materialism's field cannot therefore be restricted to the present day, it extends over the whole of sociology. But Nature itself exists for us only as a content; in experience and human practice. The dialectical analysis is valid for any content; it expresses the connection between the elements of moments of all Becoming. By incorporating the experimental sciences (physical, biological, etc.) and using them to verify itself, it can therefore discover, even in Nature, quality and quantity, quantity turning into quality, reciprocal actions, polarities and discontinuities, the complex but still analysable Becoming.

The sciences of Nature are specific. They recognize and study as such, natural, physical, biological, etc., polarities or oppositions. They use the concept as a 'trick' in order to study and modify qualities through the mediation of quantities, but they are never able to overcome these oppositions. Social science on the other hand examines the oppositions so as to overcome them. The sciences of Nature and the social sciences are specifically creative, each of them having its own method and objectives. However, the laws of the human reality cannot be entirely different from the laws of Nature. The dialectical chain of fundamental categories may therefore have a universal truth. It was only with great caution that Marx embarked on this path (as in his application of the dialectical method to economics). However, *Capital* shows how, in Marxian thought, the concrete dialectic is extended to Nature [*Capital*, Volume I], an extension carried on by Engels in *Dialectics of Nature*. Their *Correspondence* at this period (1873–4) shows that Marx followed Engels's endeavour closely and approved of it.

Thus dialectical materialism is made universal and acquires the full dimensions of a philosophy: it becomes a general conception of the world, a *Weltanschauung* and hence a renewal of philosophy.

For the materialist dialectician, universal interdependence (*Zusammenhang*) is not a formless tangle, a chaos without structure. It is only the decline of speculative thought since Hegel that has dissociated the determinations and devalued the structural elements of the Becoming: quantity, discontinuity, relative nothingness. Dialectical materialism rescues the human mind from falling back into confusion and one-sidedness. The totality of the world, the infinite–finite of Nature, has a determinable structure, and its movement can become intelligible for us without our having to attribute it to an organizing intelligence. Its order and structure emerge from reciprocal action, from the complex of conflicts and solutions, destructions and creations, transcendings and eliminations, chances and necessities, revolutions and involutions. Order emerges from the Becoming; the structure of the movement is not distinct from the movement. Relative disorders prepare a new order and make it manifest.

All reality is a totality, both one and many, scattered or coherent and open to its future, that is, to its end. Between 'moments' there cannot exist either a purely external finality or a purely internal one, either a harmony or mechanical collisions. Being elements of a totality, having been transcended and maintained within it, limited by each other and yet reciprocally determined, they are the 'ends' one of another. There exist ends without finality. Each moment contains other moments, aspects or elements that have come from its past. Reality thus overflows the mind, obliging us to delve ever deeper into it – and especially to be ever revising our principles of identity, causality and finality and making them more thorough. Being determines our consciousness of Being, and the being of our thought determines our reflection on our thought. The reality is Nature, a given content, yet one that can be apprehended in its infinite richness by the mind which moves forward, based on the praxis, and becomes more and more penetrating and supple, tending as if towards a mathematical limit (to which we are forever drawing nearer but have never reached), towards absolute knowledge, or the Idea.

The dialectic, far from being an inner movement of the mind, is real, it precedes the mind, in Being. It imposes itself on the mind. First of all we analyse the simplest and most abstract movement, that of thought that has been stripped as far as possible of all content. In this way we discover the most general categories and how they are linked together. Next, this movement must be connected up with the concrete movement, with the given content. We then become aware of the fact that the movement of the content or of Being is made clear for us in the laws of the dialectic. The contradictions in thought do not come simply from thought itself, from its ultimate incoherence or impotence, they also come from the content. Linked together they tend towards the expression of the total movement of the content and raise it to the level of consciousness and reflection.

Our quest for knowledge cannot be thought of as having been terminated by dialectical logic; quite the reverse, it must acquire a fresh impetus from it. The dialectic, a movement of thought, is true only in a mind that is in motion. In the form of a general theory of the Becoming and its laws, or of a theory of knowledge, or of concrete logic, dialectical materialism can only be an instrument of research and action, never a dogma. It does not define, it locates the two elements of human existence: Being and consciousness. It places them in order: Being (Nature) has priority, but consciousness comes first for man. Whatever has appeared in time can be erected, by man and for man, into a superior value. Nor, as a doctrine, can dialectical materialism be enclosed within an exhaustive definition. It is defined negatively, by being opposed to those doctrines that limit human existence, either from without or within, by subordinating it to some external existence or else by reducing it to a one-sided element or partial experience seen as being privileged and definitive. Dialectical materialism asserts that the equalization of thought and Being cannot be reduced to an idea, but must be achieved concretely, that is, in life, as the concrete power of the mind over Being.

Dialectical thinking has never ceased to evolve nor new aspects of it to appear, both in the lifetime and the writings of Marx and Engels, and since. Every truth is relative to a certain stage of the analysis and of thought, to a certain social content. It preserves its truth only by being transcended. We must go on constantly deepening our awareness of the content and extending the content itself. In the past as in the present, our knowledge has been limited by the limitation of the content and of the social form. Every doctrine, and this includes dialectical materialism, stems from this limitation, which is not that of the human mind in general but the limitation of man's present state. It is at the precise moment when it becomes aware of its own dialectical nature that thought must distinguish with the utmost care what, in the dialectical movement of ideas, comes from the actual content and what from the present form of thought. The exposition of dialectical materialism does not pretend to put an end to the forward march of knowledge or to offer a closed totality, of which all previous systems had been no more than the inadequate expression. However, with our modern awareness of human potential and of the problem of man, the limitation of thought changes in character. No expression of dialectical materialism can be definitive, but, instead of being incompatible and conflicting with each other, it may perhaps be possible for these expressions to be integrated into an open totality, perpetually in the process of being transcended, precisely in so far as they will be expressing the solutions to the problems facing concrete man.

For man, the relation of a particular reality to the total movement takes the form of a Problem. There is a problem whenever the Becoming carries thought and activity along and orientates them by forcing them to take account of new elements: at the moment when the Solution is tending, so to speak, to enter into reality and demanding the consciousness and the action that can realize it. It is in this sense that humanity only sets itself problems it is capable of solving. The resolution of contradictions in the transcending thus takes on its full practical significance.

The solution – the Third Term – is not an attitude of the mind. There is no substitute for practical contact with things, or effective cooperation with the demands and movements of the content.

In human terms, the energy of creation is extended and made manifest in and through the praxis, that is, the total activity of mankind, action and thought, physical labour and knowledge. The praxis is doubly creative: in its contact with realities, hence in knowledge, and in invention or discovery. Dialectical materialism seeks to transcend the doctrines which reduce the mind's activity to becoming acquainted with what has already been achieved, or which recommend it to hurl itself into the void of mystical exploration. Experience and reason, intelligence and intuition, knowing and creating, conflict with one another only if we take a one-sided view of them.

The praxis is where dialectical materialism both starts and finishes. The word itself denotes, in philosophical terms, what common sense refers to as 'real life', that life which is at once more prosaic and more dramatic than that of the speculative intellect. Dialectical materialism's aim is nothing less than the rational expression of the praxis, of the actual content of life – and, correlatively, the transformation of the present praxis into a social practice that is conscious, coherent and free. Its theoretical aim and its practical aim, knowledge and creative action, cannot be separated.

In Hegel, the inferior moments had coexisted with the superior ones, in the eternity of the Idea and the system. In this way time, history and freedom had become unreal again, having allowed themselves to be arranged into a schema that included all the established forms of law, of customs and of consciousness. In dialectical materialism negativity is more profoundly positive and dynamic in character. The Third Term, the triumphant outcome of a conflict, transforms the content of the contradiction by reassuming it; it lacks the conservative solemnity of the Hegelian synthesis. Only in this way can there be a real movement, a dramatic history and action, creation and development, liberation and liberty. The rectilinear schema of the Becoming is too simple, Hegel's triangular one too mechanical. In dialectical materialism the static representation of time *is* replaced by a vital and directly experienced notion of succession, of the action which eliminates and creates. Man can thus, perfectly rationally, set himself an objective which is both a transcending and a coming to fruition.

In Hegel, finally, the idea and the mind appear to produce themselves only because they already are. History comes to look like a bad joke. At the end of the Becoming all we find is the spiritual principle of the Becoming, which is thus only a repetition, an absurd illusion. The ordeal and misfortunes of consciousness have a ritual, magic action which causes absolute Mind to descend amongst us. But this Hegelian Mind always remains oddly narcissistic and solitary. In its contemplation of itself it obscures the living beings and dramatic movement of the world.

According to dialectical materialism men can and must set themselves a total solution. Man does not exist in advance, metaphysically. The game has not already been won; men may lose everything. The transcending is never inevitable. But it is for this precise reason that the question of Man and of Mind acquires an infinite tragic significance, and that those who can sense this will give up their solitude in order to enter in to an authentic spiritual community.

Prolegomenas

(from *Métaphilosophie: Prolégomènes* (Paris: Les Éditions de Minuit, 1965), pp. 7–19; new edn (Paris: Syllepse, 2000), pp. 23–32)

The reader is asked to cast an eye over the tables included below, then to consult the text and finally to go back to the tables, which will then take on their full meaning.

If this reader thinks he sees contradictions (in the text or the tables) he is also asked to take a second look. Contradictions in things and people sometimes get confused with inconsistencies on the author's part. If a close examination convinces the reader that there are such inconsistencies, the author would be glad to have them drawn to his attention.

TABLE OF FORMS, SYSTEMS AND STRUCTURES

Preliminary Comment

The primary purpose of this table – which is probably incomplete – is to show the *unequal development* of forms, systems and structures, that is to say, the entanglement of endings and beginnings, of 're-structurations' and 're-structurations', that history offers us. The forms, systems and structures under consideration are the products of *praxis* or the work [*oeuvres*] of *poiesis*. It is important not to dissociate the two aspects of the creative capacity. This table is designed to show how works and products have been laid down (secreted) by activity throughout the course of its history and how they become broken or dissolved. This presentation could be directly linked with a well-known passage from Engels: 'The family represents an active principle ... by contrast, kinship systems of consanguinity, on the contrary, are passive; Recording the progress made by the family at long intervals apart, and only changing radically when the family has radically changed. "And", Marx adds, "the same is true of the political, juridical, religious and philosophical systems in general."'[1] I leave aside the living human body, as a network, a system of systems, a hierarchy of self-regulations, and the cortex, the organ of accumulation, experience and memory. I similarly leave aside the earth as a set of self-regulating processes (atmosphere, rain, climates, soils, etc.). I take a number of propositions as accepted. These forms of stability exist and constitute the 'real'. They are traversed by a vast conflictual (dialectical) becoming, which philosophies have called 'cosmos' or 'world', 'God' or 'divine providence', 'Spirit', 'life', 'will', etc. This becoming, at each level of stability, appears to be exhausted. It seems to be reduced to a 'residue'. Then contradictions return and becoming starts up again. It breaks or dissolves stabilities. We may seize the creative capacity within human history, under the names of 'praxis' or 'poiesis', but we have no right to construct an ontology using that as a cover. We must not 'ontologize' history.

a) So-called archaic systems. *Derived from pre-capitalist, especially agrarian, societies. Cosmogonies and mythologies of which many elements survive: symbols, proverbial expressions (modified by the influence of writing, by the predominance of signs over symbols and nowadays, by signals over signs).*

> Signs of the zodiac (*and the astrological cosmogony*),
> the symbolism of the elements (*water, fire, air, earth*),
> the languages of objects (*flowers, precious stones, the ring*),
> the symbolism of dreams,
> mythological systems (*especially the symbolism of Mother-Earth, Greek mythology, etc.*),
> spatial and temporal cycles (*governed by the number XII, the number of the circle and the sphere*),
> qualified space-time (*represented and structured by the numbers 2, 3, 4, 5, 6 and 7, in different cosmogonies and societies*).

b) Transitional systems, *attached to biological, physiological and territorial determinants, then broken by industrialization, but not without leaving remnants and traces.* These are first and foremost systems of objects:

> systems of dress (*determined by sex, age, caste or group, the region, the nation*),
> food systems (*determined by the use of a staple commodity: wheat, rice, maize, fat, oil, butter, etc.*),
> kinship systems (*reduced by simplification to the nuclear family*),
> systems of games and pastimes (*ball, football, checkerboard games, tarot and playing cards, etc.*).

c) Large constituted forms. *These forms, created by urban life, are more general than the above-mentioned systems.*

ORIGIN	BRIEF DESCRIPTION
Greece	Form of knowledge and knowledge of form: theory of the Logos (denotations); grammar, syntax, form of

	discourse, formal logic, coherence of discourse; geometry (defined, homogeneous space); 'perfect system' (*teleion sustema*): homogeneity of the octaves in music.
Greece and Rome	Rhetoric, practical use of discourse, political use of discourse, theory of rhetorical figures (code of connotations).
Rome	Formal law (governing equivalences, exchanges, contracts, transfer of goods).
From the C13th	Codification of rituals and manners (love, etiquette, etc.).
From the C15th	Shaping of spatial and temporal perception (perspective, measurement of time).
C16th and C17th	Homogeneous, infinite space-time (Galileo, Descartes, Newton).
C18th	Complex tonal system (Rameau).[2] Combinatory model of intelligence (Leibniz, Condillac,[3] etc.). Civil code (promulgated in the early nineteenth century, devised throughout the whole of the preceding period as Law, in its different senses: generalization of rules for exchanging merchandise and for 'fair' contracts, based on equivalences of goods and property).

d) Ruptures, dissolutions, destructurations (in Europe).

Renaissance	Dogmatic theology systematized.
C15th to C19th	The peasant community.
C17th and C18th	The extended patriarchal family (lineage and household), with its kinship system: relationship, neighbourhood).
C19th	Formal logic (attacked by dialectical thinking, made more flexible by scientific progress).
idem	Dogmatic and systematic philosophy (Marx's critique of the Hegelian system, *teleion sustema* of philosophy).
Late C19th and early C20th	Competitive capitalism (with its blind, spontaneous systems of self-regulation – under double pressure from monopolies and the working-class). Language, logos (fetishized and corroded, attacked by the image, etc.).
Around 1910	Classical perspective (frame of reference: the horizon; tonal system (frame of reference: the tonic); absolute space-time (frame of reference: Euclidean dimensions, the circular clock); system of nature (frame of

	reference: mechanics, spontaneity of life-forms); the 'real' and solid perception; art (fetishized and in process of dissolution like language – a process of destruction and self-destruction: Dadaism, surrealism); movement from signs towards signals.
C20th	Local and national systems of objects (dress, furnishings, food) and situations (occupations, functions and roles).
1945	Collapse of politico-philosophical systematization based on biology (racism) and territory (fascism).
1953–1956	Collapse of politico-philosophical systematization based on class ('socialism' being an entirely autonomous system, on the rise, and the 'capitalist system' another system, in decline).
2nd half of C20th	Potential or actual break-down of the city. Possible break-down of the planet (prospect of 'nuclear death' of the earth).

e) New formations:

C20th	The everyday (functionized and structured by its dissociation: work – home and private life – leisure). The 'world of the image' (radio and television; the world as performance). The car (with its requirements, the spearhead object in a 'world of objects': glamour, prestige, destruction of cities. With its codification: the 'highway code', the perfect system of the modern era). Advanced technology (technical objects) with its social underpinning (techno-bureaucracy). The survival system (surviving as a system ...).

PRAXIS

Preliminary Comments

Marx reintroduced the Greek word '*praxis*' in order to avoid the confusion surrounding the modern word 'practice'. He did not avoid contamination. The term *praxis* has several uses today. It sometimes refers to any social, i.e. human, activity (including technology and '*poiesis*', as well as theoretical knowledge). It sometimes represents the opposite of pure theory and knowledge – or those described as such – in which case, '*praxis*' is closer to 'practice' in the current sense. At other times, it refers to social activity in its narrower sense; in other words, relations between human beings, which are distinguished by a legitimate process of abstraction from relationships with nature and the material world (technology and *'poiesis'*). It is this last meaning that I shall try to define and delimit. Is it not also the meaning of the Greek word? 'Pragmata' are things in general, what is handled or treated by human beings in their active relations.

I shall develop the idea of a series of possible analyses of *praxis*. That of the Greek thinkers (determinism – chance – will) does not seem to me incompatible with the distinction between the dominated sector and the non-dominated sector, even as applied to history, any more than it seems incompatible with the difference between *repetitive praxis* and *revolutionary praxis*. The aspects of growth (technology, economics) and (social) development complement each other.

The concept of *praxis* defines it as determined, but also as open to the possible, inexhaustible by analysis. This understanding also defines *praxis* as the locus and origin of concepts. *Praxis* in the strict sense would thus be the human 'real', as long as it is not separated either from history and historical trends or from the possible. All *praxis* takes place within a history; it creates history. History as a whole can thus be understood as a history of *praxis*; it can be thought of as tending towards complete knowledge (knowledge to the outer limit) of human development. I shall offer some stages, some moments:

1. *Division of labour.* Inequality between forms of work. A widening split between groups working with material things (shepherds, farmers, artisans, manual workers) and those operating on other groups of human beings (soldiers, priests, administrators, shopkeepers, teachers, etc.). Inequality between functions and the struggle for relative social surplus production (in times of scarcity).
2. *Exchange and trade* (trade in people and trade in merchandise). Money, the market and language. Universalization of merchandise, logical rationality (social use of the *concept*).
3. *From powers to power*, from social functions to the state of civil servants, notables, chiefs and kings. The political and the State. Political use of discourse (as a means of action).
4. *Classes and class struggles* as major groupings independent of territoriality. Challenges and fights between groups and classes. Tactics and strategy, instruments of war (including ideologies).
5. *From logical rationality to analytical rationality and dialectical reason.* Grasp of society as a single whole (in the social domain of work, at the point of its promotion as concept and revolutionary reality – in the State at the moment, at its apogee, in which its decline can just be discerned).

6. *Construction and consolidation of the everyday* (which supposes: extreme division of labour, corresponding with a praxis of analytical reason – widespread arrogation of functions and general functionalization, etc.). Ambiguities of the everyday.
7. *Technological and bureaucratic praxis.* Society as a network of self-regulations.

POIESIS

I shall call human activity thus in so far as it *appropriates* 'nature' (*physis*) around and *within* the human being (its own *nature*: sense, sensibility and sensory perception, needs and desires, etc.). *Poiesis* is thus the creator of works [*oeuvres*]. It includes the foundation of institutions, and decisions with consequences that are limitless, even if sometimes unnoticed for long periods. Thus, not all creation is *poiesis*, but all *poiesis* is creation. 'Poetry' narrows the meaning of the word. And another point: technology and technical invention will remain outside the field of *poiesis*. Technologies may well master 'nature' (the external world), and thus be necessary, but they are not sufficient to enable human beings to appropriate their own nature. A vital distinction in determining the limits of technology within modernity and in correctly defining technological alienation.

1. *Foundation of the village* (generally attributed to women, encompassing: settled agriculture, a fixed habitation (the house), pottery, weaving, basketry, the beginnings of education of the young, etc.).
2. *The town in general* (as spontaneously created by social, religious and political participation, and encompassing: meeting-places, monuments around which the population gathers (ceremonies, processions); agitation, or on the contrary *catharsis*, produced at public gatherings, etc.).
3. *The Greek polis* (foundation of the *agora*, a place of free assembly).
4. *The Roman 'urbs'* (foundation of the *forum*, a place for assembly subject to restrictions).
5. *The* (Platonic) *idea of absolute love* (the unique love of one unique being for another unique being: in western Europe in the thirteenth century).
6. *The medieval town and the project of accumulation* (objects, goods, wealth, technologies and forms of knowledge, the process of accumulation gradually extended until it constitutes capital).
7. *Foundation of ethnic groups, peoples and nationalities* (large groups attached to a territory, possession of that territory, styles of dress, diet, etc.).
8. *The notion of the total man*, transcending the division of labour (Fourier).[4]
9. *Unity of negations* to constitute a new totality (Marx), the working-class carrying within itself radical negativity.

10. *Psychoanalysis* (inasmuch as it presents a new form of catharsis, based on the transparency of individual minds, on direct communication between equal human beings, without having recourse to magical operations, systems of prestige or influence, opaque symbols or concepts with sharp divisions, and thus offers a way of elucidating conflicts).

11. *The decision to change everyday life.* The programme for repossessing 'moments', 'residues', art having ceased to be an end in itself or a specialist, emancipated activity, thus becoming a means of transforming the everyday and a tool for 'real' life. Thus constitution of the 'total', 'worldly' or 'universal' man.

Restitution in their eminent 'reality' and force of moments already achieved. Creation of new moments (or if one so wished to put it, new situations). Declaration of war on the 'cybernanthrope',[5] a parody of the total man (this is a single and indivisible poetic act which then has to be brought into praxis and its practical consequences elucidated).

MIMESIS

Preliminary Comments

The concept of *mimesis* is not the same as that of *imitation*. Mimesis is not a psychological phenomenon but a sociological one (containing the psychological, but going beyond it). In this sense, mimesis can be defined as an aspect or a level of praxis. But it has to be founded, created. Situated midway between repetition and earth-shaking (revolutionary) invention, it is related to *poiesis*. It is the mixed concept par excellence, or the concept of mix, median, intermediate, mediating, middle. With language as such, or, rather, discourse. We ascribe to mimesis any activity that follows a given form, and which also adds to its form. It thus depends on an initial perception, apprehension or intuition of form. After that it is more or less identical. It eventually gives way to a kind of formalism that can misdirect the use and function of form. It may also give way to a certain conformism, the apogee and paroxysm of mimesis. Contrary to current misapprehensions, individualism in no way excludes mimicry or imitation, which are facets of mimesis. On the contrary. Every grain of the 'sand of humanity' imitates the other grains, while thinking it is alone, and separate.

The form taken by mimesis may be logical, legal, ceremonial, gestural or ritual.

Mimesis is thus not reducible to imitative repetition. It is inherent in educability, that is, in the relationship of master and disciple, teacher and pupil, parents and children. It permits exemplarity, filiation and affiliation. It is also inherent in the relationship of legislator and citizen – the relationship of a prince with his subjects or of gods with their worshippers. Fashion is only a minor aspect of mimesis. Should we say that it secretes structures? That it lays down systems like solid concretions along the way? Yes, as long as we do not separate mimesis from praxis and poiesis and keep in view the uneven, chequered and conflictual character of becoming.

1. *Initial formation of an 'imago mundi'*, a model of the city, the temple, houses, perhaps clothes (circular or spherical, rectangular or square). Use of the forms thus perceived.
2. *Influence of partial signifying systems* (semiological systems): formulas of politeness, legal formalities, social formalisms, forms of love, of etiquette, rituals, conventions, procedures.
3. *General form of the reproduction* of objects, situations, activities. Therefore, a form of accumulation of things that have been transformed into merchandise, wealth, processes and techniques.
4. *Formation of 'human reality'*, studied by the sciences devoted to it: roles, attitudes, functions. Growing importance of models ('patterns');
   Conformism and conformity.
   The reign of idols.
5. *Simulation and the simulacrum as a method of thinking and living*. The rise of a new type within the human species, the antagonist of the total man: the cybernanthrope (caricature, simulacrum, parody, inverse image of the total man).

IRREDUCIBLES

Every activity that becomes autonomous tends to turn itself into a system, a 'world'. As a result, this world forms, expels, represents a 'residue'.

In the course of an analysis that will attempt to capture the relationships among the terms studied (systems – forms, functions and structures – praxis, poiesis, mimesis) in a sketch of the whole history of mankind, I shall have an opportunity to show these 'irreducibilities'. At the same time, I shall show that each residual element (from the point of view of a power that constitutes a 'world') contains something valuable and essential. I shall end on the decision on which is based an action, a strategy: a gathering together of 'residues', their alliance to create '*poietically*' in *praxis*, a universe that is more real, more true (more universal) than the worlds of specialized powers.

Power [Puissance]	Residue
Religion	Vitality (natural, carnal).
Philosophy	The non-philosophical (the everyday, the ludic).

The political	Private life (deprived of everything that the political has assumed for itself).
The state and the static [*l'étatique*]	The singular and singularities. Liberty.
Centralization	Forms of decentralization (ethnic, national, regional, local).
Mathematics (number and measurement)	Drama.
Structure	Time. History. Dialectical movement. The tragic.
Technology and technocracy	The 'out-of-the-ordinary'. The imaginary.
Cybernetics	Desire. Subjectivity.
Art (turned into culture, a diet for mass consumption)	'Creativity'. Style. (Mastery of the everyday and its metamorphosis).
Bureaucracy	The individual.
The organization	The deviant. The original. Moments and situations.
Reason and rationality (technical or pragmatic)	The 'irrational'. The natural.
Adaptation	Character. The non-mimetic.
The notion of 'normal'	
Mimesis	The poietic capacity.
Language [*la langue*] and discourse	Speech [*la parole*]. The unsayable and the not-said.
Signification (sign, signifier, signified)	The insignificant.
The nuclear threat	The state of survival. Possible life after death.

Marxian Thought and Sociology

(from *The Sociology of Marx*, tr. Norbert Guterman (Harmondsworth: Penguin, 1968 [1966]) pp. 14–24)

Marx is still in many quarters looked upon as an economist. He is believed to have championed a certain 'economic determinism,' according to which the level of development of the productive forces mechanically or automatically determines the other relations and forms that constitute social life, property relations, institutions, ideas. For allegedly holding such a view he is sometimes criticized, sometimes approved. But (it should hardly be necessary to point out yet another time) this interpretation overlooks the subtitle of *Capital*, which was a '*Critique* of Political Economy'. After all, wasn't it capitalism that founded itself upon economic reality: commodities, money, surplus value, profit? By contrast with capitalism, in which the mediation of money changes relations between persons into the quantitative relations that obtain between abstract things, medieval society was founded on direct relations among human beings, relations between masters and serfs – no doubt relations of bondage, but perfectly clear ones. Once society has been transformed, human relations will again become clear and direct, only without servility.[1] As for political economy as a science, it is the study of a certain praxis how goods in short supply are distributed among groups unequal in size, influence, function, and place in the social structure. Political economy must be superseded, is capable of surmounting itself. This should be achieved in and by a society living in abundance, making full use of its technological potentialities. The process entails the overcoming of law – that aggregate of norms and rules governing the distribution of products and activities in a society that has not yet achieved abundance. Consequently, political economy is merely the science of scarcity. To be sure, every society had and still has an economic 'foundation' or 'base'. This base determines social relations, however, only to the extent that it limits the activities of groups and individuals, it imposes shackles on them; it arrests their potentialities by limiting them. In giving rein to their potentialities, individuals – as representatives of groups and classes – undertake things on their own initiative, which may or may not succeed, but which assign economic reality a more complex, higher, more varied place in the social whole. For all that, the transformation of capitalist society calls for a modification of the economic base – in the relations of production and ownership, in the organization of work, and in the social division of labour.

Capital is a study of a specific society, namely bourgeois or middle-class society, and a specific mode of production, namely capitalism. It considers these two aspects of one and the same reality, taken as a whole. Competitive capitalism is here grasped theoretically the better to be described and challenged. As a description, Marx's work deals with this society's self-regulative mechanisms, the balancing mechanisms that tend to uphold its various structures: how the average rate of profit is arrived at; how reproduction on a progressively increasing scale is proportioned. Competitive capitalism constitutes a system. Within it arises a specific *form* of the product of human labour: the commodity. The specifically capitalist relations of production and ownership determine a specific *structure* of both the productive forces and the social forces. As a challenge, this work shows how the proletariat is led to become conscious of capitalism in the course of its struggles with the bourgeoisie, the dominant class. Marx goes farther than this, and demonstrates that competitive capitalism is fated to disappear. Two socio-economic forces threaten it, tend to break up its internal structures: the working-class and the monopolies (the latter resulting from the inevitable concentration and centralization of capital). In short, though *Capital* contains an economic theory, it is not a treatise on political economy. It contains something else, and more important: a way of superseding political economy, through radical criticism of it. The economic or, more accurately, the *economistic* interpretation distorts this work when it cuts down its real scope to a single aspect, at the same time truncating the conceptual range of the work.

'We recognize only one science, the science of history,' Marx wrote in *The German Ideology* (1845). This work, composed in collaboration with Engels, expounds the principles of so-called 'historical materialism'. Any 'historicizing' interpretation of Marxian thought must take this as its starting point. At first glimpse, the formula just quoted seems clear. It says that history is a fundamental matter for knowledge: the science of man. However, as we scrutinize it more closely, we may wonder what Marx meant. How could he grant such a privileged status to history? And what did he mean by 'history'?

Indeed, if, as proclaimed, history is the only science of human reality, how could Marx have devoted himself to economic studies? Why should he have bothered? Must we conclude that his method and outlook changed, that he shifted from historicism to economism, from one specialized science (overestimated at a certain moment) to another specialized science?

These questions are answered in the preface and afterword to *Capital*, as well as in the work itself. This work expounds the development of competitive capitalism as a whole – its formation, expansion, apogee and inevitable disintegration. It starts from this hypothesis, which the work as a whole is intended to verify: capitalist society, like any other reality, comes into being, grows, declines and dies. This is true of natural realities, social realities, individuals, ideas, institutions. The history of competitive capitalism unfolds on many planes and at different levels. The work contains some political economy (theories of the commodity, money, rate of profit, capital accumulation, etc.); some history proper (chiefly of England, the English middle classes and English capitalism), some sociology (pre-capitalist societies are discussed, also the bourgeois family, social classes viewed from the inside, etc). May we not say that Marx conceived and projected a *total history,* one that history in the strict sense – history as a field of knowledge, a science – cannot encompass? History as a process and history as a science do not coincide, though they converge. By historical reality, or 'historicity,' we denote the process by which man is formed, what he produces (in the broadest and strongest sense) by himself, through his practical activity. Man is born of nature: he comes into being, he emerges, he asserts himself. What he becomes is a result of his own efforts, his struggles against nature and against himself. In the course of this dramatic process, forms and systems make their appearance. The formation of social man, like that of biological man, is marked by periods of relative stability, relatively stable structures. These, too, are eventually drawn into the process of change, are sooner or later dissolved or destroyed; yet they endured for a time, they were part of history, and deserve to be studied for their own sake.

Man, both as individual and as member of society, thus comes to look upon himself as a historical being: his 'essence' is historical and unfolds within history. He constitutes, creates, produces himself in the domain of praxis. There is nothing in him that is not a product of interaction among individuals, groups, classes, societies. The historian, however, can grasp only some aspects of this total history, though he can and should try to grasp them more and more in depth. Mankind's 'socio-economic formation' (as Marx calls it) simply has too many aspects, exhibits too many differences and goes on at too many levels to be treated by a single discipline. The economist, the psychologist, the demographer, the anthropologist, all have their contributions to make. And the sociologist as well.

According to the interpretation still too widely accepted in the Soviet Union, historical materialism is a kind of general sociology, corresponding to what is so termed in capitalist countries, to be sure in a broader and truer sense. According to this 'establishment' Marxism, historical materialism formulates the laws that govern all societies, the universal laws of development as applied to history – dynamic contradictions, discontinuous qualitative changes and gradual quantitative changes.

This interpretation of Marx is one of the less satisfactory ones. For how are the universal laws of dialectics that materialist sociology would apply to social development to be conceived? There are two possibilities. Either they are held to be part of philosophy, in which case historical materialism is viewed as part of dialectical materialism, and as such open to the criticism levelled against philosophical systems in general. Then the temptation is to deduce the general features from philosophy, abstractly, dogmatically. This is regression to the theoretical level of Hegelianism, or even farther back. Alternatively, the universal laws of dialectics are linked with methodology, in which case they serve as conceptual tools for analysing actually existing societies, no matter what contents, experiences, facts they may consist of. Concrete sociology, still to be constituted on the basis of the dialectical method Hegel elaborated and Marx transformed, would deal with contents, facts, experimental data. If so, historical materialism may be viewed as an introduction to sociology, but not as sociology. Furthermore, the thesis we are rejecting here neglects the dialectical analysis of development in all its various aspects: the processes, the contents are separated from the forms they produce, the systems, the structures. We have, on the one hand, the process of growth (considered quantitatively, economically, in terms of material production), and, on the other hand, development (considered qualitatively, socially, in terms of the progressive complexity and richness of human relations). The idea of change or becoming remains pretty crude, well-nigh metaphysical, for all the pretentious talk about concrete history, materialism, dialectics and science.

Marx did not formulate a philosophy of history: on this score, too, he broke with Hegelianism. His originality was to conceive, as a totality, the production of man by his own efforts, his own labour, starting from nature and from need in order to achieve enjoyment (the appropriation of his own nature). Thus Marx conceived of a historical science that would avoid the limitations of narrative and institutional history. Such a science, in collaboration with other sciences, was to consider the development of man in all its aspects, at every level of his practical activity. The term 'historical materialism' does not designate a philosophy of history but the genesis of mankind as a totality, object of every science of human reality and goal of action. It must be emphasized that this conception of mankind's development does not come down to a history of culture, any more than to an economic history. Moreover, Marx pointedly refrains from giving a definition of the human being. He expects mankind to define itself in praxis. How can man be separated from nature with which he maintains a dialectical relationship – unity and scission, struggle and alliance? Man's destiny is to transform nature, to appropriate it as his own, both around and inside himself.

Having discarded the economist and historicist interpretations of Marxism, are we to adopt a sociological interpretation? Are we to view Marx as a sociologist? Such an interpretation would be just as inadequate as the others, though it has been fairly widespread in Germany and Austria. It began by getting rid of the philosophy attributed to Marx, without, however, analysing the meaning of philosophy in its full implications, and without formulating any thesis of how it is to be overcome (i.e. fully translated into practice). As a result, this interpretation arbitrarily mutilated Marx's thought, giving rise to endless discussions culminating in a new Byzantinism or Scholasticism. From this point of view, Marxism falls into line with Comte's positivism. Marxist thought is dulled, loses its cutting edge. Exercise of dialectical method gives way to the worship of 'facts', critical challenge is subordinated to description. In *Capital,* the use made of the key concept of totality is never allowed to overshadow the essential dialectical contradiction. On the contrary: the principle of contradiction takes on a sharpness it had lost in Hegel's systematization; Marx keeps multiplying and emphasizing the contradictions between men and works, otherness and alienation, groups and classes, substructures and superstructures. The sociologizers, on the other hand, are led by their treatment of society as a whole to play down the contradictions. Classes and class struggles are blurred. So-called 'society' is readily identified with the nation and the nation-state. This allegedly Marxian sociologism fitted only too well into the ideological and political framework Marx criticized so vigorously in his comments on the Gotha programme (1875). Every positivist sociology presenting itself as 'Marxist' has always tended to reformism. Hence its bad reputation among some and its attraction for others. Today this sociology is becoming overtly conservative, whereas originally – as practised, for instance, by Saint-Simon and Fourier, who belonged to the left wing of romanticism – it did not separate knowledge from criticism.

For quite a number of reasons, then, we shall not make a sociologist out of Marx. Anyone who ascribes such a thesis to us on the basis of the title of this little book either never opened it or is acting in bad faith. We mention the possibility because far worse things than this have occurred in the context of such discussions. *Marx is not a sociologist, but there is a sociology in Marx.*

To interpret this seemingly inconsistent statement, we must keep in mind two groups of concepts and arguments:

1. Marx asserts the unity of knowledge and reality, of man and nature, and of the social sciences and the physical sciences. He explores a totality in process of becoming and in its present stage of development, a totality comprising levels and aspects which are now complementary, now distinct, now contradictory. As such, his theory therefore is not history, not sociology, not psychology, etc., but comprehends these approaches, these aspects, these various levels of the whole. Therein lies its originality, its novelty and its lasting interest.

Since the end of the nineteenth century, there has been a tendency to view the writings of Marx, and *Capital* especially, in terms of the individual sciences; actually, it is only since his day that they have become specialized in a system of academic compartmentalization we may be sure Marx would have opposed. *Capital,* which is theoretically all of a piece, has been reduced to a treatise on history, on political economy, on sociology, even on philosophy. Marxian thought is simply too broad in scope to fit into the narrow (and ever narrower) categories of latter-day philosophy, political economy, history and sociology. Nor is it correct to refer to it as 'interdisciplinary' – a conception recently advanced (not without risk of confusion) – to remedy the disadvantages of a latter-day division of labour in the social sciences. Marxian investigation bears upon a differentiated totality and centres around a single theme – the dialectical interrelations between men active in society and their multifarious, contradictory accomplishments.

2. The specialization and compartmentalization that have gone on in the sciences of humanity since Marx's exposure of competitive capitalism are not devoid of meaning. The totality of human knowledge can no longer be encompassed as it could in Marx's epoch, at once from the inside and from the outside (both as a reality and as a possibility), critically and descriptively. All the same we cannot endorse this breaking up of the social sciences. It encourages us to forget the totality: society as a whole, the totality of human efforts. Of course, human reality is growing steadily more complex, and this mounting complexity is part of history in the broader sense. We are dealing with a broken-up totality, fragments of which confront one another and sometimes separate when they do not enter into conflict – the capitalist 'world', the socialist 'world', the undeveloped 'world', the various cultures, the diverse forms of the state. It has even been suggested that the concepts 'world' and 'the worldwide' might replace the concept totality to signify the extension of technology into a planetary scale. With such questions of terminology still pending, the indispensable presuppositions in the social sciences remain the unity of knowledge and the total character of reality. Thus it is possible to recognize in Marx's works a sociology of the family, of the city and the countryside, of subgroups, classes, and whole societies, of knowledge, of the state, etc. And this can be done at such a level of analysis and exposition as not to encroach upon the rights of the other sciences – political economy, history, demography, psychology. On the other hand, it is possible to continue Marx's own effort, starting from *Capital* and embracing its method, by inquiring into the genesis of so-called 'modern' society, its fragmentations and contradictions.

Beyond Structuralism

(from *Au-delà du structuralisme* (Paris: Anthropos, 1971), pp. 20–5)

The cutting-edge of knowledge operates far beyond structuralism. And has done for a long time. 'All contemporary thinking is polarised by a debate whose end-terms, opposing each other under the colours of Plato and Nietzsche respectively, are: seriousness and play, the foundation and concealment, the centre and its absence, the origin and the ever-present, the here-and-now and the after-the-event, the complete and the supplementary, the one and the missing or the excessive, the soul beyond the body and inscription, the referent and the literal effect, sense and significance, the figure and the trace, connectedness and collapse of support, the confrontation of subject-object and their mutual inclusion in a process of concatenation both formal and material, being and its difference, the near [*le present*] and the far-away. This debate is not about structuralism as a linguistic method or a theory of the phenomena of language, but transcends them in all directions.'[1] This is not, however, to retreat into formless dialectical thinking, simple liberalism, or naïve and perverse historicism.

Thinking took up a position beyond structuralism as a doctrine (ideology and/or knowledge) as soon as it was formulated, as soon as we got a sense of its specific traits, in relation to a certain period of time. Today we are formulating what has been preserved from that period, but also what has been lost or mislaid.

Let's make a list of what has been gained. The 'Subject' of the philosophers has been interrogated and tortured, but has not confessed. Substance, 'thinking thought'? Intentionality? No. A mirror effect? Then where does its destructive and creative force come from? Without doubt 'presence/absence', that old philosophical notion, made more concrete, sometimes dramatized, sometimes de-dramatized on the basis of linguistics. Let's also put on the credit side of the structuralist period a more refined use of concepts and thus a subtler critique of their abuse. Then an awareness of new contradictions: between *reduction* and *systematization* on the one hand and *differences* on the other, the plural or *multiple* nature of any field explored. By denying contradictions in the name of coherence, the structuralist movement has given rise to those contradictions.

More fundamentally, it is not enough to think of structuralism as an abuse of language, and a leaning towards it as a kind of mania or an intellectual tic.

There is no way of moving beyond structuralism except by understanding it as such. Hence the ultra-structuralist project for a general *Systematics*. From that perspective, we're no longer looking for a System or The System. We no longer wish to adopt a System. We study systems, actual or possible, real or virtual. We are creating the science of systems as such: systems for action and decision-making, systems of thought and values. These systems and sub-systems are multiple and various but scarcely different in the precise extent to which they are governed by parallel principles: coherent totalization, centralization, institutionalization. There are mental systems and social systems, agrarian systems and industrial or urban systems, legal, contractual, fiscal, philosophical and governmental systems, etc. etc. A comparative and comprehensive science of systems requires a critical mistrust of any attempt at, or temptation by, systematization. The science of systems, the pinnacle of dialectical thinking, can only be achieved in the name of the anti-system. It is the coherent form of the anti-system, the only systematization it permits itself. In its own way, it belongs to the 'credit' side of the balance-sheet, and to the fruits of that experience.

There are a number of texts that attack Louis Althusser and neo-Marxism.[2] They are particularly virulent. Why? Because the polemic over Marxism recast in the structuralist mode has worsened, to the same extent that neo-Marxism expresses and signifies, theoretically and practically, the failures of Marxism *by concealing them*. It substitutes epistemological retreat and withdrawal into scientism for an analysis of actual failures and contradictions.

The first of these articles on Althusser shows how structuralist thought offers a *critique from the right* (in the Leninist sense) of a currently vulgar, would-be Marxist conception of historicity. Whereas this conception – basically Hegelian – calls for a *critique from the left*. We should not, of course, take these words, 'left critique', to mean a critique made by the 'left', in the name of the existing political 'left', but understand them in their Marxist and Leninist usage, as a 'radical critique'. The worldwide process of social and mental transformation requires a thoroughgoing critique of the concepts and conceptions of the preceding period, and in particular, its conception of history. In this vital domain, it's time to break with fetishism, that's to say the Western (or better, Eurocentric) conceptions of a narrow rationalism and naturalism, elevated into a supreme historical truth, a philosophico-political absolute. A generally accepted radical critique of historicity must include an analysis of history considered as a cultural or political (ideological) institution. In that light, structuralism is *symptomatic*: of a crisis in historical thought that needs to be elucidated in order to signal a possible solution or to find one.

Another article underlines the role of three concepts – form, function and structure – in *Capital*. Its underlying thesis: these concepts are of *equal* methodological and theoretical importance. To privilege any one of them is to constitute and to create an *ideology*: formalism, functionalism, structuralism. These three concepts, *taken together*, form the theoretical field in which the analysis of *Capital* takes place. They simultaneously define the system of references and the system of concepts (exchange value, commodities, division of labour, contract, surplus value) articulated around, and addressing, the history of capitalism. Each of these ideologies (the abuse of each concept) has had its hour, its success, and then has run out. *Ideology* has thus tried every blind alley. And we were obliged to denounce them, while risking being taken for 'nostalgics'.

One of the paradoxes of neo-Marxism, and not the least of them, is that these works have been well received in countries whose central problems are still those of growth. In Latin America, for example. In fact, the position taken by Althusser only makes sense, in so far as it has any, in countries that are economically and technologically advanced. In such countries, Marxist thought has to compete with a host of sciences and technological practices that have developed outside it, without it, sometimes against it: linguistics, psychoanalysis, economic modelling, etc. This confrontation cannot be avoided, but has to be handled in various ways. One way is to undertake a radical (dialectical) critique of these theoretical and practical domains while at the same time making a radical auto-critique of Marxist thought, which has not been able to respond to social needs or the demands of practice in those countries. Another approach would be to accept without further ado steps already taken to define for each domain an established knowledge, i.e. an epistemology, and to demand that Marxist thought submit to the same procedure and provide its own epistemology. That's Althusser's approach. Based as it is on the demands of non-Marxist theory and linked neither with revolutionary practice nor with social practice in general, this approach leads to the disintegration and elimination of Marxist thought. Some demand that it justify itself as a tactical withdrawal, others welcome it as a sign of ongoing disintegration.

The basic question is not to free science from ideology but to free political strategy from the obstacles in its way: pressure from obsolete institutions and those with aims other than revolution. As strategy is worked out, some ideological elements may have a favourable effect, and others prove to be 'catalysts'. *Scientism* lumps them together, which is a serious strategic (political) error. Theory can only be developed as theory of praxis. Taken on its own, it attaches itself to nuclei or kernels that become irrevocably dried out.

Nothing today can replace the study of actual developments, that is to say, the analysis of praxis. There have been some new developments since Marx. For instance:
a) economic growth in capitalist countries, without the disruption of capitalist relations of production, managed and directed by the bourgeoisie as a class;
b) hence quantitative growth without qualitative development, a formula that to some extent suits the majority of so-called socialist countries;

c) the growing importance of urban phenomena, still poorly understood and even worse handled in the present context of thought, ideology and relations of production;
d) the prodigious expansion of the 'world of commodities', etc., etc.

These developments can only be analysed and understood according to Marx's concepts and theories, including the beginning of *Capital* (marking, according to Althusser, the influence of Hegel). How are we to understand anything at all in today's world without reference to the theory of exchange value and commodities, or to the contradiction between use value and exchange value? This does not mean that we are free to neglect the circulation of capital, its organic composition, or the theory of surplus value, nor, either, to forget the theory of imperialism, including the changes that have taken place in the modern world over half a century.

The reduction of Marxism to an epistemology is to sideline practice and its problems. It subjects Marxist thought to an absolute scientific criterion, a fetishistic philosophy of 'pure' knowledge. But no branch of knowledge, even mathematical set theory, can meet that sort of criterion; systematized philosophy brings back a *scientific ideology of the absolute*, which it presents as a *purification of all ideology*. What follows is the disintegration of Marxism, the self-destruction of knowledge (which is always *relative*).

Marxist thought can only move forward by combating this 'philosophism' and by showing the reasons for its appeal. It is seductive because it is another form of dogmatism, while sparing its adherents the ordeal of contact with actual facts – with praxis. The technique of cutting-and-editing is just the thing to justify the dismemberment of Marxist thought, under the pretext of 'rigour'.

The elimination of Marxism goes hand in hand with the elimination of the dialectic. This has been attempted from several points of view:
a) Elimination of history for no other reason than the unscientific character of the 'object' (in fact, if one suggests that the 'object' has to be cut and put back together anatomically, following a 'model', it follows that history does not exist and it is pointless to proceed any further).
b) Elimination of the tragic nature of life and action, by taking the tragic out of thought, literature and art, at the very moment when genocide is becoming widespread, the threat of a third world war is hanging over us and violence is rife. This reduction can be understood only as a defensive reaction, a clumsy withdrawal into abstract intellectualism.
c) Replacement of the dialectical methodology, accused of being 'unscientific', by *techniques* elevated into method and epistemology; cutting-and-editing, logistical calculation, cybernetic programming. It is, of course, only an arbitrary decision that elevates these techniques (valuable in themselves) into methods.

This narrowness cannot be maintained for long. Have the contradictions of the modern world been resolved? No. And therefore we will not be able to go for much longer without a method capable of grasping them. And that's not all. The old contradictions, those analysed by Marx, have sometimes become blurred but they have not disappeared (in particular those between the forces of production and capitalist relations of production and property). New contradictions are intensifying them. Between the period when the former seemed to have been resolved and today, when the latter are making the world situation worse, there was a period of stagnation, a pause. In that interim period, there was a belief that 'structural' techniques could replace the dialectical analysis of contradictions. The failure of that attempt is beginning to make itself clearly apparent.

Paris, February 1971.

Hegel, Marx, Nietzsche

(from *Hegel, Marx, Nietzsche ou le royaume des ombres* (Paris: Castermann, 1975), pp. 9–12, 46–52)

1. Without initially calling upon more than a basic knowledge of other fields and brief observations, we may state the following propositions:

a) *The modern world is Hegelian.* It was Hegel, in fact, who developed the political theory of the nation-state, pursuing its every implication to the limit. He asserted the State's supreme reality and value. Hegelianism proposes as a principle the connection between knowledge and power; it legitimates it. Of course, the number of nation-states is always increasing (approximately 150). They cover the face of the earth. It may be true that nations and nation-states are no more than fronts or façades, concealing larger capitalist phenomena, such as the world market and multinational companies, but these façades are no less a reality: no longer ends in themselves but effective instruments and structures. Whatever its underlying ideology, the State asserts itself everywhere, making inextricable use of knowledge and force, its reality and its value. The defined and defining character of the State is confirmed by the political consciousness it imposes – in other words, its conservative and even counter-revolutionary character – no matter what its official ideology, which may even be 'revolutionary'. From this perspective, the State engulfs and subordinates the reality Hegel calls 'civil society', that is to say, social relations. The State takes it upon itself to contain and define civilization.

b) *The modern world is Marxist.* In fact, for several decades, the central concerns of the so-called public authorities have been economic growth, seen as the basis for national existence and independence, and, therefore, industrialization and production. This brings with it problems in the relationship of the working-class (productive workers) with the nation-state, as well as a new relationship between knowledge and production, and therefore between knowledge and the powers that control production. It is neither obvious nor certain that knowledge is subordinate to power and that the State can expect to exist for ever. Rational planning, achieved by various methods, direct or indirect, complete or partial, is the order of the day. In the space of a century, industry and its effects have changed the world, that is, society, more (if not for the better) than have ideas, political projects, dreams or utopias. Which is more or less what Marx foresaw and predicted.

c) *The modern world is Nietzschean.* If there was anyone who wanted to 'change the world', it was Nietzsche, although the words themselves are attributed to Rimbaud.[1] If there was someone who wanted 'it all, and now', it was him. Protests and challenges to the status quo are fired off from all directions. Individual life and lived experience [vécu] reassert themselves against political pressures, 'productivism' and economism. When it is not putting one policy in opposition to another, protest finds support in poetry, music and the theatre, and also in the hope and expectation of the extraordinary: the surreal, the supernatural, the superhuman. Civilization preoccupies many people – more than the state or society. Despite the efforts of political forces to declare themselves above ordinary experience, to make society subordinate and to gain control over art, art represents the preserve of contestation, a resource for protest. And this despite what pushes it towards decline. It embodies the fervent spirit of Nietzschean revolt: the obstinate defence of civilization against State, social and moral pressures.

2. None of these propositions, in itself, looks like a paradox. That the modern world is Hegelian can be demonstrated or refuted using standard procedures. Anyone wanting to prove it must, as far as possible, reconstruct Hegel's philosophical and political system, on the basis of the texts. Then he will study the influence of this doctrine and its penetration of political life by various routes, such as the academy, the interpretation of events, the subsequent elucidation of the blind activity of statesmen. The same goes for Marx and for Nietzsche.

But the triple enunciation has something intolerably paradoxical about it. How can the modern world be one thing and at the same time, another? How can it be governed by theories that are different, or in several respects contradictory or actually incompatible?

It can no longer be a matter of influence, any more than reference. If the modern world 'is' both this and at the same time that (Hegelian and Nietzschean...), then it can no longer be about ideologies that would seem to hover, shadowy or bright, like clouds shot through with rays of light, high above social and political practice. Such a statement obliges us to grasp and define new relationships between theories (doctrines) and between theories and practice. If this triplicity means anything, it means that all three – Hegel, Marx, Nietzsche – grasped 'something' about the modern world, something that was in the process of becoming. And it means that in so far as each doctrine has attained a coherence (Hegelianism, Marxism or Nietzscheanism), it has declared what it was that it grasped, and by so doing, has contributed to what was coming into being at the end of the nineteenth century, and thus leading into the twentieth century and beyond. In such a way that the encounter between important works goes through a mediation, modernity, which they illuminate and which illuminates them. In a previous book,[2] these doctrines were compared with historicism and historicity. Here, we broaden our critical analysis while still striving to keep it concrete.

If it is true that Hegelian thought focuses on a single word, a single concept: the State – while Marxist thought puts great emphasis on the social, on *society*, that Nietzsche finally meditated on *civilization* and its values, the paradox gives us a glimpse of a meaning still awaiting discovery: a triple determination of the modern, and that this involves multiple and perhaps endless conflicts within what we call human 'reality'. We offer this as a hypothesis sufficiently broad to be called strategic.

3. To study Hegel, Marx or Nietzsche in isolation in their texts is not very productive; every possible textual connection has been explored, every deconstruction and reconstruction offered, without the authenticity of such an interpretation asserting itself. There seems to be as little interest left in the notion of studying them in context, situating them within the history of philosophy, the history of ideas or history in general, as there is in doing textual analysis. As for situating them within the history of philosophy, general history or the history of ideas, the appeal of such a contextual study seems as exhausted as that of textual analysis.

What remains, therefore, is to grasp their relations with the modern world, taking that as our point of reference, our central object of analysis, our common measure (or mediation) between the various doctrines and ideologies involved. The 'contextual' thus takes on a breadth and scope, a wealth of known and unknown quantities, that it was denied when reduced to a specialized or generalized historical discipline. How did Hegel, how did Marx, how did Nietzsche catch modernity by surprise in its nascent state, in its tendencies? How did they grasp what was 'taking root'? How did they fix on a particular aspect or define a moment among contradictory aspects and moments?

Three stars, one constellation. Their brilliance sometimes coincides, sometimes eclipses one another. They produce interference. Sometimes they cast more light, sometimes less. They rise or sink toward the horizon, grow closer together or further apart. Now one seems to be in the ascendant, now another.

The sentences above have only a merely metaphorical or symbolic import. They suggest a direction, a general setting. They affirm (and it remains to be demonstrated) that the greatness of the works and the men under consideration no longer resembles that of classical philosophers such as Plato and Aristotle, Descartes and Kant, who were building a great architecture of concepts. This 'greatness' lies in a particular relationship with the 'real', with practice. It is thus not in the domain of philology which can be represented through language. It is new, and *metaphilosophical*, and has itself to define itself by deciphering the enigmatic: modernity.

[...]

10. In order to pursue the comparison between the members of the Hegel–Marx–Nietzsche triad, and between these three magisterial systems of

thought about the modernity they tried to grasp, we must eliminate political obstacles and hypotheses. This point and this position are worth stressing.[3]

a) *Hegel and Hegelianism can be accused of reaction, pure and simple. A 'right-wing' politics that offered itself not only as Realpolitik* but also as true, could, theoretically speaking, find justification in his work in an analysis of the 'real', of the nation and the actual country, and of their essential institutions. This would legitimate not only the State and the apparatus of the State, but also its political apparatus and the predominance of the Statesman over all other 'moments' of knowledge or culture.

For we find this in Hegel: theorization and rationalization of the political event [*fait*]. With him, justification of the State goes with justification of a 'state of affairs' in which the totality of the real stops, stagnates and becomes blocked.

If that was all there was in Hegel, would he deserve confrontation? Would there be grounds for a case? No. First of all, Hegelianism, with theorization contains both an admission and a denunciation of that 'state of affairs'. It enables it to be analysed. Secondly, Hegel, who claimed to be, and believed himself a defender of freedom, also rejected and refuted this limit case, stagnation and the display of the already accomplished. He conceived of a compromise between authority and liberty that purported to be harmonious. Only the liberal State allows free play to its 'moments' and gives its limbs suppleness. It alone regenerates itself and reproduces itself autodynamically, with an immanent, rational vitality. In Hegelianism, a backward-looking appeal to what has been accomplished, to unchecked violence, shows there is no ultimate balance, that is incomplete or a failure. If for the past 150 years the State has revealed its 'worst side', Hegelianism cannot be held responsible for the State as Hegel theorized it. More symptom than cause Hegelianism cannot be scrapped as easily as the legalistic historicism of someone like Savigny, for example.[4] Hegelianism can be used (and some have not hesitated to use it) to defend an attachment to the past on historicist, nationalist, even chauvinist grounds. These interpretations and distortions must appear as part of the full case, but they are not enough to prevent a case being made.

b) And the same goes for Marx, and Stalinism. If there is a 'revisionist' ideology in relation to Marx's thought, it must surely be that dark incubus. It is true that Stalinist mystifiers used the word 'revisionist' as an insult to cover their ideological operations (based, it goes without saying and with no need for it to be stated openly, on the economic, social and political 'realities' of the USSR after Lenin). The Stalinists were adept at clouding the issue, dubbing Hegel, for example, a 'philosopher of feudal reaction', while they themselves were Hegelians or even super-Hegelians. The fact that following a proletarian revolution class struggle leads to the strengthening and further centralization of the State is perhaps a 'historical necessity', or an inevitable outcome of socio-political practice in an under-industrialized country, but that has nothing to do with Marx's thinking. Indeed, if this thesis is *true* in the theoretical sense of the word, then so-called Marxist thought collapses. It crumbles away, for all that well-meaning people pick up the pieces and try to build something from the debris.

One can quote against these pseudo-theory texts by Marx, Engels and Lenin, so numerous that they fill volumes. Furthermore, the violent controversies stirred up by Stalinism and the anti-Stalinist opposition exposed an internal contradiction within the revolutionary movement and the working-class movement itself. This appeared as soon as Saint-Simon and Fourier.[5] Fourier cheerfully dispenses with the State, while Saint-Simon no less blithely contradicts himself, sometimes predicting the coming of an efficient State because it is led by 'industrialists' (producers and scholars), sometimes that state control will be replaced by direct management of things themselves. This contradiction came to a head in Europe around 1870. Since historians and political orators pore tenderly over the working-class movement in order to remove, or at least attenuate, its contradictions, they have ignored the dual process that led in France to the Commune and in Germany to the formation of the Social-Democratic Party. The French movement boldly attacked and brought down the State in 1871, when the workers of Paris marched 'to storm the heavens'. German socialism, by contrast, under the influence of Lassalle,[6] a Hegelian, accepted the State, and became part of it. As we know, Bismarck saw that process of integration as a brilliant political strategy. Do we need yet another reminder of the content of the *Critique of the Gotha Programme,* and of Marx's caution in hardly referring in that important text (his political testament) to the Paris Commune, although he entirely approved of it? Contradiction thus appears in both Marx's thinking and his works.

Hence the terrible bitterness of the last sentence in that text: 'Dixi et salvavi animam meam' (I spoke, and saved my soul).

The fact that State socialism has triumphed in the working-class movement in Europe and throughout the world means that movement has abandoned Marxism and Leninism, that 'Lassallism' has taken it over, that Marxism has become an ideology, a philosophy subservient to the State, a *public service* in the Hegelian sense. Marx is in no way responsible for this state of affairs, apart from the fact that he left unresolved a critically important conflict.

c) Finally, the same goes for Nietzsche and German National Socialism. A process of fanatical falsification has twisted and dragged Nietzsche's texts in the direction of fascist ideology. Of course, there are plenty of ambiguous passages analysing the will to power, and Nietzsche sometimes admires some dubious heroes – adventurers, condottieri and conquistadors. Marx could just as easily be described as an anti-Semite, because he published *The Jewish Question*! With his radical critique, his fundamental refusal, rejection and refutation of the *libido dominandi,* Nietzsche envisaged all aspects, all its disguises, political and non-political: imperial and imperialist behaviour, Machiavellianism, military ambition and action, but also goodness, charitable action and 'good works', to the point of self-abnegation and humility.

As for Nietzsche's success, that is to say, the reception of his theoretical analysis as ideology, is concerned, its nature has changed; 'immoralists' or would-be anarchists in the early twentieth century, then fascists and politicians and now philosophers, 'Nietzscheans' or those who would call themselves such have lapsed into various kinds of misunderstanding. These errors of interpretation ought to be included in the evidence. They are not directly attributable to the author.

This rejection of political understanding involves the devaluation of the political as such, and this must be emphasized. There is nothing definitive about the political criterion which, during the Stalinist and fascist era, was presented as an *absolute* criterion. It changes, it falls. For a short time it takes on a 'total' appearance because it is imposed by the twin means of ideological persuasion and violence. It leads to errors that later appear in all their ridiculousness.

11. 'Would it be an obsession with triads, or a caricatural imitation of the model thus described, that makes you limit yourself to three works and three thinkers, and place Hegel, Marx and Nietzsche at the threshold of modernity, and above it? Why not others?'

It is open to anyone to claim that the honour roll of the departed ends with Freud, or Heidegger, or even with Lenin or Mao Tse-Tung, or indeed, with Wilhelm Reich or Georges Bataille, etc.[7]

Take Freud and his work. Why not include him in this governing constellation?

His analytical thinking is all the more powerful for being based on clinical observation and therapeutic practice. That clinical practice (often effective but at other times futile or harmful) has a 'real' existence. It is an established fact that it has conceptualized sexuality, so long a no-go area, and brought it into the realms of language. As far as practice is concerned, the connections of Marxist thought with social practice and revolutionary practice (endeavours and setbacks) mean that it is well placed to respond to 'practicists'. Only Nietzschean thought suffers from this comparison, because it is linked only with a practice of *speech*. Unless, that is, it is related to the mediocre practice of writing. Psychoanalysis, on the other hand, has created a livelihood, a profession with its place in the social division of labour, and one that from the beginning has tended to become institutionalized. In such a situation, partial (clinical) practice creates an ideology that tries to justify the practice by exceeding it, by addressing every issue and aspiring to totality.

Hence the feebleness of psychoanalysis; the formless combination of a linguistic technique with fragmentary pieces of knowledge, representations asserted beyond their sphere of validity, by reduction or extrapolation. This ideology conveys its own myth, the unconscious, that bag of tricks that contains anything you care to put in it: the body, memory, individual and collective histories, language, culture and its products or remnants, and so on and so forth. Finally, and especially, Freud grasped, described and analysed only the *libido sentiendi*. Post-Freudian psychoanalysis touches only indirectly on the *libido dominandi*, so thoroughly explored by Nietzsche. It ignores completely the *libido sciendi*, the domain of knowing, the *social* status of knowledge. Why? Because although Freud was influenced by search for the unfathomable [*la recherche abyssale*] (Schopenhauer), he never abandoned the Hegelian system of knowledge. He thus had a poor acquaintance with the great underground tradition, that clandestine heritage that is the glory of European thought and makes the dead or rotten branches of the Logos flourish anew. For this reason, psychoanalysis does not go as far, analytically, as Augustine, Jansen, La Rochefoucauld, Pascal or Nietzsche.[8] When Freud stands trembling with excitement at his discovery that sex and sexuality lead only to defeat and failure, tragedy and pathos, and thus to the pathological, he is returning to the ancient theme of *concordia discors* or *discordis concors*. And adding little to it, apart from clinical efforts to cure neuroses. Do psychoanalysts succeed in doing that? Do they master the terrible *negative* power of language – through language? That's another question.

If knowledge perceives the desire in the depths of the unfathomable 'being' it also calls into question knowing: itself. For Nietzsche, who pursued this problem to its furthest limits, desire, a force whose energy is contained in the whole body (not just the genitals), which becomes 'supreme greatness' and arises out of and within the body, expresses itself as dance, and song, and then as the desire for eternity, the eternal itself. It has nothing to do with humble sexual libido, or even with Plato's Eros. 'Meine weise Sehnsucht' [My wise longing], says Zarathustra – wisdom on fire, desire on the mountains, desire with trembling wings, this passionate reason cries out and laughs.[9]

As part of this investigation, it would be interesting to study the movements that perturb religions and religious institutions, especially the Catholic Church, rather than psychoanalysis, a 'modernist' ideology that is a trifle arrogant.

Did not Nietzsche himself see the success of psychoanalysis as a new symptom of decadence, a disease that was taking hold, a form of European nihilism? Indeed! There is certainly something morbid in this new avatar of Judeo-Christianity, which attempts to recycle itself by salvaging the curse placed on sex, but which in its language and concepts preserves all the 'signs of the non-body'. Psychoanalysis, as theory and ideology, practice and (discursive) technique has managed neither to restore the total body nor prevent the phallic from taking on an 'object' existence.[10] Furthermore, the ideological breakthrough by psychoanalysis continues to overshadow Nietzschean thought by relegating it to a no-go area that replaces the former one (sex) and is in fact the zone of the *libido dominandi*. The result is that as ideology, psychoanalysis serves the established order in a number of ways: by hindering the critique of power and the State, by displacing thought and giving it a different centre, and so on and so forth.

'And what about Heidegger?', demands an interrogative voice, slightly hostile. This philosopher is absent from the constellation for several reasons. He follows the triadic model in the most simplistic way: Being – its eclipse – its resurrection or resurgence. That history of Being (the creative force, the Word, the Spirit) passes as original to people who are not familiar with the eternal Gospel. It obscures the more concrete history of Hegel and Marx, without attaining the power of Nietzsche's critique of history. Heidegger's philosophy, a disguised, barely secularized theodicy, strives to rescue traditional philosophy without subjecting it to a radical critique. Although he touches on it, Heidegger evades the notion of *metaphilosophy*. He substitutes for it so-called fundamental ontology, a variant, whether we like it or not, of metaphysics. It is true that he offers a contribution to the critical analysis of modernity; he was among the first to perceive and foresee the dangers inherent in overvaluing technology and to understand that *domination* over nature (by knowledge and technology) becomes domination *over men* and is not the same as the *appropriation* of nature because it tends to destroy it. Heidegger speaks (writes) an admirable prose, almost too elegant, because for him, Being resides – and this saves it from endless wandering – in language (the Word) and architectural constructions (temples, palaces, monuments and buildings). From this admirable (the word is to be taken ironically) idea, the philosopher draws a disturbing apologia for the German language. This prevents his making a radical critique of the Western (European) Logos, although he verges on it. What he says about and against Nietzsche is not convincing – whether he goes further and deeper, or follows the truthful and deceptive shimmering surfaces of consciousness – better than his predecessor.

As for other contemporary 'thinkers' what have they done but put into circulation the small change of Hegel, Marx and Nietzsche, along with a few counterfeit coins?[11] This judgement will be seen as severe. In fact, there is nothing pejorative about it; it means that theoretical battles and ideological trials of strength are not waged without pain.

Triads and Dyads

(from *La Présence et l'absence* (Paris: Castermann, 1980) pp. 143, 225–31)

The problematic: Thought that is reflective, that philosophizes, has long put the accent on dyads. In the ancient Greek world: wet and dry, big and small, order and disorder, finite and infinite. Then there are the pairs that form the paradigm of Western philosophy: subject–object, continuous–discontinuous, open–closed, etc. Finally, in the modern era, the binary oppositions of signifier and signified, knowledge and non-knowledge, centre and periphery, etc. But a triadic structure long present within the Western logos has emerged since Hegel. Is this triadic structure having a decisive impact? Perhaps, but it is also possible that it will break down, that practice or knowledge will destroy it.

The dialogue between friendship and hatred, the grapplings [*les corps à corps*] of love or combat, offer moments of incomparable intensity, of presence. But the relationship between two entities (duality, opposition, contrariety, dyad) vanishes as it takes shape, turning into image and reflection, a mirror effect, a rivalry that is derisory to the primacy of either one. Hence the annihilation of one by the other, or sometimes their arrival at the logical compromise of mutual representation.

Might not three-term relationships be inexhaustible? Wherever the infinite touches the finite there are three dimensions, for example, those of space, music (melody, harmony, rhythm), language (syntagma, paradigm, symbolism), etc.

Is there ever a two-term relationship, except in representation? There are always Three. There is always the Other.

TABLE OF TRIADS (grouped together)

Form	Dogmatism	Empiricism	Positivism
Structure	Nihilism	Speculation	Negativism
Function	Relativism	Theory	Overcoming
Abstraction	Totality	Globality	Displacement
Reduction	Contradiction	Critique	Substitution
Restitution	Possibility	Utopia	Representation

Syntagma	Centrality	Knowledge	Knowing
Paradigm	Periphery	Misapprehension	Having
Symbol	Mediation	Ignorance	Ability
	Sentiendi	Sensoriality	Homogeneity
Libido	Cognoscendi	Sensibility	Fragmentation
	Dominandi	Sensuality	Hierarchy

Representing – Represented – Representation

	Analytical	Praxis	Melody
Thought:	Positive	Doxa	Rhythm
	Operative	Poiesis	Harmony
Thing	Presence	History	Philosophy
Product	Absence	Space	Scientism
Work	Representation	Worldliness	Metaphilosophy
Identity	Subject	Raw material	
Contradiction	Object	Processed material	Etc.
Difference	Unit	Production	

[...]

PRESENCE AND ABSENCE

1. In speaking (and I do mean speaking) of presence and absence I shall not forget the ordeals of real life: the terrible presences of the enemy in fights to the death – the terrible absences of the loved one when one is in love ...
2. This does not mean we can put the 'imaginary' everywhere. This word is becoming (or, rather, becoming again) magical. It fills the empty spaces in thought, like 'the unconscious' or 'culture'.
3. Presence and absence cannot be thought of as two sides, recto and verso, of one mental (or social or natural) phenomenon. Such oscillations, or flickerings, of the notorious 'signifier-signified' pairing in particular, have been overused. By this process, the intelligentsia that has withdrawn from action has, cleverly enough, extended its own apologia and discourse. Moreover, as two terms were not enough, a third had to be introduced: the unconscious, the imagination, culture. Just like that.

In this text, we had to get out of the 'representing-represented' pair, in order to grasp the third term, representation, by taking analysis further.
4. The third term, here, is the *other*, with all that implies (*alterity*, the relation with the present/absent other – *alteration* – *alienation*).

5. We (Who? That remains to be seen) often look for presence elsewhere than in the *oeuvre*, in love, in the concept. *We* are thus liable to find only the shadow, the simulacrum, etc. Which is not to say that these attempts to go beyond representations are any the less meaningful or important. They show how the route circumvents or subverts the goal, how *we* think the issue.

6. This is all the more so since presence has no substantiality, contrary to what the metaphysical tradition tells us. The philosophical figure of the Substantial also subverts and circumvents the goal; it is only a representation. And presence? It always manifests itself in a form, but the form, taken on its own, is empty, and thus absence. Content taken on its own is formless, and thus absence. Form and content, when separated, are evasions of presence. This presupposes and implies an act: the *poietic act*. And that also implies an attachment to *being*, to the fact of being and the possibility of a plenitude that is never fixed, never definitive. Presence, which is a *moment* and not pure form or substance, rewards an act that takes risks; to be 'at stake' and 'to win' imply that the 'subject' thus created transcends both seriousness and play; that it ceases to play when the game becomes serious.

Presence is achieved only through effort, which precedes surprise, the flower of life (the Rose without why).[1] To encounter a person or a work, we have to go out to meet them, or it, a meeting that fulfils expectation. Presence is not met with except as part of a scenario, which it interrupts. It evolves within representations, and transcends them. Just like the theatre!

7. Play, like knowledge, like work, like the search for love (for the Other) are only moments in which absence reveals itself, and presence appears. The poietic act cannot avoid them, but traverses them. This movement is always liable to stop at a representation (what we call 'blockage').

Examples of so-called 'balance' (which are alienating and factitious), circles and loops, are no less dangerous for movement than are 'blockages'. On the individual as well as the social level, representations that 'motivate' or 'inhibit' over a long period set up a pattern of armour–armature–closure. A protection against anxiety and dissolution, these are defences but they are nonetheless traps, decoys, illusions of power. And thus dissimulated and dissimulating absences. Simulacrum and dissimulation go together. A recent but little publicized discovery: presence, as power and creation, are all simulations. And the representation of the simulacrum conceals failure.

8. Are these psychological questions? Psychoanalytical? Ethical? Philosophical? Ontological? Yes – all of these. And no – something different. Psychologically speaking, presence is arrived at by various routes: by *impregnation* (in childhood and adolescence, i.e. during the period of 'education') and by *choice* (later, by accepting a risk, with a greater or lesser degree of lucidity).

9. The role of the will-to-power remains enigmatic. It is, it seems, impossible to avoid it. It cannot be circumvented, and both desire and poietic

activity include it as an element or moment. But it also has to be deflected, *re-futed*. Otherwise, the relationship with the 'other' remains one of domination, and the 'other' becomes object, instrument, servant, etc.

10. Once analysis of the 'presence–absence' relationship as a binary, and therefore logical and linguistic phenomenon, reducible to a pertinent opposition, has been eliminated, what route remains open? Description, analysis and statement of this relationship as a dialectical movement. Which is to say, unity and contradiction. No absolute presence. Flight of presence, which never becomes substance. Magical character of 'substantification'. No absolute absence. No vacuum or pure nothingness, even in (after) death. Presence is not absence, however. And conversely. On the one hand, at the extreme, the limit, there is the anxiety that attaches itself to a shadow, a double, a distant echo, a simulation. On the other hand, at the limit, there is a plenitude, a richness (never possessed). Between the two, teeming re-presentations, acting as mediators and intermediates. They are ambiguous; the gap into which re-presentations flock is also the space for conflicts.

11. *Absence*? How to represent it, since representation fills the voids of absence? The sign, which one misuses, expresses absence – the existence of the designated absent – and assigns it. Signs offer the illusion of naming that which escapes naming. They name what is distant and thereby distance it all the further. Hence the equivocal, negative character, even lethal and murderous, of language, already noted by Hegel.

The image invites access to presence. It wishes to *sur-prise* or *re-prise* a lost presence, or to *sus-pend* absence. Hence its magical aspect, which compensates for the destructive and auto-destructive effect of the verb (Apollonian).

Presence is sought by the Dionysian route: drunkenness, trance; but it is also by this route that absence and the flight of presence are discovered. Exorcising absence, imitating presence to bring it into being, these magical actions elude poietic action, the action of love, creation, knowledge. Intoxication of the senses leads to disenchantment: empty hands, empty head. The *oeuvre* – no . . .

12. In such a world, where there is no longer (or never truly has been) either base or basis, where language itself (in which in the West we thought we had seen an installation) gives way, where the ground begins to sway (reference systems collapse and emancipated capacities and powers assert themselves in and for themselves), what is called 'abnormality', 'psychological defect' or 'neurosis' becomes normal. The simulation of 'presence' without faith or credibility removes it, especially in politics. We mime the substantial by using representations; which allows us to 'present' the political, the economic, the technological, etc., as truths, as absolutes. Consistence is obtained via advertising and propaganda, in the general expectation and search for some sort of 'substantiality'. Truth operates to the full as representation, ideology, myth and mystification.

Henceforth 'normal' man has every form of mental illness. By turns, he is schizophrenic, paranoid, maniacal, etc., with their corresponding representations. But he does not settle on (in) any single one.

The person who is mentally ill has one illness only, a single neurosis, which may turn into psychosis if it becomes fixed. The only treatment: to find again a presence. Which one? How? Everyone does all he can to open up access to presence, by as many means as possible. In general: imitating it, simulating it, in order to achieve it.

13. The terms of classical philosophy: the Same and the Other, Subject and Object, the One and the All, can be recognized in Presence-Absence; they are all there but do not merge: unity in difference, totality without a fixed system, without transcendence or immanence. Terms in relation one with another cease to refer to one another in an infinite regress, as in Leibnizian monadology (monads being nothing but the relationship between monads); they cease their redundant repetition. They make a connection with productive and creative practice, which transcends classical philosophy. The Other ceases to modify, to alienate the Same. The Same ceases to impose on the Other its logico-tautological law. When does alienation begin? When the ordeal of alterity exceeds the forces, when presence becomes lost in representation; when absence is accepted and the 'subject' is defined by emptiness and the defence against emptiness.

To obtain the gifts of chance and chance encounters, risks must be taken – the risks of failure, poverty, vain pursuit, the risk that the moment of presence will end, leaving behind it wounds and nostalgia. Suffering must be accepted, which is less profound than joy (Nietzsche), but slips despair into joy's place when joy is lost in time. It is true that despair, a moment of poietic action, is different from anguish, that emptiness from which there is no escape. Those who refuse to take the risk because they do not wish to suffer, no longer wish to feel joy. Who has desired it to the full, apart from the philosophers, the founders of religion, certain mystics, certain revolutionaries? They all fall into the neutrality of ambiguous representations, into magical gestures that substitute fantasies and phantoms for presence ...

14. Still borrowing the themes and categories of classical philosophy, even its problematic: presence is neither origin (attached to a *terminus a quo*) nor end (attached to a *terminus ad quem*). Its origin and its end lie in itself. Has it no history? Yes, its own history – of moments, of contact. It 'is', first possible, then actualized, or, rather, carried out; and yet it 'is' not in the classical sense of substance, of 'being' held and held back.

Although the final reference point, it does not 'function' as a frame of reference, a principle of decoding-coding. To keep hold of it by defining it thus is to cause it to escape, without the stimulation of absence becoming manifest. Knowledge also has its magic and may substitute a magical operation – possession of the object – for poietic action. Here we are dealing with the unity of the 'subject' and the 'object', but *as act* and not as representation. This act seizes in a single apperception *both* what constitutes it as 'subject' (with no pre-existence as substance) *and* what it perceives as 'object' (in the luminous field of consciousness). This unity of subject and object does not *precede* the difference between them, in nature or the unconscious; but nor is it situated *beyond* it, in a transcendent truth or a higher spirituality. It is situated *in the difference*. It differs as much from abstract identity (tautology, equivalence) as from contradiction through incoherence or incompatibility, i.e. the popular conception of the dialectic.

It is true that there is that which precedes the everyday (survival without the resources necessary in order to live) and what lies beyond the everyday (life freed from everyday constraints). There's what *precedes* the political (lack of political awareness) and *what lies beyond* it (critique of the political). Presence and absence are not situated like that. 'Before' and 'beyond' are ruled by representations that fill the void and mask both presence and absence.

15. *Prey to absence* ... Naked humanity beset by signs? Plagued by the vampirism of words and things? No. Modern man as prey to absence. A surprising paradox among paradoxes: exchange, communication, information, endless discourse, discourse about discourse, have denuded this 'man' without essence or generic definition, stripped him of nature and powers, dispossessed him of his body, which he attempts (women rather than 'man') to reconquer. The disappearance of points of reference, the breakdown of unity as it is lived and conceptualized, the predominance of representations leave him prey to an absence that is hardly experienced as such and is fraught with resentment.

Radical critique, initiated by Nietzsche and taken to its furthest limit by Artaud[2] and others, declares: 'In order to create the new, to clear out entirely the space of invention, let us begin with a guerrilla war of signs; let us destroy exchange, established modes of communication, these parodies, these simulacra; let us abolish ideology; let us pit the logic of signs against symbols and images; let us revolutionize discourse, the social body of signifiers, the illusory life at the heart of signs; let us deny their crazy illusion that they offer a totality in the form of vocabulary, nomenclature, the word; let us bombard the channels of signification, every kind of *medium* ...'

And now? And then? The approach is familiar: a taste for the worst, an attraction towards absolute negativity, the vertigo of nothingness. They will dig a gulf from which they will never find a way out ...

Is the real problem not to recognize and reveal what presence is and what it is not – absence? To restore the present to the heart of the actual.

16. *Presence and absence.* First lived, then transferred to language and the concept, which reacts with lived experience. What about presence? To start with lets call it a 'thing', a 'being', an 'oeuvre' (but none of these words fully elucidates the act) which reveals itself, so that it can be seen, grasped and loved (or hated!). It can be a (human) person, a 'thing' (a tree, a flower, a

stone), or several persons, a place (a rural landscape, a city), a building (monument), a piece of music or an event. The variety of presences is infinite, but the word has a universal and univocal import: intensification of experience, a force that is persuasive without being brutal (whether in the form of irruption, impregnation, choice, etc.).

Space thus conceptualized is defined as the play of absences and presences, represented by the alternation of light and shade, the luminous and the nocturnal. 'Objects' in space simulate the appearance and disappearance of presences in the most profound way. Time is thus punctuated by presences. They give it rhythm, but it also contains things that are not what they seem, representations that simulate/dissimulate.

17. *Critiques of metaphysics and mysticism.* The philosophers and certain mystics have prospected the way of presence. Meta-physics is meta-phorical: it delves too deeply, in the conceived. Mysticism enquires closer to hand, in the lived, but differs from metaphysics only in this orientation. Their respective methodologies, in the East as well as in the West, end up as the representation of an (onto-logical) centre of the 'real' or the 'spiritual', while claiming to capture it and install themselves within it. This centre is defined as either: a) a complete and always present, substantial Being around which everything else turns, devalued and demeaned in relation to this absolute presence; or, b) a void, an emptiness, a nothingness, an equally absolute absence.

Between this negativism and dogmatism lies the way of the poietic act: the act of overcoming. What is overcome? A (substitute) pseudo-presence or over-presence of re-presentations transposed into models (philosophical, metaphysical or mystical).

Is there an eternal moment, both spring and sun? Nietzsche himself both thought and said so (cf. *The Gay Science*, p. 341).[3] These moments would seem to have their symbol in the City and the home, the heart, or the mountain-tops ... There are certainly moments that are to a greater or lesser degree profound or sublime, but still relative: the minute at which I would say 'Stop' seldom comes ...

18. *Absence and pathology.* Absence, as a moment, has nothing pathogenic about it. On the contrary: it provokes, it incites. Pathology comes from the cessation of movement, from fixity in absence and emptiness, from the feeling of never escaping it, a state of nothingness. When every 'object' (thing, being, *oeuvre*) is replaced by its ghostly double, when absence disappears through ceasing to appear as such and when as a result, the maelstrom of anxiety opens up, then a pathological state arises.

Twelve Theses on Logic and Dialectic

(from *Logique formelle, logique dialectique*, 3rd edn (Paris: Terrains Éditions Sociales, 1982, Preface)

1. Neither logic nor the dialectic can be defined as superstructures of this or that society, this or that mode of production. Nor can they be attached to religious or philosophical ideologies. Linked in their discovery and elaboration with ideologies and even with institutions, at some point in the course of historical time they became detached from them, without being reduced to pure, abstract, timeless forms persisting over centuries. Nor can they be reduced to a simple methodology, gnoseology or pure theory of knowledge. On the one hand they are related to practice and on the other, to theory (concepts) and thought that seeks itself, and believes it finds or recognizes itself in a system, which sooner or later collapses.

2. Dialectical thinking emerges in Heraclitus through direct, immediate contact with the world. His poetical language proclaims his perceptions about fire, the river, the rainbow, etc., that is, becoming, conflicts, oppositions, creation and destruction. This introduction to the dialectic still preserves its meaning and flavour. And that raises a question: 'Having passed through all the mediating processes that he has himself produced, that he has managed to turn against himself (alienation), of which the latest is technology, does not the social, thinking, acting man rediscover a relationship with the world in immediacy?' '*Man*' here does not refer to any essence, any defined subject, any more than it does to a humanist ideology. The question of the rediscovery of immediacy with the world is raised in terms of contemporary 'universality', interrogation of what is possible or impossible, contradictions within societies, exploration of nature and the universe, etc. It should be pointed out that the dialectic cannot be conceived of only as deriving from Heraclitus but also from his confrontation with Parmenides; the conflict between them marked the inception and the source of the great philosophical questions that have been asked through the centuries: 'The Same and the Other – repetition and becoming – positivity and negativity – order and disorder – life and death ...'

3. Logic and its problems are not only problems of *form*, but ontological, cosmo-logical, anthropo-logical questions. The theory of forms cannot forget that every form presents itself first as a content that is worked up, developed and thus becomes form, in such a way that it eventually

appears to pre-date the content. Was this not true of the Greek conception of the universe, developed by Aristotle as the concept of order and necessity, translated into formal deduction?

4. Logic is first considered formally, but its form cannot be separated from a content that it seizes or receives from facts, from practice and sooner or later, from becoming. The formal refers to 'something', which it appropriates but which nevertheless escapes it. Is this relationship not doubly dialectical: the relationship of form with content and of content with temporality, i.e. becoming? At the same time, the dialectic – the dialectical movement of knowledge and thought – has first to be studied formally. Dialectical thought also is defined by a form, by rules and laws. It contradicts logic, but does not abolish it; it does not fall into absurdity. The dialectic does not permit us to make contradictory statements, at the same time, about the same subject; it does not allow us to say this sheet of paper is both black and white. Hence an axiom: 'The theory of contradictions cannot be contradictory.' However, formal analysis reveals the defining characteristics of dialectical thought, which fundamentally distinguish it from logic. Logic tries to confine itself to one term: identity and its implications. In order not to be tautological, its relationship with content forces logical thinking to introduce differences, i.e. a second term. This is not without its difficulties. $A = A$; that's obvious, but not very useful. A is B; that's much more complex and harder to define logically. We're in the mediating area between logic and dialectics, and sooner or later, dialectic introduces *three* terms. Dialectic resolves itself into neither a single term nor two different terms. The introduction of the third term reveals a transformation in thought, its evolution in the world that is in process of becoming. The third term indicates both the contradictory complexity of the real and the movement that springs from contradiction and moves towards going beyond it. (An illustration of this idea: in Marx, the triad 'work/capital/profits-from-the-earth's-products'. In music, the triad, 'rhythm/melody/harmony', etc.).

5. The logical form detaches itself and is studied as such. It is not only joined with external contents, but is product and producer. It produces abstractions that join up and tend towards the concrete via the logico-mathematical route. These abstractions, linked together, serve as mediation between the form and the real. Active, these mediations help to create the real, that is, not only to define it as such, in and through science, but actually to make it, to produce it. Philosophy has long attributed this production to the activity of the 'subject' or 'subjects'. Logic, or the logical, invests itself in the real and its production, while the dialectical becoming removes this reality – the reality of the Same – by dissolving it. Logic becomes part of practice: projects and coherent strategies, operational logic, operating systems, and nowadays, 'software', i.e. logical machines, etc. The logical form is thus connected with its effects: consistency, stability, coherence, systematization, etc. Logic thus sets up its empire both in the area of

knowledge, as a theory that is stable in terms of rigour, proof, truth and reality, and in practice. It provides and ensures homogeneity in knowledge and practice. Its tendency is to *totalize*, but it never succeeds in this, either in applied forms of logic or in so-called systems analysis or epistemology. Within the empire it tries to establish, logic starts out as a tool, then becomes a machine and even a machine for producing machines.

6. The logical form (identity) produces repetition: A is A. With everything it engenders, the logical form is connected with the dogmatic assertion of the *Being* and the *real*, and consequently with the philosophical questioning of the Same and the Other: 'What is the Same, i.e. that which persists, is repeated, continues? What is the Other, which changes the Same and makes it a world [*qui modifie et qui mondifie le Même*]? And what is becoming? How can there be repetition and becoming, continuity and discontinuity, appearances and disappearances? Which is appearance, the Same or the Other? Could the Same be mechanism? The substantial or the Essential? Law? Or Being? ...'

7. Classical philosophy from Plato to Hegel, and its overcoming today, turn on these central questions, to which Hegel provided only incomplete answers: 'What is identity, or the identical? Being or void? Substance or tautology? Why such questions if identity is obvious, intelligible, true and the image of Truth itself?' It is a question all the more disquieting in that identity is connected with the repetition, equivalency and ambiguity of the word 'Being' (sometimes copula, sometimes substance). But we can safely say that identity is triple or triadic: a) Logical identity, A is A, repetitive, long taken as the criterion or model of absolute truth (the transcendent deity of the theologians and metaphysicians declares and defines himself in a neat phrase: 'I am that I am.'). b) Concrete identity, of the Same that maintains itself against becoming: the 'being [étant]', defined objects, consciousness, concepts, 'I am myself' ... Groups of human beings seek, find and lose their identity. This identity persists, and seeks to persist, even though it is relative. c) Dialectical identity: 'I is an other' ... 'I only see, and am, in relation to the other ... All that is becomes other.' This is the figure of the relative, found in relationships, in the world, in becoming; it is the Same in thrall to the Other, defining itself by it, carried by it, that is, by contradictions.

8. While logic believes it is relegating logical identity to the absurd, dialectical contradiction penetrates its very heart; it installs itself there as becoming stable, difference within the indifferent. Becoming removes all that resists it by using repetition and equivalence. So that what is non-equivalent in equivalence responds to and corresponds with what is non-identical in identity (as it is in the world of exchanges and merchandise). And furthermore, logic or the logical cannot be conceived of without recourse to the dialectic(al). The attempt fails because logic can only be theorized via its other. Logic is not yet thought, but the form and rules of speech and actions through which thought seeks itself. The dialectic is the fertilization of the

logical, at the heart of logic. The logic-dialectic nexus brings with it conflicts in the course of which logic tends to eliminate dialectic, but it does not succeed, or succeeds only partially, although logicians think it is for ever – for all eternity! The relationship of logic and dialectic is thus itself dialectical.

9. The contradiction that goes unnoticed, unstated as such, is called a *paradox*. Thought in search of itself has been both stimulated and blocked by paradoxes, from Epimenides's paradox of the liar[1] to more recent examples: the paradoxes of set theory, or Gödel's theorem.[2] The terms 'paradox' and 'paradoxical' occur ever more frequently in contemporary writing. What is not paradoxical? Our contemporaries have lost the sense of the dialectic and thus that of logic. Specialized branches of logic proliferate – down to the 'logic of the unconscious' – as do paradoxes and situations described as paradoxical. In this way, the work of the negative continues, in turmoil and confusion. The negative and the dialectic are denied, but return to the scene as the paradoxical.

10. The negative carries on its work in the modern world, with paradoxes and crises, risks and threats. Might it not be the negative that constitutes a totality of the various elements and fragments of today's world?

11. Logic has established its empire within the world of capitalist production. The use of this theoretical and practical tool has played an important part in the unexpected flexibility of this mode of production and particularly its capacity for technological initiative, including cybernetics and computing. The empire of logic is circumscribed by and in the capitalist mode of production. Logical empiricism [*L'empirisme logique*] (pun intentional)[3] is therefore coming into its own as the philosophy of this mode of production, as the theorization of a truth that is both factual and propositional. Its success is in direct proportion to the triumph and pressures of the world market – an immense network of equivalences (monetary, etc.) and non-equivalences (inequalities).

12. Contradictions – ancient and modern, cumulative or specific – gnaw away at this empire and the societies that make it up. The dialectic, both theory and practice, continues its work [*oeuvre*]. It is important to note, however, that dialectical thinking remains at the level of ideas as long as there is no living force to carry through the work of the negative and resolve contradictions by overcoming them. Today these forces manifest themselves on a *world* scale. Might it not be in this sense that the relationship of thought with the world returns to the foreground, thus overcoming classical philosophy, in which reflexive thought related mainly to itself, its cumulative experience and its history? This does not abolish any specific moment – the national, for example – but subordinates every such moment to the world dialectic. The struggle of logic and dialectic is thus, at the theoretical level, a higher form of 'classic' struggles in thought and society.

April 1982

State

(from *Le Retour de la dialectique* (Paris: Éditions Sociales, 1986), pp. 17–21)

THE POLITICAL OR POLITICS [*LE OU LA POLITIQUE*]

Why begin with this word, the State? Because the State, and everything that it concerns and implies, is to be found at the heart of modernity and the so-called modern world. Except for those who get lost in detail, and find the 'isolated fact' easy to grasp and the only object of knowledge. At the opening of this collection of essays stands the State: the largest of these pieces of a puzzle – the world puzzle – and the most weighty.

From the outset, we have to make a distinction (which is common, by the way) between *politics* [la politique] (ideology, speeches and gossip, wheeling and dealing) and *the political* [le politique], the sphere of decision-making, including the supreme decision: war. Now the lack of a theory of *the political* means that the activity and decisions of the politician are doomed to be 'ad hoc'. It means a lack of strategy. Conversely, if there is strategy, there is theory, often implicit, unexpressed, latent. The 'ad hoc' can succeed for a while, because pragmatism and improvisation do not necessarily or swiftly lead to failure. Failure comes, sooner or later. Something that seldom worries statesmen, who are always preoccupied with the present or the near future; which distinguishes them from the *political thinker*, who tries to see in the long term, by drawing from an analysis of a particular *conjuncture* a pre-figuration of what may be to come, and tries, strategically, to produce tactics.

THE STATE AND POLITICAL POWER

For a long time now, it has been impossible not to notice the effects of political power, which is at the centre of political life, and also of social and economic activity. Which is not to say that this power can control everything at will, even under the rule of a monarch. But all the same, nothing is done without him – even the plots that are hatched against him. That's a hoary and slightly silly comparison, but it still makes some sense: political power is like the sun; everyone can see it, nobody can look straight at it, it has taken centuries to 'discover' it and it's not finished yet!

And besides, we're not talking about 'power' in general, a metaphysical entity brought into fashion by speculative philosophers who have diluted the concept by finding it all over the place, in every form of 'subordination', and by forgetting about it where power has its 'real' seat: in the state, in constitutions and institutions. The result is that *political* power has sometimes been fetishised and worshipped, sometimes misunderstood, unknown, while nothing has escaped the minute analysts of relations of dependency and domination between men and women, parents and children, human beings and animals, etc.

How is political power exercised? How does a form of power become established and how does it endure? How do 'free' citizens, members of a political 'community' (the people, the nation, the homeland) allow themselves to be stripped of the capacity to make decisions, when a decision affects them? That's an aspect of History that is not negligible – and it's a kind of *measure* of democracy. One which can be appreciated by the degree of knowledge among the 'citizens', and their involvement in what affects them. After endless expert studies, endless tiresome experiments, most of these questions are still open. Should they be left to specialists who belong neither among the politicians nor among the political 'thinkers'? No. Their study is part of a larger project. It is an extension of classical philosophy.

A BRIEF HISTORY OF THE STATE

Like everything that 'exists', the State was born, and grew up. One can assume that it will decline and disappear. Could it be that this decline has started? Might it be coinciding with the apogee and becoming worldly, and thus the apparent triumph, of the state level [*étatique*]? The question must be asked. Whatever the case, the State has a history, that of its generalization (becoming worldly) today.

There have been societies without a State, a favourite topic lately among scholars in specialized disciplines (anthropology, ethnology), who substitute such 'cases' (which are not without interest) for a critical analysis of the worldwide and of modernity. Marx would have shelved them, in a slightly simplistic way, under 'primitive communism' and its relics. Nowadays, such societies are no more than historical fossils or traces.

Given that the State had a beginning – how and why? The 'conditions' (broad, vague word) of political power today seem more complex than to Marx and Engels a century ago: differences and oppositions (struggles) between classes, of course, but also wealth to plunder, populations to dominate (and exploit) by conquest and violence – sometimes a way of getting rid of dangerous people, even dealing with overpopulation, by sending them off to war, etc.

The State, war and violence are as inextricably connected in historical time as (political) power and classes, although violence does not explain everything! Can we conclude from this that history, far from being oriented in a specific direction, is nothing but a bloody chaos, 'told by an idiot, full of sound and fury' (Shakespeare)?[1] No. Nevertheless, the idea of a precisely oriented determinism, an axis with no critical points of bifurcation, sudden divergence, or different possibilities (contradictions) cannot be accepted without close critical examination or further precisions and additions. Furthermore, political history, the history of the state, always involves relations of force, and thus violence, latent or avowed – struggles to win, exert and retain political power; this implies economic *conjunctures*, which are not reducible to *structures*. If these political struggles do not lead to war (civil or 'foreign'), is that not a definition of democracy? Can such a history form an 'object' of knowledge? It could be argued that it has a *rationality*, as long as we broaden the traditional concept of reason. Can it offer a mode of action, or a model for it? That's another story.

Political power comes from way back; it dates from before the State-as-institution, constituted as such. Conquerors, warlords, held power (or if you prefer, potency [*puissance*]) over subject peoples. They usually needed an 'apparatus' to extract tribute from those they enslaved; hence the concept of the 'tributary mode of production', which Marx did not classify among 'modes of production', although the 'Asiatic mode of production' comes close to it. The need for such an apparatus seems to have meant the end of 'military democracy', i.e. the election of a warlord by his warriors. In antiquity, the city-state was no less important than slavery, and involved particular relationships between city and countryside, commerce and plunder, oceans and continents. In the genesis of the modern State, the 'military-feudal' form covers a long period, right up to the twentieth century (the Austro-Hungarian empire, the Tsarist empire, the Ottoman empire, the Chinese empire, etc.).

Should not history make a clear distinction between the pre-national state and the nation-state, the prototype of contemporary representation? Which introduces the idea of the post-national or transnational State.

Several forms of polity (multinational or pre-national) have coexisted or still coexist with the nation-state, which may itself be 'imperial' (England, the USA, etc.). Just as the city-state politically accompanies the 'slave mode of production' but is not its logical result, so the empire-state, which retains medieval (feudal) aspects, accompanies the rise of capitalism without resulting from it. Some typical nation-states (England, France) were democratic at home and imperialist abroad. The multinational imperio-military state (Austro-Hungarian, etc.) only breaks up through violence: war. Nevertheless, the figure of the nation-state dominates historical narratives (history), as a 'state of right', since Hegel, and presents itself as the direction, decisive phase and finality of historical time (real history).

The nation and the nation-state, as supreme values and truths, are generally accepted without further examination, a critique of the criteria used seems like sacrilege. Can a thesis that dogmatically makes an absolute of what is a historical phase, hold sway in the era of the worldwide, the transnational, and also of decentralization and differences within homogeneity? It's a tricky question, impossible to answer; would not the 'national', and nationality, take on a 'cultural' or 'politico-cultural' tinge as they gradually begin to transcend geographical, historical and political determinations and determinisms? This needs a closer look!

Becoming and the Historical

(from *Le Retour de la dialectique* (Paris: Éditions Sociales, 1986), pp. 40–42)

The philosophical concept of becoming [*le devenir*], vast and universal in scope, encompasses those of time and history. Is it not the source of the notion of *historical time*, while experience and everyday life show only the repetitive, including repetitions of catastrophes, acts of brutality, abrupt interventions and interruptions?

Philosophically speaking, becoming remains enigmatic. And as for time?

Is it God? In the presence of God? Outside God? The divine itself? Theologians have never been sure. And why should this or that thing appear or disappear? Why birth, why growth, why decline, ageing and death? What have philosophers since Heraclitus had to say on the subject? Most of them have avoided the question of Time in favour of the changeless – the holy – eternal Truth; in favour of Being, of the defined and definitive Real. Those who have tried to explore Time have said there is the Same and the Other, Repetition and Difference, the One and the Many, the Finite and the Infinite. Between these carefully weighed terms might there be, not intervals, but fractures, cuts, perhaps even chasms, yawning gulfs? But that doesn't take us very far. We expected more of philosophy!

Unitary approaches eliminate time: via Being, Substance, the Eternal, the True, the Absolute, the Identical; this position, so common among metaphysicians that it appears to be the source of philosophy, involves rejection and of becoming in appearance, illusion, error and evil. As far as *binary* approaches go, they are better able to grasp (some would say, save) movement and change. Philosophers have made lists of significant oppositions that at least interrogate becoming, even if they fail to apprehend it: the Same and the Other (mentioned already, but figuring in the genesis of almost all types of philosophy), knowledge and recognition, mobility and rest, relative and absolute, etc. These opposed pairs sometimes open up a path to knowledge: the large and the small, the continuous and the discontinuous, odd and even, linear and cyclical, etc., etc. Near at hand, the oppositions between inside and outside, open and closed, structure and conjuncture, etc., have a wide scope.

Although they appear to be 'dialectical', these opposed pairs do no more than refer back one to the other, in an infinite regress, with a fixedness that even passes for intelligibility. A (misleading) analogy between 'dialogue' and 'dialectic' has sometimes led people to believe there is dialectical movement in any significant opposition. Nevertheless, the most 'rigorous' form of binary analysis, structuralism and the one that isolates structure has always excluded becoming, in linguistics (etymology) as well as in ethnology and sociology (nomenclatures), epistemology, etc.

Thus a theory reappears which, although it has long led an almost subterranean existence, and has emerged only recently into the daylight, has had no less currency and influence than those described above; ternary or *triadic* analysis grasps becoming (or at least comes nearer to it than the rest), which in no way rules out the possibility of further extensions, multi-dimensional analyses or the introduction of new parameters. When it was first coined, and before it became hackneyed, the Hegelian triad 'thesis–antithesis–synthesis' aspired to *construct* becoming. An illusion. It only constructed a representation. The Marxist triad 'statement–negation–negation of the negation' aims to *produce* becoming, but so far that high ambition has not been fulfilled, in particular as far as the State and the community (which was negated by history and re-established under communism) are concerned. It seems that in historical time there have been, not lacunae, surprises or unbridgeable gaps, but bifurcations, back-tracking, detours and diversions not included in the original triad. But this is not to say that the triadic hypothesis is exhausted. There is still the analytical approach: *three terms*, in a complex movement in which now one and now another is stated in opposition to one or other of the remaining two. It is not really an analysis of becoming, nor is it construction or production. But this does rule out the discovery or recognition of a direction, a *horizon* in this complex becoming. This theory takes into account what has happened over the course of a century, and does not leave becoming indeterminate. On the contrary: it offers a *strategy* (without the absolute certainty that the goal will be reached). No lacunae. No flaws, no glib continuities. Which means possibilities, uncertainties, opportunities and probabilities.

There is no shortage of exemplary cases of triadic analysis. Music (the art of time), with its three *moments*: melody, harmony and rhythm; contemporary political life, with its three aspects: state, nation, classes; nature, or matter, with its three categories: energy, space and time; and so on. Each of the above terms can be grasped in itself or in a conflictual relationship with any one of the others.

It is logical that among the terms of such triads contradictions should arise and evolve; on the other hand, in actions and activities – conflicts. We will come back to this.

For the moment, let us return to historical time, poorly defined, while retaining the proposition that it has a governing axis: the growth of forces of production – work and its history. That said, does this schema not lack the dimensions that would allow it to approach the complexity of becoming?

The Critique of Everyday Life

Introduction

From the first pre-war texts – the 1933 essay in *Avant Poste* and in *La Conscience mystifiée*, published in 1936, to the last book, *Rythmanalyse*, the last of four volumes of *Critique of Everyday Life*, completed around 1985 and published posthumously in 1992 – the *Critique* (for it is always a critique) of everyday life is a life force in the whole of Lefebvre's work. It absorbs, generates and gathers virtually the entirety of his philosophical concerns, at the centre of which is man: total man. What generates the critique of everyday life is a political imperative which lies at the heart of Lefebvre's philosophical project and which transforms itself into a philosophical imperative at the heart of a political project and back again. Each moment of its unfolding announces its *dépassement* or critical overcoming, the deployment of a renewed understanding of the human condition under capitalism and the possibilities for its emancipation through consciousness.

It is a movement which breathes outwards and then inwards. Outwards it is as the *Liberty* of the Enlightenment Project: a critique of past and present structures – here commodification, consumption, alienation, bureaucratization, for ultimately the making of another kind of citizen. As Labica has remarked, this is the citizen producer, the citizen of a civil society which has reabsorbed the State. What used to be called the dictatorship of the proletariat.[1] Inwards it is a movement of demystification and self-discovery through contemplations both formal and dream-like on consciousness: aesthetics, play, love, happiness, presence and absence and finally, the senses and rhythms of the body where life lived begins and ends. In the course of its fifty years the *notion* of everyday life – for it is always a residual category and never a concept – is defined only by its critique and *autocritique*. It is accorded various registers and voices, many inconsistencies and even more unfinished definitions, but it is never about objects or specialized fields and it is certainly not about a positivist sociology of the everyday.

Lefebvre used the term sociology to describe his practice in the first two volumes of *Critique de la vie quotidienne*, published in 1947 and 1961 respectively. He was then employed at the CNRS[2] as a sociologist – indeed his was the first post of sociology in France. However, by the second volume he also makes clear that the critique of everyday life is effectively a radical transformation of the concept of *Lebenswelt* ('the lived' or 'lifeworld') and that its purpose is no less than a rehabilitation and secularization of philosophy – a metaphilosophy of the everyday for a revolutionary humanism.[3]

The aims of this particular selection of texts, besides introducing hitherto untranslated and lesser-known material are twofold. One is to suggest a tracing of the philosophical journey of the critique of everyday life from its beginnings in a post-Hegelian critique of knowledge, via its relations to Marxian theories of fetishization, alienation and consciousness, to its final but not conclusive transmutation into an epistemology of the senses. The other is to illuminate the experimental, almost unstable nature of the notion and its place in Lefebvre's academic and political career. Everyday life as a notion contains various registers and resonances: an anti-psychoanalytical undertow, an outline of what will become cultural studies, a critique of structuralism (and later, postmodernism), a conceptualization of global change, a conversation with feminism to name but a few. Without it the production of space remains a geographical conceit.

Published in 1933 before Norbert Guterman left France for New York and the New School for Social Research, the first published essay on the critique of everyday life is also the first of this section. It aims to contribute to a materialist theory of knowledge and in so doing lays out some of the major preoccupations of Lefebvre's thought for the next 50 years. Two short excerpts from the second volume of *Critique de la vie quotidienne: Fondements d'une sociologie de la quotidienneté* published almost 30 years later, in 1961, follow. In themselves they cannot represent the most rigorous and adventurous of all of Lefebvre's books on the critique of everyday life in which he compares the importance of the concept, as he there calls it, to the place of sex in Freud, labour in Marx and the dialectic in Hegel. Taken from the first chapter, the first excerpt, '*Mise au Point*' is an *autocritique* of previous writings and discusses distinctions between private and public life and the place of history in the mid-twentieth century, while the second excerpt, 'The Social Text', taken from chapter IV and entitled 'Theory of the Semantic Field', offers a language for an understanding of landscape, cityscape and the 'world of objects'.

The next two excerpts are taken from the third volume of *Critique de la vie quotidienne: De la modernité au modernisme (Pour une métaphilosophie du quotidien)* to illustrate the texture of Lefebvre's formal thought after 50 years of reflection on everyday life, a reflection which came to no definitive or decisive conclusions. Two passages on 'the end of modernity' and the notion of 'vulgarity', both obliquely addressing contemporary discussions on postmodernism and taste, are included. The section closes with an article, 'Myths of Everyday Life', published in 1962 when Lefebvre was still in Strasbourg, which not only returns to a first preoccupation with mystification via *Elle* magazine, but to another pre-war preoccupation: adulthood as a myth.

Elizabeth Lebas

Mystification: Notes for a Critique of Everyday Life

Henri Lefebvre and Norbert Guterman

(from *Avant Poste*, 2 (1933), pp. 91–107)

Preliminary Note

In idealist philosophy, the theory of knowledge has replaced ontology. But its examination of a supposed general 'possibility' of knowledge, or of its conditions, leaves out the matter of knowledge. Hegel already criticized this separation between knowing and what is known. Despite the Hegelian critique, neo-Kantian schools in France, Germany and England took up this theory of knowledge. Their efforts only sanctioned the progressive distancing of the object in bourgeois thought, its gradual disappearance, its evaporation into empirico-criticism or its running aground into 'intuition'. It could not be otherwise. The object of the theory of knowledge was form without content, essence dissociated from existence. The effort to grasp this elusive form could lead only to exposing the weakness of rationalist thought, and correlatively, to the triumph of philosophical neo-mysticism.

Bourgeois thought has proved incapable of grasping the world as a totality. Of course, with its usual tactic, this thought presents its defeat as a victory. Henceforth, we grasp this totality only by an extra-intellectual act – or we proclaim plurality. Bourgeois philosophy, with vainglorious modesty 'gives way' to specialized sciences; the real becomes the relative, which the sciences divide amongst themselves. Metaphysics is dismissed – a good excuse to get rid of materialism. And faced with the question of the 'meaning of life', we need only throw ourselves into the arms of the Church!

The real reason for this failure to seize the real is not, as people would have us believe, an excess of thought and criticism, but a deficit and a fear. Because bourgeois thought has never been able to behave critically vis-à-vis its own fundamental categories (Man, Awareness [Conscience] of Self, Subject and Object, the Eternal, etc.) it has not yet extricated itself from their fetishistic power. It has never seen its culture as a simple dialectical moment to be transcended. It has remained closed in on itself.

The materialist theory of knowledge is located first of all in objective reality. It illuminates the mystifying subjectivism of bourgeois thought by abandoning it, and by dominating it. Its object is not the covert deduction of certain categories by presupposing them in the process of deduction, and its goal. Human knowledge is an actual fact, and one with a history. In it, matter and form, the laws of the object and the laws of thought, have an indissoluble unity. Materialist philosophy is therefore not concerned with analysing the truth of abstract knowledge, it also looks for an explanation of errors that can only be moments of truth. Materialism alone offers a real theory of error – something no idealist philosophy has been able to do.

In the notes that follow, we want to contribute to this materialist theory of knowledge by analysing under the general heading 'Mystification' a number of forms of bourgeois thought – even a kind of general law of that thought.

In the end, it all comes down to a critique of everyday life, *because we deliberately take the word 'thought' in its widest sense: all the ideas people form about their lives, all attempts to unify or justify these representations.*

We want to show that, in a society divided into classes and based on exploitation, the ideologies created or maintained by the ruling class tend to become increasingly dissociated from reality and to dress it up in an appearance that is its direct opposite, instead of joining with it and becoming one of its active, creative elements.

THE UNITY OF BOURGEOIS CULTURE

We talk about bourgeois culture, in the singular. Its bourgeois nature is questioned more often than its unity. However, when we criticize, for example, the ethics of journalism, the response is, 'Yes, but look at Bergson, Paul Valéry, Marcel Proust!'.[1] And when we mock the wild abstractions of philosophy, or the terribly tenuous subtleties of art, people say, 'Maybe, but what a direct vision our great reporters have.' And in practice, we excuse bourgeois culture by denying its unity.

In fact, it presents itself as diverse. Divided by specialities: art, philosophy, science, etc. Divided by levels. Ideologies for superior beings: elegant mysticism, high philosophy, supreme forms of art. Ideologies for the 'middling sort': classic poems, essays, novels of ideas, the politics of people who aren't taken in by it. Ideologies for 'ordinary people': films, religion, newspaper leaders and official speeches.

And for each speciality, and at each level, it is a continuous series of 'genres', of 'styles', of 'revolutions'. 'I can see, sir, that this type of thing doesn't appeal to you, but here's something else you might ... ' And so on and so forth. The appearance presented is the very opposite of unity. What actual connection is there between Duhamel and Clément Vautel?[2] The very people who accept the idea of 'one' culture are later ready to present this limitless diversity as proof of fecundity.

The different forms of expression do not only separate, but actually feel contempt for each other. Criticism of one benefits another. The philosopher despises newspaper reporting. If you look down on the one, you seem automatically to endorse the other. And as for the journalistic souls, they're in clover, rolling in the facts; they smile an indulgent, almost grateful little smile when they talk about Monsieur Benda ...[3]

It's that contempt that gives the game away. It's a connection in itself. Riches, superabundance? No: dispersal, crumbling away. Diversity? No. Unity in dispersal, monotony in fragmentation.

How does it come about that in times as harsh as these, the 'high' forms of culture are not a little more combative among themselves? That they coexist so easily and so courteously, in fact, is significant. Philosophico-religious battles? What a joke! That's all over, it's all been said and done. We're tolerant. Let each have his place in the great symphony of the intellect [*de l'Esprit*]. Cardinals, rabbis, pastors, philosophers, generals, men of letters of the right and the left – anyone can be put on any committee you like, as long as he's not a communist. And just now and then, some old pedant or Young Turk is given the job of recreating the illusion of heroic struggles between 'Incompatibles': religion and reason, philosophy and photography, naturism and the top hat, etc. etc.

It's not only the coexistence of forms that were once enemies – not only juxtaposition, heaps and piles – but continuity. Between Mallarmé and Clément Vautel[4] you find every intermediate form, forms within the reach of every purse. It's the same thing between the superstitions of those who consult a clairvoyant and the most sharply honed sceptics – between Picasso and church images.

And it's not mere continuity, but a correspondence between themes, paternity and filiation. Profound themes are no more than popular themes made abstract. Valéry's poetry sublimates with a vocabulary that means its secret can only be purloined by learned professors,[5] the narcissism of petty bourgeois women, their notions about their bodies, the sea and sleep – even of poetry itself. Balancing acts and games of compensation. The pared-down abstractions and subtle passions of the rich are soberly adjusted to fit the fullness of their carnal pleasures, just as the pathetic ideas and crude feelings of the poor cloak their actual deprivation. The poles are both opposed and mutually supporting. All this diversity represents a process of opposition within a unified whole.

Division by levels and external diversity are, from the inside, a single mechanism. It's a question of clientele, which is a class question. Consumers of luxury products and consumers of mass-produced products. It is accepted that there is a popular culture for those who are not the elite. But it is the elite who control things. The structure is like one of those fish-traps with a number of chambers. Anyone who tries to get out of his compartment, explore the depths or swim upstream, simply gets deeper inside the prison. Each social group has a type of expression that comforts it and confirms it in its own identity. All is admirably done so as to maintain order. From articles in papers sold on news stands, and 'cops and robbers' films glorifying bourgeois virtues, to 'serious' poetry, writing for academics, or romances for shop assistants, their themes all find their place in this order, we find the basic categories of this bourgeois order everywhere, the wish that it would survive for ever – in the form of rational concepts, beliefs that are more or less irrational or moral, tenacious hopes, intellectual or sentimental consolations, sterile forms of despair, spiritual opiates.

On every side, order is being shored up. But it is still threatened. People want to escape from it. So we set a trap for them. Everything is on sale in the bourgeois market. You can even find ready-made and approved means of escape.

Bourgeois ideology offers hundreds of easy ways to get out of the bourgeois world – without actually leaving it. There is more than one 'out there'. The 'out there' of religion, of philosophy (via transcendence and the absolute), of art. Kingdoms of Heaven, of the Idea, or of Beauty. There are also the escape routes of outrage and romantic revolt. We escape – and by escaping we join the elite, the 'right' people, those who 'keep their own counsel'. We have been given a rank. Not only have we never escaped, we've dug ourselves deeper into order. That's the trap of the 'superior'! We should not condemn bourgeois escapism because it is escapism (if it succeeded, what would we have to say? – that would be magnificent!), but precisely because it is not, because it is one more failure, one more deception. It was Rimbaud who said, 'On ne part pas' – we never leave.[6] The 'out there' is never real. It is only *out there* in the reflection, and what's more, it honestly and sincerely fulfils it function of keeping us in the *here and now*.

The cycle of diversity is complete. Everything, including the '*superior*' – Absolute and Escape – forms part of the whole. The links between all the stitches, the unity of the woven cloth, are visible. And this internal unity of external diversity, of all these mental fireworks, reveals itself to be the unity of bourgeois order, the bourgeois order itself.

But this unity does not present itself as such. It presents itself as indifferent towards bourgeois order or the economy: as objective, neutral, impartial, disinterested.

A revolutionary critique was needed in order to demonstrate these internal characteristics of bourgeois culture. All its forms reveal themselves as *alienated* and *mystified*. They present themselves as other than they are, with a meaning that does not reflect their truth. This is already well known in relation to political economy. There are fewer and fewer dupes to believe that the experts – Rist, Rueff, Keynes and their like – offer anything but conscious, self-interested lies in the service of imperialism.[7] Bourgeois economics is no longer a science. But the same mystifying tendency expresses itself to the full in all domains; bourgeois culture as a whole is becoming an instrument of the ruling class. Although since Marx, philosophy in general may have been unmasked and although lies are cynical in political journalism and reportage, the question is still up for discussion as far as literature, art, science and culture in general are concerned. Revolutionaries themselves oscillate between global condemnation of bourgeois culture and worship of its exponents and its 'values'. The real response can only be one of dialectical critique: understanding by transcending. For bourgeois culture, like every ideology, has real content; it expresses and reflects something of the truth. The mystification lies in the presentation, use and fragmentation of that content; culture, taken as a whole, lives parasitically on this real content, which it has ceased to renew. (In the same way, bourgeois democracy still lives ideologically on its memories and the remains of its great revolutionary period, although in reality it is evolving towards a denial of its promises.) Revolutionary critique must expose this real content.

To talk about the mechanization of man, to say that machines have turned against him, has become a commonplace that only conceals the true situation. It is not only machines that have become detached from man. All the immense machinery of capitalism – ideas, values, institutions, culture – all this civilization has taken on a sort of independent existence that weighs on man and wrenches them apart from themselves; the very expression '*man*' is drenched in mystification, because man still has no real existence. Alienation, that real abstraction, that false life that exists only through him and feeds on man – the 'human' that has lost its way on the road towards his realization – inevitably is dispersal, and a mutual exteriority of the elements of culture. But in this very exteriority, the elements have unity: unity in the movement of alienation.

Revolutionary critique thus reveals and defines the unity of bourgeois culture.

BOURGEOIS VALUES

The bourgeois always has the feeling that he is but a grocer or a philistine. When revolutionaries declare themselves materialists, the cynic who in the soul of the bourgeois lives side by side with the poet, the lawyer and the pig, mutters to himself, 'What fools, who could be more materialist than me?' Then his 'inner poet' replies, yes, your life is dull, boring and disgusting, but there are always values. Up above your life, shining down upon it, there is France, or Germany, Liberty, Beauty, Truth, Love, Purity, Reason, Dynamism, Command of the High Seas, and so on.

The unique life, life as a totality present in its every form, which remains the goal and meaning of revolutionary culture – all this is incomprehensible to the bourgeois. His life is parcelled out. Action is one thing – it is first and foremost business and sharp dealing; thought is something else. When intelligence ends, will begins; what he cannot buy, he wishes to *possess* by love. And if you draw his attention to this rather ambiguous distinction, he replies, 'What do you mean? It's perfectly natural.' He does not know that his life, however compartmentalized, is still secretly unique, and is contaminated through and through by commerce and business. But no doubt he senses it, since his 'values' are there to restore him, to save him!

'Values' are that which is *worth* being *wanted*. But by definition, it is from without that they give life meaning. The bourgeois, for whom Christianity is so convenient, likes to plagiarize the familiar quotation, 'I do the evil that I do not want, I do not do the good that I want.'[8] By this tactic he keeps his share in superior values. As bourgeois culture has abandoned the idea of truth and the intelligence of the whole, so it has attached itself to 'Values', each one strictly localized, clearly distinct, which one 'wants'.

'Look here, you've got to make a living. Life's a down-to-earth business. You've got to be a slave. To live, you've got to do things that deep down you don't like doing. You'd be only too glad to give every poor chap all you've got, but you know perfectly well that would be ridiculous. You'd like to think noble thoughts, but, look, life's hard. You've got to live.' – 'But wait a minute, are you saying you're just a machine, an animal?' – 'No, but there again, the things I can't do, I respect them all the more. Take the theatre, doesn't it bring tears to my eyes when the lovers die of a broken heart? I like music, don't I? Are you telling me I don't have respect for heroes?'

Values lie outside life, the bourgeois admits it, but they lie ahead of it and above it. The column of the Jews in the desert and the Star of Bethlehem make his heart swell, too.

But it is precisely when some aspect of reality has been consumed by bourgeois life that it becomes a 'value'. Gold by devouring everything before it takes possession of what it destroys. When love was still possible, love was not glorified, it was completely natural. But when romanticism declared that love was the supreme value, that meant precisely that every man and woman could now be bought and sold. Bourgeois husbands who bought wives, and women who bought husbands began to dream of the ideal love. When capital made all men slaves, 'liberty' became a value. Over each corpse, a grand monument was raised. Regret turned into promise and hope. The man who suffered torture and death became ever more a god.

The totality of bourgeois values is nothing but a museum of mortal remains. Value. Gold stamps its seal on what it has vanquished and destroyed. Gold trumpets its pride in conquest. At the same time, it bows its head, it consoles those it has stripped bare and deceived. And if, today, people tell us that solitude is the last value and the last refuge of despair, it is because in fact there is no more solitude left, because we can no longer escape. The individual is crushed. We can no longer possess that last source of pride, our solitude, unless we buy it. Otherwise, we are trapped in the crowd; revolutionaries have known this for a long time (that's their starting point). Similarly, fascism proclaims the nation as the supreme value, at the precise moment when the nation has only a mystified reality, used by that very fascism in the service of international capital.

Values, therefore, are not ahead of and above life, but behind and below it. Philosophers and writers who proclaim values are simply saying prayers for the dead.

But perhaps we are reaching the end of the song. We can no longer, it seems, create values after solitude and nothingness. We no longer even have hopes to lose. Life no longer has meaning; it no longer has value, through being broken into a thousand mystifying values, with the result that, in order to know what life is, we have to retrace the road travelled in mystification. We have to rediscover real love, behind the love that is all protestation, real freedom behind illusory freedom. This, too, is the work of revolutionary critique. Once we have transcended this mystification, we will realize that mystification itself has been a moment of consciousness; it will have forced us, though a lie, to achieve through mystification itself a unique and true consciousness of life. Genuine revolution is increasingly becoming the only hope for humanity, the only possible source of salvation for life, even in its humblest sense.

DEATH OF THE BOURGEOIS REVOLUTIONARIES

Before the war, in the days when the 'sweet life' ruled over the boulevards, in the days when there were no problems – then bourgeois thinkers had no great difficulty in making Values supreme: Beauty, Love, Passion, Art, etc. A superficial neurosis was enough to suggest originality. Since then we have become harder and we have doubts. People have too much real anxiety. So we had to make up our minds to open our eyes and take a look around us. If you really think about it, isn't that in itself revolutionary, for a young man brought up on high culture, Wagner and his mother's migraines! True, the old gentlemen are still spiritualists, like Bergson, or still take a shamelessly old-fashioned view of economic realities. But after the war, a whole team of keen-eyed realists discovered you had to take everything in. The Chicago stockyards, a Calibanesque people,[9] Geneva or Moscow, housing estates, factories, machines and brothels, they looked at it all – and always, always with a keen eye. Not like journalists, of course not, but in depth! And they also discovered the sexual crisis, the bourgeoisie, the death-of-thought. And sometimes, even capitalism.

Perhaps, then, they should have realized that capitalism isn't a country in which you spend three weeks so that you can come back with a book. That capitalism isn't just a factory or a safe, but envelops us from every direction.

Those writers who claimed to have discovered capitalism thought they understood it without difficulty – no doubt because they had capital.

They knew – because they're decent people – that a certain Karl Marx spent his life analysing the phenomenon of capitalism. But Marx was an economist. He lacked sensitivity. He said, in many unnecessarily obscure and turgid volumes, what someone with a sensitive eye could have seen straight away.

They didn't have the modesty or patience needed to become Marxists. They preferred their purple passages and stillborn paradoxes. They were above class. They didn't feel they were inside capitalism, but ahead of it. And then, wasn't it important to maintain the dignity of intelligence, and above all, to preserve the prestige of one's own specialization? So they couldn't join the revolutionary class without reservations.

But they'd bitten off more than they could chew. They thought they could transcend capitalism but they only chopped up the phenomenon itself and its critique, i.e. Marxism; they distributed its fragments and different aspects among themselves. The *Kulturphilosophen* – Germans, French and others – talked about the decadence of the West and of the Spirit (while it was actually no more than the decadence of capitalist civilization).[10] They held forth on the depersonalization of man (without seeing it was a mere detail in the theory of alienation of Hegel and Marx). Others, again, invented 'anti-machinism', while it was only the capitalist use of machines that was in question ...

The problems of the Depression have marked the collapse of all these grand critiques; they were contributing nothing. Monsieur Duhamel represents them perfectly; his theories of the exquisite soul led to campaigns against machines, then against noise, and finally to buying a house in the suburbs.[11] Monsieur Berl killed off bourgeois thought, only to resuscitate it with 'Marianne'.[12] Monsieur Guéhenno became a democrat again ...[13]

The bourgeois revolutionaries all chickened out. Did they really want to understand capitalism? No, they only wanted to dodge, to duck and dive, and run away. They even stopped using the words 'capital' and 'bourgeois'.

Their critique served only the bourgeoisie itself. The were its left wing, its audacious wing. They appeared to be putting the modern world on trial, precisely in order to avoid actually addressing the problem of capitalism. Then they got lost in the general panic of the bourgeoisie: the end of the bourgeoisie is the end of everything. Shall we therefore save the bourgeoisie? They were the social democrats of critique (political social-democracy doesn't even have any ideas).

For some, the critique of detail, the partial truth that becomes a lie, ends up in fascism. Monsieur Drieu-la-Rochelle now puts Nietzsche up against Marx (the Nietzsche of young French girls in 1905) and the 'leader' against the depersonalized man, lost in the crowd.[14]

And that's the end of the bourgeois revolutionaries, mystifiers mystified.

A CRITIQUE OF SINCERITY

Bourgeois thought, ejected from the domain of reflection, takes refuge behind the redoubt of the immediate fact: in 'sincerity'. 'We're French because we're French,' says Berl, a Jew, with great sincerity.[15]

When ideas run out of steam, one resource is left: you can say what you like; you talk about what's going on inside, just as it comes to you. You're sincere.

In the days when the bourgeoisie was capable of creating grand constructions and great visions of the world, its thinkers would never have dreamed of presenting as arguments the mere fact of having the thoughts they had! One can hardly imagine Spinoza or Hegel putting their hands on their hearts ... This modern cult of sincerity and the immediate would it not be an admission that we no longer have anything to be really sincere about? The *fait accompli*, i.e. the bourgeois world, stands alone before bourgeois thought; then, ecstatically, people discover it as a profound and (naturally) eternal truth. It's a discovery of life itself, a thrilling fragment; this is the era of reportage. Failure is hidden, it turns into fraudulence. This is the age of sincerity!

The question of trust has to be posed precisely in the case of what requires trust. What is the value of this vast ideological construct of sincerity (impressionism, intuitionism, reportage on the inner and the outer world)? What truth does it contain, except by chance? What assurances does it offer?

The big lies, the influential ones, are lyrical, eloquent lies – the lies of politics and religion – and they require sincerity. The gestures of sincerity are imitated, they serve the liars. But there's still more: big lies always contain something that relates to many people's lives, to their 'sincere' illusions. These themes had first to be passionately lived before they could be utilized. Every great lying ideology has had 'sincere' inventors, who did not know they were lying, and who lied on a big scale, a broad canvas, without being worried by doubts or fears. Cynics are few and far between, and they are not the first to appear on the scene. If those angry buffoons, Hitler and Göring, know they're in the service of the financiers, those who gave them their ideas – from Gobineau to Feder, to Moeller van der Bruck, to Fried, to Hitler himself (in his humble beginnings) – they may very well have been 'sincere'.[16] There are naïve buffoons. Nowadays cynicism is actually a profession. No higher tribute to sincerity, but no better proof that it has no direct relationship with the truth. *If you want to create lies, it's better to be sincere!*

Why does mistrust of sincerity not form part of our basic education? Children (who perhaps suspect as much) should have to learn that tone of voice does not distinguish truth from lies, and that sincerity is a question of tone and subjective feeling. Instead of thinking sincerity is a power, instead of being devoted followers of those who are 'most sincere', we should look for what lies behind sincerity. But the decadence of bourgeois culture, and bourgeois democracy, need this value all too much. So, sincerity is in vogue. And today, with unctuous obedience to these moving 'facts', the bourgeoisie sees that the workers do not want revolution or communism, but only a job, and some bread. It senses that the world is not a happy place and can probably never be one. It establishes its good intentions.

We don't want to talk about hypocrites, but about people who are deeply, genuinely sincere. For example, people who suffer, in the spiritual sense. God-fearing folk sincerely believe they find God in their souls. They believe they have a soul. Think about that! They suffer on account of it, and long for eternity – they scratch away at it, this soul of theirs, it makes them itch when they're on their knees. Populists really think they're doing something for the people. Some rich members of the bourgeoisie think – honestly – that the spiritual revolution comes before the other kind and that material goods aren't important. And what's easier than to be a sincere democrat, who wants so, so badly for everything to be fine! There are these set ideas that more than any others give one the pleasant sensation of being sincere ... Yes, truly, many people need to deceive themselves in order to deceive others. Cynics are less common among 'thinkers' than among politicians, because bourgeois thinkers do not directly participate in power. Their lies are deeper than their consciousness. They are submerged in their social world.

It's a fine thing to have a healthy bank balance and a bit of power, and every time you're in a bit of trouble you just ask 'how much?' and sign the cheque without turning a hair. But have you never come across the poor soul who right away takes refuge in the sublime? Innocence is a great resource when you've no money. Being a large, sincere consciousness means not having an ordinary bank account, but one with the Bank of Morality, the Ideas Trust Fund, with Heaven itself. The most practical thing, of course, is to have both at once. Is not everything permitted to fine souls? Because it all depends how you do it.

Sincerity is rarely put in its proper phenomenological place. It is only an attitude, a refusal to reflect, or a feeling that arises under certain given conditions. (So nothing takes it away! The fine souls who read this won't even feel it's about them ...).

The history of philosophy teaches us what philosophers have studied under the term 'nature'; themselves and their times. Objective psychology, psychoanalysis, and the critical examination of evidence have helped us puzzle out the tricks played by consciousness. There is no truly unmediated fact, interior or exterior. Every observation is an interpretation. Every observation, up to and including those that give the greatest sense of being immediate and patently obvious, in fact contains all the thought processes of the person making it. Today the immediate method of grasping the real involves the whole of bourgeois consciousness and its contents. It involves all the categories of this bourgeois thought. It has a last trick up its sleeve:

perseverance in the bourgeois world, acknowledgement, with the most natural air in the world, of its structures and their durability. In cultural terms, even 'nonconformist' sincerity is the refuge of conformity. Only revolutionary sincerity, based on practical class action, has a connection with objectivity and truth.

MYSTIFICATION

Everything is suspect.

So what is this world? Isn't a word, a face, an act, always a mask? The person who speaks, the person who acts, does he ever really know what he is saying, what he is doing? The 'other', the other thing, is hidden behind every moment of life, and of our life. Not to be obsessed with that is to be profoundly complicit and in agreement with it; to be obsessed with it is to pursue an elusive reality that escapes every direction. But we sense it, we touch it, beneath our own consciousness. But it is always beyond our reach. This inability to grasp the real, and this escape by the real, are the characteristics, indissolubly joined together, of the consciousness and the life of our times. A general unreality and an exasperated need for who knows what permanent possession are each the cause of the other ...

This rift has its heroes, carefree or tragic. They are in need of a god, or of death. Because they have never been able to experience as real any being whom they encounter, because they have never experienced themselves as real, these tragic heroes seek, even if it has to be in suffering, something that exists, that resists, that implacably and harshly penetrates their flesh – but that nevertheless may yield to them and become their possession. Mystics, masochists, sadists, all of them men of nothingness who flee towards another nothingness and for whom death is the only reality. That is the crisis of the spirit in creatures who are, for all that, creatures of flesh and blood ...

Mystification is unquantifiable. Expression in itself (language) has been perfected to the extent that no more than a minimum amount of reality is needed. Things do not exist until they have been spoken, because they have been spoken, and their whole reality is in having been spoken. A heyday for swindlers and false prophets. We don't even notice that this marvellous technique of expression represents a total depreciation of words, since they mean nothing more than themselves. Where are the words of love that do not contain some business expression or other, and at the same time recall whole millennia of literature and oratory?

Purity is the greatest corruption, because the only people who do not sell themselves are those who can buy everything. The greatest cruelty is charity; is there anything more ignoble than the happy awareness of being 'charitable'? What is affection but the biggest trick to bind the thing one claims to love? There is not only the trickery of ideas, but trickery in all feelings, including the simple-mindedness that passes for *joie de vivre* and becomes attractive! Innocence and simple-mindedness are highly rated, and without knowing it, of course; they are sincere, so that is their due ...

Every act is so much what we didn't want, every acquisition contains such a defeat, every wild, exuberant joy a loss of self, that one can almost understand those who desperately clamour for an impossible 'salvation'. It is as if all the moments that mark an individual life – its ecstasies and experiences – are extracted under torture. Only unhappiness is profound. How are we to live? There is no easier way to lose something you desire than by truly desiring it; how rash, and at the same time, how vulnerable we are! Everything closes up on us, everyone makes common cause against us.

This tragedy is played out in the middle of the vast and dismal circus-ring of journalism and politics. Who can be surprised if at this point armament is called disarmament, if preparation for war is called peace, if rescuing banks is called the march to socialism, and so on and so forth? *All reality is enveloped in its opposite, and expresses itself as it.* Selling a country to the foreigner, domination by international capitalism, is expressed as fascist nationalism!

Today, mystification of bourgeois thought has reached its final, extreme form, because if it is to go any further, it must take as its mask its precise opposite, utilize the reality of its enemies, of its own death: the reality of revolution. That is why fascism calls itself 'revolution'. Its unreality is disguised as the supreme reality, and tries to make true reality permanently unreal.

There is perhaps no longer a single phenomenon of public, or even private life that appears in its true form. It's no longer enough to say that everything is disguised or camouflaged; everything becomes its opposite, appearance seeks to become the whole of reality and tries to make reality nothing but appearance.

FETISHISM, ALIENATION, MYSTIFICATION

The theory of *fetishism* contained in Marx's work explains how these phenomena are possible.

Capitalism is a system for producing merchandise. When it turns into merchandise, the object becomes detached from itself, so to speak. It enters a system of relationships that are expressed through it, so that in the end it seems to be the subject of these relationships, their causal agent. Relationships between men are masked by relationships between objects, human social existence is realized only by the abstract existence of their products. Objects seem to take on a life of their own. The market dominates human beings; they become the plaything of anything with which they are unfamiliar, and which sweeps them along. The market is already a machine and an inexorable destiny. People are now alienated, divided from themselves. Division of labour, labour itself, individual roles and functions, the distribution of work, culture and traditions, all impose themselves as constraints. Each person experiences the collective achievements of society as the work of an alien power.

In a society that has not gone beyond this stage of alienation, where people have not yet regained their identity, consciousness can only be uncertain, painful and conflicted: the consciousness of the slave, the devotee or the mystified. Uncertainty and torment, the 'unhappy consciousness', spring from this double source: people feel they are seized and swept along, but at the same time they sense that things could be different. They try to regain their identity, but, until the proletarian revolution, they have created only other fetishes, reflections of reflections, more external projections of themselves: religion, theology, philosophy, art, alienated culture.

The capitalist system has taken this mystification to its furthest limits; it has given rise to the mystifications of freedom, justice and democracy. (In another article we will follow the birth, development and overcoming of these themes.)[17]

This is how Marx describes this ungraspable creature, this heavy, impalpable cloud, burning and alive with the insane, indissoluble will of the fetish by which we are compelled to live: 'Capital is increasingly becoming something concrete and material, but something within which social relationships are included – something at once real and unreal, endowed with imaginary life and autonomy. It is under this form ... that Capital appears as an entity'.[18]

(to be continued)

Elucidations

(from *Critique de la vie quotidienne II: Fondements d'une sociologie de la quotidienneté* (Paris: L'Arche, 1961), pp. 7–8)

In its initial project, the critique of everyday life had as its task to summarize an *autocritique* of the everyday. Its principal aim would have been to confront the 'real' and the 'lived' with their representations, their interpretations and their transpositions (in the spheres of art, morality, ideology and politics). The outcome of this comparison would have been a reciprocal critique of the 'real' by the imaginary, the 'lived' by its transpositions, and what is learned practically by the abstract. Similarly, a confrontation between *private life* (the individual distinguishing himself from the social, without as such the individual separating from society) and *public life* (that of the citizen, of 'historical man', social groups and the political State), and the reciprocal critique of these two fragments of the whole, were part of the agenda.

The only solution offered: 'openness', participation, that of private life to collective, social and political life, that of 'everyday man' to 'historical man', to the problematic of the totality (of global society). The political sphere, that of the State, thus gave itself the rank of supreme authority. Critique was mainly brought to bear on 'private life', seen as a 'disadvantaged area' of praxis, a backward and underdeveloped region, so to speak, within the heart of so-called 'modern' industrial and technology-driven society, within the framework of capitalism. Several chapters would have been devoted to the little magical aspects of everyday life, the innumerable little superstitions (customary rituals and gestures, proverbial expressions, horoscopes, witchcraft and devil-worship), with the intention of exterminating them by subjecting them to practical argument. Of course, it was not a question of dissolving the individual in the collective and the private in the sociopolitical, but of raising them to the collective and historical level, and so to the political level, via political consciousness. A fairly simple theory of alienation and de-alienation seemed to meet all needs. Prior to the great de-alienation, that of political revolution (which it prepared for and heralded) the opening up of private to public life, as well as active participation in history and political action, was going to de-alienate everyday man and negate his 'privation'. Without disappearing, the everyday was going to be enriched and organically bind itself to the whole: to the total man.

Elucidations

These over-simple hypotheses were sinning from a certain naïveté. And this is where a number of changes notably alter the original project. Within a few years, significant changes appeared within the configuration 'private life–political life–history–technical development'. How could the critique of everyday life ignore them? We have already referred to these changes, indicating that they were not destroying the programme, but imposing new elements. We will now pause there and look more closely at those elements.

First of all, mid-twentieth-century man (a member of an 'advanced' society) looking to Marxism for the theoretical means of understanding that society, is, vis-à-vis *history*, in the same position as Marx. He cannot accept or ratify the historical, events and processes. He denies history its 'philosophical certificate', as long as he is not a professional politician, and places himself on the scholarly level. The politician, on the other hand, espouses a strategy. He says what has to be said, in terms of that strategy. In relation to history and the historical past that weighs on the present, he has to 'save face'. Otherwise, he compromises his strategy and, of course, his political career (because another politician will be found immediately, to handle the operation better). This divorce between scholarship [*connaissance*] and politics, and the inevitable renewal of a sociology of politics that explains it as such, instead of seeing it as the supreme science, have worrying aspects. Let us move on. This is not the place to deal with it. In his time, Marx subjected politics – events, processes, strategies and tactics – to ruthless analysis. Starting from an objective appraisal of forces and potentials, assessing what had and had not been achieved in the light of what was possible, he studied decisions, errors and failures. He did not approach facts with simplified or schematized hypotheses; he recognized in them neither constant and consistent 'progress' in all domains, nor a one-sided determinism, nor an absolute necessity. Marx never considered the historical as a collection of *faits accomplis* to be universally accepted and recorded. Challenging the absolute nature of history and politics (and especially the Hegelian philosophy of history and the State), he studied what we call deviations [*dérives*].[1] He drew many lessons from the discrepancy between intentions and results.

Today we have to contest history, the history we have lived and to which we have contributed. What lays claim to be history has not gone further than man's prehistory. From decisions and actions *something else* arises, something other than what was intended and planned. Even if we agree that intervention by the revolutionary proletariat has narrowed the gap between plan and the result (which is debatable in any case), that gap has not disappeared. Far from it! Men make their history, but not as they want it.[2] They do not do what they wish, and what they do, they do not wish. There is more in the 'world' than philosophy has dreamed of.

How, then, do we propose everyday life to bridge in one leap the gulf between the lived and the historical? How are we to show it as a model of the political sphere, which intervenes in history and attempts – in the best cases – to make it and consciously set its direction? The split between private life and political consciousness is perpetuated. The two forms of consciousness sit side by side when they are able to coexist. In many cases, private consciousness gains the upper hand over a political consciousness that is obscured and itself starved of nourishment as a result of this split.

We have had to restore to the foreground the theory of the *withering away of the State*,[3] an essential Marxist theory which contemporary history (and the history of Marxism in particular) had obscured. Utopia? Probably. In reality, nowhere in the modern world is the State convincingly withering away according to the process Marx predicted and considered the future path of history.[4] If there is utopia in the theory of the withering away of the State, we can all the more easily demonstrate what is utopian in Marx's thought and refute once again, but with better arguments, some false contentions. Utopia, that is to say, the distant possible, is not an 'eschatology', a theory of the end of becoming. It is the very concrete and positive concept of a history at last oriented, directed and controlled by knowledge and will. The day when the gap between goal and outcome will narrow, or when the hour marking the end of destiny (i.e. pre-history) will strike, the withering away of the State will be near.

For the gap between *private* life and *public* life (between consciousness and political consciousness) to be reabsorbed in an overcoming, the withering away of the State or its practical prospect is an objective condition. The *private* cannot rise to the level of the *public* unless the public ceases to be located in inaccessible and mysterious domains, unless it descends towards the private to be reabsorbed into the everyday. This process of overcoming is also involved in the determination of concrete democracy. Democracy moves towards the withering away of the State and towards transcendence of the 'private-public' conflict. Or else it does not live.

How, then, today, to propose as practical aim for the private consciousness of the man in the street his recognition by historical and political man? To the degree that such mutual recognition would bring about the potential unity of the two divided parts of consciousness and praxis, it remains an abstract ideal: an idea, a 'utopia'. To the degree that such recognition can be reduced to a mere fact among other facts, it has already been achieved. In propaganda, action and especially, *raison d'Etat*, ideology and political consciousness address private consciousness. That is not in order to bridge the gulf between them and achieve fusion in overcoming. Propaganda leaves daily life, consciousness and private life intact. It takes them as objects, even as 'things'. It enters into them in order to fashion them. It does not raise them to the level of the universal. It contests them with other forms of propaganda. Is this inevitable? Of course. We're faced with destiny, that is to say, with historical necessity and chance, which have become strategic necessity and tactical calculation. Recognition has been achieved unilaterally, and unity in confusion. Hence the paradox which will have to be closely examined: the intensification and simultaneous discrediting of ideologies, and the depoliticization (however profound or however temporary) of a daily life that is astonishingly 'informed' politically, while political problems press upon us with an urgency that no one any longer denies.

Another element of both innovation and deterioration: the technical element. It forces us to formulate differently from the way it was expressed in the original project the fundamental demand of the everyday. It is now not only a matter of bringing the private into the social, via language, knowledge and the concept – of raising the everyday to the level of the historical and the political. *The critique of everyday life demands a plan, that is to say, a policy that will put the everyday on the level made possible by technology.*

The Social Text

(from *Critique de la vie quotidienne II: Fondements d'une sociologie de la quotidienneté* (Paris: L'Arche, 1961), pp. 306–12)

The social text. For the moment, we are going to present this notion, without developing its content. In fact, it will only acquire its full scope within the 'communications model'. Nevertheless, it also has a place in the theory of the semantic field. To tell the truth, the 'social text' is merely one aspect of the semantic field. It is the semantic field as it appears to everyone in daily life, in a non-conceptual or pre-conceptual (affective and perceptive) way.

It is the result of the combination, in infinitely variable proportions, of the formants mentioned above: *signals*, which tell us nothing, issue imperative commands, and repeat themselves in the exactly identical form; *symbols*, hidden and transparent, deep-seated phenomena of the social spectacle that transform it into something other than a spectacle because they have influence, because they demand or refuse participation, because they always bring surprise and the unexpected, even when they are making a reappearance; and lastly, *signs*, which bring only limited surprises and differences that are to some extent predictable.

Each of us is constantly – every day – faced with a social text. We move through it, we read it. Through this text, and through reading it, we communicate with others, with the wider [*globale*] society on the one hand and with nature on the other. At the same time, we are all part of a social text. Not only do we read, we are also read, deciphered, made plain (or not). We are all both subject and object, indivisibly (*first*, *object*; the social text encompasses us and we have to see ourselves as encompassed; *then*, *subject*; because we decipher and read the text from within, in that we see ourselves inside it, never entirely outside it).

In relation to information theory, we should say that *signals* represent redundancy of the modern social text: banality and clarity, triviality and intelligibility. *Signs* carry information. *Symbols* may be compared with the 'noise' that jostles out information, pouring forth in a familiar repertoire (codified and conventional) but at the same time enveloping information from all directions (background noise, white noise, etc.).

Still in relation to information theory, we will say that a social text is to some degree readable. Overloaded with symbolism or too full of information, too rich, or disjointed, it loses its legibility. Reduced to signals, it becomes utterly banal; it is clear, intelligible, boring; it repeats itself endlessly; it is swamped by redundancy. A good social text, readable and informative, surprises but does not overstretch its 'subjects'; it teaches them a lot, and constantly, but without overwhelming them; it is easily understood, without being trivial. The richness of a social text is thus measured by its accessible variability: by the wealth of novelty and possibility it offers individuals.

Armed with these concepts, let us analyse some forms of the social text, as we encounter them every day. The everyday reader misunderstands what is revealed upon analysis. But the informed reader realizes that he has before him part of the structures: a level of existence and reality, in which no level, of course, comprises the global reality.

In the *village* everything is symbolic, and reveals the truth of symbolism: ancient and powerful, strongly attached to things, and also to rhythms. Houses, fields, trees, sky, mountains or the sea are not simply or solely themselves. Cosmic and vital rhythms surround them; they contain subtle resonances; every 'thing' is part of a chorus. Space and soil symbolize the community; the church sets the time and symbolizes, in the cemetery, the world, life and death. In this poignantly archaic world, daily life presents itself in all simplicity, both utterly quotidian and inseparable from its resonances.

Every action, connected with some fundamental 'thing' – need, property, object, presence or absence – has symbolic import: taking bread, cutting it, opening or closing the door of the house, crossing the yard, or the garden, going out into the fields. In the village, everything abounds in life, the life of actions made more powerful by the symbols embodied in them. And it is all antiquated, outmoded, distant ...

The *landscape* also presents us with a social text, usually readable and sometimes wonderfully composed, in which man and nature – the signs of the one, the symbols of the other – meet.

If we look closely at the *city*, we will soon see how hard it is to understand this masterly *oeuvre*, created by social groups and the whole society, an *oeuvre* that bears the traces of struggles that stimulated creativity but which also tends to erase out these traces. In the big cities, symbols have lost the ubiquity they had in the village. They are localized, and condensed. But their role is not less important. Quite the contrary: everything that has, or seeks, prestige and influence, everything that organizes and dominates this enormous mass of humanity, does all it can to retain the old symbols in order to benefit from their ancient authority, or offers new symbols to give itself legitimacy. Symbolism is condensed in the monuments; churches, cathedrals, palaces, great public and private buildings are full of symbols mingled with their decoration and aesthetic style. Monuments are works [*oeuvres*] that give a city its face and its rhythm. They are its memory and the figuration of its past, the active and affective hubs of its present everyday life, prefiguration of its future. We will call them 'supra-functional' or 'trans-functional', which is not to say they have no function, or transcend function, but that they have such diverse functions that no single functionality characterizes them or exhausts their social function. In working-class districts, by contrast, and around factories, inside actual businesses – few monuments or none at all. Symbols have disappeared (which means that in a horrible way everything symbolizes power and oppression). Nature has disappeared and culture is nowhere to be seen. Here, everything is a signal: a signal of work and work-related actions, and actions that sustain the workforce.

Beside its monuments and proletarian neighbourhoods, the city presents its informative text, rich in signs and meanings. Here, analytical description should typify and specify cities: the ancient city, organizing in a majestic fashion movements still close to vital rhythms around certain monuments – the arena, the temple, the agora, the forum or the theatre; the medieval city, with its enormous vitality, where all elements are interconnected: city and country, house and street, artisanal production and forms of exchange. Let us briefly mention the *street*, that characteristic feature of the modern city. It is the street, in the large industrial city, that has the most real, most original life. It is the street that in the big city offers incomparably more choices and possibilities than in the village or hamlet, what we call 'seductions', 'temptations', opportunities, appeals, whether we're talking about objects or people, encounters or solicitations and adventures. As soon as the street loses this attraction, either because it is deserted or because, contrariwise, dense traffic makes it unbearable, the city turns into a lunar desert.

The fact is, that in the society we're looking at – that were reading – and of which we are a part, intermediaries enjoy extraordinary, sometimes outrageous privileges, to the detriment of those who have, or might have, more reality. This proposition could be based on economic analysis: the role of merchandise and money, intermediaries that become dominant, things that become fetishes, mediating processes that make themselves determinative by disguising and overwhelming the things they connect. Here, in the social text, this proposition should be directly legible. It is situated at the level of common sense and everyday argument; nevertheless, it looks paradoxical. It means that round about us, the place where we come and go, and meet – the street, the café, the station – is more important and genuinely more interesting than our homes, houses, places connected one with another. There lies the living paradox that everyday familiarity makes us accept, and whose absurdity it hides from us. Once, in the ancient or medieval city, this was not so. Circulation, of people, merchandise and vehicles, was not preponderant. The means of communication were subordinate to their ends and to human beings, as were every kind of medium and intermediary. Today, we're tempted to accept this state of affairs, and even to exaggerate it: when the street ceases to be interesting, daily life loses its interest. So, what is becoming of the city, jam-packed with cars, reduced to a system of signals?

The busy, active street, with no relation to nature apart from the sky and the clouds, or a few trees and flowers, represents the everyday in our social life. It is an almost complete representation of it, a 'digest' made interesting by being condensed. And this despite its being outside, or because it is outside, individual and social existences. A site of coming and going, of intrusion, circulation and communication, in an astonishing reversal it turns into the mirror image of the things it connects, more alive than those things. It becomes a microcosm of modern life. It plucks from obscurity all that is hidden. It makes it public. It takes away its private character and drags it across the stage of an informal theatre, where the actors are putting on a play that is also without form. The street publishes what happens elsewhere, in secret. It distorts it, but introduces it into the social text.

Like the everyday, the street changes constantly and always repeats itself. In the ceaseless alteration of times of day, people, objects and light, it tirelessly reiterates itself. The street is spectacle, almost solely spectacle, but not quite, because we are there, we walk, we stand still, we participate. The person in a hurry does not see the spectacle, but is part of it nevertheless. Almost, but not quite, pure spectacle, it is a book, or rather, an open paper, full of news, trivia, sensational stories, advertisements.[1] The street and the newspaper (analogues or homologues) join together in our everyday life, which, at the same time, they make and represent. Changing and constant, the street offers only limited surprises. The (truly) sensational, the outrageous, the absurd, the terrible and the sublime vaguely interrupt the pure, monotonously variable quasi-spectacle. Symbols go unnoticed. Who today takes seriously, or with a sense of tragedy the symbolic language of cathedrals: devils and divine figures? The street brings before our eyes a social text that is generally speaking good – dense and legible. All kinds of people mingle and get mixed up together in the street. Once, when class differences were less clear-cut than in our day, when there were 'estates' and 'castes' rather than classes, these differences were conspicuously expressed. The street was expressive. Today, these conspicuous differences have disappeared; they would make the crowds walking along the Champs Elysées or the boulevards intolerably colourful. But these social differences continue to be visible; they express meaning, through many signs and indicators scarcely visible to the casual observer. That is to say that the spectacle of the street encompasses multiple semiologies. Are faces expressive? A little, not very much. Clothes and manners signify. The spectacle of the street thus trains the eye and stimulates the faculty of observation. Think how many women, getting right inside (without knowing them) subtle systems of signs, are able at first glance to categorize another woman, assessing her shoes, stockings, hairstyle, hands and nails, jewellery and general appearance! A detailed analysis of the social text would pick up these partial systems of signs and significations, which are meshed and intertwined like the columns of a newspaper.[2]

The 'world of objects' as they present themselves in the street forms one of the most important commentaries, one of the subtlest but least well-defined system of signs. Merchandise offers itself in the street, but in so doing hides its commercial essence. It calls itself beauty, tranquillity, luxury, sensuousness. The streets of a big modern city postulate and assert the harmony of needs, desires and goods. Paradise lost is parodically regained; at every step, original unity is caricaturally recreated. Goods, things, objects are displayed; they put themselves on view to attract and arouse desire, proclaiming their aim without perceptible irony: 'To every object its desire, to each his desires, to each desire its possession and enjoyment. There are goods and desires for all, democratically, even for children, even for the not-very-well-off, but even more – everything – for the rich'. At one and the same time completely within reach, since they answer to true and false desire, and horribly inaccessible, like women who are superbly dressed and presented, objects lead their sovereign life behind display windows. In the street, the intermediary among human lives, merchandise, these exchange-values, achieves autonomy. Fetishism, taken to its extreme, acquires a sort of splendour; and the thing, the possession, the object, make their way back to symbolism via an amazing detour, by becoming symbols of wealth and pleasure without end or limit. Some streets have the beauty of museums, the same tired, dead beauty. This is where the process that changes the product – the merchandise – into a desirable and desired possession, comes full circle. Here, in this unpremeditated work of art – the street achieves the beauty of its society. Through the play of objects offered and rejected, the street becomes the place of dreams, the place where the imaginary, but also the most unsparingly real, come closest. It is where men and women, but women especially, pay court to things. Things with magical and regal powers, wonders and marvels, have the ability to transform (from the other side of the clear window-glass, in a parody of transparency in human relations) their courtiers and courtesans into things. 'Shopping' and 'window-shopping' have their magical practices, their religion, the cult of merchandise, sovereign and paramount. 'Goods', sanctified as such, are identical to their spectacle and advertising. Consumption is radiant and becomes holy. In pleasures possible and impossible, in dreams and frustrations, money proclaims more than its royalty – it proclaims its empire, its pontificate.

Far away, in the factories (factories that produce the wonderful objects, or produce the means of producing them), everything is functional, or tries to be; everything is a signal of the repetitive actions of work and its technical organization. Far away, in the workers' suburbs or on the working-class housing estates, everything is functional, a signal of the repetitive actions that maintain the workforce in its everyday life . . .

The End of Modernity?

(from *Critique de la vie quotidienne III: De la modernité au modernisme (Pour une métaphilosophie du quotidien)* [Paris: L'Arche, 1981], pp. 50–2)

It is not possible here to develop the concept of modernity and its critique to the point where we can resolve some rather serious questions. How are we to appreciate 'modern' art, in all its breadth and variety: painting and the novel (often assumed to be central), but also music, architecture, sculpture and poetry? And first of all, how are we to situate it? For Lukács, modernity and its idolization accompanied the decline of the bourgeoisie and its decomposition as a class that had previously been in the ascendant and was then bold enough to imagine that its concepts, values and norms would become universal; after Goethe and Balzac, the capacity for creativity within the ranks of bourgeois society dwindled, then disappeared.[1] For the Marxist theoretician, the works of the period of decadence bear its mark. Increasingly sophisticated technology does not prevent the lack of interest of the works or products of art, especially when they claim to 'be interesting' and their only 'interest' is merely commercial. But enough of these accusations! By contrast, for another Marxist theoretician, Adorno, modern art has aesthetic import and genuine value.[2] Of course, in Adorno's view, modern works of art do not spring up out of context, and cannot be compared with those of the Renaissance. But they still have a profound meaning; they are negative moments of their epoch, marking out transformations in society and the world. As works of 'constructive deconstruction', they bring with them, if not Truth, at least some truths about future development. They make it comprehensible, precisely in those traits that sectarian criticism sees as characteristic of decadence: the systematic use of ugliness (from Baudelaire to Beckett)[3] and its transformation into formal splendour by appropriate techniques – the absence of content and meaning, close to emptiness and nothingness, but only to flirt with them ('no cancelled trinket resonantly foolish')[4] – or the use and abuse of word and image in surrealism, in the return to rhetoric, etc.

The debate between these two interpretations of modernity will never be concluded. This is partly due to the place ascribed to the negative in the dialectical movement. Neither Marx nor Engels, still less Lenin, pay much attention to the negative. Hegel certainly goes further than the dialecticians who came after him by putting emphasis on the profound 'work of the negative'. If you think the negative consists only of the inverse and converse of the positive, and that therefore it creates nothing because all it does is dissolve and decompose the positive to make way for what is to come, then Lukacs's peremptory critique of modernity and modern art flows from that. If, on the other hand, you admit that the moment of the negative creates something new, that it brings it to life and develops its seeds through the dissolution of what now exists, then you will take Adorno's position.

Today, this unresolved debate is receding with modernity itself. Modernity has the appearance of an ideology, that is, a series of representations, all more or less elaborated, that might be thought to conceal a practice. Modernity was promising. What did it promise? Happiness, the satisfaction of all needs. This promise of happiness – no longer through beauty but through advanced technology – was supposed to be realized in the everyday. In fact, the ideology of modernity replaced the everyday as the site of continuity by offering the illusion of a break with the previous era. Once this illusion had faded and modernity had been thrown out, debates about its essence and importance lost some of their interest. What remains from this period is a general drift from a concrete derived from nature towards the abstract-concrete as mode of social existence, this including the work of art. The predominance of the abstract in modern art accompanies the extension of the world of merchandise and merchandise as a world, along with the unlimited power of money and capital, very abstract and terribly concrete at one and the same time. The work of art thus loses its previous status: closeness to and even imitation of nature; it detaches and extricates itself from naturalism. This is equally true of the momentary victory of the most abstract signs – for example, the writing on coins and bank notes – over the remains of concrete systems of reference.

Recession brought with it the separation of modernity and modernism. Modernity as ideology may be coming to an end, but modernism as technological practice goes from strength to strength. That is what, for the moment, is taking over from modernity in a potential transformation of the everyday. In short, modernity as ideology now looks like an episode in the development and implementation of the capitalist mode of production. In a contradictory way, that ideology has provoked a contestation all of its own; the reckless promise of the new – immediately and at all costs – has brought about a return to the archaic and the retro, and the optimism of modernity has been tinged with nihilism. From that massive confusion emerges modernism: a clear field for the deployment of technology – the declaration of the end of ideologies (the ideology of the end of ideologies) but the arrival of new myths, to which we must return, such as the myth of transparency in society, the State and political activity.

How can we avoid concluding that the choice is a false one: either modernity or postmodernity? Posed this way, the question misses the essential point: technological modernism, its reach, its capacity to act in the everyday. And the related problem, at once theoretical and political, of control over technology. Meanwhile, the everyday continues.

On Vulgarity

(from *Critique de la vie quotidienne III: De la modernité au modernisme (Pour une métaphilosophie du quotidien)* [Paris: L'Arche, 1981], pp. 74–8)

It is hard to define; but who could deny its 'reality', especially since it consists of a certain way of being 'real' and of understanding the 'real'? Nowadays, it is contrasted with *distinction*; but this distinction is itself an aspect of vulgarity. Nothing is more vulgar than distinction and the wish to distinguish oneself (to *be* distinguished); ethical-aesthetic judgement and sociological fact, vulgarity does not emanate from popular gestures and words, but from the everyday as it is secreted and decreed by the middle classes: a certain 'realism' about money, clothes, behaviour and gratifications, a realism that flaunts and asserts itself, which is part of the 'vulgar'. The everyday is limited to what is there; it has no horizons, no resonance, it congratulates itself on its limitations and retreats into them. It parades need, the object of need and the satisfaction of need; this is its 'behaviour', a self-satisfied conditioned reflex, a way of behaving that lasts throughout a lifetime and imbues it with its own tonality: vulgarity. And this makes suspect and forbidden all forms of rupture, and prohibits all change by identifying 'what is' with wisdom and good sense. Realism – dense, vulgar and producer of vulgarity – stifles the very sighs of the creature it oppresses: the dream, the call to what is 'other' or 'elsewhere', the protestations of those who in the everyday – women, children, deviants – are the irredeemable lived, demanding 'something else'. The extraordinary that pierces through the ordinary, the extra-quotidian [*extraquotidian*] that ruptures the everyday [*quotidien*] (the 'passions', the appeal that is heard through interdictions and maledictions, interjections and exclamations, curses and insults), the vulgar rejects it, denies its existence, ridicules it, and reduces it to nothing. Impermeable, invulnerable, inaccessible, the vulgar being forms a shell around itself, which protects it from all but the most common ills. The only part of the everyday that vulgarity keeps is the trivial. It does not confine itself to one utterance, but relates to something more hidden and essential. Does satisfaction not have something *cumulative* about it? Not in the same way as knowledge, but in some analogous way? Satisfactions accumulate; needs, by producing and reproducing themselves, and producing and reproducing their objects, create the density of the vulgar. This does not mean that unease, imagination or anxiety tear the 'subject' away from vulgarity; a thwarted person can still be vulgar in his anxiety.

Vulgarity is not restricted to the everyday and to those who concentrate the trivial within it. Certain 'reflections' that try to pass for thinking become tainted by vulgarity and carry its mark as well as aspects of behaviour rooted in habits. The vulgarity of complacent knowledge has traditional names, which 'scientific' and 'technological' apologias for it make us forget: fussiness, pedantry, complexity. Once, we used to say 'philistinism' and Schumann wrote his 'March against the Philistines'.[1] The enormous and lasting success of psychoanalysis has not prevented discussions 'centred' on sexuality from descending into vulgarity; there is something deeply vulgar in the attention paid to 'sexual matters' and 'sexual relations', to sex in general or to 'sexuality'. Nowadays, after Nietzsche, no doctrine deserves to have a following unless it advances the idea of a new (superior) type of man, society or civilization. Freud brought to language, to ideas and (it is always worth remembering, to avoid misunderstandings) to theory a 'reality' that had until then remained unrecognized, disregarded, even anathematized. Freud's thinking does not descend into vulgarity, but it can lead to it. Here, intellectual triviality meets social triviality, the triviality of unhappy adolescents who talk endlessly about sex, and cast shamefaced glances at the opposite sex and the sexual apparatus of their peers. This 'reality' does not cause doubt, nor the everyday problems that it poses (itself); but such a 'reality', or rather, such a 'realism', are inherent to vulgarity. Should not the theorization of this 'reality' be understood *as a symptom*, as a sign of the malaise that haunts Western, Judeo-Christian – capitalist and bourgeois – or scientific and technical society? Can psychoanalysis, a symptom and symbol of a failure that goes well beyond the sexual, guarantee that an acceptable 'everyday' can be established on the basis of the language and knowledge of the 'unconscious'? Is it not precisely this implied – never fulfilled – promise, this failure of prophesy, that discredits theory? And of course, vulgar Marxism is not exempt from this.

Is it a question here of giving 'vulgarity' philosophical status, as Sartre tried to do for certain notions like that of the 'bastard' [*salaud*], or the 'gaze of the other'? Not exactly. It is a question of bringing within the theory of the everyday what is generally thought of as belonging to subjective judgement: vulgarity, boredom, malaise. The so-called social and human 'sciences' do not take account of these things. So boredom does not exist for sociologists, as a social fact. Wrongly so! And as for going from feeling-bad to being-bad,[2] philosophically understood, that is another operation entirely.

Neither Marx and so-called 'Marxist' thought, nor Freud and psychology and psychoanalysis have escaped the great illusion of the nineteenth and part of the twentieth century: the confusion (even their identification in the name of Truth) between the lived and knowledge. From this deceptive point of view, to live is to know – to learn and to know is to live. The lived and the conceived become identical. Knowledge, confused with 'being', focused on the 'real', defining it and thus controlling it, has a predominance that is at one and the same time methodological, practical and ontological. Social and practical man becomes according to the Cartesian precept the master and proprietor of Nature, through work and knowledge; he thus defines and realizes his full existence. That's according to Marx. If I know what I feel and perceive, if I attain what in 'me' escaped 'my' knowledge, and followed its own course outside my consciousness or without it, I achieve a satisfying, normal situation: deliverance and health. That's according to Freud. As if knowledge had this bearing: not simply to grasp the unknown 'object', whether nature or the unconscious, but to realize the 'subject'. Which would thus be constituted through knowledge, experienced as such.

Many empty discussions take this position, which practically falls into an extreme vulgarity. There is the vulgarity of the specialist who knows the things that fall within his narrow competence, but knows nothing of the world. There is also the vulgarity of the technocrat who cultivates only the kind of successful performance with which he is familiar and whose only link with other fields is via the most trivial commonplace.

The attitude that calls itself rational, and privileges the conceived to the point of hypostatizing it, causes a strong reaction, which stands in direct confrontation with what motivates it: the fetishism of the absurd, the cult of the irrational. Thought thus makes a loop and comes full circle.

Hence also a problematic without answers, and endless disputes, in the course of which theory degrades into vulgarity. On the Marxists' side: are superstructures a simple reflection of the base? If they reflect the base, how can they take effective action? What is the base? Forces of production, or social relations? What relations? On the Freudians' side: does psychoanalysis have concepts? Which ones? Does the psychoanalyst apply these concepts or does the treatment of 'patients' take a course that in practice is indifferent to concepts? Where, if not from knowledge and its transfer, does the power of the analyst over the patient (a power that in principle is beneficial) come from? Does this process take place at the cognitive level or in the emotions? And so on and so forth.

'Marxism' has thus not been spared the fate of philosophies of pure knowledge. Revolution through knowledge, transmitted by the political party, brought by it to the working-class *from the outside* (Lenin) – this revolution has failed.[3] The outcome is a situation that seems favourable neither to theory, nor the political party, nor the working-class; the latter cannot constitute itself into an *autonomous*, self-determining 'political subject' through knowledge (of economics, of its own condition, etc.) alone. Hence the tiresome *vulgarization* of Marxist thinking. We waited in vain for the 'working-class', which had not yet achieved the status of a 'class for itself', according to Marx, to assimilate the simplified knowledge it was being offered.[4] This knowledge still belongs to – it is almost their (collective) property – groups narrower than a 'class', to an elite stratum of professionals, members of the 'political class', bound up with the autonomization of the apparatuses of government and the State. This situation in turn is bound up with the autonomization of technology.

The transformation of the social by knowledge and in knowledge ends in the reversal of the project; knowledge promulgates itself autonomously, thus consolidating the existing state of affairs, known and acknowledged as such. Must we remind ourselves here that the critique of everyday life proposes a different route: to take lived experience as the starting point, and elucidate it in order to transform it – instead of starting from the conceived in order to impose it? But at the same time, without belittling or rejecting knowledge.

Myths in Everyday Life

(from *Cahiers Internationaux de Sociologie*, XXXIII (1962))

Let us briefly remind ourselves of the definition of the everyday. In our opinion, it concerns a level in contemporary society defined by: 1) the gap between this level and levels above it (those of the State, technology, high culture); 2) the intersection between the non-dominated sector of reality and the dominated sector; 3) transformation of objects into appropriated goods.

Let us ignore other features of the 'ordinariness' of everyday life, which cannot, in our opinion, be defined or grasped in an 'ordinary' fashion.

In this vast and ill-defined zone of the everyday a mass of multiple and interrelated dialectical movements evolve and confront each other; for example, dialectic movements of need and desire. Desire, constructed through culture and language, cannot do without need, because a desire without a need is a pure sham. In this perpetual conflict between desire and need, there is a dialectical unity between the two, while at the same time perpetual opposition and contradiction. So there you have one dialectical movement among others, that of need and desire. Another one from among so many: the serious and the frivolous. What is serious? What is frivolous? It often appears that what presents itself as frivolous, or manifests itself as frivolity, is also the most serious, the essence of seriousness, in fact, as with everything to do with love.

The everyday is thus one of the sites of multiple confrontation between the natural (what comes from nature and is part of all social constructions) and the artificial (what comes from culture, inasmuch as this culture is precisely detached from nature and opposed to nature).

It is also the site of confrontation between the private and the public.

We thus see a series of intertwined conflicts and dialectical movements, of which I have named only a few: need/desire, natural/artificial, serious/frivolous, private/public, etc. It is also the site where, for the somewhat crude mentality, interpretations abound – for example, the notions of good and bad luck that play such a large role in everyday life and which are subjective interpretations, themselves blind and contingent, of necessity and chance.

I should like to emphasize one point: in industrial society, the everyday manifests itself as a discrete *level*. In previous societies, everyday life was incomparably more integrated into the culture as a whole – into religious life, for example; it was not separate from it. In our society there is an increasing disparity between the level of the everyday and higher levels – those of politics and the State, high technology, or high culture, for instance. This gap is widening and helps to define the everyday as such, as a level. Furthermore, at the same time as it is gradually becoming defined as a level, the everyday is spreading and levelling out throughout industrial society, in all countries, and in all the cultures that are subordinate to industrial society; and it is becoming uniform, in other words, defined.

I have indicated some broad features of the everyday, an everyday that teems with myths. We need only open a weekly magazine. This morning, I bought a copy of *Elle*, of which I am a devoted reader. I bought it with you in mind, and from page one onwards, I found myths by the dozen. 'What a great idea! Wear your favourite colours.' There's an understanding that we're only referring to preferences that already exist, whereas in fact, they're going to be created for us. In whose name? By what means are these choices, these suggestions, going to be imposed on us? The text tells us. It goes on: 'Liz is looking for her unattainable love.' Eternal, absolute love continues to exist in a society which in every other respect forbids, prohibits and opposes it. But in extraordinarily privileged cases, the case for example, of Liz Taylor, who is still searching for this unattainable love, a myth appears once removed.[1]

To continue. Here we have a story. We don't know if it's a story in the literary or the journalistic sense of the word, just a story for you unspecified ladies who believe in love at first sight. The unspecified nature of the words used is carefully calculated, and reveals a fleeting glimpse of another form of the myth of absolute love: love at first sight. And here we move from the dream to the practical, because one feature of this mythology of modern times is perpetual movement from dream to reality (and it's a feature I have tried to pin down elsewhere) with the result that reality is lived at the level of dream and the dream is read, dreamed, as if it were reality. In your house: practical white-wood and fine old furniture. And, more practical still, the 'pull-out card'. Here we find a major element of contemporary mythology: the technical seen and presented not in its technological or scientific guise, but as myth, as something all-powerful. Thus we have a pull-out menu card for 'healthy eating'. Lastly, to end with a kind of mythical restitution of the most obscure metaphysics, an enquiry from Marianne K.: 'Are we to believe in thought transmission?' A sociological study, please.

On every page we find modern mythology, in all its glory.

Look at this lovely creature. She's beautiful. The text reads: 'The ideal woman doesn't find her path strewn with roses, she makes them bloom.' A prodigious comment, because its about a magical power of creation attributed, in today's world, to the 'eternal feminine'.[2] Not only does the myth of the eternal feminine persist, alongside the myth of absolute love, but the two are very precisely related: the ideal woman makes roses bloom.

And so on and so forth, on every page. And I haven't even come to the horoscopes, which you undoubtedly read. Myself, I don't miss a single one.

Another page reads, 'Keep that morning freshness', with a picture of a young man wearing the eternal smile of a man utterly satisfied with life. Just look at the delightful creatures that have entered our lives! 'Keep that morning freshness.' By using lotion X after shaving. We'll ignore the product itself (it's not important) but the accompanying text has an immediate impact: it's the omnipotence of technology. Technology is omnipotent. With it, anything is possible. Put your trust in technology, that is, in the products of modern technology, which are involved in all of our everyday chores – all those demeaning, tiresome chores, like going to the office, taking the metro, sweeping floors, doing pieces of writing – and all those boring everyday things will be imbued with morning freshness if you put your trust in modern technology.

So here you see, in a simple example, a manifestation of this very diverse mythology. I could also refer to the book by Roland Barthes, but my methodological interpretation is slightly different from his.[3] I think it would be interesting to take advantage of the presence of my friend Norbert Guterman, who does not come to Paris very often, and to pursue the analysis further. Long ago, we wrote a book together entitled *La Conscience mystifiée*, in which we did in fact use a method for analysing modern myths.[4] It was not precisely the semantic method; our method was more (as today's fashionable language would put it) diachronic than synchronic.[5] If you like, we'll come back to it in a moment in the course of our discussion.

These mythologies of the everyday are difficult to distinguish from the innumerable superstitions given ritual form in everyday life. The origins of these superstitions are obscure, and maybe to rediscover them, we ought, perhaps, to cite the work of psychoanalysts on different types of symbolism. On 'touching wood', Freud said wood is *materia*, primordial matter, and in *materia* there is *mater*, an interpretation I find slightly forced.[6] Memmi, who has a soft spot for psychoanalysis, will perhaps have something to tell us about it.[7] We sometimes wonder, is it pagan or is it Christian? To look for the sources of these minute rituals of everyday life would mean going back to the origins of society, and that is where we can construct – and have already started to do so – a kind of ethnography or ethnology of contemporary society.

Myths are different from symbolism or rituals – which rarely have the character of myth, properly speaking, as defined by specialists in mythology. The mythic story is often absent, although something may make it appear.

It is difficult to distinguish the mythical from the ideological; in the case of good or bad luck, for example, myths surrounding luck are frequently confused with ideologies.

Myths have multiple functions, but they are rarely recognized. In the quotidian they have as primary meaning and effect to maintain and contain human beings within the narrow limits of the everyday. They exert ceaseless pressure; they have a kind of negative power, a power of repression; one makes do with the banality and triviality of everyday life. And this is not because they reveal these things, but because they conceal them and frequently transform the everyday. They provide a false image of it, and on it they base an aesthetic, or a quasi-ethic. They mix adaptation in the illusory dimension of the imaginary with acceptance in the practical dimension of the everyday. We dream our real lives.

For the people who live in the everyday, there are, somewhere, very high up, wise men, experts, who know what is to be done and in whose hands they can leave everything. These 'top-down' myths are the myths of power, and in this they're like the most ancient myths, because, speaking for myself, I believe most of the ancient myths are myths of power, including those that involve the father and fatherhood.

It is possible to distinguish 'top-down' myths from those that spring from the everyday 'bottom-up' and spread and propagate themselves from the everyday. All the myths arising from the level of the everyday turn on the notion of satisfaction, satisfying act, satisfaction attained or achieved in the form of privileged acts. 'Consume this or that product. Go to see this or that. Believe in life, be fundamentally optimistic.' They turn on what I would call the myth of the smile in the modern world, and the myth of niceness. These are the myths of happiness in the consumer society, the society that is coming up over our horizon.

On the basis of this rather crude classification, I could take most of the myths of the everyday and try to put them into one category or another. I shall limit myself to recalling one or two. First of all, myths of love. As far as love goes, it's agreed nowadays that it's a big failure. When it occurs in literature, in films, it's always about failure, except in a few privileged, exceptional cases, which are presented in a mythic way, and generally limited to the 'elect': kings, queens, princesses and stars. A grand failure, with a few rare examples of success, haunting exceptions. However, it is agreed that the person who is starting out in life – the young man or woman (and that's where the myth is, where it comes right down to the everyday) – it's agreed that someone who is just starting out has every chance of succeeding; that despite the risk of failure, the person setting out in life is blessed with fortune and favour, and that in any case, failure has nothing to do with them, because they're starting out, because they're beginning. Provided of course that they do what they're told, this young man or woman, that they read the problem pages and follow as closely as they can the advice given there, carry it out to the letter, then they'll have good fortune, and good fortune will bring favour, ardour, success. They will enjoy perfect love.

Then there is the myth of woman. Here I'm getting onto slippery ground, but it has to be admitted that myths of woman persist, in their entirety, in a way that is otherwise ambiguous, and I will labour the point that ambiguity is the fundamental category of everyday life. You either believe in these myths or you don't; you behave as if you believed in them, and at the same time you believe in them without doing so. The eternal feminine survives; it can transform the everyday, not only for the man associated with this divine creature, but for woman herself; if she is able to cultivate the eternal feminine living within her, the everyday will be transformed into splendour and beauty. On the one hand, there is the fascinating *femme fatale*, on the other, the woman as victim [*femme victime*], seduced and weak; they coexist in constant ambiguity and the strangest thing is to try to understand how these myths of the eternal feminine accord with the real progress made by women in society, with their real activities, because this is the problem the editors of women's magazines set themselves every week: how to combine and connect these myths with an everyday reality that is hard and unforgiving and in which women obviously carve out a place for themselves as best they can. These images of femininity become firmly established; however, they are images that come from a time when women were subordinate and submissive. What is wonderful is to see how these images survive in an era when women are not just carving out their place by every means possible, but asserting their priority and pre-eminence and somewhat confusedly – as everyone in sociology knows – working towards the creation of a new matriarchy. So we see myths of female weakness transformed into women's strength in a period when their desire for power is bursting forth.

We live in these complex ambiguities of ancient myths, which persist in the everyday to mask it, transform and transpose it. Two ambiguities coexist: an ambiguity of consciousness and an ambiguous consciousness, since the modern woman is both everyday and divine, immanent and transcendent, mediatory and fundamental, weak and strong – to say the least!

On the question of masculinity and femininity, we could continue our analysis, to refine it and perhaps reach the point where the mythic, the ideological and the utopian meet. The mythic relates to origins, foundations, Eve, Aphrodite; the ideological relates to interpretation, women's real role in contemporary society, what can be said about it, the critiques that can be made of it, the projects that can be built around women; lastly, the utopian relates to happiness and the absolute as we dream and half-dream it, mingled with reality at the level of half-dreaming.

I should now like to mention some other aspects of everyday myth. The first is what I would call 'family folklore'. Here, I descend into the everyday in the sense of the trivial, but I in no way separate this level from the one I have analysed or attempted to analyse, because every family has its own lore about its origins – its ancestors and what they did or did not do. This lore is transmitted and transformed in the process, and it forms part of the most precious inheritance passed down to children, who carefully collect it, if only later to say the exact opposite, or to make fun of Dad and the ancestors. In this family lore is the story (belatedly fictionalized to some extent) of how one's parents met, how they fell in love, or out of love, and how they lived. A family folklore stuffed with myths. These are the myths about the past.

On the same level, there are myths about the future: what we will do, what we would do. What we would do if we were rich, if this person or that left us an inheritance, if we won the lottery jackpot (the lottery in many respects expresses the way myth enters everyday life through our dreams, and is the source of an almost endless procession of dreams). What would I do if I were rich? What career will such or such a child follow? All the myths about the future ...

There are also myths about the present. Think about advertising. A study ought be made of its actual methods, the way it has long since given up the 'conditioned reflex' – although it still makes considerable use of repeated slogans – to concentrate almost exclusively on image and myth. Advertising today uses symbols. It is the symbol of whiteness – with everything suggested by it, everything associated with purity and virginity, everything that is spiritually immaculate – it is whiteness as symbol that sells one detergent or another, and the public 'goes along with it'. They buy. Advertising stakes everything on images of beauty, and glory, on all the symbols communicated via everyday life, where they are therefore effective, because it 'works', and the statistics are there to prove it.

I could continue this analysis, but before I conclude, I should like to dwell on one of the great myths of our time, the one that plays the most important role in everyday life, especially in the life of children and adolescents: the myth of adulthood.

I shall make a distinction between chronological adults and adulthood [*les adultes d'âge – et l'âge adulte*], which seems quite different to me. We present adulthood to children and young people as a goal to be attained. It is understood that after a series of initiations for which, by the way, they are responsible because initiation ceremonies have disappeared, they will reach adulthood, and that adulthood is the supreme test. Once they've turned that corner, they'll be sailing in new waters – calmer, wider and more beautiful. Who tells young people, boys and girls, that? Why adults, of course! You and me. Now I contend that adulthood is a myth and a myth presented by adults to their juniors, because nothing entitles us to say there is an age that could possess this 'initiatory' power. What do we see when we, sociologists, study actual social life? We see young people, adolescents, children, in their various age-groups, as they call them, and belonging to this or that social group (students, apprentices, etc.), actually reaching adulthood. And what does adulthood mean? It means that a social group, well organized and also possessing a number of usually solid structures, takes control of the life of the person who has reached adulthood and subordinates and integrates him firmly into itself. Such well-organized groups include, for example, the army, the university, the civil service. From the moment adults are firmly integrated into one of these groups we see them turn into very important people, decorated, beribboned and frequently childish. So adulthood is a myth, because it infantilizes adults in the very process of integrating them with terrible force into a social structure. This is one of the great myths of our everyday life, and we adults are perhaps also its victims. (With honourable exceptions, of course.) I believe it is one of our society's most oppressive myths, and that's why I'm on the side of everyone, young or not-so-young, who does not believe in adulthood.

The analysis of everyday life leads us to a radical critique, a radical questioning of the everyday in contemporary society: industrial and technological society, and so-called 'consumer' society. There, also, we have several great myths, but I shall not discuss them here.

To conclude, I should like to sum up my analysis as follows: nature has been the privileged site of myths – ancient myths are located in the relationship between man and nature, but in so far as man was weak in the face of nature; nature is where the mythic story unfolded. Myths set in nature translated into natural terms the actions of civil powers and the birth of political powers, as well as human weakness in the face of those powers. That weakness was projected, so to speak, onto nature. Today, the everyday has become the site of human weakness. It has become the site of men's powerlessness vis-à-vis themselves. It is the site where men's (and that means our own) non-appropriation of our own nature and powers appears – not obviously, but rather in a veiled and thus deeper way – and that is why this weakness encourages myths to flourish.

Strasbourg, Faculté des lettres et Sciences humaines

The Country and the City

Introduction

Though now better known for his writings on the city and the urban, Lefebvre entered the CNRS in 1948 to undertake research on rural sociology. Questions concerning the peasantry and agrarian reform had interested him since the 1930s. He submitted his doctoral thesis in rural sociology and his book on the *Vallée de Campan*, based on research carried out from 1941 to 1952, focused on a valley in the Western Pyrenees.[1] Another major piece of rural research, the *Manuel de sociologie rurale*, was stolen from a car and never found or rewritten.[2] Several articles outlining his sociological and methodological approaches were published in *Du Rural à l'urbain* which is a collection of articles on the rural and the urban written from 1949 to 1969, and recently republished.[3] As in many of his writings, he combines the sociological and historical. He commented in the Introduction that an interest in worldwide agrarian issues was pursued through detailed local fieldwork.[4] Articles on the rural world covered 'social classes in the countryside', 'theory of land rent and rural sociology', 'problems of rural sociology' and 'perspectives on rural sociology', the last of which we include in this section. This article elucidates his methodological three-stage approach of regression-progression which he frequently deploys elsewhere, as in *The Production of Space*.[5] Sartre adopted this method of returning to the past before moving back to the present in order to progress through to the future in his *Critique of Dialectical Reason*.[6] Hess also comments that it was a method used by Freud in his analysis of the unconscious.[7]

By the late 1950s Lefebvre saw that the most relevant issues concerning the relationship of philosophy and the non-philosophical world had moved onto issues of everydayness, everyday life and modernity, especially in the urban arena. Near Navarrenx, the new town of Lacq-Mourenx had emerged from green fields in the early 1960s to house workers in a major energy development. Some would call this the *Texas béarnais* [Béarn being the old name of the province] to describe the rapid shift from the rural to the urban. Lefebvre himself examined the urban problems of the new working-class in the town. Urbanization raised all kinds of new questions about historical periodizations, contradictions of development, conflicts between integration and segregation, and the relationship between the urban and the State.[8]

One of his principal preoccupations was the fluctuating dialectical relationship between desire and need in a period of rapid modernization and expansion of consumption in France in the 1960s after the resolution of two major colonial wars and a period of political instability. He had coined the term 'the bureaucratic society of consumption',[9] which was to be taken up by students in the 1968 events. Of his writings on needs, one of the most insightful in relation to housing was his introduction to a study of *the habitat pavillionnaire* (detached house or bungalow) which was undertaken by a group at the Institut de Sociologie Urbaine (ISU)[10] of which he was director. These were studies that critiqued the functional dimension of architectural and urban analyses of housing that were common in the 1960s. His introduction outlines the epistemological and methodological underpinnings of the studies and explores the meaning and sense of what it is to inhabit a dwelling. In it, he acknowledges the influence of Bachelard, Barthes, Foucault and Heidegger.

During the 1960s and the early 1970s, he was heavily involved in architectural and neighbourhood projects. Towards the end of the 1960s, and just before the events of 1968, he devoted some attention to the new urbanism and the right to the city. He felt that we couldn't any longer contemplate a new urbanism. *Le Droit à la ville* was extremely influential in France amongst a wide range of disciplines and professionals. One can see its impact in subsequent slogans such as 'Changer la Ville, changer la vie'[11] [Change the city, change life] in the mid-1970s in France. His concern with rights can be traced in much of his work.[12]

The article *Les Autres Paris* [The other Parises], which formed the text for a short film called *Le Droit à la ville,* reflects his love of wandering through the various sectors of a city in which he had spent most of his life. This was published in *Espaces et Sociétés*, a journal he had founded with Anatole Kopp in 1970, but then left in 1974. After the early 1970s he ceased to write specifically on the urban, although he returned to it through the lens of urban rhythms, as with his relationship to the noises and rhythms of his Paris neighbourhood (see 'Seen from the Window', a contemplative piece written at the end of his life) and, more generally, Mediterranean cities.[13] Instead, from the mid-1970s, he directed his energy to the production of space and then theoretical reflections on the State.

La Révolution urbaine [The Urban Revolution] was read in more narrowly academic circles and by English-speaking theoreticians, such as David Harvey,[14] and fed through to a radical urban geography and sociology. In this section we are including a chapter on levels and dimensions, which asserts the priority of habitation in relation to the urban and the State, on the one hand, and lays the foundation for the subsequent *The Production of Space* on the other.

Eleonore Kofman

Perspectives on Rural Sociology

(from *Cahiers Internationaux de Sociologie*, XIV (1953), pp. 22–40; repr. in *Du Rural à l'urbain*, 3ᵉ édn (Paris: Anthropos, 2001), pp. 63–78)

An earlier article in *Cahiers Internationaux de Sociologie*[1] set out some of the problems of rural sociology. It is now time to develop an overall picture of this branch of sociology, and to present – and offer for discussion – the outline of a manual or study on the subject.

We may speak of a 'world' of the peasantry, not in the sense that peasant reality constitutes a world *apart,* but on account of its extraordinary variety and peculiar characteristics.

We insist again on an (apparent) paradox: this world was long neglected, especially at a time when it dominated the life of society, quantitatively and qualitatively. As long as 'urban' experience, with its institutions and ideologies – its successive modes of production, and their superstructures – had a rural basis and rested on a vast agricultural base, people in ruling-class circles paid scant attention to country people. They thought about them as much we do about our stomach or our liver when we are feeling well! Peasant life appeared to be one of those familiar realities that seem natural, and are not studied until much later. Hegel's aphorism should appear at the beginning of any methodology of the social sciences: *'What is familiar is not necessarily understood.'*[2] A truth that holds good for actions in everyday life – for example, buying or selling some object or other – for actions at work, for social life as a whole, or even for the life of country people.

The rural world became an object of scientific study from the moment it posed *practical* problems.

In France, towards the middle of the nineteenth century, the splitting up of lands and inheritances, the division of property and rural exodus began to worry the authorities. The creation of a national market brings with it a reorganization of agriculture: concentration of holdings, commercialization and specialization of production. Later, the questions raised by the world market, then by modern technology, are superimposed on existing ones: price protection, profitability, the introduction of mechanization. Gradually, familiar but little understood conditions are judged worthy of interest and academic study.

Rural sociology developed in the United States; it is clear that the reason for this was the rural problem, and it has been a major preoccupation of successive governments.[3]

Today, the 'peasant problem' is raised or arises under many forms. *Agrarian reform* has taken place, or will take place, everywhere: in the peoples' democracies, China, Mexico, Egypt, Italy, Japan, India, etc., not to mention the great transformations of agriculture in the USSR. Of course, these reforms and transformations are profoundly different under different conditions and political systems. This does not mean that they are any the less an indication of the scale, throughout today's world, of agrarian problems.

But sociologists have gone from studying primitive people to studying urban and industrial cultures, while leapfrogging, so to speak, over this phenomenon, which is so vast in both time and space. In France, the study of rural life was initiated by historians and geographers.[4] But we must now go back to their work, and both make it concrete and integrate it into an overarching concept, which sociology alone, seen as the study of the totality of the social process and its laws, can provide.

One cannot over-emphasize the fact that large *entities* (national and world markets, social and political structures) have played a major part in transforming agrarian structures. National and global markets led to *specialization* (on the national scale, we could cite the vineyards of the Midi, and on the world scale, coffee plantations in Brazil). Social and political organization, government policy, plans – or the lack of plans, or their failure – have acted and reacted on the remotest places on the planet. There isn't a peasant farmer today, even in Africa or Asia, who is not affected by world events.

But nor should we neglect the other aspect of reality, which contradicts the previous one: agriculture brings with it residues, survivals from the distant past. And this especially in backward or underdeveloped countries, and those that lack planning, i.e. colonial countries, but also in 'Western' European countries. In a single region, the Pyrenees, one may observe both phenomena side by side: the most archaic cultivation methods using the hoe ('laya' on the Spanish side),[5] the Roman swing-plough, the tractor, remnants of the agrarian community (collective holding and use of pasture), modern cooperatives and large-scale mechanized farming.

The rural world thus presents a twofold complexity:

a) *Horizontal complexity.* In agrarian formations and structures of the same historical date – especially those determined by large-scale contemporary social and political phenomena – we see essential differences, which reach the point of antagonism.

Thus, the borderline case of agrarian capitalism, with its highly mechanized methods of cultivation, is to be found in the USA. The 'owner' or capitalist farmer, owning the latest machinery, can spend at least half the year in town. He goes to his farm at ploughing time, employing seasonal workers and using advanced technology, and once his crop is harvested and sold, he returns to his home in town.

At the other extreme, just as highly mechanized and technically advanced, but with a completely different social structure, we find the Soviet *kolkhoz* and *sovkhoz*, and the future 'agri-towns' (*kolkhoz* villages grouped together in a single cluster).[6]

Between these two poles, we find intermediate situations. J. Chombart de Lauwe has recently published an interesting study of the CUMA (Coopératives pour l'Utilisation en commun de Matériel Agricole en France [Cooperatives for sharing the use of agricultural equipment in France]).[7] Production cooperatives, like those in Emilia (the region of Bologna in Italy), or those in the peoples' democracies, are other intermediate or transitional forms, lying somewhere between the 'poles' described above.

In each case and on each level, it is possible to make a sociological study that takes a *comparative* approach to technology, its relationship with the human community and social structure, agricultural productivity and population movements – in other words, of *conditions* as a whole.

b) *Vertical complexity*. Today's rural world offers for observation and analysis formations that *differ in age and date* but which coexist. As we noted above, this paradoxical juxtaposition – the archaic alongside the ultra-modern – is sometimes seen within a limited geographical area. Another example: North Africa, where pastoral nomadism or semi-nomadism, with its huts (*noualas*) that a man can carry on his back, coexists with highly developed technology. In the rural world, even more clearly than in the craft industries, nothing has entirely disappeared. And the mere fact that these archaisms and 'sociological fossils' have been preserved – relatively speaking, and allowing for various forms of influence or degeneration, and a greater or lesser degree of integration of the archaic into recent structures – this fact itself poses many problems.

The two kinds of complexity – the one we call *horizontal* and the one we call *vertical* but could call *historical* – intertwine, intersect and interact; hence a confused mass of facts that only a sound *methodology* can disentangle. We have at the same time to determine the objects and objectives of rural sociology – and to define its relationship with its ancillary fields and disciplines: human geography, political economy, ecology, statistics, etc.

Rural sociology developed primarily in the United States. We know why. Every American university has a chair in rural sociology and there are already many manuals, textbooks and research studies.

But something strikes you when you read these publications: the lack of reference to a *history*.

Take the case of a major collaborative work, *Rural Life in the USA* (Knopf, 1942).[8] From the historical point of view, it includes only one demographic study, dealing with settlement, colonization and rural population movements during industrialization (pp. 13–36). This statistical section is interesting (see pp. 27–29, on the national origins of immigrant farm workers), but it is in no respect a rural history.

These studies do not even refer to the defining characteristic of America's brief rural history: colonization (in the broad sense: settlement by colonists) and settlement on *free* land. Marxists make the distinction between the *Prussian* form of colonization (colonization of appropriated land) and the *American* form. In the latter case, there is no tradition of feudal landed property. Until the coming of large capitalist holdings, and the involvement of banks and trusts, tenant farming is rare; medium-sized farms are the norm, and the small producer does not have to pay *dues* to the owner whose land he works. So there is no parasitic class taking a significant part of the national income. There are no *feudal* obstacles to the growth of productive forces; capitalism is able to grow more quickly, until its *internal* contradictions strangle its development. It is precisely this factor that explains the extraordinary economic growth of the USA during the nineteenth century. American economists and sociologists are therefore unable even to study seriously the conditions for this growth, whose results they note empirically. They do not explore the formation of the domestic market, nor the specific characteristics of an agricultural system that has produced vast quantities while remaining for the most part extensive, and of relatively low productivity (by acre or hectare cultivated).

The fact that the land was settled from the *towns*, and its consequences, have not been studied. In Europe, agriculture has preceded industry and towns grew up in a rural context. The Italian or French peasant [*paysan*] is basically a 'pagan [*païen*]' (*paganus*). Peasant life has its own customs, habits and traditions. To some extent, one may speak of a peasant 'culture'. But the American countryside took its cultural models ('patterns') from the town. Such peasant culture as there is does not have traditional roots; it merely reflects the urban culture in a degraded or gradually integrated form ('acculturation'). There is no conflict between country traditions, habits and customs, on the one hand, and religion on the other. In the absence of an original peasant 'culture' (all the more so given the slow adoption of scientific culture by isolated country-people) religion is the only potent ideology in the countryside. It is therefore no surprise to find American rural sociologists producing minutely detailed studies of the church as a social institution,[9] making a denominational break-down of the population,[10] or tracing the radius of church influence in a given rural 'community', compared with the area visited by the postman or the doctor.

It is clear that the problems of rural sociology present themselves differently in the 'historical countries' and in the USA.

The purely descriptive and empirical method could only emerge in a country without a history, or more precisely, of little historical 'thickness'.

There, human life is simply laid down on the land flat, so to speak. So sociologists simplify the problem of methodology. Empiricism and statistical formalism become characteristic of their work. We have seen that this method is not adequate, even for a 'non-historical' country with few historical foundations or 'sediments' in its immediate given reality.[11]

As a result, as far as France and the major part of the rural world are concerned, we find ourselves facing a methodological problem: *the relationship between sociology and history*, given that we are dealing with a reality that has a history – one which preserves and juxtaposes within itself archaic and 'modern' formations.

The problem is a tricky one, because it is a question of not allowing history to absorb sociology, and on the other hand, not allowing rural sociology to avoid competing with history, as an *ancillary* discipline. Sociology has to take as its starting point current reality, and its *description*. But when this reality has historical 'thickness', how are we to ignore it? The problem is made even more difficult by the situation noted above.

It is *historians* who have developed and disseminated certain concepts which, if found to be valid, would dominate rural sociology.

Thus, Marc Bloch has spoken of an *agrarian regime* or an *agrarian civilization*. According to him there is a clash, in France, between two major forms of agrarian civilization which we could, *faute de mieux*, call those of the North and the South.[12] He characterizes these basic agrarian civilizations or structures in terms of contrasts:

North	**South**
Community disciplines	Individualism
Plough	Swing plough
Long fields	Irregular fields
Open fields	Enclosures
Triennial crop rotation	Biennial crop rotation

The concept of an agrarian regime corresponds with the geographers' concept of the 'way of life'. Whether scholars from the school of human geography passed it on to the historians or whether they took it from them (as far as France is concerned) is of little importance here. What *is* important, is that the two concepts are very closely connected, both referring to very ancient, stable, or more precisely *static* configurations which diverge only under pressure of mechanization. They are thus archaic, or almost, and 'natural' (as long as one does not apply them to collective representations of this or that race, country or people).[13]

A subtler analysis dissolves fixed oppositions and static differences between structures. It substitutes a profoundly different model for contrasts between agrarian 'regimes'. For example, we find triennial crop rotation in the south of France and biennial rotation in the north and east, especially in Alsace. In the south, we find biennial rotation with fallow and with continuous cultivation (no fallow); and similarly in the north, triennial rotation with or without fallow. Continuous cultivation represents technical progress, better use of land and increased productivity. In each region, depending on geographical conditions, and also on social relations and political events, there was growth – faster or slower, curbed or accelerated by differing conditions – in the productive forces, with instances of stagnation, retardation or regression.

If agrarian structures were fixed and discrete, as historians and geographers have believed, the sociologist could do no more than describe in detail what scholars in those fields were able to define as a whole.

If there are no agrarian 'regimes', 'civilizations', or 'ways of life', but a process of growth – unequal, and subject to complex conditions – of productive forces, sociology regains all at once a domain, an objective method and the right to an overall view of the facts.

[...]

We talk about: 'gradual, accelerated, interrupted or retarded development of the forces of production'. But that model should not be taken to suggest some sort of poorly differentiated *continuity* between different rural realities.

We suspect the presence, beneath present-day phenomena, of radical transformations and ancient upheavals. For example, the eastern part of the Pyrenees (Catalonia and Roussillon) was repopulated in a new way following the Moorish invasions. The introduction of sharecropping in Tuscany overturned the pre-existing structure, and so on. We see signs of enormous and enduring conflicts, in different forms, like that between small and large holdings (the Gallo-Roman *latifundia*; seigniorial domains; large capitalist farms).[14]

We know that at least three times in France, grandiose 'agrarian reforms' changed the structure: the barbarian invasions – the emancipation of the serfs – the sale of property belonging to émigrés and the clergy.

The 'agrarian revolution' that began in the eighteenth century immediately set the pattern for the appearance of today's French countryside. And especially the economic development of northern France, with its attendant consequences.

Sociology absorbed by history? Definitely not. The sociologist has first to observe, and analyse, in order to explain. He uses history as an ancillary, subordinate science in the study of the social process *as a whole*.

[...]

We therefore suggest a very simple method, using ancillary techniques, and consisting of several moments:

a) *Descriptive.* Observation, but with an eye informed by experience and by a general theory. In the foreground: participant observation in the field. Careful use of survey techniques (interviews, questionnaires, statistics).
b) *Analytico-regressive.* Analysis of reality as described. Attempt to give it a precise *date* (so as not to be limited to an account turning on undated 'archaisms' that are not compared one with another).
c) *Historico-genetic.* Studies of changes in this or that previously *dated* structure, by further (internal or external) development and by its subordination to overall structures. Attempt to reach a genetic classification of formations and structures, in the framework of the overall structure. Thus an attempt to return to the contemporary as previously described, in order to rediscover the present, but as elucidated, understood: *explained.*

Take *sharecropping* as an example. First we need to *describe* it exactly (rent paid in kind, crops shared with the landowner, obligations in addition to rent, etc.); then to *date* it (it is contemporary with the creation of the urban market, the bourgeoisie, but where capitalism develops, it gives way to tenant farming; it thus has a semi-feudal origin), then to *explain* its transformations and preservation (economic backwardness where it is practised, lack of capital, etc.).

We could also take as examples the village community, with its survivals, or the peasant family, with its specific features, etc.

These studies call for a general framework, a conception of overall process (let us stress again the need to be aware of interaction between structures, and the influence of recent structures on old ones that are subordinate to them or integrated into them).

A) We first find the *rural* or *village community.* These terms refer not to something mystical, or 'pre-logical', but to an historical and social fact that is found everywhere.[15] Human beings, weak in the face of nature, and with only rudimentary tools and techniques, have long needed to form highly cohesive social groups in order to perform agricultural tasks: ground-clearing, building dykes, irrigating, cultivating (and frequently, tending livestock, etc.). The peasant group was therefore highly organized, held together by *collective disciplines*; it had *collective characteristics*, of widely varying types.

Then the peasant community slowly began to be differentiated, and dissociated. Advances in agriculture brought about its dissolution, also in very diverse forms, but showing common features (affirmation of private property, differentiation between classes, local leaders, the introduction of exchange and money, subordination to successive modes of production).

In the peasant community, we note first of all the predominance of ties of *kinship.* When they lose their force, they give way to ties of *territoriality*, based on residence, wealth, property, prestige and authority. We thus go from the extended to the restricted (male-dominated) family and relationships of *proximity.*

But the history of the peasant community is still more complex than this schema would suggest. It is subject to pressure from successive modes of production and from administrative, fiscal, legal and political institutions. Sometimes it gives way, sometimes it resists; until it is dissolved by individualism (based on competition, the market economy, etc.) it manifests extraordinary vitality.

In our view, the Middle Ages in Europe and the disappearance of the medieval (feudal) mode of production cannot be understood unless we take account of a resurgence in the peasant community, and its profound resistance to the grip of feudal lords. Only in this way can we explain the notions of *custom* and *customary law*, which are so important in the study of agrarian society. All custom implies a form of social support – the community – and resistance to 'exactions', that is, what acts outside (*ex-agere*) custom.

B) *Slave and feudal modes of production.* It is impossible to study peasant conditions in Africa, the West Indies or the American South without reference to slavery, and its survivals or consequences.

It is important to be familiar with the different varieties of feudal modes of production (the *Asiatic* mode, based on ownership of water and the irrigation system – the *Islamic*, based on domination of the surrounding countryside by artisanal and commercial urban centres – the *European*, based on landed property) in order to be able to explain the current situation of the peasantry in many countries (including the southern parts of Italy and France, etc.).

The complexity of this situation only emerges if it is approached in a number of different ways. For example, the south of France preserved *roman* law, or was penetrated by it very soon after its reappearance, and at the same time, it is the part of France where *customs* have been preserved best (including local dialects and patois, etc.).

C) *Capitalism* entails an agricultural revolution, very advanced in England, less complete in France and Italy. In France it involved agrarian reform (causing small and medium holdings to be restructured, extended or created, depending on circumstances). Then it led to concentration of the ownership of good land, situated near markets (producing the maximum income). It led to the dominance of tenant farming over sharecropping, to individualism, mechanization, industrialization of agriculture, etc. How are we to study agrarian conditions without constant reference to this mode of production?

Slave and feudal modes of production have been partially superimposed on earlier agrarian structures (even though they encouraged the formation of 'latifundia' and large domains). That is why these 'communal' structures were able to survive or regenerate. But since its beginnings, the capitalist mode of production (the economy of money and the market) drastically changed agrarian structures, from within and from without. In a hundred ways, the capitalist form of private property subordinated to itself previous forms: those of the clan or tribe, communal or feudal. This fact emerges clearly from the study of the agrarian structure of 'underdeveloped' countries: colonial or semi-colonial countries, backward sectors in capitalist countries.

D) The industrialization of agriculture, the introduction of mechanization, large-scale agricultural production and increased productivity are all today moving in opposite directions: capitalism and socialism.

Socialist transformation of agriculture takes place in three stages: agrarian reform–cooperation–creation, not yet clearly envisaged, of 'agro-cities'.

Each of these stages evolves differently depending on the country concerned. In particular, agricultural cooperation (production cooperatives and the *kolkhoz*, which is very different from a production cooperative) is established at village level, that is, it involves a kind of revival – on a very different plane, with new technical resources and an equally new structure – of the agrarian community, proximity relationships, collective disciplines, etc.

In this way, we arrive at an overall view of peasant conditions. They could be compared with a fan, displaying and juxtaposing forms of varying ages, if this image did not conceal the constant interaction between formations, and their subordination to 'ensembles' (new structures; the world capitalist and socialist market, etc.).

This overall view shows agricultural development *lagging behind* industrial development – a gap that only the socialist structure is able to close – something that needs to be studied in its own right.

This general picture encompasses *contradictions* (notably the intense struggle, throughout history, between large and small-scale farming) and *survivals* in the ideological (survivals of agrarian myths, folk traditions, etc.) and structural (the village, the peasant family, etc.) domains.

From this general picture we get the outline for a study or manual of *Rural Sociology*.[16]

It must begin with an investigation of current ensembles and recent (capitalist and collectivist) structures and of the (capitalist and collectivist) global market, etc.

It will involve a study of the agrarian community, its dissolution, survivals and resurgences, emphasizing the movement from kinship ties to those of territoriality (the latter emerging victorious from the conflict) and also stressing differentiations, hierarchies, proximity relationships, etc.

From this overall study we can derive a typology of *villages* (communities that are still alive – communities in decay – individualist villages – villages affected or modified by proximity to a commercial or industrial town, by large-scale land ownership, or by cooperation). Major chapters will be devoted to the peasant *family*: to the position of women, children (elder and younger), old people and the very aged, in the different types of villages and families.

The problem of class (or stratification) in the countryside demands a detailed study of the modes of tenure and the ways the land is farmed (sharecropping, tenant farming, small or medium-sized holdings, etc.).

Lastly, we must always situate the peasant group studied (usually the village) in relation to larger structures and institutions: hamlet and town, province and nation.

Peasant 'culture' (in the *cultural* sense) will in the end have to be defined concretely. To the extent that the peasantry produces a 'culture', or a contribution to culture, we are not talking about an *ideology* properly speaking (even though this peasant contribution may have an ideological content that only philosophers or theoreticians coming from another, more developed social structure are able to reveal). We are talking about a culture without concepts, orally transmitted, consisting almost entirely of anecdotes, stories, interpretations of ritual and magic, and illustrations that serve to influence practice, preserve or adapt customs and govern emotions and actions by acting directly on them.

We then realize that the peasant contribution to the history of ideologies – confused, diffused and formulated by city people – has been considerable. In particular, the great agrarian myths (the Earth Mother) have informed poetry, art, philosophy, from the dawn of time to our own day. Again, the Christian heresies had a largely agrarian base (continuations and memories of the peasant community). From this point of view, rural sociology can make a substantial contribution to the study of ideas, that is, to philosophy.

Preface to the Study of the Habitat of the 'Pavillon'[1]

('Préface' in Henri Raymond, Marie-Geneviève Raymond, Nicole Haumont and M. Coornaert, *L'Habitat pavillonnaire* (Paris: Éditions du CRU [Centre de recherche d'urbanisme], 1966), pp. 3–13, 14–23; reprinted as 'Introduction à l'étude de l'habitat pavillonnaire' in *Du Rural à l'urbain*, 3ᵉ édn (Paris: Anthropos, 2001), pp. 159–70, 171–80)[2]

In the last ten years or so, analytical and technical thinking has been brought to bear on questions that have been given the name 'town planning' [*urbanisme*]. One function and objective of the human being in his social life has been methodically defined: to house himself, in other words, to own a certain space in which to organize his 'private', individual, family life. We have coined a new word to express this phenomenon: 'habitat'.

Today it can confidently be said of many texts (among which those of Le Corbusier and his school are the best known)[3] that they are specific, tend towards sociological positivism and raise more problems than they solve. The motive behind them rejects what, in our Western culture, was, and still is, called 'depth', in the study of man, the city or society in general. This tendency is not peculiar to sociologists, or experts in architecture and town planning. It is to be found in many other fields, including literature and the social sciences. The rejection of traditional philosophical speculation, without its being used to find new ways of arriving at the many dimensions of the 'human phenomenon', leads to a superficiality that is accepted, deliberate, advertised as such and identified with the predominance of technical and scientific problems.

Sociology that calls itself empiricist and positivist immediately finds itself in a 'revolving door', in other words, a vicious circle. On the one hand, good arguments are made for saying that before people are housed we have to know their needs, and that to study them means seeing individuals and small groups in the context of ever larger entities: society, culture. On the other hand, we come to isolate, within this global context, a number of partial functions, forms or systems, among which habitat, housing, is at the forefront. Going round and round in this circle, a certain sociology that prides itself on being very scientific utters smug banalities on needs, on family life in the home, on neighbourhood life, etc.

Is it by chance, as they say, that during the same period, historians have pored over vanished forms of the City in order to recover their forgotten features? Or that the most 'profound' philosophers have tried to reach a definition of 'habitation'? We are indebted to Gaston Bachelard, in his 'poetics of space', for some memorable pages on the House.[4] And habitation or dwelling [*l'habiter*] plays an essential part in Martin Heidegger's teaching. The earth is the dwelling of man, that exceptional 'being' among 'beings' (those that 'be'), as his language is the Dwelling [*la Demeure*] of absolute Being.[5] This philosopher, who claims no longer to be a metaphysician, and rejects the label 'existentialist', stuck on him by ill-informed readers, asks the fundamental question: 'What does it mean to dwell?' According to him, there is a connection between building, dwelling, thinking (and speaking). Dwelling, in its essence, is poetic. It is a fundamental feature of the human condition, not an accidental form or a determined function. Discussing Hölderlin's fine poem, 'poetically man dwells',[6] Heidegger states that what the Poet says does not in any way refer to present conditions of dwelling. It does not say that to dwell means to house oneself. We are, he says, faced with a double demand and a double movement: to think through the deeper existence of the human being by taking dwelling and the dwelling as our starting-point – thinking of the essence of Poetry as a form of 'building', a way of 'making dwell' [*faire habiter*] *par excellence*.

The Poet constructs the dwelling of the human being, that is, the Being in man. 'If we search for the essence of Poetry, in this direction, we will discover the essence of dwelling'.[7] It could be, says Heidegger, that our dwellings that lack poetry, our inability to take the measure of man and his heart, spring from a strange kind of excess: a rage for measurement and calculation.

The strange, oneiric, unique house Bachelard tells us about, this house that brings together in its unity of the dream the dispersed fragments of the Ego, is a traditional house, a patriarchal dwelling [*demeure*], packed with symbols and full of attics and mysterious corners. The philosopher could say of this house: 'It is one of the strongest forces for integrating man's thought, his memories and dreams ... It keeps man safe through earthly and heavenly storms ... It is body and soul.' This house is disappearing. We no longer have the skills or capacity to build houses like it. It is all too easy to note this disappearance and positivism wins hands down. Heidegger, now, shows us a world ravaged by technology, that through its ravages leads towards another dream, another (as yet unperceived) world. He warns us: a lodging built on the basis of economic or technological dictates is as far removed from dwelling as the language of machines is from poetry. He does not tell us how to construct, 'here and now', buildings and cities.

Is our situation not tragic, both in praxis and in theoretical thinking? On the one hand we have banality, a description of the things sight observes and which confirm its observation and imprison thought in the set of observations known as 'science'; this science deals with the *fait accompli*, and all it derives from it is a knowledge and a critique that are deliberately superficial. This approach, which amasses and accumulates facts, calls itself 'operative'. It is; its models and concepts are developed in such a way as to permit rapid application, at the lowest cost (of time, space, money and thought). It is easy to construct buildings or 'housing estates' according to the rules of this operative thought. It is less certain that the residents will be 'satisfied', and less still that the life they lead in them is worth living. Would not the worst thing be for them to be satisfied with very little, to adapt? But on the other hand, there is depth, the intimation of a 'total' being of man, but this depth is not put to use. There is nothing 'operative' about it. How are we to get out of this impasse?

The contradiction is all the more difficult to resolve in that it cannot be isolated. It is connected with a more general 'problematic', in steps that are easy to reconstruct. What is the relationship between the new sciences of society and the ancient philosophical tradition? What are the precise relationships between facts, conceptions and theories, in these sciences? And so on.

The study presented here by the *Institut de Sociologie Urbaine* certainly does not claim to solve these problems. But it has an aim. It proceeds from an awareness of the problems and their contradictory terms, not from an option deliberated for such and such of these terms. It thus seeks a route by way of which a solution could be sketched out, to appear on the horizon once the route was opened. And this would enable the bringing together of research and exploration, while in fact they too often diverge, research straying into dead-ends, and exploration endlessly retreating or arbitrarily declaring itself.

First point (or, if you prefer, first step, first statement, first hypothesis). Habitation is an anthropological fact. The material habitation, the dwelling, the fact of settling on the ground (or detaching oneself from it), the fact of becoming rooted (or uprooted), the fact of living here or there (and consequently of leaving, going elsewhere), all these facts and phenomena are inherent in what it is to be human.[8] They make up an ensemble that is both coherent and shot through by contradictions, by virtual or real conflicts. *Homo* (man as species) can call himself *faber, sapiens, loquens, ludens, ridens* or whatever ... He is defined by a given number of attributes, whose denotations and connotations (that is, their significations and resonances) are broad enough to cover the many manifestations of the 'entity' under consideration. The list of these attributes of man as a species may be inexhaustible. Habitation is among these attributes, or as we might also put it, dimensions.

This formulation calls for immediate correction. If we think of *habitation* as an anthropological trait, that does not mean that it comes under a specific discipline, anthropology, which is supposed to study the attributes of the human species (man as a man) as constants and invariables. This conception, which is quite widespread today, cannot be accepted. For as long as they have led a social existence, i.e. as a species, with their specific traits, human beings have had a habitation. Their modalities have profoundly changed; there is a history of habitation and of habitations. The similarity between a hut and a detached house should not be pursued to the point of erasing their differences.[9] Habitations have changed with society, with the mode of production, even if certain features (the enclosure of a space, for example) remain relatively constant. Habitation has changed according to these totalities, which constitute culture, civilization, and society on a global scale: relations and modes of production, structures and superstructures.

Such are the transformations, that one can now imagine, even experience, the way of life of another human (or rather, superhuman) being, which would amount only to wandering, a worldwide, supra-terrestrial peregrination, a deliberate uprooting after each settling-down. Or, indeed, would find its only dwelling in poetry. Under these rubrics we will continue to exclude both 'sociologism' and an ontology that proffers its eternal verities about roots and rootedness. If at the outset we state that habitation is a dimension of man (as human being), it is not in order to privilege it. Every attempt to define the human by a single dimension or attribute fails under attack from critical thinking. Similarly with any attempt to reduce to static combinations the dynamics that make history. Therefore, let no one assume the right to determine the fate of society by setting for its members rules for their habitations, or modes of habitation. Invention and discovery must remain possible. The dwelling is an open place. In a mode of habitation preferable to others, the human being must be able to affirm himself and call himself *faber, sapiens, ludens, ridens, amans, creator*, etc., in turn. There may be traits that belong to all human beings by virtue of their membership of the species and the condition (for example, the fact of being born weak and naked, of experiencing growth and learning, of maturing, ageing and dying) but the place and importance of these traits for habitation, their hierarchy, have changed from one society to another, as has their mutual interaction. In other words, the fact of having a specific age and sex is one of the general characteristics of the individuals who make up the human race; but relationships between age and sex have changed in different societies, as has the inscription of these facts in habitation. With these changes relationships were transformed, such as those of proximity and distance (social, within groups), intimacy and estrangement, closeness and separation – relationships that form part of social practice, i.e. habitation, and which are indicated or signified by objects of everyday use.

Habitation consists first of objects, by the products of practical activity: moveable or immovable property. They form a characteristic ensemble, or ensembles, within societies. They exist objectively, or if you will, 'objectally', before they signify; but they do not exist without signifying. The word 'before' indicates a kind of logical priority rather than previousness in time.

We ought to posit habitation as an inherent function of every society, every social organism; but a signifying function is straightaway added to this practical function. Moveable and immovable property constitutes habitation, embracing and signifying social relations.

Second point. The manner of inhabiting, the mode or modalities of habitation, are expressed in language.

That proposition is a truism. What would people talk about, what would language express, if not the way of life, including habitation, of a given society? There is first of all a practical function, let us say, then the addition of significations and meanings. Analysis distinguishes what is given as inseparable; and similarly, in practice, significations and meanings may appear in objects in common use before practical functions. Once the use of objects has been learned, there is no need to think about it, and consciousness focuses on their significations, which tell about social status, the conditions and relations of groups and individuals in groups.[10]

Unfortunately, ways of life are expressed in spoken language, which leaves no traces. Written evidence is thus incomplete, purged of part of what interests us. Language is not solely devoted to expressing habitation. We also find there food, clothing, games, as well as memories of events and remarks on a host of economic and political activities. Language thus encompasses 'systems' that overlap, and that cannot close. Everyday life requires a constant translation into ordinary language of the systems of signs comprised by objects used as habitation, clothing, food. He who does not know how to translate is ignorant or deviant, or a foreigner. At the same time, we can only agree with Maxime Rodinson when he writes, at the end of a very thorough-going and genuinely sociological study of a society as vast and significant as our own, and yet different: 'Man-who-feeds-himself, man-who-clothes-himself, man-the-producer and man-the-thinker do not co-exist.' We're clearly talking about the 'same' man, whose activities affect each other.[11] While it is true that notions of globality and totality, of the 'total' man, and of interaction within this totality, are not without their problems, this is not a sufficient reason to abandon them. Partial systems of objects, acts and signs (things and words) are creations of social man. It is the individual members of a society, inserted into praxis, caught in a global whole, who eat, drink, play and inhabit. Individuals and groups form an active, constant link between society as a whole on the one hand, and partial systems on the other, language serving them as medium, intermediary and milieu.

And language? Languages? They can be thought of as systems of systems, but no partial systems can be closed. We thus have to extract them from language (from the language) by means of a series of difficult operations that cannot be performed successfully without a method. This method uncovers a scientific abstraction, in its own way concrete: the code relating to some sensory or verbal message, the one that has as its frame of reference the modes of play, habitation, dress and loving of a given society.

The difficulty arises from the fact that the operation would be precise only if the partial ensemble in question formed a closed system (a 'corpus'). Now, none of the partial systems, let us say, nor all of them taken together, namely language, can be closed. Moreover, relations of production, the (technical and social) division of labour comprehensively dominate the language without quite entering the vocabulary. Only some of the outcomes of these relations enter the vocabulary or the morphology. The biological, for example, enters more easily than the social, properly speaking, paradoxical though that may appear. In language, the social phenomenon par excellence, which 'reflects' social life, essential social relationships remain 'unconscious', or 'supra-conscious', as does the totality of society, culture and civilization itself. They await the knowledge that alone can formulate them by developing concepts. Lastly, if 'man' or 'the total man' presents a problem, it is perhaps because he creates meaning (or seeks meanings).

The great social, ideological and political struggles, and their strategies, do not take place on the level of partial systems that are allowed to enter everyday practice and pass into language. All the more, then, must the linguist or sociologist study the importance of partial systems, and their changing hierarchies.

Third point (or third approach). Habitation expresses itself 'objectively' in a ensemble of the creations, products and things that make up a partial system: the house, the city or the urban area. Each object is part of the whole, and carries its stamp; it testifies to the style (or lack of style) of the whole. It has signification and meaning in the palpable whole that offers us a social text. At the same time, habitation is expressed in a set of words, or locutions.

For habitation, as for dressing, 'feeding oneself' or playing, there is thus a double system: palpable and verbal, 'objectal' and semantic. What is the relationship between the two systems? In principle, they should correspond. In fact, it is unusual for the correspondence to be exact, unambiguous, word for word. Language is not a 'bag of words', or a 'bag of things', on the scale of a partial system any more than that of the whole society and its language. There are always gaps, discrepancies, even hiatuses between the two systems, which prevents our seeing them as two aspects of a single system. They do not develop according to the same law, nor to one that is internal to each of them. Events that alter or overturn society act differently on objects and the language, and on the various partial systems. A given material cause, a given formal (ideological) reason, may change this partial system or that group of words or objects, sooner or later, by acting predominantly on objects or predominantly on words.

It would be too easy to arrive at the semantic system of habitation (words and connected words) by speaking of the semiological system (objects relating to habitation and their significations). None of these messages supplies the code that would enable us to decipher the other, automatically. There are not amongst them reciprocal relationships of code and message, or language and meta-language. They are two distinct social texts, which have to be studied and analysed as such without thereby separating them, using correspondences that are already traceable and which have been traced.

Another complexity: habitation cannot be looked at globally, even though it has to be studied as a 'whole' (as a partial system). It consists of *levels*, including language. In his study of those societies, as large as ours and sufficiently different to throw light on it, that are grouped under the name 'Islam', Jacques Berque has shown that the Muslim city is a 'city of signs'. The functions of a city according to Islamic ethics, namely exchange and bearing witness, take place in an architectural ensemble of significations, and at the same time, in its economic and political activity and in a hierarchy of proximities around its monuments, the chief of them being the mosque.[12] In an ensemble of that kind, both 'objectal' and subjective, habitation by individuals and families represents only one element: the house. It inserts itself, and is articulated with broader levels. It is essential, but at the same time, subordinate. In order to grasp it, here too we have to extract and abstract a partial system, one element and level in larger systems that are themselves partial, open, never complete, never closed.

This is an indication of how far we have to refine our concepts of 'system', signification, ensemble, totality, etc.

The technique most often used by sociologists, the questionnaire, is not appropriate in a study of this kind. Of course, many precautions are taken and it aspires to scientific precision. But as we know, the questions asked are usually closed ones, to which the respondent answers 'yes' or 'no'. The questionnaire is 'administered' to a sample chosen according to strict rules. After being coded, the data is analysed by machine. Numbers – percentages, correlations – are retrieved. What have we obtained? Is it not the case that the questions asked were formulated within a system of significations (belonging to the sociologist, to another, unseen person), in such a way that the respondent conforms to it when responding by the very fact of responding? The questionnaire is a precise but narrow tool, and may also be suspect. It allows us to call 'scientific' what is an interpretation, and at best, a partial conceptualization. Questionnaires and apparently rigorous data analysis are sometimes authorized in order to match pseudo-concepts to pseudo-facts.

The approaches recalled above have this consequence: only non-directive interviewing can give a proper account of habitation. The people concerned must be allowed to speak, and the interview is oriented towards the specific activity the researcher is studying (in this case, habitation), leaving scope for free expression. The only constraints are the interviewer, an 'absence/presence', and the tape-recorder, another 'absence/presence'.

A major methodological problem arises here. Questionnaires are precise, but not far-reaching. Non-directive interviews give deeper insight into 'human beings'. Who would not grant that? But more than one sociologist would argue that it is impossible to gain knowledge from non-directive interviews. What lies 'deep' cannot be 'collected'; the methodological conduct of research therefore demands that we avoid it. How are we get out of this bind, which reflects on the methodological level the general theoretical problem of steering a course between metaphysics and positivist triviality?

Here we suggest an approach. The interview, although necessary, is not enough. And printed forms alone, even detailed ones, breaking down the social setting of the interview under headings, would not make it so. Detailed description is important: of houses, moveable and immovable property, clothing, faces and behaviour. Knowledge can only be obtained by comparing, on the one hand, hard data, which the sociologist perceives and tries to grasp as a whole, and on the other, the places, times and things perceived by those concerned. Let us make this point very clear. The objects connected with habitation (as with dressing, or 'feeding oneself') do not form a language, but a coherent sub-category, a group: a (partial and semiological) system. The words linked with habitation form a semantic group. There are two messages: one of words, one of objects. Comparison between them, which does not presuppose the spontaneous or automatic decoding of one text by the other, and rests on scientific experimentation, not on the subjectivity of the scientist, enables us to emerge from the verbal interview with an objective understanding of it. Research is not imprisoned in it, and does not emerge from it in the name of a hermeneutics (interpretation) which would be unable to constitute itself as knowledge but would be an extension of philosophy. A methodological paradox: recourse to the twofold system, the twofold definition of the specific activity being studied – in this case, habitation – enables us to break the circle. The only procedures that get confused by a 'words–things' dualism are those of a unilateral way of thinking. The system of objects enables us to delimit and analyse the system of verbal significations, and conversely.

Every page of such a study ought to be fully illustrated, the sociologist's scientific discourse referring back to these two texts, which he brings together in a coherent argument: interviews, and hard data (arrangements of places, privileged sites, areas given over to the private and to the social, photographs of surrounding walls and façades, etc.). This illustration would be indispensable, just as the data reproduced have been indispensable for understanding the statements of those concerned. However, this 'objectal' equivalent of verbal statements would still not include time, periods of time and the rhythms of life, of which the division of spaces is the palpable expression. At present, we have no means of illustrating and making palpable the abstract 'times' divided up by analysis.

[. . .]

Without a doubt, the city has exploded; its classic forms (the ancient or medieval city) are receding in time. That does not mean that the urban area, with its forms and functions, old or new structures, has disappeared. The 'urban fabric' (a rather vague but useful expression) has taken on new forms; it is assuming new functions, acquiring new structures. Among the forms taken by the excrescences springing up on the periphery, which are being added to the centres of cities, when the centre has not disappeared or become too run down, we all know the residential sections, the 'districts' of individual houses, the new developments and housing estates. There are few more striking contrasts than the easily observable one between detached houses and new estates.

Literary authors and sociologists have gone overboard about Housing Estates, which have been, and still are, the subject of many studies. But note how little the *pavillon* has been studied. Writers have usually limited themselves, on aesthetic or ethical grounds, to noting the ugliness and poor planning of residential suburbs [*banlieues pavillonnaires*], mocking the petty bourgeois traits of their residents, and pointing out the slightly ridiculous illusions that the setting so poorly conceals. The 'suburban habitat' seemed scarcely to merit academic study. Guy Palmade's conclusions on 'French attitudes to housing'[13] seemed as final as they were severe. The *pavillon* indicates an essential individualism; its occupants want above all to preserve the 'me', the private personality. 'The contrast between the outside world and the inner world gives housing its meaning.' The image of the detached house corresponds with an ideal involving the wish for protection and isolation, the need for identification and confirmation of the self, the need for contact with nature, in short, the requirement of isolation. A kind of magical attitude idealizes and promotes the *pavillon*; in it, resistance to change and the triumph of individualist isolation take on the status of myth. This leads to condemnation. However, sociological research would seem to show that a majority (80 per cent) of French people of whatever age, status, socio-professional category or income bracket, would like to live in a *pavillon*. This majority is bigger among manual workers and in lower income brackets than among middle-managers and higher income brackets.

How are we to explain this phenomenon? Is it really nothing but a myth? An ideology? A recrudescence of individualism? A revival of myth? If there is a myth, are we talking about an old reality become mythic, like the patriarchal and predominantly rural house described by Bachelard? If it's an ideology, how and why has it become so widespread? Where does it come from?

Sociologists have hardly ever asked themselves these questions. They usually explained the attraction of the *pavillon* only in terms of the real or imaginary disadvantages of 'housing estates' and 'collective' housing in modern cities overwhelmed by the huge influx of new populations and bursting out into suburbs and peripheral areas.

The chief virtue of the ISU team (and especially of M. Henri Raymond) was not to show contempt for 'suburbanites' [*pavillonaires*], but to see their way of habitation as worthy of the kind of sociological study that demands sophisticated methods and technical procedures. What seemed insignificant or trivial revealed a meaning. Might this not be a route to explore?

As we were saying, the contrast between 'the *pavillon* habitat' and housing estates is striking. Let us spell out some aspects of this contrast. In a detached house (no doubt in a small-minded way) modern man 'dwells poetically'. By that we understand that his 'inhabiting' is in some way his creative work. The space in which he is able to organize it according to his own tastes and patterns is somewhat malleable. It lends itself to rearrangement. This is not so with the space provided for tenants or co-owners on an estate; that space is rigid, inflexible. It is difficult, often impossible (and almost always prohibited) to convert it. Space in a detached house allows the family group and its individual members to appropriate to some extent the conditions of their own existence. They can alter, add or subtract, superimpose their own ideas (symbols, organization) on what is provided. Their environment thus acquires meaning for them; there is a system of signification, even a double system: semantic and semiological, in words and in objects.

The concept of *appropriation* is one of the most important handed down to us by centuries of philosophical discussion. The action of human groups on the physical and natural environment has two modes, two attributes: domination and appropriation. They ought to go together, but are often separated. Domination of physical nature, the result of technological processes, ravages nature while allowing societies to substitute its products for nature itself. Appropriation does not ravage nature, but transforms it – the body and biological life provided, and the time and space – into human property. Appropriation is the goal, the direction, the purpose of social life. Without appropriation, technical domination over nature tends towards absurdity as it increases. Without appropriation, there can be economic and technical growth, but social development, properly speaking, remains nil.

In former times (antiquity or the Middle Ages) the city brought a spontaneous appropriation, limited but concrete, of space and time. 'On the human scale', as has so often been said, space and time become creations that can be compared with works of art. When growing cities exceeded their original 'scale', this spontaneous appropriation disappeared. At different periods there were attempts to replace it with reasoned rationality. Is it not remarkable that since ancient Greece, rational planning should have accompanied both the growth of the city and the decline of urban civilization? Reasoned (rational, or better, rationalized) planning has never succeeded in penetrating the secret of qualitative appropriation of time-space, or of reproducing it to fit the quantitative requirements of what is called 'excessive' urban growth. For over 2,000 years, so-called rational planning has proceeded in sudden breakthroughs, straight lines or quarterings, geometric patterns, combinations of homogeneous elements, abstract quantification. We do not have to look very long at the new estates and their features in order to confirm this statement. Appropriation is disappearing, while the power of technology, including its power to ravage, increases 'excessively'. And more: the concept of appropriation has become blurred and degraded. Who understands it? The word suggests trivialities. As if any open space whatever could correspond to the agora, the forum, the market, the place of entertainment!

Now, the *pavillon* offers us an example – a trivial one, but never mind – of that 'poetics' of space and time that in different periods, societies and social groups is either allied with social practice or dissociated from it. Appropriation of palpable reality, in other words, is always a social fact, but is not to be confused with the forms, functions and structures of society. It is an aspect of social practice (praxis), but a second and superior aspect, which is translated into language by meanings. The modes of appropriation, their relationship with the whole society and the social groups that make it up are highly dialectical, that is, conflictual, complex, changing. A further example: the street. Who does not acknowledge the attraction of a busy street, its interest for the eye, the imagination and the mind? Furthermore, it is not easy to analyse this attraction. The street is an appropriated, and thus 'socialized' space, within the setting of a city, for the benefit of multiple, open groups without exclusivity or the need for membership.

It is thus not enough to emphasize the relative plasticity of space of the *pavillon*, or to note the way it is arranged. Attention must also be paid to appropriation, describing and showing the reasons for it, picking out its complementary aspects and its meaning. This can only be done using the techniques and methods mentioned above: interviews, the double approach and a comparison between the semiological (palpable objects) and the semantic (verbal).

It is no longer necessary to show the importance for academic disciplines of the concept of levels. But is this term not sometimes used in a vague, that is, falsely precise, sense? In fact, it is used to mean all sorts of things, just like 'structure', 'function' and 'form'. However, linguistics and its related disciplines, semantics and semiology, use these terms, 'level' in particular, with undeniable rigour.

Mme Nicole Haumont's paper defines levels clearly and distinctly: within each level secondary levels, also articulated, appear. The whole set forms a sort of grid. Theory and epistemology, which come later, will add depth to these concepts and show the connections between them.

We can distinguish:

A) *Appropriation of space in the* pavillon, that is, the socialization of individual space and the simultaneous individualization of social space. This specific activity takes place in a remarkable way: affective and symbolic. The ages and sexes take from the available space the part that 'belongs' to them, which then attracts one group and repels the other, which plays a role and in which each person plays a role. Analysis of this level falls into three levels: marking, enclosure, arrangement (to be thought of dynamically: with movements, and spaces for putting aside or for replacing others). Putting it another way: symbols, contrasts, order. On this level, tendencies and elemental, almost biological drives operate (though subject to a cultural system). They are linked with those semi-constants (modified by society, culture and civilization), that are the province of social anthropology: youth and old age, the masculine and feminine elements of groups and of life. That way, the most individualized and singular aspect of *pavillon* existence reaches broader and more general levels; and it is here that architecture and planning have lessons to learn from studying it. The question, 'What does it mean to inhabit?' remains open.

B) *The world of the* pavillon *as utopia*. What do those who live in it expect from it? Nothing less than happiness. Many people experience it like that, forgetting the disadvantages, arguing them away. This happiness, in which fiction and reality are as thoroughly mixed as water and wine in a glass, ought to be attained via nature, a healthy and regular life and normality, all connected in this utopia with the *pavillon*.

In her analysis, Mme Haumont avoids using words such as a *magical* attitude. It is a question of significations, connotations, added to a form of praxis, a mode of social existence, and to the affective and symbolic appropriation of space.

This is why, in the 'world of the *pavillon*' more than elsewhere, every object is an element in a system. The object is not only loaded with symbols, it is a sign. Rather than being functionally adapted for use, it is caught in the system of signs. This is equally true of the garden, the lawn, the flower-pot, as the decoration of the façade, or of furniture and ornaments.

Here the focus turns to the curious problem of presence-absence, which haunts research on systems of significations. A system or sub-system, whether of objects or words, both is and is not self-sufficient. It is self-sufficient; it is complete whole. Each element refers to all the others. It looks as full as an egg. Look at it a bit longer and a bit more closely: see, it empties itself. A host of questions, posed technically by linguists and tragically by philosophers, now arises. We ask: Who? For whom? Why? How? The system is not self-sufficient. This 'whole' is partial, and open. It refers to 'something else': purpose, on the one hand, and the 'subject', on the other, and beyond these two terms lies the totality and the meaning. Every occupant of a *pavillon*, every 'subject' (individual and family) believes they find in objects their own thoroughly 'personalized' microcosm, and their own happiness. But these microcosms, these 'systems' share a strange resemblance. The same suppliers sell these goods, these objects, these houses in the 'Normandy', 'Basque' or 'modern' style. Every subject could move somewhere else and feel just as comfortable. He would experience the same happiness, half imaginary, half real. Everywhere, the goal – happiness – is presented in the same way, that is to say, it is indicated, signified, but indicated in its absence: reduced to signification. What is signified – happiness, the person – is eluded or elided, and appears only as nature or 'naturality' (fountains, flowers, the sun and the sky, etc.).[14] Work (and creativity), material production and its relations (and the activity that produces created works) are put into suspension, put aside. Meaning equals absurdity. In 'naturality' we find, recreating themselves in an odd sort of waking dream, 'lived' happiness and the consciousness that lives it, the illusion and the real. This waking dream is the discourse of the owner of the *pavillon*, his everyday discourse, poor as others see it, but rich for him.

Time disappears from this illusory microcosm, as it does from all systems. Or rather, it loses its point and cutting edge, its menace. It turns into safety. In a detached house, the occupant does not feel himself age. Time goes by gently, naturally. For each member of the family group, time is identified with the physical house, spaces marked out and allocated, some beneficial, others unfavourable. Relationships between members change into relationships between objects, and are 'naturalized'. One such privileged object (the television set) governs the little world of objects and relations within the group.

To a greater extent, and better than elsewhere, in the *pavillon* the resident consumes significations. In its way, this 'world of the *pavillon*' is abstract, while he is so concrete on the affective and symbolic level. In its way, it is very modern, while he seems a little old fashioned. At the utopian level, the consumer of the detached house is intensely absorbed, not by things, but by signs. Sociological study cannot proceed without a thoroughgoing analysis of this misunderstanding (a veritable denial) of a reality that is both signified and left out (present-absent). Here everything is real and everything is utopian, without a clear difference; everything is nearby and everything is far away; everything is 'lived' and everything is imaginary (lived in the world of the image and the sign). These tendencies are especially marked in the 'world of the *pavillon*' in contrast with the 'world' of new housing estates, where everything is combinative, in series, neat and tidy, where the image and the imaginary emerge against a background of rigidity.

This utopian level could be called 'mythic' since it involves constant reference to 'naturality', i.e. a myth of nature, a naturalization of the human. As Roland Barthes says, we naturalize the cultural.

Analysis thus breaks the utopian level down into secondary levels. Arrows point to invisible 'realities', half real and half imaginary: the status of happiness, safety and rootedness, personality and naturality. These are the latent contents, in the social 'unconscious' or 'imaginary', of the great dream pursued by people living in detached houses, as interviews show. It is a dream that is all the more constant because it is in its way rationalized, and because objections to it are foreseeable.

C) *Ideology*. That there is an ideology of the *pavillon* – of that there is no doubt. That it coincides with the other levels, that is, determines life in the *pavillon* in general, that it creates symbolism and utopianism – the work presented to the reader here forbids us to admit. The ideology of the occupants of such houses and of those who prefer them to other ways of inhabiting, is an ideology, i.e. a set of representations. Nothing more, nothing less. A set of representations justifies, explains, completes a way of social living; it cannot create it in practice, and does not coincide with it.

The currency of this ideology in France poses new problems. Does a different ideology rule in the residential suburbs of Britain or the United States? Are we talking about cultural phenomena? Or models (patterns)? Or the 'basic personality' of a society and a country where such a model holds sway, tends to become implanted and to mould people, for better or worse?

The ideology of *pavillon* living involves a consciousness of property and the property-owner that may conflict with other forms of consciousness (in particular with 'class consciousness', in the frequent cases where the owner is working-class). Usually, this conflict remains in the latent state. Nevertheless, it has an effect. The 'bourgeoisie-proletariat' contradiction turns into the oppositions: 'poor-rich' or 'small-big' (property-owners).

This ideology presupposes a confusion, even an identification, of individual and family consciousness with property. It is therefore never without a form of alienation, and at its limit, 'reification'. Alienation and its extreme case, reification, here belong less to things than to a signification that receives from the ideology an addition, an 'over-determination', as the psychoanalysts say. The added signification here comes from the figure of the Owner-occupier, which completes that of the consumer, the suburban dreamer. This ideology of property does not exclude the concrete appropriation of time and space, at the affective and symbolic level. It indicates and sets its limits, enabling us to understand how those involved do not see their boundaries, the narrow limits of their horizons. It does not seem to suburbanites that they are stuck in social isolation; they have not chosen it. Instead, it seems to have a rather nice name: liberty, as envisaged in the Civil Code, where it is more or less completely identified with property.

It is possible that the ideology preceded the other aspects and levels of the '*pavillon* world'. It is probable that it created them without actually coinciding with them. In this microcosm, it represents a globality or a totality: contemporary society. It is here, and in this way, that Mme N. Haumont's study spills over into ideological and political history.

Psycho-sociological and thus sociological study has discovered the common denominator of Suburbanites [*Pavillonaires*], the thing that virtually or actually links them together. It has revealed their microcosm. It emerges that 'suburbanites' do not form a social group or a homogeneous ensemble. Lastly, it emerges that the social existence of sectors (or 'districts') of detached housing varies according to the urban area with which they are associated, their distance from the city centre, their amenities, and their function, when it is more than purely residential. They cannot be studied sociologically apart from the city and without a study of its problems. Psycho-sociology leads to sociology, without which there is a theoretical or methodological rupture. Are we to blame the ISU team for not starting from sociology? To go from the more homogeneous to the less, from unity to differences, from less marked differences to the more notable, is not an approach that can be faulted on epistemological grounds. The important thing is to begin.

Mme Marie-Geneviève Raymond's research partly fills this gap, and at the same time goes further into the historical and sociological study of the phenomenon of detached housing than the above propositions. The history of the detached house and its ideology that she presents is a highly original contribution to the political, social, economic and ideological history of France. In it, we read how the *pavillon* and its image and 'values' were literally launched before the appearance of the methods of 'launching' currently used by advertising. For reasons of high politics (itself linked with ethical values) the '*pavillon*' brand has been the subject of market research *avant la lettre*, and of intense and successful propaganda. A political strategy has produced an ideology, which was given a more (or less) complete 'reception', for different reasons and motivations, by different groups and classes. Its impact was such that it introduced a contradiction into French society: a conflict between the individual and the social (the 'collective'). This conflict appears in fields and sectors other than habitat, where it takes a particularly acute form.

French society is thus seen, on the global scale, in a new light. Political history and the history of ideas, psycho-sociology and the sociology of habitation, converge in a movement towards the acquisition of new knowledges.

[. . .]

Levels and Dimensions

(from *La Révolution urbaine* (Paris: Gallimard, 1970), pp. 105–10, 113–38)

As it currently offers itself for analysis (or, alternatively, resists it) urban phenomena show some methodologically familiar features: dimensions and levels. They help us to introduce a degree of order into confused discussions on the city and urban issues, discussions that mix up texts and contexts, levels and dimensions. We could say they enable us to establish clear codes, juxtaposed or superimposed, by which to decipher the message (the urban phenomenon considered as message). Or we could call them the vocabulary (readings) of the text and writing of the city, that is, the plan, on the one hand, and on the other, 'urban things' – palpable, visible, readable in context. Can we say there is a reading at the geographical level, an economic reading, a sociological reading, and so on, of the text of the city? Probably. It is clear that to organize facts using concepts does not exclude other forms of discourse, classifications, readings or sequences (geopolitical, organizational and administrative, technological, etc.). We have previously taken a position on the problem of convergence, provisionally at least.

Diachronically, on the space-time axis, we have clearly indicated (without going to the point of total rupture) the levels reached by the economic and social unit, or, as is often said, using a rather vague word, by 'society'. In short, the *rural*, the *industrial* and the *urban* come one after the other. Now we come to a synchronic table dealing with the last term. We will distinguish, in the present day, a *global* level, which we will call G, a *mixed* level, which we will indicate by M, and a *private* level (P), the level of 'habitation'.

On the global level we see the operation of power, the State, as will and representation.[1] As will: State power and the men who hold this power have a political strategy or strategies. As representation: politicians have an ideologically justified political conception of space (or a lack of conception that gives a free rein to those who offer their own images of time and space). At this level, *logics* and strategies come into play, of which we could say, with some reservations, that they are 'class logics', because they usually consist of a strategy pursued to its furthest consequences. In this sense, with some reservations, we could speak of a 'socio-logic' and an 'ideo-logic'. Political power has (ideological and sociological) tools at its disposal. It has the ability to act, and can alter the distribution of resources, revenue, and the 'value' created by productive work (i.e. surplus value). As we know, there are two main strategies in capitalist countries today: *neo-liberalism* (leaving the maximum initiative to private business, and as far as urbanism is concerned, to property developers and banks) and *neo-dirigism* (emphasizing 'broad brush' planning and, as far as urban development goes, encouraging action by experts and technocrats, by state capitalism). We also know there are compromises; neo-liberalism leaves certain place for the public 'sector' and for concerted action by state services; neo-dirigism encroaches only prudently on the 'private sector'. And lastly, we know that diversified sectors and strategies can coexist, with a tendency towards dirigism, even socialism, in agriculture, liberalism in the property market and (prudent) planning in industry, with circumspect control over the movement of capital, etc. This global level is the level of *the most general, and thus the most abstract, relationships*, but also the most essential: the capital market, and the politics of space. This means it responds all the more, and better, to the practico-sensory and the immediate. This global level, which is both social (politics) and mental (logic and strategy) projects itself into part of the built domain: buildings, monuments, large-scale development projects, new towns. It also projects itself into the non-built domain: roads and motorways, the general management of traffic and transport, the urban fabric and neutral spaces, conservation of 'nature', sites, etc. It is thus the level of what we will call *institutional space* (with its corollary, institutional planning). Which presupposes, if not a system or systems of fully explicit activity, then at least systematized activity (or so-called concerted actions, carried out systematically). The fact that such logics, such unitary systems, are only possible at the level of government and the State shows that the old city–country distinction is in process of disappearing. That does not mean it is obsolete. We may even wonder whether the State, which claims to undertake this mission, is capable of carrying it off. The *social* division of work, that which goes through the market (of products, capital and work itself), seems no longer to function spontaneously. It calls for control by a higher power of organization, the State. Conversely, this power, the supreme institution, tends to perpetuate its own conditions and maintain the distinction between manual and intellectual work, as well as that between rulers and ruled, and perhaps between the city and country. We might then ask if it does not here introduce new contradictions within the State. Will it not, as will, transcend the city–country distinction? This would lead to its strengthening the centres of decision-making until it turned the hearts of cities into citadels of power. Will it not, at the same time, represent urbanization and general territorial development in a decentralized way, and then separate it into zones, some of which will be doomed to stagnate and decline, and return to 'nature'? It thus seems that the State organizes unequal development, in order to use it to achieve global homogeneity.

Level M (mixed, mediating or intermediary) is the specifically urban level. It is that of the 'city', in the current usage of the word. Let us suppose that thought works by detracting (subtracting) from the plan of a city (it needs to be large enough to give this *abstraction* meaning) on the one hand what belongs to the global level (the level of the State and society), i.e. buildings like ministries, prefectures and cathedrals, and on the other hand, what belongs to level P, private buildings. There will remain on the plan a domain that is both built and not built: streets, squares, avenues, public buildings like town halls, parish churches, schools, etc. By removing the global, we have mentally taken away all that belongs directly to the higher institutions and authorities. What remains before our minds has a form related to the site (immediate surroundings) and the situation (broader surroundings, global conditions). This specifically urban ensemble presents a unity characteristic of the social 'real', the grouping 'forms–functions–structures'. In this connection we can speak of double functions (*in* the city and *of* the city: urban functions in relation to the surrounding area and internal functions) and double structures (for example, those of 'services', commerce, transport, some 'serving' the surrounding area – villages, hamlets, small towns – and the others serving urban life as such).

Let us move on to level P, which appears (wrongly) to be modest, if not negligible. Here, only the built domain, and buildings, can be taken into account (housing: blocks of flats, large and small detached houses, shanty towns and collections of temporary structures).

[. . .]

We have already emphasized the relationship between the 'human being' grasped analytically, and the form he is given and receives from his 'habitation'. Knowledge accumulated by philosophy tells us that this being is all contradiction: desire and reason, spontaneity and rationality. Anthropology, supported by other partial forms of knowledge, and psychology and/or sociology, teaches us there are different ages and sexes. The simplicity of these statements is merely apparent. The coexistence of different ages, necessary for the existence of a collective group or 'subject' (family, neighbourhood and friendships) is no less indispensable to the actual (social) perception of time. This time has nothing in common with clock time. It is the time of an ordeal, that of finitude, which makes every instant serious and every moment precious. An infant is not born as a *tabula rasa*, but it is nonetheless formless. It can only move towards that form, that maturity, that marks its end (in the multiple senses of 'goal', 'direction', 'fulfilment', 'perfection', 'term', 'termination', 'conclusion'). Maturity is achievement, and already death. The adult may not behave arrogantly because he has achieved his goal. Childhood and adolescence, and young adulthood, which are poor in terms of 'reality', awkward and pretentious, even stupid (see the works of Gombrowicz),[2] are immeasurably rich in terms of the greatest and most deceptive of riches: possibility. How to create a 'habitation' that will give form without impoverishing, a shell that will allow the young to grow without becoming prematurely closed up? How is this ambiguous 'human being' – who will only escape ambiguity via old age, scarcely formed and yet magnificent, contradictory, but in such a way that no side of the contradiction can overcome the other without serious damage, and so that the 'being' must nevertheless escape the contradictory situation – to be offered a 'dwelling place'? These problems in themselves presuppose a subversive way of thinking that turns the 'model' of the adult upside down, shatters the myth of Paternity, and dethrones maturity as an 'end'. This, posed properly (that is, bringing together scientific disciplines and metaphilosophical meditation) is the problematic of 'habitation'. This level is no less complex than the others because it is 'micro'. A very remarkable and strange form of ideology, derived from Cartesianism and a degenerate form of analytical thinking, identifies the small with the simple, the large with the complex. Habitation can no longer be studied as a residue, the trace or product of supposedly 'superior' levels. It must be – it can already be – seen as a source, a foundation, an essential functionality and transfunctionality. Theoretically and practically, we are moving towards a reversal of the situation, an inversion of meanings; what seemed subordinate comes, or comes back, into the foreground. The predominance of the global, the logical and the strategic is still part of the 'upside down world' which we have to put back. We are attempting from urban reality here a form of *decoding* which is the opposite of the usual one, starting from *habitation* and not from the *monumental* (which is, however, not dismissed, but reconsidered). The dialectical and conflictual movement itself (both theoretical and practical) of habitat and habitation comes into the foreground. In this analysis, it is not ruled out that the semiologist may have more than a little to say, whether it is about understanding the prevalent non-verbal signs and symbols found inside and outside 'dwellings', or, indeed, the words and phrases in the discourse (monologues or dialogues) of architects and urbanists. Nevertheless, critical analysis cannot restrict itself to semiology and methods taken from linguistics. Other concepts will inevitably be used. There is no reason to neglect the relationships (which seem *misunderstood*, and not simply unknown) between Eros and Logos, desire and space, sexuality and society. It may be true that in the industrial age, the 'reality principle' overcame the 'pleasure principle', but is not the time coming for its revenge, in urban society? Does not sexuality belong to the 'extra-social social' – social, because it is shaped, fashioned, cultivated and alienated by society, and 'extra-social' because desire, tending towards anomie, calls itself (and becomes) a mystery, something strange, a secret, even a crime, in order to evade social norms and forms? Love, conjugal or otherwise, seeks 'intimacy'. All the more intense and passionate because it feels guilty and knows it is hounded, its only 'sociality' and sociability are in opposition to society. How is this situation of the 'human being', incomplete and full of contradictory virtualities, to be expressed in architectural and planning terms? At the so-called highest level, objects form a system. This is the socio-logical level. Each object communicates to each action its system of significations, which come to it from the world of merchandise of which it is the vehicle. Each object contaminates each action – that is only too true. Nevertheless, these systems do not have the full and complete character suggested by the idea of a logic of space, or of the thing. There are weak spots, voids, lacunae everywhere. And conflicts, including those between logics and strategies. The logic of space, subjected to the constraints of growth, the logic of urbanism, that of political space and housing, collide and are sometimes smashed one against the other. Similarly, the logic of things (objects) and that of play (or games). As social logics are located on different levels, fissures persist or open up between them. Desire passes through these fissures. Otherwise, formless 'human matter' would soon be subjugated to an absolute form, guaranteed and controlled by a State firmly enthroned on the mass of 'subjects' and 'objects'. Otherwise, everyday living would become irrevocably uniform. And even subversion would become unthinkable!

Alongside the distinction between levels, we can introduce:

A. *The dimensions of the urban phenomenon,* this word referring not to the phenomenon's size, but its essential 'properties', namely:

1. *Social relations projected on the ground.* Including the most abstract, those that derive from merchandise and the market, from contracts or quasi-contracts between 'agents' on the global scale. The urban phenomenon and urban space, may, from this angle, be seen as 'concrete abstractions'. We have already made the point that this dimension itself harbours multiplicities (different markets, juxtaposed, superimposed, in conflict or not: products, capital, work, created works and symbols, housing and land).

2. The urban phenomenon and urban space are not only a *projection of social relations* but *the site and terrain where strategies confront one another.* They are in no way ends or goals, but the tools and means of action. They include what belongs specifically to level M, namely urban institutions, bodies and 'agents' (notables and local leaders).

3. For all that, the urban phenomenon and urban space still have a specific reality and vitality. That is to say, there is *urban practice*, which is not reduced to global ideologies or institutions, involving space and its organization – nor to particular activities called 'urbanistic', which serve as the means for ends that are often unknown.

B. Differences and distinctions involving the *topological* properties of urban space, properties designated as such, constituting theoretically a network or system of permanent opposites (a paradigm):
– the private and the public
– the high and the low
– the open and the closed
– the symmetrical and the asymmetrical
– the dominated and the residual, etc.

Here we find a very familiar form of analysis by dimensions: the *symbolic* dimension, which normally refers to monuments, and hence to present or past ideologies and institutions – the *paradigmatic*, the set of system of opposite – the *syntagmatic*, linkages (a journey).

Starting from the distinction between *levels* and introducing relevant opposites among them, it is not impossible to construct a *grid of urban space*. We will assign to each level an index of the appropriate topological properties. Thus, what relates to the global (G) and the public, normally built high (h+) includes wide open spaces and others that are firmly closed (O–), sites of power, or divinity, or both together. Sometimes this space belonging to grandeur is marked by pronounced symmetries (s+) and sometimes it leaves asymmetrical elements 'free' (s–).[3] We will not present this space grid in more detail here. Why? Because it will appear in a work devoted not to the urban phenomenon in general, but to the analysis and politics of space, and urban topology. And also because it might have the effect of masking what the present analysis contributes, and its position. The essence, the foundation, the meaning, come from the level of 'habitation'. Not from the other levels. Now, in the grid (taken by itself) the levels all appear to be governed by an overall coherence, a logic of space. That point of view cannot be explained without an immediate *critique*.

It follows from the above that the *importance* of the levels is relative. For politicians, the level of the State is obviously decisive. In fact, it is the level of decision-making, at least on paper, bureaucratically speaking. Such people have a strong tendency (i.e. a tendency based on force) to conceptualize the phenomenon's other levels and dimensions in relation to their own knowledge (representations) and power (will). It is at this level that industrial practice, that of the firm, becomes an ideology (representation) and will (reductive). The State and the people from the State are thus 'reductive' in their essence, and often in an aggressive position. All the more, and so much the better, in that, during the *critical phase*, the levels and dimensions tend to merge. The city explodes; the urban comes into being; total urbanization is coming; but at the same time, the old structures (institutions and ideologies connected with earlier forms, functions and structures) defend themselves, and adapt to new situations. The second level (M) may appear to be essential. To present it as such, is it not to act on the theoretical level as a defender of cities as they are? While, in fact, it is nothing but the (mixed) intermediary between, on the one hand, society, the State, powers and knowledges on the global scale, institutions and ideologies, and on the other, *habitation*. If the global seeks to govern the local, if generality aspires to absorb particularities, then the middle (mixed, M) level may act as: the terrain for attack and defence, for struggle. It is still a means. It cannot become an end, except provisionally and for a strategy that means spreading out its cards and showing its hand. To protect existing urban institutions?

Maybe. To promote them? To take them as criterion and model? What for? To extend to (virtual and possible) urban society the institutions and ideologies derived from the (old-style) city? No. Impossible. *Urban reform* may proceed in this way, but a more profound, more radical (i.e. grasping things from the root), and thus more revolutionary, way of thinking asserts the lasting primacy of *habitation.*

In short, the two critical phases that the urban has gone through in historical time may be defined as follows. First phase: the agrarian (agricultural production, rural life, peasant society), which was long dominant, is subordinated. To what? To an urban reality at first driven but then soon ravaged by commerce and industry. A second about-turn, a second inversion of meaning: dominant industry is subordinated to urban reality; but a form of subversion enters that reality: the level considered minor since the beginning – namely *habitation* – becomes the essential. It can no longer be considered as an effect, or a result, or an accident, in relation to the specific level of the urban, still less so in relation to the global, which has remained subordinate to the industrial period (to the 'productivist' ideology, to political space subjected to the demands of growth). The *urban* is defined by the unity of these two levels, the latter being predominant (sign P). Due to confusion in the critical phase, this inversion of meaning can now be conceptualized and planned. To aim for it does not mean to achieve it. Confusion is equally favourable to adverse undertakings, whose extent we will measure. In the perspective suggested here, we have *primacy of the urban* and *priority of habitation.* This priority requires freedom to invent and the establishment of novel relationships between planner and architect, architecture having the last word. Architecture answers a confused social *demand*, which until now has not been able to become a *social command*. The subversion in question (theoretically) lies in this proposition: the implicit *demand* will become an explicit *command*. Until now, social command has come from industrial growth, i.e. from the ideologies and institutions established on level G, the level of the State. In other words, the planner obeys the requirements of industrialization, even if he expresses reluctance and can see or wants something different. As for the architect, he *condenses* (as in 'social condensation', as the word was used by Soviet architects between 1920 and 1925) existing social relations.[4] Like it or not, he builds under constraints of funding (wages and salaries) and of norms and values, i.e. according to class criteria that lead to segregation even when there is an honest desire for integration and mixing. More generally, the architect finds himself trapped in the 'world of merchandise', without realizing it is a world. Unconsciously, that is, with a good conscience, he subordinates use to exchange and use-values to exchange-value. Social command is imperious and the sole demand that emerges is nothing but a direct or indirect expression of this command. If it aspires to be something else, this confused demand is repressed. This is not an argument for abandoning ancient cities and the 'virtual urban' in the face of the attacks made against them. On the contrary. While level M is defined only as a *mediator* (mixed) and not as central or essential, it is for that very reason both the terrain of struggle and what is at stake.

Are we not going from one paradox to another? Indeed. Unspoken paradoxes proliferate, and those who utter them do not believe them. In the same way, those who predict disasters or upheavals do not cause them. Some people, with false or genuine naïveté, blame the weather-forecaster when there is a storm. With general urbanization and the spread of cities, there is a wish to destroy urban reality. Is that not a paradox? An empty challenge? An ideology? Probably. But this ideology inspires many projects, all with very different motivations.

Attacks on the 'city' are nothing new. Let us summarize its enemies' arguments. As early as 1925, Soviet theorists were harshly judging the big city, the metropolis that had not yet been given the name *Megalopolis*. They saw the metropolis as a capitalist creation, a result of manoeuvres by the bourgeoisie the better to dominate the working-class. This was not wrong, but it was only relatively true, and for a short time. They demonstrated its defects with sharpness. It is a line of argument that has been frequently repeated, even in the United States. The big city, monstrous and tentacular, is always political. It is the most favourable milieu for the establishment of authoritarian power, in which organization and 'over-organization' rule. The big city sanctifies inequality. Between order that is hard to tolerate and ever-threatening chaos, power, of whatever kind it is – the power of the State – will always choose order. The big city has only one problem: numbers. It is inevitable that a mass society will emerge within it, and this involves control over the masses and thus permanent violence and repression. What are we to think about the 'city–country' opposition? That it is insurmountable, and that interaction proves disastrous. The countryside knows it is in the service of the city, and the city poisons nature; it devours it while recreating it in the imagination so that this illusion of activity can survive. Urban order contains and disguises an underlying disorder. The big city is nothing but vice, pollution, sickness (mental, moral, social). The alienation of the city embraces and perpetuates all forms of alienation. In it, and through it, segregation becomes general: by class, by district, by profession, by age, by ethnic group, by sex. Crowd and solitude. Space in the city becomes scarce; an expensive luxury and a privilege, maintained and sustained by a form of practice (the 'centre') and by strategies. Of course, the city becomes rich. It attracts to itself all forms of wealth, and monopolizes culture in the same way as it concentrates power. It collapses from its wealth. The more it concentrates the means to live, the more unliveable it becomes. What makes for happiness in the city? The intense life of the big city? The proliferation of pleasures and leisure activities? Mystifications and myths. If there is a link between social relations and space, between places and human groups, we ought, in order to achieve cohesion, radically to modify the structures of space. And in any case, has urban space a structure? If the big city is not segregation and separation, is it not at least a chaotic tangle? Concepts that appear to denote places and qualities of space in fact denote only the social relations housed in an indifferent space: neighbourhood, environment, etc.

Going a little further, there is an idea that only the village – or the parish – had a social and spatial structure that allowed a human group to *appropriate* the conditions of its existence (environment, occupied places, organization of time). It is true that these harmonious (social) organisms (or that pass for such) also displayed a strict hierarchy, an equilibrium between castes. This meant that only space was entirely full of meaning, completely *signifying* and openly announcing to everyone (that is, to each member of a caste, age-group or sex) what was prohibited and what was permitted. The place determined the role. The equilibrium of the community demanded virtues: respect, submission and custom perceived as absolute. All this disappears in the big city.

Without going as far as to fetishize community (of the tribe, village or parish), or speaking of the 'non-city', around 1925 some Soviet theorists were formulating the problem of the *optimum*, a question that has been endlessly discussed since. How are we to determine or calculate (in terms of area or population) the optimum city? Using what criteria? Attempts to do so have always met with serious objections. Supposing that the 'administrable' (in what bureaucratic framework?) – and therefore desirable – optimum population was set at around 300,000, it would be very unusual if such a city could support a major university, a large theatre, an opera house, hospital services whose technical resources make them expensive, and so on.

We have recently seen projects in which major French highways would become the streets of a future megalopolis, delivering on the one hand neighbourhood life and a centrality of a certain kind (at junctions and crossroads), and on the other, natural areas and 'virgin' spaces, distinct from industrial zones. This just goes to show that in this field the only thinking is utopian! Projects like that anticipate the generalized urbanization. In that case, why reduce urban space to rural space, by building urban society along old roads? Why this retreat into the past, which is not identical with the detour made by communitarian ideology (fed by a form of ethnology), but is not distinguished from it?

Arguments against the 'urban' and for the 'non-city', and the principles derived from them, are more moral than based on the connection between the real and the possible. The problems are not well formulated. Without reopening the debate, it is enough to note that widespread urbanization and the growth of the urban fabric has overtaken them. Society now faces problems of a different order: either urban chaos – or urban society, conceived as such. More concretely, the attack on the (old) city and against the (virtual) urban – confused, deliberately or not, one with the other – takes place at two levels: from the higher level (G) and from the lower level (P).

The attack from above, so to speak, involves a global project in which the national territory is subjected to 'development' as decreed by industrialization. Two requirements and two premises: the entire space has to be planned – individual features of sites and locations have to disappear under general, technologically-driven constraints. Then, *mobility* becomes essential for a population subject to changing constraints, determined by a list of variables: energy sources, raw materials, etc. Residential mobility, always low in itself, will dissolve into a higher rate of industrial mobility (thus, the Lorraine iron and steel industry is moving, with its investments and workforce, to Dunkirk, the port where the ore arrives from Mauritania; Mourenx will disappear or be converted when its gas-fields are exhausted, etc.)[5] From this point of view, it is unacceptable for 'labour deposits' to remain unexploited on the grounds that they are tied to the soil, immobilized under layers of history, under the pretext of being 'rooted', etc. These harsh truths will apply on a world scale, wherever economic, financial and technological pressures undermine structures (local, regional and national) that resist them, ineffectually.

At level P, motivations, which are very varied, nevertheless converge with technological and technocratic concerns. The taste for nomadism and the ephemeral, the need constantly to travel, will replace the old, settled existence in the home, the traditional attachment to one's place of birth. What does the human being need? Shelter. No matter where. Y. Friedman builds supports and units (boxes) that can be put together to make a room, several rooms, large or small – a temporary combination.[6] This offers the prospect of making widespread and democratic the luxurious life of millionaires who go from palace to palace, from one grand house to the next, or live on board their yachts. Which makes the world their oyster. Or so it would seem.

From above or below, this would mean both the end of habitation and the end of the urban as places and as collections of opposites, centres. This ending of the urban would result from *industrial organization* as a system of acts and decisions – from the end of *historical value*, as far as values are concerned – and from the *transformation of everyday life* as far as cultural *patterns* or models are concerned.

Among the forms of resistance to this double pressure, it is important to distinguish between reactionary and revolutionary forces. In other words, the critique sometimes comes from the 'right' and sometimes from the 'left'. The same is true of the second order *critique of the critique*. We see a critique of the city in the name of the old community (tribe, village, province) as a 'right' critique and, contrariwise, the critique made here of the city (and the non-city) as a 'left' critique. It is the traditionalists, the voices of parochialism and a somewhat 'folkloric' regionalism that protest against the disappearance of the city. Protest that arises from *particularities*, and usually originates in the countryside, cannot be confused with either a challenge to repressive authorities, or with awareness of and challenges to *differences*. The affirmation of differences may include (selectively, i.e. in the course of a critical examination of their coherence and authenticity) ethnic, linguistic, local and regional particularities, but on another level, where differences are perceived and conceived of as such, i.e. in their interrelationships, and not in isolation, as particularities. The fact that conflicts may arise between differences and particularities, just as between possibilities and existing interests, can hardly be avoided. It remains the case that the urban is defined as the place where differences become known to one another, and in acknowledging one another, are put to the test: validated or invalidated. Attacks on it envisage, coldly or cheerfully, the disappearance of differences, often identified or confused with 'traditional' particularities. Ideology, industrial, technocratic or individualist, is homogenizing.

It will be difficult for the defenders-in-training of urban society to avoid all ambiguity, to open up a path that cannot be misappropriated. Take the question of the centre and centrality. There is not a city or an urban reality without a centre. And that's not all; as we have said, urban space is defined by the vector 'zero'; it is a space where virtually every point may attract to itself *everything* around it: things, created works, people. At every point, the time-space vector, the distance between the contained and the container, may become zero. This is *impossible* (u-topian) but characterizes the dialectical movement (immanent contradiction) of urban space-time. Thus it is theoretically forbidden not to defend urban concentration, with its dangers of saturation and disorder, and its opportunities for encounters, information, convergences. To attack and destroy it is the result of empiricism that starts by destroying thinking. Thus the centre cannot but be dispersed into partial, mobile centralities (multi-centrality) whose specific relationships are to be determined in context. This being so, we are in danger of defending decision-making structures, centres of power, in which there is a massive concentration (giving them enormous density) of the elements of wealth and power. There are no places of leisure or entertainment, celebration, knowledge, oral and written communication, invention or creation, without centrality. But as long as certain production and property relations are not changed, centrality will fall prey to those who use and benefit from those relations. It will be at best 'elitist', at worst under military and police control. What is to be done, other than to accept ambiguity and contradictions, in other words, the *dialectical* character of the situation and its processes? To accept the situation does not mean to ratify the dictatorship of power centres and authoritarian forms of planning. Far from it. Or rather, the reverse.

As far as *mobility* goes, we note the superficial character of the social and professional mobility sought by planners (improver-removers). We are not talking about the intense mobility that can take place only near a centre, but about a movement of people or industrial plant that leaves social relations intact. Such mobility may certainly produce chaos; there seems to be a greater danger of seeing it produce 'equilibrium' or 'stability', since movements of people and their activities are heavily programmed and 'structured'. This disorder is not that of information and encounters, but of boredom and neurosis. It is no less true that a contradiction arises, which the activity known as 'town planning' tries to resolve: order and disorder, equilibrium and movement, stability and mobility. How would it succeed in doing so, other than by concentrating its constraints and imposing homogeneity, a *politics of space*, a rigorous form of programming that gets rid of symbols, information and play, all at once? Planners come out of it badly, offering temporary constructions that last: a monotonous morphology, an unchanging environment for people who pass through because they want to go somewhere else and actually find something different. From this perspective, moreover, the planner and the architect merge. The architect easily sees himself as a planner, or else the other way round. Both, combined or in competition, take orders and obey a uniform social command. Acting in concert, they soon abandon their little scrap of utopia, the touch of madness that could still mark their work and leave them open to suspicions of ill will, disobedience, non-conformity. The politics of space involves a strategy that brings levels and dimensions into line. Order? It clothes itself in morality and 'scientism'. The tyranny of the right angle becomes conflated with that of industrialization and the neo-capitalist State. This was always the orientation of Gropius's great project, when he conceived of 'logical and systematic coordination in the handling of architectural problems', when he envisaged, when the Bauhaus was founded, a 'total' *architectonics*, which could be passed on through 'coherent, operational and systematised' teaching.[7]

As for residential nomadism, which invokes the splendours of the ephemeral, what does it represent but an extreme and in its way utopian form of individualism? The ephemeral would seem to be reduced to a change of box (for living in). To offer, like Y. Friedman, liberation through nomadism, and that in the form of a habitat in the pure state, set on metal supports with steel panels (a giant Meccano set), is ludicrous.[8] If the ephemeral, as can be imagined, is soon to be promoted, what might it consist of? In activity by groups that are also ephemeral, and would invent and create works. Their *oeuvres*. In which their life and existence would come into being and be exhausted in momentarily freeing itself from the everyday. What works? Which groups? The answer would make pointless the fundamental question – that of creation. These groups, if they appear, will invent their moments and their acts, their space and their time, their works. Probably at the level of habitation, or starting from that level (but not remaining there, i.e. creating an appropriate model of urban space). Neither the failure nor the success of some attempts in this direction – to pierce through the system or systems of things and make possible the impossible – proves anything. These attempts would be effective only in the course of the revolutionary restoration of an upside-down world; they are and will be the work of groups who are probably dubbed 'leftist', and whose ideas existing society will try to take over. Unless *movement* wins out and takes society in other directions. And what about initiatives by architects and planners? It would be naïve today to think like Hans Meyer, in 1928, when he replaced Gropius as Director of the Bauhaus: 'To build is to organise social, psychological, technological and economic life.'[9] The role of architect as demiurge is part of urban mythology and/or ideology, which are hard to separate. Moreover, Gropius thought on a grand scale when he suggested that the architect-coordinator pull all problems together, and progress 'from a functional study of the house to that of the street, from the street to the city and finally to regional and national planning'. Unfortunately for that project, the converse happened: structural planning put the lower steps and levels under its own constraints. Can this situation be reversed? The possible is today impossible, bound up with transformative actions within society. It is not for the architect to 'define a new conception of life', to enable the individual to develop on a higher level by relieving him of the weight of the everyday, as Gropius believed. It is for a new conception of life to make possible the work of the architect, who will continue to act as a 'social condenser', not of capitalist social relations and the commanding order that reflects them, but of relations in motion and new relations in the process of development. He may even be able to act as a 'social accelerator'; but the conjuncture that could bring that about must be examined very carefully, so that we are not duped by words – by appearances.

Following this sequence of arguments, the spatio-temporal diagram looks like this:

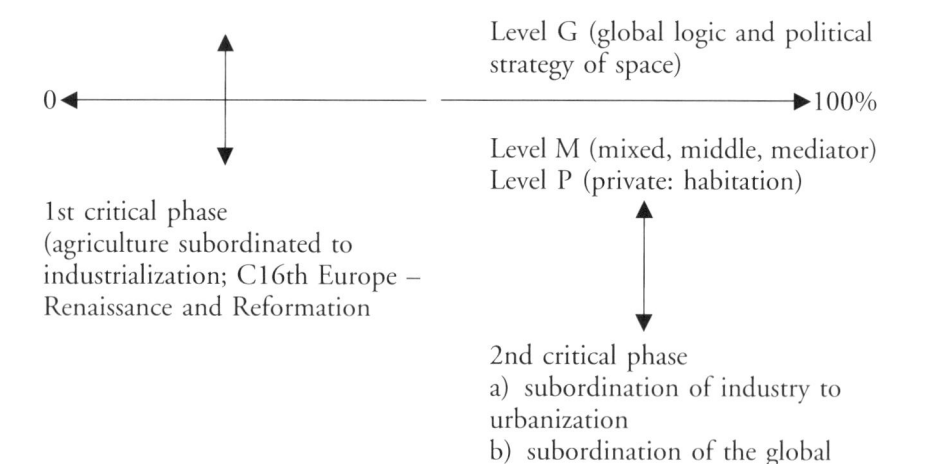

Level G (global logic and political strategy of space)

0 ←————————————————→ 100%

Level M (mixed, middle, mediator)
Level P (private: habitation)

1st critical phase
(agriculture subordinated to industrialization; C16th Europe – Renaissance and Reformation

2nd critical phase
a) subordination of industry to urbanization
b) subordination of the global to the urban and the urban to habitation

There is a double reversal: the subordination of urban reality to its antecedents and conditions, and the subjection of habitation to supposedly higher levels of social practice. Hence a *fundamental* (from the bottom and from the foundation) reorganization.

An especially bold, yet very simple, interpretation of Marxist thought sees in Marx's work (in *Capital,* and also the so-called philosophical and political works) an account of a *world turned upside down* and a proposal for *re-inverting* it, that is, to put it back on its feet.[10] It is not just Hegelian philosophy and dialectic that have their head down below and their feet in the air, very encumbered (alienated) by this situation, whose strangeness has been diluted or eliminated by custom. The upside-down world, according to Marx, is a society:

a) in which the intermediary supplants the producer (worker) and the creator (artist, inventor, producer of knowledge and ideas) and in which he is able to enrich himself at their expense by harnessing the results of their activity and leaving in poverty those who have taken the risk of creating something. Who are these intermediaries? Merchants, and the many others who manage to plug into the circuit connecting production with consumption and vice versa. In the front rank: the capitalist, whether a landlord or a producer;
b) in which the State (which ought to serve the whole society and diffuse through it its organizational capacity and rationality) comes to do precisely the opposite: it reinforces the exploitation of society as a whole, sets itself up above it and declares itself the vital essence of social life and its *structure*, while being no more than an accident (a *superstructure*);
c) in which the bureaucracy can acquire interests of its own and the means to serve them, and where skill and knowledge become the criteria for appointment to the bureaucracy;
d) in which as a result, effects pass for causes, and the end becomes the means and the means the end.

We have only added a few articles to the theory of the upside-down world, which support the project for re-inverting this world, and contribute to the Marxist project for a revolution in industrial organization through a project for urban revolution. It is not difficult to show that any other interpretation of Marxist thought is precisely that, an interpretation, a weaker version, designed to manage this or that institution or aspect of the upside-down world: the State, philosophy, division of labour, the existing morphology, etc. It is just as easy to show that without total subversion of that sort, including the kind that foregrounds problems relating to the actual places where social relations take place, what is said about these relations is nothing but ideological talk. We are happy to repeat, after Marx, that 'man' in his 'essence' does not reside in the isolated individual but consists of a set of relations or concrete (practical) social relationships. With the result that generic Man (man in general) is only an abstraction. What system of reference enables us to discover the features of the personal? For a long time, it was *biological*; we borrowed from the theory of Pavlovian reflexes, the physiology of the brain.[11] The cortico-visceral defined the personal. The system was, and still is today, most frequently *technological* (and therefore economic). It is in relation to productive work that we conceive of and determine the relations that make up consciousness (of personal life), to the extent that we are not chattering in a vacuum and are making the effort to achieve a *praxis*. Who would deny that references to industrial practice or biology are meaningful? The reference to desire, to 'the unconscious', is no less so, unless we fetishize the unconscious by substantializing it. But can we study these questions, questions of conscience and the development of the individual (in the group closest to him, or those of which he forms a part, i.e. from the family to the world) without taking into account the morphology and the forms presented by *places*, by the relationship between these places and institutions (school, university, army, State, etc.)? Speculations of this kind survive as a wild abstraction, covered by a mask or veil of philosophy.[12] The introduction of topology (analytical consideration of *topoi* in mental and social space) enables us to preserve the philosophical breadth of conceptions, by eliminating the effects of the philosophizing (speculative) attitude.

The Other Parises

(from *Espaces et Sociétés*, 13/14 (Octobre 1974–Janvier 1975), pp. 185–90, 192)

This text served as the basis for the film 'Le Droit à la Ville', a 26-minute 16 mm colour documentary directed by Jean-Louis Bertucelli. Henri Lefebvre was involved in creating the film, which was produced by the Établissement Public du Centre Beaubourg, Centre de Création Industrielle. Produced by PAV and Elisabeth Tamaroff Auclaire. Distributed by PAV, 39 rue Dareau, Paris 14ème.

There is a trite Paris, a Paris that is easily available. For tourists? Not only for them. Many Parisians take on trust a conventional representation of their city: the acceptable, presentable, and therefore 'normal' and 'self-evident' Paris. Culture does not play much of a part. How many 'cultured' Parisians do no more than glance at the *Semaine de Paris* or the weeklies, to find out what is going on in France's capital?

At one time, everyone was involved in their family and with those living nearby, and they knew their neighbourhood because that is where they lived a village life, or something like it. (In the original form of social practice, in the old peasant societies, 'the environment' still had an *immediate* character: there were no intervening forms of mediation, or rather, if there were, they remained remote.) A narrow life, but not without its attractions: each individual feels himself supported, under close supervision, but assisted. Those are the days of which we talk or sing nostalgically: 'How pretty was my village; my Paris, our Paris ... We all spoke the same language, you could be sure of being understood!'

Today, in a Paris that has spread out in an endless suburbia, there are dizzying swarms of people from all over the world: students, tourists, people passing through, travellers staying for a while, businessmen, etc. Is it a Tower of Babel or the great Babylon? In the legendary, monstrous city, everyone has some route of his own (from flat to school, the office, the factory) and does not know the rest very well. These familiar journeys are part of the everyday, practical and reassuring, narrower in many respects than the old neighbourhood life. And the representation (image) of the city? You would have to be a bit naïve to think the prevailing image resembles the one formed in a stroller's mind. To wander through a modern city pursuing the 'reveries of a solitary stroller'[1] is pleasant, no more, and soon becomes disappointing, unless it is accompanied by other interests and forms of curiosity. Representation of the city, for the great majority of people, is restricted to banalities about the big department stores, about places that are 'in' or 'out', to be visited or avoided. Urban reality, in its complication and complexity, becomes schematized. In earlier times, monuments played an important practical role: they organized their surroundings, and attracted or repelled clearly defined categories of people. The parish church, for example. Without losing this role, monuments have acquired an *iconic* role. They act both as useful landmarks and as symbols. In the over-extended fabric of the city, they are key points, tying the 'weave' to the earth, and holding the gaze within a series of horizons and perspectives. Attacked from all sides by the proliferation of buildings, large and small, Monumentality defends itself and takes on a new meaning, paradoxically concrete within an invading abstraction, the abstraction of anonymous places and impersonal comings and goings.

Paris has the Eiffel Tower as its icon. Is there anyone who does not know that? It is a strange fate, for a strange symbol; the work of an engineer who was audacious for his time (almost a century ago now!) has suffered a displacement. From the technical point of view, the tower is outmoded. Constructed as a large building, metal's challenge to stone and the engineer's challenge to architects, it has come to look like a monument, a work of architecture. In less than a century, the technical object that in its time represented a technological manifesto has turned into a work of art; aesthetic qualities are attributed to it: elegance, slenderness, feminine appeal. Through the medium of its icon, the visible Paris attributes these qualities to itself. All over the world, people have become accustomed to seeing the tower above Paris, and Paris at the foot of the tower. The association has become unarguable: Paris has become an 'environment' of the Eiffel Tower; hence its popularity, expressed in all sorts of photographs, postcards, and more or less outrageously 'kitschy' objects. But the Tower has not entirely lost the properties of a technological object. As an icon, it seems rational. Around it lies a city based on reason, with Cartesian lines and horizons, occupying a homogeneous space, without awkward roughnesses.

The process by which a privileged object is charged with such power to signify leads to the simplification of the schema, to an extreme degree of poverty: Paris on view as spectacle, from the top of the Tower, at its feet, all around it. The spectator (tourist or native Parisian) forgets that the city made a generous gift of its qualities to the icon, and that the spectacle – trivial yet charming – has no right to substitute itself for this reality. Which is what icons and Symbols do all the time, relying on a certain practical utility and the need for landmarks and representations.

The Eiffel Tower has rivals: other monuments offer themselves as candidates for the role of icon: Notre-Dame, Sacré-Coeur, the Arc de Triomphe, etc., etc. When one of these candidates is successful, an icon is declared: luminous, edifying, impoverishing. Paris is transformed into a religious city, a military city, a political city. And it is those things too (but it is all of that – and other things as well!)

A city can be settled and grow on the basis of a simple plan and of structures defined once and for all: a grid, for example, with this or that square or rectangle taking on a function, a movement, according to constant laws: the church or the temple, the palace of the ruler or the prince, the place set aside for traders, etc. This is the case with many cities in Asia and Latin America. Other cities have a more flexible form, a binary structure: the city of the rich and the city of the poor, the political city and the city of working people, the castle and the labourers, etc.

Paris has had the historical good fortune to have a form that is complex without being rigid (though orientations and directions are assigned to it), that is to say, a *ternary* structure or organization. In so-called historical time-space, there have been from the beginning three 'Parises', intimately linked together through the combined action of many forms of energy: the political Paris, the Paris of knowledge and the Paris of commerce, production and wealth.

The Paris of Knowledge?

This is the so-called Latin quarter (the Quarter!), curiously established on top of Paris 'in the country', since its streets follow the earliest routes by which the first denizen-citizens went from the city to their fields, pastures, mills, orchards and vineyards. 'Culture' installs itself on top of 'nature', and the streets and alleyways have kept the twists and turns of country lanes. They thus have a character that for a long time meant they were destined to be lived in by poor people, by a population that was unruly but to some extent protected: scholars and those who associate with them. Today, this allows a curious kind of hijacking in the interests of an international (cosmopolitan) 'elite'.

The Paris of knowledge, of 'culture', is constantly expanding, though the relocation of some of the *grandes écoles* and the opening up of the universities may modify and slow down its own growth. Today it stretches from La Halle aux Vins to rue du Bac, from the banks of the Seine to boulevard Montparnasse,[2] with some curious interruptions (fashion boutiques and off-the-peg outlets, art and craft shops).

Political Paris?

Originally located in the Cité (the Palace of so-called Justice, the policing centre of the capital and of France),[3] it quickly spread far towards the west.

Why? Because the eastern part of the city acquired, very early on, a military vocation (if one can call it that). It's the dangerous direction, where the enemy comes from. Trade goes from south to north and north to south. Towards the east there are forts and fortifications, (the Bastille), barracks, stores of armaments (the Arsenal), depots and warehouses, places believed, rightly or wrongly, to be unhealthy (the Marais, which was only later occupied by gardens and the town-houses of the aristocracy).[4] Thus, at a very early date, political Paris developed westwards, creating extensions such as the Louvre, the present district of ministries and embassies (rue de Grenelle, rue Saint-Dominique, rue de l'Université, etc.).[5] Place de la Concorde, place de Grève (with the Hôtel de Ville), place des Victoires and place de l'Étoile, like the Invalides and the Champ-de-Mars, were linked to political Paris, with its military additions.[6] Political Paris was also monarchical, then imperial, then imperialist Paris, the Paris of the centralized State. It retains the splendour of its royal character. In this Paris, monumentality rules.

The Paris of Business, Commerce and Production?

It took shape around Les Halles and the major trade routes (to England and Flanders: rue Saint-Denis and rue Saint-Martin),[7] with these markers: the stock exchange, the financial exchange, the Banque de France – places given over to merchandise and money, first commercial then industrial and financial capital, but also with places devoted to production, especially in the Marais, where the rising nineteenth-century bourgeoisie vandalized this area of town-houses, parks and gardens in order to take it over. Here, and here most of all, the functional asserted itself; it would have taken over, had not concern for prestige preserved a certain monumentality. Unitary structure creates monotony, 'uniformity', binary structure an opposition that is strongly marked but stubbornly repeated. Threefold or ternary structure ensures an extraordinary diversification of space. The three Parises saw themselves grow in the course of terrible struggles (including a number of revolutions) of which the city was both the scene and the issue at stake. Can that be overemphasized? Historians have often talked about political struggles as though they were waged in abstract space. The best writers on the past have described the city (the faubourg Saint-Antoine and its artisans, Montmartre with its exuberant lower class population, Belleville and the workers 'deported' by Haussmann)[8] as the theatre of conflict. Nevertheless, you have only to study the Marais and the 'historic centre' a little to realize how the victorious bourgeoisie carved up the existing space and quartered, shattered and rearranged it to suit its own requirements. And how this process has not stopped since, but still continues today.

Whatever the case may be, anyone who passes through one of Paris's diversified spaces should not forget about the others, if he claims to have a mental 'image of the city', however inaccurate. It is not just about a confused memory of junctions, directions or functions, but of spaces that are described differently by powerful social groups, in active competition. For each Parisian space, the 'environment' is the other spaces; each Paris is surrounded by the rest. Have the rivalries and conflicts that marked and differentiated spaces now disappeared? They may sometimes have become attenuated, but the prospect of 'student' Paris being one day reabsorbed into a Paris of international 'culture' remains a distant possibility; the 'Quarter' is still disturbing. As far as commercial and financial space goes, it too tries to invade the space of prestige and political power, both in Les Halles and La Défense in the Wild West.[9] Political space, which aims to erect the State above society, strikes back, blow for blow.

Where does the trite, 'ordinary' Paris persist, outside our mental images? In the prosperous neighbourhoods, no question of it, with their modern, straight streets and perfectly aligned façades that create noble, monotonous vistas; in the Paris of Napoleon and Haussmann, to be specific.

This seems to call for comment, including a history of the façade and the way houses are aligned and grouped together according to the laws of perspective. For centuries, neither the façade nor strict alignment were very important. Straight lines had not yet supplanted either curves or the play of imagination in the sequence of buildings. Something of this survives in the old streets (for example, the rue des Archives: bends, widened pavements, trees, pavement cafés, etc.).[10] In the Middle Ages one side of artisans' and merchants' houses faced the street (awnings, shops), but life was lived in an inside courtyard or a garden. By then, monuments had façades (which they did not have in ancient Greece, when all their sides were of equal importance). The façades of monuments dominate a square or an immediate neighbourhood, allowing those who control them to see a certain space and to be seen, when they so design. Later, private buildings (noblemen's residences, bourgeois houses) imitated the monumental façade on a smaller, meaner scale; under official rules that imposed vistas, alas, façades (which showed less and less variety) were juxtaposed and individuality was confined to mouldings and stuck-on decoration. In the bourgeois era, under the planning regimes of Napoleon (Haussmann), the façade reaches its apogee and demonstrates its absurdity. Vistas consist of almost identical façades. Differences, now increasingly *within* vistas, cease to be visible or perceptible despite the praiseworthy or risible efforts of architects racking their brains to design them. Made to be seen, the façade gets lost in the 'visibility' of the avenue, the street, the anonymous location. It is easy to take a street (let's say, rue d'Assas) and demonstrate: the sequence of façades, their age, generation and variety, the pleasure and monotony of rigid perspective, the decline and fall of the façade among recent buildings (functional, technical, specialized, etc.).[11]

But the façade has yet another meaning. Built to be seen (and to allow one to see out, from balconies, windows and openings), the façade is a lie. What lies behind this show, under this decoration? What are these rigidly straight, perspectival, streets hiding? The interior volumes behind the ornamental surface contain many surprises. Whoever penetrates under this cover, discovers something different: sometimes charming, more often wretched; in short, the things people passing by under the gaze of the windows do not see. Already, in each apartment, the 'formal' rooms, where visitors are received, the sitting room, the dining room, the rooms overlooking the street and opening on to the façade, conceal those where everyday activities considered unworthy of daylight, even shameful, take place: the kitchen, the bathroom, the 'W.C.', etc.

The ordering into perspective is also a 'staging' of everyday life; it organizes it; the *scene* determines the *ob-scene*, what is not done here, but there: we do not undress in the street or the sitting room, we make love in the marital bed (officially); we eat in the dining room, but we do not prepare meals there. The casting of roles in everyday life is not functional, in the functionalist sense, but it stipulates actions in space very strictly, for purposes of camouflage and representation, in a quasi-theatrical way; furnishings and styles of furniture (the glass-fronted cabinet, the double bed, the chest of drawers, the sideboard, the table, etc.) obey this quotidian order and emphasize it by monumentally organizing space down to the gestural detail. Such is the order that is concealed but also revealed (because it is prescribed) by the façade.

The façade thus has many 'properties'; it is much more than a simple surface, covered to a greater or lesser extent in ornamentation. It characterizes a way of life. It determines urban space and its use (the 'uses' that take place in it). It has power; it contains a latent violence, a capacity for repression, not only in its visibility/readability, but also in the dissociation between what is hidden and what is displayed, and thus the private and the public, a dissociation that reveals specific social relations: those of bourgeois society and the capitalist mode of production during their ascendancy in the nineteenth century, in France, in Paris.

Also hidden, and hard to read, although decipherable to the experienced eye (but not to others), there is the Paris of wealth and power. This ubiquitous and disguised city, the true 'capital' (of capital), presents both the ideal 'ego' (dictated by the places where everyone would wish to live, because those who do not belong to the 'establishment' dream of finding fulfilment in these privileged places) and the 'ideal' of the ego (the role of superiority and talent, which demands some innate gifts and some acquired qualities).

The big bosses, the truly wealthy, the Olympian deities, do not reveal themselves. The places they fill with their presence and power, from which they exert their influence, are not seen. Certain clues give them away: private parks and gardens, monumental gateways and entrances, signs of luxury and especially those essential luxuries: available space, available time. A palace is hidden away in a modest street, behind a plain-looking wall (rue Monsieur, for example);[12] super-elite residences like this are not even visible from the street (the house of Dr Dalsace, rue Saint-Guillaume).[13] The powers of state are housed in '*hotels*' – townhouses whose size and importance is not always apparent (the palace of the archbishop of Paris, rue Barbet de Jouy).[14]

Above working-class Paris and the Paris of the middle classes, semi-bourgeoisie, above the 'knowledge quarter' and the business district stands power, the Paris of the Establishment, the ruling Elite, of the old grand bourgeoisie and the new, of the *dolce vita* and of power exercised for its own sake. But how are they to be reached or penetrated? The keen eye can at least guess at them, sense them, trace their outline in space.

Below ordinary, everyday Paris lies underground Paris. Are we talking about the sewers? The catacombs? 'Evacuations', including those of human remains, the dead, the mad? The Paris of the unconscious and the unconscious of Paris? Yes, if you like, but first and foremost, the city of poverty, of the deserving and undeserving poor. Marginal Paris? Those words mean nothing. There are many kinds of poverty in a big city, and many poor areas in the larger Paris. Metaphors like 'marginality', or 'underground life' help to disguise what someone wants to hide.

Working-class neighbourhoods have a 'liveliness' that makes them interesting and which we would like to find elsewhere, even to take it into the 'desert' of the gentrified districts by employing 'cultural community workers'. The spontaneous liveliness of working-class communities between the Belleville and Couronnes metro stations, for example, has no need of such 'workers'.[15] What does it hide? Can it be attributed simply to 'life', or vitality?

First of all, without entirely hiding them, it contains rivalries, frequently intense struggles (connected with the class struggle and the position of 'workers' under capitalism) which nevertheless have a pronounced ethnic character. In these 'lively quarters', Arabs and Jews, immigrants and returned ex-pats actually live in a state of great tension, often if not always on the brink of confrontations, fights and brawls.

The ghettos of foreign workers do not fall within conventional categories: liveliness, city life. And on the 'picturesque' quality of these quarters, this is what one of those rare North Africans who has lived the life of an immigrant in France, and can express himself in writing, has to say. The France of today, imitating the most repugnant aspects of its American model, turns 'the abominable into a market value and disguised slavery into a practice'. In the ghettos, the victims of racial and spatial segregation defend themselves in their own way; what comes from outside is seen as the enemy, the agent of repression; whether it is a journalist (who may be well-intentioned), a film-maker or a sociologist, people speak to him in a 'doctored' language. How are we to penetrate these citadels of anger and hostile silence, or capture in rational concepts a bubbling ferment that evades the usual criteria by which social and political forces are recognized? 'Immigrant ghettos are the domain of a powerful, impenetrable darkness', wrote Mustapha Sala, in an unpublished text. It is where agents of the countries of origin, representatives of the traffickers, the cops, members of the 'resistance', and the mafias that deal in everything that can be traded (including women) come into confrontation. The ghetto speaks a language that is unintelligible; its sufferings as well as its oases of celebration and enchantment, are inaccessible; the organization of space eludes study as it eludes the 'values' of a foreign, that is, French, society.

The underground Parises lead a life that is 'infra-everyday' compared with that of 'normal' people, and yet everyday, adapted both to poverty and to rejection (of capitalism, of the West, and of 'Frenchness').

The foreigners' and immigrant ghettos are not the only ones. There are the ghettos of the hippies (often seen basking in the sunshine, on the *quais*), those of the beggars, prostitutes, the drug-users. Are they ghettos? Isolated 'pockets'? Signposted routes? 'Specialized' spaces? There is an infinite number of nuances between 'abnormal' and 'normal' life, between the bland and the exciting, the ordinary and the tragic. Sometimes the extraordinary reveals itself within the ordinary. Usually, it is not about a place, but about a well- or less well-placed event – a news item.

It is not easy to describe Paris and its transformations without invoking the past; without falling into nostalgia and striking up a lament for a paradise lost. Once, fifty years ago, everywhere (Paris and the Ile de France, the French countryside and the whole of France, and nature cultivated in the French way, etc.) was more beautiful. A hundred, or two hundred years ago, beauty reigned – the beauty of nature and medieval or monarchical splendour.

None of this yearning for the past; a hundred years ago, tuberculosis held sway along with beauty in the slums of Paris. What was the Belle Epoque? A bourgeois myth, an ideology designed to mask the present by exculpating the bourgeoisie, by attributing to an enigmatic 'decadence' or a no less enigmatic 'modernity' the ravages of speculation, concentration and the will to power.

Nevertheless, it is difficult to show Paris and talk about it without noting the traces of its lost splendour. Monuments (and symbols) betray the past, because they create a belief in enduring beauty, while life – a form of life – has disappeared for ever, and its traces tell us practically nothing. Apart from making us dream.

[. . .]

What are the reasons for this loss? We know them: cars, offices and the rule of bureaucracy, specialization and functionalization of places, the primacy of profit, the embourgeoisification of the city, the desertification of the elegant quarters and the gentrification of old quarters, etc. These converging causes and reasons have a disastrous result, so unacceptable that one asks oneself, after the briefest reflection, how 'that can be', and why 'that can continue'. It reaches the point where both the young and the artistic elite invade what is left of the poor areas (rue Saint-Denis and the streets around it, and the recently formed ghettos). Why? 'The abominable acquires a market value.' We come full circle. The young people who open craft shops in rue Saint-Denis, buying and selling the most heterogeneous objects (anything whatsoever can be bought and sold) are doing no more than the tourists who swoop down on the ancient hill-towns around the Mediterranean. They consume, they destroy what they love (or say they love).

Something will come of all this. What? The eye will see it before the mind can express it, unless we're making a rash error of judgement.

History, Time and Space

Introduction

With the contemporary interest in questions of spatiality within social theory, there is a continual danger that questions of temporality are pushed to one side. In terms of existing translations of Lefebvre's writings, evidenced perhaps by his adoption within the discipline of geography, it might seem that the spatial took precedence over the temporal. However, as we seek to show here, Lefebvre not only wrote widely on the notion of time, but his thinking about spatiality always follows from his thinking about time. The selections chosen demonstrate the complexity of philosophical influences at work in his thinking about time and space and focus on four main areas: the theory of moments, the question of history, the notion of rhythm and that of the world.

The first piece here, 'The Inventory', taken from Lefebvre's autobiographical *La Somme et le reste* [The Sum and the Remainder] discusses the notion of moments. It therefore has an affinity with Nietzsche's deployment of the *Augenblick*, a moment or literally a 'blink of the eye', in *Thus Spoke Zarathustra*, which Heidegger discussed at length in lectures delivered in the late 1930s but not published until after Lefebvre's work here.[1] The discussion of the repetition of moments is a useful complement to the work on everyday life, bringing to mind the 'everyday' repetitiveness of the mundane. This selection also demonstrates Lefebvre's interest in questions of love, which has recently been highlighted in Rob Shields's *Lefebvre, Love and Struggle: Spatial Dialectics*.[2] As with the selection 'Being a Communist' in the 'Politics' section below, it should be remembered that *La Somme et le reste* was Lefebvre's 'confessions', written not long after he had left the PCF.

The discussion of becoming and history, which should be supplemented with the piece in the 'Marxism and Philosophy' section, comes from the 1970 book *La Fin de l'histoire* [The End of History]. In this work Lefebvre takes Hegel, Marx and Nietzsche as his principal interlocutors, just as he would five years later in the book devoted to them.[3] Coming a decade after, and in opposition to, Daniel Bell's polemical *The End of Ideology: On the Exhaustion of Political Ideas in the 1950s*[4] Lefebvre discusses the notion of an 'end', both a conclusion and a goal, and relates this to discussions in the three German thinkers. Of course the title 'The End of History' also predates Francis Fukuyama's famous article of 1989, and the subsequent bestseller of the early 1990s.[5] However, far from sharing Fukuyama's blithe optimism at the prospect of a post-historical liberal age, Lefebvre anticipates many of the objections that have been raised, and looks at the notion of 'end' with a much more progressive sense. This piece also shows Lefebvre – following from the selections in 'Marxism and Philosophy' – further reworking the notion of dialectics, and, particularly here, the integration of Nietzschean notions of overcoming.

One brief excerpt from Lefebvre's study of the Paris Commune is also included, as a glimpse of Lefebvre the historian. As was mentioned in the general introduction, Lefebvre included long passages of intellectual history in his studies of literary and philosophical figures in the French tradition, but he also wrote studies of two major Parisian events – those of May 1968 and March 1871. His study of May 1968, long regarded as a classic first-hand account, is already available in English,[6] so we have chosen to provide an extract from *La Proclamation de la commune* [The Proclamation of the Commune], which focuses on the notion of style. His study – like that of May 1968 – is of a 'moment', but with a spatial as well as temporal context – a situation or a spectacle. Lefebvre had been close to the Situationists around the time he wrote this, though they were later to break acrimoniously. Among other things it shows Lefebvre's notion of a festival being deployed as an alternative to everyday life. Kristin Ross's excellent study, *The Emergence of Social Space: Rimbaud and the Paris Commune*, was influenced by this work.[7]

The notion of rhythm – already known from the two pieces included in *Writings of Cities* on the streets of Paris ('Seen from the Window') and Mediterranean cities, and first proposed in the second volume of *Critique de la vie quotidienne*[8] – is further explored in 'The Rhythmanalytical Project' included here. This piece was coauthored with Catherine Régulier, a young communist who had first collaborated with Lefebvre in a long, rambling and at times flirtatious interview published as *La Revolution n'est plus ce qu'elle était* [The Revolution is No Longer What it Was].[9] Régulier became Lefebvre's last wife, and the work on rhythms was a joint venture. 'The Rhythmanalytical Project' preceded the book *Rhythmanalysis* by a few years, and covers some of the same ground, though naturally in much less detail. A full translation of *Rhythmanalysis* is forthcoming from Continuum.[10] In rhythm, space and time find another mode of union, and the misleading imbalance of one over the other is finally laid to rest in an analysis of everyday and city life. Here Lefebvre does not so much suggest an ending as a new cycle of work.

A somewhat different section comes from Lefebvre's epic *De l'État*, a four volume tour de force written immediately after *The Production of Space*, which discusses Marxist State theory, the role of the State in the contemporary world, and economic policy. One of its most interesting notions is the way the State operates on the world stage or at the worldwide scale. Although much of his work anticipates and influences contemporary theorization of 'globalization' we have resisted the temptation to use that word to translate Lefebvre's *mondialisation*. We have therefore rendered *mondial* as 'worldwide', and *mondialisation* as 'making-worldly' – a process or an event.

Of all Lefebvre's many books, perhaps *The Production of Space*, translated in 1991, has had the most impact in the Anglophone world. One of the aims of this section is to complement it with texts that both precede and follow it, but which also showcase its limitations and partial nature. One of the central texts in this section is therefore the 'Preface to the New Edition', written for the third edition of 1986. Its omission in the English translation of *The Production of Space* was a serious one, as here Lefebvre seeks both to clarify the key arguments of the book and to suggest several issues that he had left out.

Stuart Elden

The Inventory

(from *La Somme et le reste* (Paris: Méridiens Klincksieck, 1989 [1959]), pp. 642–55)

Human life (the praxis of man, indivisibly individual and social being) includes no basic elements or attributes other than those which emerge from the origins of life and physical nature: struggle, play, food, love and reproduction, rest. Let us look at the meaning of the words 'human nature' dialectically. Neither for man in general, nor for the specific individual, is there a fixed nature, a strictly determined essence, a kind of biological preformation of what he may and must become. Every man is therefore – virtually – every nature. He has only to recognize possibilities and apply them to himself. While some of these possibilities will be more nearly within his reach than others, and while there exist inclinations or gifts, this given 'essence' represents no more than access by one route or another to a more complete existence. We have thought it equally necessary to eliminate the idea of pure plasticity as that of innate endowment. Furthermore, what differs completely – between animal and man, between individuals, between cultures and civilizations, between classes and groups – is the order imposed on innate chaos. It is the way of dividing up moments, perceiving them and distinguishing between them, placing them in a hierarchy, moving from one to another, uniting them.

In socio-individual man, a living and organizing reason tends to separate out what in animal life was mixed up (let us say, for example, rest and struggle) and also to connect what was separated (let us say, grace and power). This reason *has an aim*. Its work meets many obstacles, arising both from immediate, spontaneous life that suddenly reasserts its demands, and from the social distribution of goods and objects, which are not subjected to the order that this reason attempts to impose.

From living reason at work in civilization, we will say here that it is inclined to constitute 'moments'. We will not use the ambiguous terms 'domains' or 'regions' because we are not talking about a theory of knowledge [*connaissance*] or an ontology (or a critique of ontology), but about the study of a reality that first presents itself at a *sociological* level, at which the individual is not separate from the social.

Let us consider the *moment of play*. The highest civilizations, as they become more refined, tend to create forms of play which are specifically nothing but play. Earlier, in the childhood of societies as in that of individuals and in the animal kingdom, it is difficult to distinguish play from action, work, or fighting [*lutte*]; it is mixed up with them; the child plays while working or works while playing; ethnographers study societies in which play is a prelude to fighting, or in which dance combines movements of love and war with play, etc. In advanced civilizations, play constitutes a moment. It is not isolated. Figures of war or love are integrated, but are subject to the rules governing the particular game. Thus, chess represents a pitched battle between royal armies, but the configurations are rigorously defined on the field of play. So, card games include configurations of love, but subject to rules of necessity and chance. These particular games do not come into being suddenly, produced by an abstract will to play. The abstract will to play creates only games without depth or reality: trivial social games. True games derive from magical and cosmic objects. These objects changed their positions as civilization developed, and became subordinate to play as such, while retaining something of the role they originally played in the totality. The movement of magical objects towards games obviously involves radical transformations, such as a very specific kind of formalization: the 'rules of the game'. The game has its specific categories: the rule, the partner, the stake, the risk and the wager, luck, skill, strategy. The sphere of these categories, the borderlines of play, are not fixed. There is no guard to give the order, 'Play stops here, the serious starts here.' The borderlines of moments depend on the moments and on men. Anything can be played at and become a game. Love can be played at and be presented as a game (but then it is not, is no longer or has not yet become love). The actor plays, the playwright is played (but the actor has a profession; neither art nor theatre is described as a game). Social life can be feigned, mimicked – played; but then frivolity wins out over real interests, those which make social life interesting. Game-playing, with categories of its own, reveals one modality of presence. My partner shows himself to me playing, as a player; and while I may be able to discover in the course of the game the qualities or faults that I see in him in other circumstances, he may appear very different then from the way he does at other times. Finally, because it has its own categories, a game presents a world. I may enter into it to the point of allowing myself to be caught in it. Because a game *is* a moment, it sets a trap. I become a player. It presents something: an abyss, a potential vertigo. There is an absolute in the moment of the game; and this absolute, like every reality or moment taken to the absolute, represents a specific form of alienation.

This substantiality without substance (in the ontological sense) which is conveyed by the existence of an absolute at the heart of the relative, is expressed as all substantiality by a tautology at one and the same time meaningful and empty: 'the game is the game'. This proposition, in appearance identical but empty as logical identity, is categorically not reducible to a pleonasm. In its first part, the game is presented as a specific activity; in the second part, it is a game, all the categories of this specific activity are condensed, which then have to be clarified; in this way identity opens out indefinitely into a non-identity that says what play is: what games are. Play thus has to do with logic, formalism and formalization, and yet it is anything but form and formalism. It is much more about abyss and vertigo, mesmerism, infernal pleasure: alienation. Elementary activity, arising from the murky depths of nature, has taken this transparent form in order to rediscover its murky depths.

The problem of the *moment of rest* has recently been posed, and in a curious way, using a wide and obscure vocabulary. We talk about 'relaxation' and 'unwinding', conflating ideology, myth and need. Techniques for resting have existed for as long as civilization has existed, but are rather poorly defined and utilised. Only now do we realise that a science of rest, organizing the objective and subjective conditions of this 'moment', has to be created. Resting is not easy for human beings, whose 'essence' is activity. It is not enough to lie down in order to relax, to close one's eyes and block one's ears to achieve relief or peace. The absence of movement is not in itself methodical relaxation, because it leaves most of the muscles of the body with residual tensions and poorly proportioned. In short, our civilization tries to create the moment of rest consciously and rationally. It institutes it through the use of various elements, some material, some not: bodily techniques, places in which to rest, soothing sounds, etc. The moment of rest as we confusedly try to create it in the 'modern world' cannot be reduced to relaxation. *Re-creation* in and through leisure takes many forms, which are sociological in nature and studied by the sociologist.

About the *moment of justice*, I have already said almost everything I have to say. Justice and judgement are not formed in nature. This moment exists only in civilized man. To the extent that for a long period of time, ontological thought projected it into the absolute being: God, the supreme Judge. All of life has to do with justice and judgement; however, judgement is no more than a moment. For a long time it was extrapolated into eternity, in the form of the supreme and final judgement. This colossal image, which enlarged the figure of the Judge to the scale of the universe, is becoming blurred. (One day I should like to write a novel in which to bring this magnificent image back to life. It would be called 'The Last Judgement'. One day, some day, at a given hour or minute, the last judgement begins; but the people do not know that; they have not heard the angels' trumpet. But slowly, slowly, they begin to see their suppressed memories again; actions and events that they had forgotten return with a sour taste to their lips and their consciousness; they begin to show through, one in place of another, beneath their words, beneath their pretences and their masks; they reclaim their past, while their shameful secrets are revealed, their slips becoming more frequent, then their confessions. Slowly, slowly. The Last Judgement has all the time in the world. When the Judge arrives, men will already have judged one another, in their everyday lives: husbands and wives, children, parents and friends, naked, already damned or already saved. The great Judge has only to carry out the supreme sentence. I should like the novel to take place in the household of a distinguished, right-thinking person, and why shouldn't he be a politician of the MRP[1] sort? Let's end the digression here.) There is no longer a supreme Judge, and that's why our consciences are obsessed by the themes of Judge, Trial and guilt. The moment of justice is also defined by a form, a procedure: summons, court appearance, testimony and cross-examination, indictments, pleas, deliberation, application of the law, sentence and the execution of the sentence. This or that partial moment may be missing, or their order may be reversed – it doesn't much matter. This form is more or less the same in the individual as in the social consciousness. And [for] me, as around me, the ceremonial of justice unwinds with the same gravity and the same absurdity, internal or external. Justice has its machinery and its Time. In both cases, for want of an absolute Judge, the Judge is always both judge and party to the case. Justice is not of this world, and there is no other world. Justice is a modality (and no more than a modality) of presence. It succeeds neither in totally justifying itself, nor in imposing itself, nor in fully legitimizing the sentence, nor in fully ensuring its execution, except when it is unjust. Justice is an absolute, around which we become dizzy. Like every absolute, this one makes demands and alienates. There is an absolute of justice, just as ungraspable as others, as compelling, as urgent; however, as a moment, justice is necessary. I should like to show here how Brecht drew an important dramatic form from the moment of justice, ceremonial becoming spectacle and subordinating to itself the elements of this spectacle: the dramatic moment corresponding with the court appearance, dialogue with testimony and cross-examination, denouement defined by the sentence and the central character with the Judge.[2] The absence of the Judge, and the end of the great image of the Last Judgement have led to a major dramatic form. It is a reflection of the despair that no longer believes in the Judge and recreates him in fictional form. Social life may offer a sketch of its basic elements and broad outlines, but a thinker is still needed to grasp them and formulate them within a specific set of circumstances.

There is the *moment of poetry*, resting solidly on the form of language. An object, a being, a fugitive impression, thus receives the privilege of an unbearable, unbelievable, inexplicable burden of presence. A smile or a tear, a house or a tree become a whole world. They really are, for the moment that lasts, and which fixing themselves in words will recur and be repeated almost indefinitely in the future. In this way a smile or a cloud become eternal. In this way the poet evokes a specific feeling, which can only be expressed by a tautology, 'poetry is poetry [*la poésie, c'est la poésie*]', this parallelism, with its rich content, being capable of infinite explication. It defines the poetic moment, and its manner of proceeding: melody and sense, the excessive emotional burden of the object, signifying the poet's whole sensibility. Hence the misunderstanding between lyric poetry and the sense of the serious, so clearly seen in the recent Pasternak affair.[3] For a slightly old-fashioned romantic like him, the fall of a leaf is as important as the fall of a State. It was Amiel, I think, who said that in connection with German romantic poetry.[4] We can imagine such a poet writing a very beautiful, very pure poem on the fall of a leaf, declaring that it is of crucial importance to him, more important than a world war or a revolution. The moment of poetry is essential to the poet and the person who listens to him. If the poet wished to sing of his love, and the smile or the kiss of his beloved, without thereby revealing in it a whole world, he would not write a good love poem. 'But it's not real! It's not true! It's a joke! The fall of a leaf is of no importance! There are millions, billions of women; there's nothing special about this one's smile or her kiss.' Quite so! Quite so! On second thoughts, the Soviets should be forgiven for many things. In this 'modern' world they represent an enormous mass of seriousness not deprived of weightiness. That's the way it is. You have to take people as they are. You can explain, but explanation is not important here. For the serious, weighty mind, instants and moments are of equal merit; they're closely examined for their usefulness, using political criteria. Boredom obviously leads to pedantry. When serious-mindedness takes the poet utterly seriously and exclaims, 'No, look, you're being frivolous, socialism forbids us attaching so much importance to a kiss, or trying to move people's hearts with the fall of a leaf ...' , and when this serious-mindedness contemplates the abuse of power, then the situation becomes delicate. We then have to restore the rights of the moment of poetry and the powers of lightness as a moment. The poet does not lie; he does not deceive. He reveals a presence, transferring to it the power that comes from a totality that surpasses it and surpasses himself: language. He uses magic spells. But do we still burn witches and wizards in the twentieth century?

What therefore, would moments be? They are limited in number, although the list cannot be declared closed: play, love, work, rest, struggle, knowledge, poetry ... If the number proved unlimited, they would no longer be moments. However, we cannot stop enumerating them, since it is always possible to discover or to constitute a 'moment', in principle, at least, and since there are perhaps 'moments' in individual life. Theory ought, if it is to be consistent, to declare a criterion. What is a 'moment'? What is not? It is not obliged to undertake the task of making an exhaustive list. In order for it to present a coherence that would make it acceptable, it is better to indicate and emphasize a few general characteristics of these 'moments'.

First of all, a moment defines a form and is defined by a form. Wherever the word 'moment' is used in a more or less precise sense, it refers to a certain constancy over time, an element common to a number of instants, events, situations and dialectical movements (as in 'historical moment', 'negative moment' or 'moment of reflection'). It thus tends to refer to a structural element that thought must not separate from the conjunctural without precaution. The word clearly designates a *form*, but this form is specific to each case. What is the form of play? The whole set of rules and conventions (categories of the game). What is the form of justice? An external or internal ritual, a ceremonial that governs the sequence of events, the bond, the summoning or indictment of defendants and witnesses, their appearance in court, etc. What is the form of love? A code of etiquette that prescribes the manner and style, the progression from courtship (declaration, avowal) to acts of possession and voluptuous pleasures. This etiquette excludes brutality and in principle includes shared pleasure as the goal of love. With necessary strictness, it sets – allowing for eventualities and the unexpected – the role of the kiss, of conversation, of boldness, respect, discretion, modesty, immodesty, abandon, renewal, etc.

While the word 'form', behind its false precision, is one of the most confused in our vocabulary, we may say (in the hope that we are making a statement that makes some sense at least), that every civilization is a *creator of forms*. In this it differs from *society* (which consists of an economic structure, a mode of production, property relations, etc.) and *culture* (which consists of forms of knowledge, of matter learned and facts retained, and of accepted works). It is essential that we connect these three terms without confusing them, and clearly distinguish between them without separating them. Civilization creates forms whose historical developments would be worth following. Thus we have formality in speech and ritual in gesture, courtesy and politeness, as modes of contact and communication. The long, winding road from archaic societies to civilizations (or civilization in general) allows natural gestures to be stylized and organized into a set of significant gestures. Social groups take as their starting point magical words and actions, designed to protect a moment, to disarm enmities and to place this moment under the sign of harmony or poetry (formulas that thus become rituals of everyday social life: greeting, blessing, shaking hands). This means that the theory of civilization does not cover the whole of reality (praxis). It does not encroach on either the study of society (from economy to ideology) or the study of culture, even though it must take them into account and cannot be separated from them.

The relationship between such forms with content differs from the relationship between content and form in knowledge or productive praxis. The form of civilization allows the introduction of widely differing material elements; it governs their order and succession, not their materiality. Thus, the summons dictates that certain characters will come before the court, or where the tribunal is concerned, a consciousness of events, impressions, ideas, decisions, remote or immediate feelings. The form, independent of the materiality of the content, does not impose itself on it or distort it; it allows it a degree of freedom, while at the same time assigning it a role and a place within the whole. The material elements of which these forms preside over their making and valorization; can they also be taken from the totality of praxis? Praxis taken as a whole comes under justice, it falls within the sphere of judgement, although justice and judgement represent no more than a moment. An individual's entire life may be affected by his love, and his love may become coextensive with his life, even though love is only a modality of presence. The ritual and ceremonial elaborated and stylized within a given civilization (and by specific social groups, peoples and classes, within an historical context) leave nothing out of their stylization – neither everyday objects, nor gestures, nor works of art, despite the fact that the ritual in question was created in daily life and in direct, everyday relationships. The unrigorous forms described here are not completely stable; they oscillate between the extremes of seriousness and frivolity, conventional artificiality and almost spontaneous nature. Despite these oscillations, they continue to have a specific existence, and are confirmed through circumstantial elements.

Each moment, which is a partial totality, reflects or refracts a totality (global praxis), including the dialectical relationships of society with itself, and the relations of social man with nature (in and around him). Each moment perceives the others and is distinguished from them by the modality of apperception.

From such a viewpoint, a rigid boundary between nature and society (or nature and culture) is no longer conceivable. The germs that develop into 'moments' exist in the deepest parts of nature, animate or inanimate. Nevertheless, they lie shrouded, buried, at one and the same time mingled together and separated. The forms of civilization take their elements from nature, from natural instincts and needs. They insert the natural into the structures of the civilized consciousness. Thus, civilization 'reflects' nature, material or living; but the relationship involved is radically different from a passive reflection. It extracts natural elements from nature in order to profoundly metamorphose them by inserting them into forms: into a human order. 'Instincts' can be recognized in it, but sometimes transposed in such a way that their vital animal reality hardly survives in their human form. The process of formation and formalization – in the sense indicated above – involves the distance created by the power of society over nature (man's power over nature). Civilization, in recovering the natural, making up the distance, closing the loop and recreating the totality, is thus still determined by a distancing of the human and of the natural. There is no barrier, but a space and a time in which forms or 'moments' are created. Not without conflicts between the natural and the 'created', between which there is no separation. This relationship between nature and society is without an ontology. Being is reflected in social man – in the totality – and not in a privileged act of reflection. Life reflects life, and not pure thought.

These moments thus first appear as *sociological* realities. Their categories also are categories pertaining to sociology. So the categories of play and games can only be arrived at sociologically. Only sociology is capable of studying the social distribution of games, the groups that play such and such a game, etc. The same goes for love, or rest, or knowing. In those areas there is a sociology of forms, still poorly developed. Could we call it 'structural sociology'? The term seems shocking. Sociology studies the formation of 'moments'; rather than moments, it deals with the groups who create them. 'Moments' and the theory of moments are on another level, that of philosophy. There is therefore something imprecise and improper about the phrase 'structural sociology'.

The theory of moments excludes the idea of a boundary between nature and society (or nature and culture); it also includes the idea of a reciprocal immanence between the sociological and the individual. There is no separation between them. The moments that an individual person can experience are developed (formed or formalized) by the whole of the society of which he is a member, or by some social group that spreads its collective creation (such as ritual, or the form of feelings, etc.) throughout society. These realities pertaining to sociology constitute 'moments' in as far as nature and the natural must also form part of the structures of social consciousness. This mutual immanence does not lead to confusion between the psychological and the collective. They are not 'the same thing', all the more so since it is not a question of 'things'. Individual consciousness opens onto 'moments' that are also part of social consciousness. Conflicts are always possible, as individual consciousness may reject the form that has been developed socially and historically. It may aspire to other forms. It chooses between propositions that reach it from outside. It alters them, and each one selects differently from the 'others' the material elements that become part of forms. It also alters – adapts, amends – their forms. The unity of the individual and the social is manifested in these very conflicts. This dialectical unity can only tend towards an overcoming. From this viewpoint, civilization is conceived of as what arises from conflicts between the individual and the social in their dialectical unity, and it tries to resolve the conflict on the basis of the material and formal elements that constitute the given problem.

Moments, which are social relationships and forms of individualized consciousness, are also forms of communication. The modalities of the presence constituted by them 'present' or 'presentify' in a single unity nature, others and oneself. The form in which I present myself to the other is also that in which the other presents himself to me. So, in a game, each partner presents himself to the other as playing. As the act does not differ from its communication, its communicability is complete. The fact that my partner does not know my game is part of the game and does not constitute an impenetrable reality, falling outside communication in and through the form.

Such a conception goes beyond pluralism as well as totalitarianism. Distinguishing between a multiplicity of moments, theory belongs to a form of pluralism; all the more so in that it claims to be neither exhaustive nor closed. It takes into account a variety of different modes of presence and activity; but each modality of presence is itself determined as a partial totality, open to the totality and a 'perspective' on it, immanent in this totality. The idea of the natural and social whole, or rather, this whole as such, concretely considered, manifests itself and is understood in a number of different attributes and modes: games and play, love, knowledge, justice, rest, etc. None of these modes is metaphysically privileged. By going beyond 'ontologism', we go beyond the antinomies that derive from it and in particular, those that separated the whole from the parts by setting up the multiple in opposition to the total, or conversely. The theory of moments thus repeats with a new meaning the theory of the 'total man'.

Need we stop here to show that theory attempts to overcome the opposition between the circumstantial and the structural, while leaving a place for each of these aspects of becoming? It is more interesting to show how it overcomes (or aims to overcome) the opposition between ontology and axiology. It excludes ontology, but conceives of 'being' as reflected by the human totality or the total man. It excludes the antimony between observing (or discovering) and creating or establishing. The moment I am going to live, I must recreate it in order to live it; I discover it, but as form, in such a way that, in order to make this form my own, I have to reinvent it by reinventing the arrangement of its elements. It is 'valid' for me; I receive it, but not as something imposed; I 'pose' it for myself, and at the same time I expend my activity in it. So, when I play, I accept the rules of the game and make myself a player, to the full extent. I recreate, reinvent the game through the way I play it, and in a new way on each occasion. Discovery and observation, fact and value, frequency and prescriptiveness thus cease to be mutually exclusive.

The 'moment' thus conceived of has its memory and specific time. Repetition is an important aspect of this 'temporality'. The repetition of moments forces us to refine the concept of repetition. It frees itself from psychology or metaphysics. It is no longer repetition of an 'ontic' or ontological nature; nor it is any more a repetition copied to the letter from the phenomena of memory, pushed as far as they will go. The re-presentation of a form, rediscovered and reinvented on each occasion, exceeds previous conceptions of repetition. And furthermore, it includes them; because it also involves the return and reintegration at a high level – individual and social – of elements of the past and the surpassed. In a general sense, the concept of repetition has to be re-examined and refined in confrontation with the theory of forms. Whether psychological or metaphysical, this concept was too close to materiality. Repetition of a form differs from material repetition; what's more, material stability, equilibrium and consistency (when observed) should not be confused with formal repetition. Which at this point introduces the project of a general theory of forms, that would finally make a clear distinction between the different uses of this term and the specificities of form.

As for alienation, its concept has a place in the theory of moments. Each moment, a modality of presence, offers an absolute for thinking and living. The criterion *reductio ad absurdum* [*le critère par l'absurde*] for the 'moment' could even be determined in this way. The moment can be raised to the status of an absolute, or, rather: A MOMENT IS WHAT IS SET UP AS AN ABSOLUTE. There is no moment except in so far as it embraces and aims to constitute an absolute. It is possible for every moment to become hypertrophied, or hypostatized. There is an absolute of play. This absolute alienates and defines a specific alienation. To play is a normal or normalizing activity; the *player* is an alienated person [*un aliéné*].[5] In any case, there is no clear separation within the moment. The alienated person locks himself in the moment; he makes himself its prisoner; by pushing it to its highest point, he becomes lost in it; his consciousness and his being lose their way in it. There is no demarcation separating love from the madness of love. And yet, although there is no border between them, there is a fundamental difference between moment and alienation. The form of communication becomes a form of isolation and incommunicability. The modality of presence is transformed into a modality of absence. The mode of being or the attribute of existence is transformed into annihilation [*néantisation*]. Action changes into passion, all the more indistinct the 'purer' and nearer to the absolute it is. The absolute is thus defined as a constant temptation, within each moment.

The possibility of this temptation of the absolute emerges as soon as the 'temporary' structure is created. If it wished to avoid it, active liberty would settle at the level of everyday life, which offers first of all a mixing of moments: their indispensable, rich (natural and social) material elements and even some formal elements, stylized but still lacking their most delicate structure. Attempts at 'structuration' appear and develop at the everyday level. And yet something further is needed: regulation and control. The everyday is necessary but not sufficient. In it, virtual moments are both mixed together and separated. It re-presents on its own level certain characteristics of natural life. An intervention has to be made in order to add to it an aspect or dimension that can be defined in various ways: style, order, liberty, civilization, but also, perhaps, *philosophy*? This intervention could well be represented, on the level of everyday life, by a better distribution of its elements and instants into 'moments', in such a way as to intensify the vital performance of the everyday, its capacity for communication, for information, and also, and especially, for enjoyment, by defining new modes of enjoyment in natural and social life. The theory of moments is thus not situated outside the everyday, but can be seen as articulated with it by uniting with critique in order to introduce into it what is lacking to its richness. It can thus be seen as tending to overcome at the heart of the everyday, in a new form of particular pleasure united with the whole, the old oppositions of lightness and heaviness, the serious and the lack of seriousness.

While the 'absolutization' of the separated moment is alienating, mixing and ambiguity also play an alienating role. Theory indicates a direction and a form of (individual) liberty. From the point of view that concerns us here, it is formed in constant struggle against the alienation that lies in wait for it. If absolute choice leads to mutilation, and thus alienation, to not choose, to hesitate indefinitely, to remain in a state of formless chaos, is also to risk the alienation of liberty. Liberty cannot make itself effective if it presents itself as arbitrary. It has to use the means and mediations offered to it by everydayness. It is formed by forming 'moments', by taking from here and there the material elements on which form is able to confer a higher order. It extricates itself from ambiguity and admixture, without, however, entering completely into a moment; it reserves for itself possibilities, choices and options, disengagement and commitment. The theory of moments thus includes a certain notion of liberty: a form of liberty that does not exclude other forms on other levels.

This is the time to repeat that the 'theory of moments' neither claims to be nor presents itself as exhaustive. As a perspective on the totality, it is located on a particular level: the theory of civilization, the theory of forms. It takes elements from other levels, other theories; far from contesting them, it allows them to express their specificities. Thus, it does not encroach on the study of the economic-social formation (the analysis of society considered as a mode of production, with its ideological repercussions) or of culture (knowledge as social fact). In particular, considerations about alienation take nothing away from the theory of fetishism and economic reification. Considerations about liberty in no way eliminate other aspects of liberty. The theory of moments thus respects the sciences of human reality. Nevertheless, it is more closely related to sociology than to political economy, for example.

Is it then to be considered a philosophy? A philosophy of presence? Or the outline of a new type of philosophy?

Time and History

(from *La Fin de l'histoire* (Paris: Éditions de Minuit, 1970), pp. 190–1, 195–6, 200–2, 205–6, 211–13, 215–16, 225–9; 2ᵉ édn (Paris: Anthropos, 2001), pp. 162–3, 167–8, 172–4, 176–7, 182–3, 185–6, 193–7)

16. THE CONCEPT OF TIME

We explain the concept of time by saying it has nothing in common with 'lived' time, that it is mentally constructed, that it differs from the 'lived' as much as a real dog differs from the concept 'dog' (which doesn't bark). This thesis calls for a number of reservations:

a) It leads to the restoration of speculative philosophy and even of metaphysics. Removing all reference to praxis, it justifies abstract constructions, in the non-scientific meaning of the word. If thought does not even have the opportunity to challenge its models with some form of practice, who is going to check it? Theory turns in on itself and justifies a strategic withdrawal on the part of the action whose failures it disguises. The old philosophical concept of 'pure' knowledge is re-formed. One eliminates. Marxism is sold off. The mental is separated from the social. A philosophically schizoid state comes on the scene again.

b) In fact, in traditional metaphysics, we find the (well-known) hypothesis that intelligible space has nothing in common with real space. Intelligible space is not extensive. Conceptual time will quickly become atemporal, if it is not so to start with. Because the concept 'dog' does not bark, we forget that a concept (in comprehensiveness and in extension) indicates the type and specific differences (how the dog differs from other animals, how different breeds of dog differ from one another). Which brings us back to practice.

c) In this metaphysical hypothesis, history is eliminated. Just like that. Knowledge of so-called historical time is said to have nothing in common with 'lived' time. Atemporal knowledge of time is said to consist only of dogmatic speculation, something that holds some surprises.

d) The concept of time, if it is not in time (lived, subjected, blind), consists nonetheless of a coherent discourse on time. It may not be able to pass for a 'reflection' of time, but it is no less truth of time. As a result, while it exists as a theoretical concept and can be shown, it gathers together all the characteristics of becoming, which elude those (conscious and active 'subjects') that exist in time. For example: continuity and/or discontinuity, rhythms and measures, predictability and/or unpredictability, spontaneity and/or reflection, etc. Each of these traits corresponds with a blind lived experience [*un vécu aveugle*]. Totality eludes the lived, because the lived never reaches it. It should be noted that 'lived' time is not only mental (subjective) time. It is also social time, biological time, physical and cosmic time, cyclic or linear time. Already plural (differential).

[…]

20. ON THE EVENT

In rational conceptions of historical becoming (that is to say, in Marxism in particular) what does the event represent? A privileged instant, that of a crisis. When there was a revolutionary event, that decisive moment enabled the leap forward, the hour of birth through (more or less brutal) violence. In all cases and all situations, the event was conceived of as an end result. Various causes and arguments converged in it, explaining it fully. The event was thus defined as an expression: of a relationship of forces, a conflictual tension that had come to a head, an explosive situation that had reached maturity. The event was scarcely at all seen as arising from an already existing virtuality, from a possibility striving for realization. For example, in the historical study of the Paris Commune, the category of the possible never came up; the virtualities of social practice (of French society) appeared by way of the effervescence of the City and the urban proletariat. And now, as for the event in the real, we did not realize that we were emptying it of its meaning: the presence of the possible (therefore a temporary impossibility).

In this rationalist conception, there is nothing fortuitous about the event, unless it is its breaking out at this or that instant. It incarnates historical necessity, oriented towards a distant goal that is visible neither in the causes nor in the arguments and motivations for the event. Thus the action of the proletariat tends towards economic growth, towards the destruction of obstacles to the rapid increase of productive forces; but it does not know that and acts for liberty, for peace, against oppression. The imperatives of history end up in the event and explain it, but for the historian, not the actor.

During the simultaneous crisis of historical thought and historical reality, the event frequently appears to be the outcome of chance and circumstances. We expect it to evaporate and disappear without a trace. However, if it is historical, it will leave traces. And we're going to become attached to this henceforth privileged phenomenon: the trace. And we shall try to understand the so-called historical event in terms of a series of things, revealed by traces.

That said: May 1968. The event overthrew the structures and even more, the superstructures of existing society, not just the University but 'values' and value systems: information, institutions dealing with health, the law, the judiciary, town planning [*l'urbanisme*], the arts, etc. It may come about that this society recreates its superstructures via the institutional route, but it may also be the case that it never succeeds in regaining its 'values' and lives (or survives) on long-questioned 'values'. Whatever may happen, these products or *oeuvres* of history have been severely shaken by an event whose historical character is thus defined. Is this a trace?

That character is ambiguous, that is, rich in meanings, complex. At the same time, students and their allies revealed the maladapted, out-dated, features of French society – and they have glimpsed, through radical ('leftist') critique, other ways of living, those of urban society transforming everyday life. They tried to free themselves from the past, but in the name of a certain historical consciousness still alive in them, in consciousness and culture (the Paris Commune). An outcome of the history that masks it? That denies it? But is it a trace?

[...]

25. ON WORLDWIDE HISTORY ('WELTGESCHICHTE')[1]

We should not forget that worldwide history is also the making-worldly [*mondialisation*] of history. Might not this metamorphosis have a deeper meaning than the one we generally attribute to it by seeing it as a continuity?

Should it not be seen as having (at least) two phases:

Phase I: Forces in 'unconscious' convergence (industrialization, technology, knowledge, neo-capitalism, sometimes revolutions) push towards *homogenization*. Among these homogenizing forces, which are destructive of natural particularities and of nature as a whole, are accumulation (of knowledges, technologies, forms of wealth), an increasingly exclusive preoccupation with growth (economism), the primacy of technology and its assertion as a model, and proclaimed (systematic) philosophy and historicity.

Phase II: There are forms of resistance to the process of homogenization, residues, irreducible originalities. A higher level of knowledge and developed forms of consciousness come into being in the course of phase I; they struggle in their own – revolutionary – way to manifest themselves, moving towards forms of divergence and *differences*. As homogenization appears, differences and awareness of differences emerge simultaneously. Knowledge accompanies this process, which is at the same time both double and single. It marks out the road of spontaneity, and confirms it.

Phase I is linked with the process of industrialization. Phase II (it is also the theoretical hypothesis) would be linked with the process of urbanization (at first subordinate to industrialization, then coming into the foreground and tending to form urban society).

If the hypothesis is proved correct, there is now an intense, though unconscious, struggle between the forces of homogenization and the forces of differentiation.

Phase I is historical, even today. Phase II, although originating in history, would be trans-historical. History, present but in the process of being overcome, is conceived and perceived as a totality, by the very fact of this overcoming. It is there, an enormous mass of causes and reasons, which brings us to where we are but soon abandons us so that we can go further. Elsewhere.

26. THE PERIOD OF TRANSITION AND THE EXIT FROM HISTORY

Marx's political legacy, the *Critique of the Gotha Programme*, puts forward this concept and defines certain features of the period of transition (from capitalism to communism).[2] Since then, theoreticians have never stopped thinking about this period, or explaining and enriching the concept.

It would seem paradoxical that structuralism, which leaps over transitions, accentuates breaks and discontinuities and tends to conceive of modes of production as coherent wholes (to the extent that the passage from one mode of production to another becomes all the more intelligible in that it signifies the disappearance of a type of intelligibility) – it would seem paradoxical but not inconceivable that this period, in which immobilism is fetishized, brings about a deepening of the concept of transition.

Why not add another transitional feature to those offered by Marx? *The transitional period – is the end of history.* Let's give this proposition a thought. Are we talking about abolishing history? About declaring history as knowledge finished and writing off historical thought and historical reflection? Absolutely not. No more than of abolishing philosophy, either. The point is a different idea altogether. The end of history is not its abolition by 'epistemological' decree.

We can no longer avoid Nietzschean hypotheses. Taking the drama out of the situation, Marx said something like: 'Look, people will no longer need this opium, religion; the world will have other savours; this point of honour, this soul of a soulless world, and this illusory encyclopaedic knowledge will lose their meanings ...' Now, it is in the midst of tragedy, genocide and huge massacres that religion and morality are coming to an end. And history. And, doubtless, the State. Is the economy the only explanation for the chaos of the modern world, its satisfactions and its discontents, the pursuit of security and massacres? No, definitely not. The generic man, in the anthropological sense, creates himself, fulfils himself, overcomes himself, declares Marx. Perhaps the human race is merely a failure, adds Nietzsche, thoughtfully. If it is man's task to overcome himself, is it not another 'being' he has to have in his sights? To what lands is this strange procession leading us? Is it a certainty that beyond all the obstacles there will be a Promised Land, the land of milk and honey, the Blessed Isles?[3] The end of history could be its violent destruction, its self-destruction. Tragedy retrieves its values. That's the least we can say.

[...]

29. THE OVERCOMING OF HISTORY

On this road, that of a differential form of thought (and, why not, a differential history, which could be substituted retrospectively for homogenizing history, which is taken to be the history of originalities and their change into differences, which would stop dismissing divergences and subjecting the formation of ideas to identical models and models of identity, which would no longer centre them on a thesis and a position of rationality), an enormous scholasticism shuts off the horizon. This complicated (but not complex) thinking comments endlessly on the preceding period: industrialization, military and totalitarian objectives, models, projections, ideologies. It sometimes believes it is opposing it, when in fact it is prolonging it. An already long list of impertinent oppositions gets longer still:
– rationalism versus reason,
– nationalism versus nations,[4] individualism versus the individual, structuralism versus structure, formalism versus form,
– functionalism versus function, urbanism versus the urban,
– scientism versus science, growth versus development, the original versus difference,
– verbalism versus communication, historicism versus becoming,
– etc.

[...]

34. APPROPRIATION

The Marxist notion of appropriation has been abandoned. For most of the time, those who took it into account identified it with de-alienation (the end of alienation). Which restricts the scope of the concept and its active (positive, as they say) content. Even the radical critique implied in the concept (the critique of property as non-appropriation, caricature, parody, prohibition of concrete appropriation) has become blurred. In fact, we are not dealing with a simple concept borrowed by Marx from Hegel, taken up in the course of the 'deconstruction' of Hegelianism in order to make critical use of it. This concept has many more requirements. It awaits, it calls for a complete theory, one intended to supplant other theories. The lack of such a theory, thus far, has a meaning, and is not without reason.

a) Mastery over natural processes, domination of physical nature and the search for the means, skills and techniques to be used to achieve them, set their mark on a long period of time. It begins with the origins of 'man' (that these origins are related to the invention of tools, the organization of labour, language, the incest taboo, is a subsidiary question). Accumulation (of wealth and resources, knowledges and technologies – in short, of capital) is organized during this historical period. This period, the era of industrialization, of history and the great historical struggles for conquest and domination over nature (the struggle against nature being accompanied by intense struggles between nations, peoples, classes and fractions of classes), this period is drawing to an end. It is ending in contempt hidden behind knowledge, in a form of madness whereby reason and unreason are the same: the sacrifice of a considerable part of the earth's resources in order to gain possession of one of the ghastliest of all the piles of pebbles rattling around in space.[5] Let's move on.

b) A new period, with its problematic, its thematic and its categories (concepts) is on the horizon: the period of appropriation. Psychoanalysis, a clumsy effort, but evidence of a change of direction, and sport, which is incomplete and specialized, tending to form a hierarchy parallel with or superimposed on others, herald the appropriation of desire, the appropriation of the body, of time and space, and of new possibilities.

Thesis: The period of appropriation, a post-historical period, cannot be thought except in terms of urban society. We are already entering into that society and that period. Signs and symptoms: urban guerrilla warfare, as well as huge gatherings of 'non-violent' youth, eager for contacts, encounters, love, eroticism, sexual enjoyment, joy and oblivion.

(If it proves that Heidegger glimpsed the importance of difference and appropriation, we will be able to say, using his model, that the urban follows technology on the path of being and its development. But one may object that these still philosophical propositions are not of great importance in throwing light on praxis ...).

[...]

36. THE MEANING OF HISTORY

The meaning of history, therefore, is to end: not to give way to metaphysics or religion: to immobilism or eternity. Its meaning is to overcome itself (by *Überwinden*[6] rather than by a sober, calm *Aufheben*[7]). How could there be historicity without overcoming? Hegel and Marx asserted it with every conceivable and probing argument. If history consists of overcomings, in other words, if it has a meaning, then may it not, must it not, itself be overcome? The meaning of history is to allow us to move from the discourse of history (Hegel) to discourse *on* history, which reveals it and goes further. The meaning of history was to unite meaning and truth to their dissociation. After which, meaning continues with the search for meaning, but it is no longer truth – the same, old truth – that seeks itself; and it is no longer history. The negation, for not having the 'pure' character assumed by Hegelian-Marxist negativity, for not having tragic and uncertain aspects, is no less dialectical. Dialectical movement does not lose its rights with the end of history. On the contrary: it recovers, discovers and extends them. In the end, we conceive of history, defined as such, according to the general theory of dialectical movement, which includes the historical as such.

The end of history reveals history and historicity; it makes them visible as they were, their features having become blurred since the historical moment at which history came to the foreground. At that moment, the sociohistorical process was profoundly creative, both innovative and totalizing, in praxis and in knowledge. The end of history takes back this double characteristic. It enables an overall look over the period that has passed, and on theory and practice during that period. This view over history is not limited to history as science or 'scientificity'. It covers the whole range of fragmented knowledges, and the implications and consequences of fragmentation. This analytical and synthesizing view is also capable of scanning the horizon.

It is an intellectual (and practical, in other words, political) attitude, separated by a vast distance from the one that rejects history because it is tainted by subjectivism. Another, no less considerable, distance, separates it from the vain effort to arrive at history again from the starting point of subjectivity, to renew it as a science and prolong its existence as reality. These attitudes and efforts are to be found everywhere, in more, or less, coherent forms. They can easily be recognized in the work of the most distinguished ideologues of our day.

[...]

SUMMARY AND CONCLUSIONS

Let us now cast our eyes back over the whole scene, whereas, to begin with, we were concentrating on the horizon. In keeping with our original announcement, our journey soon brought us to a central place, a dominant position from which we could study the whole landscape and chose the best route (not the shortest, or the most comfortable) to go forward. (These topographical figures are actually a little more than metaphors, as we already know.)

We originally set out to present a problematic and a set of themes that were highly centred. In fact, the end of history enables us to understand how some dominant influences – those of the Hegel–Marx–Nietzsche triad – oppose and reinforce one another. The mistake would now be to leave these works side by side, to study them in isolation – or to subject them to a preliminary systematization. Careful thought avoids these errors by identifying the problematic these three thinkers have in common. Each of them in his own way put forward the end of history.

But this central theme does not only occur in the study of the ideas that have marked a century and a half of European history (and non-history). The end of history also involves contemporary culture, the dimensions of consciousness (including the consciousness of the working-class and/or the absence of a consciousness itself).

The question of the end of history contained another question: the relationship between the State and history. From which we put forward three hypotheses:

1st hypothesis: The hypothesis of perpetuity. A parody of historicity continues. The State (and the series of States) is consolidated. Strategies and tactics (mixed up together, with three players or more) lead to changes in relations of force, without anything other than local conflicts taking place. Absolute politics rules the world. Note that this hypothesis must be examined and not that it be accepted; in fact, the rotting away of the State – of a specific state or States in general – may replace a rational, controlled withering away, such as Marx predicted.[8] But not without risks.

2nd hypothesis: That of catastrophe. It is not only historical discourse that continues, but history itself reaches its tragic dénouement. Degradation of the revolution and consolidation of the State do not prevent the eruption of barbarous, spontaneous forces. Whether the outcome be a world war or a limited war between (socialist or non-socialist) countries, strategic games leave the field of play; this is no longer history, but the self-destruction of history (planetary self-destruction and the death of the human race may follow in the wake of the abstract death of man, the death of God, and the theoretical death of historicity).

3rd hypothesis: This one, and this one alone, is positive. But also u-topian (with the addition that now more than ever there is no thought without u-topia, in other words, without an exploration of the possible and the impossible, i.e. the possible-impossible conceived of dialectically). This path assumes that the Cyclopean forces dominating the world impose neither their wills nor their representations. This positive hypothesis is formulated thus: there is a way out of history, putting it another way, an opening, an escape. The notion of a transitional phase or period, handed down by Marx and a valuable part of his political legacy, this notion may be deepened, enriched, and possibly realized in a form of practice.

On the one hand, and to a certain extent, history continues. It must be brought to a successful conclusion. How can we imagine a sudden end – other than as a catastrophe – of historical time? However, new things appear, which no longer have to do with historicity. The transitional period is conceived as an interaction of the historical and the trans-historical. In the course of this dramatic transition, history itself is imagined as a complete whole, in process of being overcome. It is no longer dominant, but in decline, but not without having supplied the conditions for its overcoming.

More specifically, two phases are intertwined:

A) The phase characterized by the accumulation of knowledges, technologies, resources and wealth, of capital (also in the 'socialist countries'). A phase also defined by mastery over nature and the substitution of mental and social space for the space of natural particularities. Hence the predominance of growth, technical expertise and a defined and limited rationality. This phase A is the historical period, which unleashes homogenizing forces on an ever larger and more destructive scale.

Class struggle begins in this phase. At first, it involves a duration that is homogenous or tends towards homogeneity, as well as unitary goals and methods (strategies). It thus tends towards this unity, using techniques of constraint: dogmatism or discipline. Later, it involves the inverse and the reversal of this process.

B) Gradually, even during this period, the accent shifts to what resists, to 'irreducible' residues, to homogenization. These are originally particularities, but are transformed in the course of and through their resistance. Humiliated or humble by origin, crushed and overwhelmed, particularities survive. Sometimes they fall into folklore; they are often confirmed and affirmed by resistance. They become practically theoretical, raising themselves to the level of difference.

We thus enter a new problematic: that of difference. The theme of difference is discovered and elaborated on all sides. It prompts us to pose the question in all its breadth, to conceive of categories that make it possible to strengthen forms of resistance and give them a meaning, even to define the new type of intelligibility (and rationality).

It is thus impossible to eliminate history.

Neither theoretically nor practically can it disappear from one day to the next. The tasks of history, if we can express ourselves that way, are not completed. Industrialization has still to be brought to a conclusion by putting an end to it and without seeing in it an unlimited future. The same goes for the class struggle. History extends as far as the transitional period, it is a constituent element in it. Whether we're talking about history as discourse or as action, as a search or as acquired culture, it persists; *but its end acquires a meaning.* It is not the meaning of history that is important and on which the question hangs, it is the meaning of its end. This end fills an epoch.

The Leninist distinction remains crucial. Right critique uses the deficiencies of historicity and the crisis of historical thinking to announce the death of history. Which leads to nihilism. Which prevents theoretical understanding and blocks the exit of history. Left critique, on the other hand, gives these deficiencies, and the crisis, meaning. It attempts to overcome the situation, first at the theoretical level, and in practice at the same time or later on. It shows the way.

The present phase would thus be that of conflict (intense but still, and more than ever, dialectical) between homogenizing and differentiating forces. Dialectical analysis is more than ever indispensable for a clear approach to the tangle of contradictions. Violence takes on a new meaning. Is it not likely to be that of affirmation, often premature, often naïve, attached or fixed onto particularities in their terminal phase, but 'positive' in a new, trans-historical sense of the word?

Hegel is right. A homogenizing force is dominant, the same everywhere, imposing the Same (philosophically speaking) everywhere, against the different (perceived and conceived meta-philosophically). The sovereign State rules, and its law crushes all forms of resistance.

Yes, but Hegel is wrong, and the neo-Hegelians are exploiting the situation. They disguise the depth of the conflicts, which Marx alone foresaw. In fact, Marx predicted and even determined the broad lines of the transition,[9] in particular, the shaking to its foundations of that colossus with feet of clay: state domination. Was this inevitable? Here we come upon the inevitable u-topia, which alone enables us to think and act. What a surprise: the enormous reality, the colossal weight of things is transformed into a strange unreality, when this dimension of transparent awareness comes into play!

But after all, Nietzsche has his position of eminence. It is he who inaugurated thinking on and pursuit of the different, who proclaimed the diversity of values and meanings, and who in consequence opens the way to affirmation within difference.

Trans-historical concepts related to differential conceptions of thought, action and affirmation are already manifesting themselves. Among these concepts, one is for the moment taking centre-stage: that of the possible-impossible. It is not a question of the trivial distinction between what may (be done, happen, etc.) and what may not (happen, come about, etc.). In a more profoundly dialectical way, the impossible arises and shows itself in the heart of the possible. And conversely, of course. There is no communication that does not include in its possibility the project of the impossible: to say everything. There is no love that does not presuppose absolute love. No knowledge that does not posit absolute knowledge, the inconceivable unlimited and infinite.

Exploration of the possible-impossible has another name: u-topia. There is no thought, today more than ever, without this exploration, and the discoverer does not turn away his gaze from obstacles, especially if he wishes to circumvent them. This consciousness of the possible-impossible replaces consciousness of the past. A cause of the double crisis, that of historical consciousness and that of historical practice, exploration of the possible-impossible brings back lucidity. It situates reflection and meditation on their proper territory once again. There is no place without an other place and the other place, without the elsewhere and the nowhere. No topia without u-topia. No topology nor typology without imaginary. No countryside or landscape without roads, without the search for a way out. No journey without a project (and vice versa). The Same cannot affirm itself without the Other; the Other (the different and the elsewhere) reveals itself through the Same, and attains itself by passing through the Identical. The struggle to differ starts but will not end with history.

The Style of the Commune

(from *La Proclamation de la commune: 26 mars 1871* (Paris: Gallimard, 1965), pp. 20–3)

The Paris Commune? It was for one thing an immense, epic festival [*fête*],[1] a festival that the people of Paris, essence and symbol of the French people and the people in general, gave both to itself and to the world. A spring festival in the Cité, a festival of the disinherited and the proletarians, a revolutionary festival and festival of the Revolution, a total festival, the greatest of modern times, which unfolded at first in magnificence and joy.

The historic day of the 18th March 1871 brings to an end the passivity and resignation that, without denting the official powers, had prevailed during the Empire, during the war and even during the siege of Paris.[2] These forces erupt with epic calm. The people of Paris break down the barriers, flood the streets; in its warm and fraternal mass, it envelops those who must fight against it, the soldiers of established power. It disarms them. The collective hero, the popular genius, rises up in his youth and native vigour. He has vanquished simply by the fact that he has appeared. Surprised by his victory, he metamorphoses it into splendour. He rejoices, he contemplates his awakening and transforms his power into beauty. He renews the vows made with consciousness, with the palaces and monuments of the city, with power which had so long evaded him. And it is truly a festival, a long festival, which goes on from the day of the 18th March to that of the 26th (the elections) and of the 28th March (the proclamation of the Commune) and beyond with magnificently ordered ceremonial and solemnity.

Later, or at the same time, the people take pleasure in their own festival and change it into a spectacle. It occasionally goes too far and makes mistakes, as the spectacle it gives to itself also diverts it from itself. Then, as in any real festival, pure drama appears and closes in. The popular festival apparently changes character. In truth, it continues; it gives way to pain. We know that Tragedy and Drama are bloody festivals, during which defeat, sacrifice and the death of the superhuman hero who has defied destiny are performed. Misfortune is changed into greatness and defeat becomes a lesson in power and hope in the purified heart of its despicable fears. Hercules, tamer of monsters, struggles to prevent the venomous tissue from enveloping his body. He flexes all his muscles. In vain. He then prepares the pyre. Then comes death and the triumph of destiny and misfortune, defeat and the final holocaust; but the funeral cortège has not lost the epic sense of the Festival. Those who have fought to the cry of *Liberty or Death* prefer death to capitulation and the certainty of servitude. They are still fighting, desperately, insanely with boundless courage; afterwards they light with their own hands the pyre on which they want to be consumed and disappear. The tragedy ends in a blaze and disaster worthy of itself.[3] Pursuing the titanic defiance to the end and final outcome, the people of Paris envisage the end of Paris and want to die with what is for them more than a theatre set and more than a setting: its city, its body.

And so the Festival becomes drama and tragedy, absolute tragedy, Promethean drama played without a trace of frivolity, tragedy where the protagonist, the chorus and the public are uniquely one. But, from the outset, the Festival contained the drama; the drama taking on its primordial meaning: a real and collective festival, a festival lived by the people and for the people, a colossal festival accompanied by the voluntary sacrifice of the principal actor in the course of his defeat, tragedy.

When we define the style of the Commune in this way, at one and the same time work [*oeuvre*] and act, all we do is go back to Liebknecht's expression on the '*horrible and epic tragedy of the Commune*'.[4] We will not for all that omit other aspects of the events; we will not forget either previous events or circumstances, or relations between men and groups and the ideas which entered into the action, or finally the requirements of the historical analysis and account. But we propose to show how Paris lived its revolutionary passion. We shall see why and how the scattered and divided city became a community of actions and how, during the Festival, the community became communion, on the then largest conceivable scale. And how the people acclaimed the symbols of disalienated and disalienating labour, the fall of oppressive power, the end of alienation. And how it acclaimed the world of work, that is to say, work as world and creator of worlds. And how, during this immense festival something rents asunder the opaque veils of customary social life, rises from the deep, cuts through the accumulated layers of the inert and the obscure, comes to light and opens up. What was it? A basic will to change the world and life as it is, and things as they are, a spontaneity conveying the highest thought, a total revolutionary project. A general and delirious 'all or nothing'. A vital and absolute wager on the possible and the impossible . . .

The Revolution as act was to coincide with the results of the Revolution. One would have leapt in a single leap from blind necessity into the joyous reign of Liberty, into a great festival without end. At the same time free labour was to be born having become a game, a great game with arms, with life and death.

'*Spiritual visions! Interpretations! Romantic visions! Literature, but not history!*' To anticipate these objections, in fact normal and natural, we can now introduce texts and documents.

The Rhythmanalytical Project

Henri Lefebvre and Catherine Régulier

(from *Communications*, 41 (1985), pp. 191–9)

RHYTHMS AND EVERYDAY LIFE

In a forthcoming publication we will show the relationship between everyday life and rhythms, that is, the way social time actually behaves.[1] The study of rhythms that we will attempt to make is an integral part of the study of everyday life. It expands some aspects of it. Everyday life is governed by abstract, quantitative time, the time of clocks and watches. This kind of time gradually gained dominion in the West after the invention of clocks, as they became part of social practice. This homogeneous and desacralized time emerged victorious as soon as it provided *a means of measuring working time*. From that historic moment, it became the time of the everyday, subordinating other aspects of daily life to the spatial organization of work: times for sleep and waking, times for meals and private life, relationships between adults and children, entertainment and leisure, relationships in the home. However, everyday life is shot through and cut across by the larger rhythms of life and the cosmos: days and nights, months and seasons, and more specifically still, biological rhythms. In everyday life, this results in constant interaction between these rhythms and the repetitive processes linked with homogeneous time.

We will ignore some aspects of this interaction, for example, traditional connections between social time and religious beliefs and prescriptions. We will concern ourselves here only with the rhythmic aspect of daily time. The study of everyday life has already brought out this banal and yet little-known difference between the cyclic and the linear, between rhythmic time and the time of abrupt repetitions. Such repetition is wearying, exhausting and tiresome, while the recurrence of a cycle seems like an event, or an advent. Its beginning, which is after all only a recommencement, always has the freshness of a discovery and invention. Dawn always has a magical charm, and hunger and thirst renew themselves as if by magic. The everyday

The Rhythmanalytical Project

is at once the location, the theatre and the issue at stake in a conflict between the great eternal rhythms and the processes imposed by the socio-economic organisation of production, consumption, circulation and habitat. The study of everyday life shows how and why social time is itself a social product. Like all products, like space, time is split and divided into use and use-value on the one hand, and exchange and exchange-value on the other. On the one hand it is sold and on the other it is lived.

Hence a series of hypotheses which serve as a starting point for rhythmanalysis.

First, everyday time is measured in two ways, or, rather, it is both measurement and measured. On the one hand, the basic, cyclic rhythms are preserved, and on the other, the quantified time of clocks and watches imposes monotonous repetitions. Cycles enliven repetition, by cutting across it. Could it not be this double measure that has enabled the everyday to establish itself in modern times, to become stable and, as it were, institutionalized?

Secondly, there is the dark and bitter struggle around time and the use of time. That struggle has the most surprising ramifications. So-called natural rhythms change for many reasons, technological or socio-economic, in a way that demands detailed research. For example, there is an increase in night-time activity, which disrupts circadian rhythms. As if daytime were not long enough to carry out repetitive tasks, social practice gradually eats into the hours of darkness. At the weekend, instead of the traditional 'seventh day' of rest and piety, we have 'Saturday night fever'.

Thirdly, quantified time is subject to a very widespread law of this society; it becomes both uniform and monotonous while at the same time dispersed and fragmented. Like space, it is divided into lots and parcels: journeys (themselves fragmented), various forms of work, entertainment, leisure. There isn't time to do everything, but every 'thing to do' has its time. These fragments have a hierarchy, but work remains to a large extent (despite its devaluation, resisted by practical re-evaluation in times of unemployment) the essence, the point to which we seek to refer everything else. Nevertheless, disturbances of rhythm proliferate as do so-called nervous problems. It is not incorrect to say that nerves and brain have their rhythms, just like the senses and mental activity.

From the rhythmanalytical perspective, we can describe 'day-times' and the employment of time according to social category, sex or age. It is worth noting that objects are consumers of time, they inscribe themselves in its use with their own demands. A washing machine uses up its fragment of time (running and maintenance), just as it occupies its fragment of space. Mealtimes spring from social convention, since they differ from country to country. But, if you eat at midday and at eight o'clock in the evening, you will eventually feel hungry at those times. It takes perhaps ten years to train the body to these rhythms, and it is not unusual for children to reject social rhythms. As far as mental concentration and its attendant activities (reading, writing, analytical thought) are concerned, they too have their own rhythms, created by habit, i.e. by a more or less amicable compromise between the repetitive, the cyclic and what happens. Forms of behaviour acquired from a particular division of time and from clearly defined rhythms still give the impression of spontaneity. Automatism or spontaneity? We ascribe to an internal need something that results from external constraints. Someone who wakes at six in the morning because his work has given him this rhythm may perhaps still be tired and in need of sleep. In the long or short term does this interaction between the repetitive and the rhythmic not result in dispossession of one's own body? This dispossession has been noted and emphasized many times, without our having grasped all its causes.

In everyday life, what is relative, in social relations, thus appears to each 'subject' to be necessary and absolute, essential and authentic. If we introduce a new element into everyday time, its structure totters and threatens to collapse, thus showing it was neither necessary nor authentic. Falling in love, becoming an insomniac or a bulimic puts a person into a different everyday world …

The rhythmic organization of daily time is in a sense what is most personal, most internal. And it is also what is most external (which corresponds with a famous dictum of Hegel's.) We're not talking about an illusion or an ideology, but a reality. The rhythms we have acquired are both internal and social. During one day in the modern world, everyone does roughly the same thing at roughly the same times, but each person is really doing it alone.

The 'cyclic' and the 'linear' are categories, i.e. notions or concepts. Each of those two words designates – denotes – a great diversity of facts and phenomena. Cyclic movements and processes, waveforms, vibrations, revolutions and rotations are innumerable, from the microscopic to the astronomical, molecules to galaxies: heartbeats and blinking or breathing, the alternation of days and nights, months and seasons, and so on. As for the 'linear', it designates any series of identical phenomena, separated by an interval of time: hammer blows, the fall of a drop of water, the noise produced by an engine, etc. Connotation does not disappear into denotation in the case of these terms. The cyclic is perceived rather favourably; it comes from the cosmos, the global, the natural. Everyone can picture the waves of the sea (a good image, full of meaning), or sound-waves, or circadian and monthly cycles. The linear, on the other hand, is pictured only as monotonous, wearying, even unbearable.

Relationships between the cyclic and the linear – interactions, interferences, domination of the one by the other or rebellion by the one against the other – are not simple; there is an antagonistic unity amongst them. They interpenetrate, but in constant conflict, sometimes as compromise, sometimes as disturbance. Nevertheless, there is between them an indissoluble

The Rhythmanalytical Project 193

unity; the clock's repetitive tick-tock measures the cycle of hours and days, and vice versa. In industry, where linear repetition tends to be predominant, the struggle is intense.

Given that the cyclic and the linear are categories of time and rhythm with general characteristics (including measurement, of the one by the other, which makes each of them a *measured measure*), are there no other categories? Other characteristic features of time and rhythm? Other forms of time?

The time that we shall provisionally call 'appropriated' has its own characteristics. Whether normal or exceptional, it is a time that forgets time, a time during which time no longer counts/is counted. It appears or occurs when an activity brings a kind of plenitude, whether that activity is banal (a job, a piece of work) refined (meditation, contemplation), spontaneous (play, in children but also in adults) or sophisticated. This activity is in harmony with itself and with the world. It has some of the features of self-creation and of a gift, rather than an obligation or an imposition from outside. It *is* in time; it *is* a time, but it does not reflect on it.

To put the question of rhythms clearly, let us return to everyday life, and the description of a day. The usage of time fragments it, parcels it out. A minute description of these parcels represents a certain kind of realism; it studies the activities connected with food, dress, cleaning, transport, etc. It cites the products used. Such a description will seem scientific; but, it bypasses the object itself, which is not the number of periods of time passed in this way, but the way they are linked in time, and thus their rhythm. The essential will get lost, to the advantage of the accidental, even (or especially) if the study of the fragments makes it possible to theorize some of the structures of the everyday.

WHAT IS RHYTHM?

Everyone thinks he knows what this word means. In fact, everyone perceives it in an empirical way that is very different from knowledge; rhythm is part of the 'lived', but that does not mean that it is part of the 'known'. There's a big gap between an observation and a definition, and an even bigger one between grasping a rhythm – the rhythm of a tune, of breathing, or the beating of the heart – and being able to conceive of the simultaneous intertwining of several rhythms, their unity in diversity. And yet each of us *is* this union of various phenomena, whose aspects are subordinated to action towards the outside world, oriented to the external, to the Other and to the World, to the point where they elude us. We are only conscious of most of our rhythms when we begin to suffer from some irregularity. It is in the organic, psychological and social unity of the 'perceiver', oriented towards the perceived, i.e. towards objects, surroundings and other people, that the rhythms composing this unity exist. An analysis is therefore necessary in order to distinguish between them and compare them. We're talking here about hunger and thirst, sleeping and waking, sexual and mental activity, etc.

For there to be rhythm, there has to be repetition in a movement, but not just any repetition. The monotonous, identical duplication of the same noise no more creates a rhythm than does some object moving along its trajectory, for example, a falling stone. Although our ear and doubtless also our brain, tend to introduce a rhythm into any repetition, even if it is completely linear. For there to be rhythm, the movement has to have strong and weak beats, which recur according to a rule or law – long and short beats, repeated in a recognizable way – pauses, silences, blanks, recommencements and intervals, all with regularity. Rhythm therefore has a differentiated time, a qualified duration. As well as repetitions, hiatuses and recommencements in that time. Thus it has a measure, but an *internal measure*, which is clearly distinguished from, though not separate from *external* measure, and time *t* (clock or metronome time) only exists as a homogeneous and quantitative paradigm. External measure can and must be superimposed on internal measure in a reciprocal action, but they cannot be conflated. They have neither the same beginning, nor the same end or purpose. This double measure is part of the definition of rhythm and its essence, irreducible to a simple formula, but on the contrary, involving complex (dialectical) relationships. Thus, only a non-mechanical movement can have rhythm; this means that everything purely mechanical belongs to the domain of the quantitative, abstractly detached from quality. However, this statement needs some qualification. For example, there is a close relationship between rhythms and the wave phenomena studied by mathematics and physics. Sounds, these elements of musical movement, with their properties and combinations, their place on the scale of sounds (that is, on the continuum from low to high, intensity and tone), their pitch and vibrational frequency – result from complex vibrations: wave movements that form part of chords and harmonies. We will return to this later, and explore more fully the relationship of musicality and rhythm. For the moment, it is enough to note that rhythm presupposes:

a) Clearly marked, strongly accented and thus contrasting temporal elements, like strong and weak beats.

b) An overall movement that takes with it all these elements (for example, a waltz rhythm, which may be fast or slow). By this double aspect, rhythm enters within a general construction of time, movement and becoming. And therefore within its philosophical problematic: repetition and becoming, relationship of Self and Other. It is worth noting at this point that since rhythm includes a measure, it implies memory of some kind. While mechanical repetition works by reproducing the instant which precedes it, rhythm preserves both the measure that initiates the process and its repetition in an altered form, thus with its multiplicity and plurality. And without repeating precisely the 'same', but subjecting it to alterity, even alteration, that is, difference.

To grasp rhythm and polyrhythm in a sensory, pre-conceptual but active way, we have only to look carefully at the surface of the sea. Waves come in succession, taking shape close to shore, cliff or embankment. These waves have a rhythm, which depends on the season, the water and the winds, but also on the sea that carries them and brings them ashore. Every sea has its rhythms, and the rhythm of the Mediterranean is not that of the oceans. But look closely at each wave. It is constantly changing. As it nears the shore, it takes the force of the backwash; it carries with it many smaller waves, right down to the minute shivering motions which it governs but which do not always go in its own direction. Waves and waveforms are defined by frequency, amplitude and the energy displaced. Watching waves, you can easily see what physicists call the superposition of small movements. Large, powerful waves crash one upon another, creating jets of spray; they clash loudly together. Little waves criss-cross, absorbing one another and merging rather than breaking. If there is a current or solid objects with a motion of their own, you may have a sense that this is a polyrhythmic field, and even glimpse the relationships between these complex processes and trajectories, between bodies and waveforms, and so on.

Now, we do not yet have a general theory of rhythms. Habitual ways of thinking, mentioned earlier, have long separated time from space, in spite of contemporary theories in physics that propose a connection between the two. So far, these theories have failed to offer a unifying concept that would also enable us to understand diversities (differences).

And now comes the rhythmanalytical hypothesis. Think about the body. Your body. It's made up of a bundle of rhythms. Why not say, a 'bouquet', or a 'garland'? Because these words connote an aesthetic arrangement, as if nature, like an artist, had intentionally organized and arranged the harmony and beauty of bodies. That's perhaps not wrong, but premature at this point. The living – polyrhythmic – body is made up of various rhythms, with each 'part', each organ or function having its own, in perpetual interaction, in a balance that is probably 'quasi-stable', always in jeopardy but usually restored, except when there is some sort of trouble. How? By a simple mechanism? By homeostasis, as in cybernetics? Or more subtly, for example, through a hierarchical arrangement of centres, with one higher centre that organizes relational activity? That is one of our questions. But the body's environment, social as well as cosmic, is also a bundle of rhythms ('bundles' in the sense in which we say, without being pejorative, that a complex chord, consisting of various notes and tones, is a 'bundle' of sounds). Now look around you at this meadow, this garden, these trees, these houses. They present themselves, offer themselves simultaneously to your vision. Now this simultaneity is only to a certain extent mere appearance, surface, spectacle. Go deeper. Don't be afraid to disturb this surface or set its limpidity in motion. Be like the wind that shakes these trees. Let your gaze be penetrating, be more than just reflecting. Let it transgress a little its limits. Then you'll notice at once that each plant, each tree has its rhythm. Several in fact: leaves, flowers, fruits or seeds. The flowers on this cherry tree come out at the same time as the leaves, which will last longer than the fruits, and in the autumn they will not all fall at the same time. From now on you will experience every being or creature, every body, animate or inanimate, 'symphonically' or 'polyrhythmically'. You will grasp it in its time-space, in its place and in the form it takes next [*son devenir proche*], and this is true of houses and buildings, of towns and landscapes.

Is simultaneity deceptive? Does synchronicity go too far? Yes and no. No: the quasi-obliteration of distances in time and space by modern means of communication is surely not without importance. You have only to 'see' the interest aroused by live television news broadcasts. You are present at the event the moment it happens. You see massacres, and dead bodies, you watch explosions. Missiles and rockets are fired before your very eyes, heading for their targets. You're there! But no, you're not there. You have the vague impression of being there. Subjectivity! You're in your armchair in front of the small *screen*, which is well named because it hides what it shows. Simultaneity does not only conceal dramas – or tragedy. It masks time, and diachrony. And what about history? What about origins? Not only these, but also the diversity of places, and rhythms, and therefore of countries and peoples. It is the 'mirror' error and deceptive corollary of false simultaneity: the constant throwback to history. Because we're talking about present times!

From this preliminary overview, the outcome is that the living body can and should be seen in terms of the interaction of the organs within it, each one having their rhythm but subject to a spatio-temporal whole. Furthermore, this human body is the locus and seat of interaction between the biological, the physiological (nature) and the social (often called the 'cultural'), and each of these areas, each of these dimensions, has its own specificity, and thus its space-time: its rhythm. Hence the inevitable shocks (stresses), disorders and disturbances within this whole, whose stability is never absolutely guaranteed.

Hence the importance of scales, proportions and rhythms. In order to conceptualize physical reality and its relationship with human physiological and sensory reality, modern philosophy has offered two models: the Kantian, or neo-Kantian, and the empirical or positivist. In the case of the former, phenomena – the flux of sensations – are classified, arranged, organized under a priori categories, i.e. categories interior to the subject and consciousness, including time and space. The thing-in-itself (the noumenal) eludes the grasp of this 'subject'. According to empiricism and positivism, sensory data fall of their own accord into relationships of simultaneity, involvement, linkage. 'If A implies B and B implies C, then A implies C.' There is no need for other categories than those of logic, or the logical, which are in fact not categories but self-evident experiential data, transcribed in formal language.

But consciousness, from Newton to Einstein and contemporary physics, follows another route, also marked out in certain philosophies, such as Feuerbach's. It is correct to say that we perceive our relationship with the things of nature as with created objects, in a word, with realities. This means we have to distinguish between appearances – which themselves have a reality – and what there really is in these things. For example, they seem inert (this wooden table, this pencil, etc.) and yet they move, if only within the earth's movement; they contain motion and energy, they change, and so on. As with physical reality, so with social relations; this immobile object in front of me is the product of labour; the whole mercantile chain is concealed within it, this material and social object. As a result, we have to go beyond facts, phenomena, the flux of direct sensations, but the phenomenon or sensory fact, within or beyond is determined internally or purely a priori, as the Kantian tradition believed.

Our *scale* determines our location, our place in the space-time of the universe; what we perceive of it, and what serves as a point of departure for both practice and theoretical knowledge. The *micro* as well as the *macro* eludes us, although we can gradually attain them through knowledge and their relationship with the known. Our rhythms insert us into a vast and infinitely complex world, which imposes on us our experience and the elements of that experience. Consider light, for example. We perceive it, not as a waveform carrying particles, but as something wondrous that transforms things, as the illumination of objects, a play on the surface of all that exists. This subjective aspect nevertheless includes an objectivity that has enabled us to arrive, after centuries of research and calculations, at the physical reality underlying the phenomena of light, yet without exhaustively defining that reality.

The ghostly presence of wave motion (coupled with its trajectories, or, alternatively, in no relationship with them) extends indefinitely, perhaps infinitely, from the macro to the micro, from molecular motion to the motion of the meta-galaxies. Relativist thought obliges us to reject all fixed or definitive references. A system of reference can only be provisional and conjunctural, and today we can berate Einstein for refuting the absolute laws of Newtonian space and time, while at the same time retaining one absolute, one constant in the universe: the speed of light.

In this immense spectral presence we grasp and perceive only what corresponds to our own rhythms, the rhythms of our organs, including, according to the individual, two variable and uncertain areas: one within our normal perception, towards the micro, and the other beyond it, towards the macro (sound and ultrasound, infrared and ultraviolet waves, etc.). Moreover, we could conceive of beings whose perceptual field might be wider. Above all, we can make devices that extend this field in practice. But this is not to say it does not survive, with its limits, its markers, its boundaries.

Man (the species): his physical and physiological existence is indeed the measure of the world, as in the old saying of Protagoras.[3] It is not only that our knowledge is relative to our constitution, it is that the world that offers itself to us (nature, the earth, and what we call the sky, the body and its role in social relations, etc.) is relative to that constitution. Not to a priori categories, but to our senses and the instruments we have at our disposal. More philosophically: another scale, would determine another world. The same one? Probably, but grasped differently.

Without knowing it (which does not mean 'unconsciously'), the human species takes from within the universe those movements that match its own. The ear, the eyes, and the gaze, the hands, are by no means passive devices that merely register or record. What is fashioned, formed, produced, establishes itself on a scale which we must also understand is in no way accidental or arbitrary. This is the scale of the earth, of accidents on the terrestrial surface and the cycles that unfold there. This does not mean that production is limited to reproducing things and objects supplied by nature. What is created does not take its place against this scale; it either overcomes or transfigures it.

Paris, March 1983

The Worldwide Experience

(from *De l'Etat, Vol. IV: Les contradictions de l'état moderne* (Paris: Collection 10/18, Union Générale d'Éditions, 1978), pp. 413–22, 435–41)

The Revolution had been relied upon to create the 'world' and 'worldliness' [*le «monde» et la «mondialité»*]. It was the *worldwide revolution* [*la révolution mondiale*].[1] Today we have to realize that the worldwide and worldliness, with its hazardous and unforeseen features, constitutes the 'revolution' itself, instead of concluding it.

But what is revolution? What is the worldwide? After an initial look we notice the prodigious complexity of the movement: the worldwide market, generalization of state power, generalized but processed information, unbridled demography and technology, space, the Third World and minorities, ethnic groups, women, peasants, youth, etc. The working-class movement set out by Marx and Marxism as (fundamentally and essentially) privileged, would only be a movement among others, important, or the most important, but the generator of contradictions, and not the only one. Which requires a reconsideration of the 'worldwide'.

That having been said, the concept of the *worldwide* made itself known. It detaches itself slowly, but not without difficulties, from the historical. Concept rather than metaphor? Of course, but with a new meaning, placing emphasis on the possible and not on the 'real'.

We do not have to examine here certain important and maybe decisive aspects of the 'worldwide', such as the 'aero-politics' of information. One only has to mention them. Information reserves more than one surprise.[2] From these elements should now be drawn, aspects and moments, the concept of the worldwide, present from the outset, in this work: now this concept, this point of departure and anchorage point is far from explanation. It appeared *dialectically* as what is shown, designated, given rise to, *produced* by the whole of present-day forces and as what they conceal, inhibit, forbid and thwart. Which poses without resolving it the question of the *worldwide* as possible-impossible, as out-of-reach virtuality. For whom? For those who carry along the movements which engender these very same virtualities.

The worldwide paradoxically appears on the horizon as possibilities already partially (sketchily) realized, induced and produced, but also resisted and thwarted by the forces in action in modernity. Conversely, the worldwide tends to break obstacles, explode boundaries and drag along that which opposes it. We already know how the State is becoming worldwide [*se mondialise*] and at the same time opposes the worldwide. The nation states, attached to a territory, managers of this space, arbitrate and act as dominant power from and by this space. They manage it as *eminent* owners [*propriétaires* éminents], almost in the way this word meant under the *ancien régime*, whereby the written rights and powers of the nobles and the king were superimposed upon the common rights of the peasants, 'commoners', holders of perpetual usufruct.[3] An analogous superimposition governs the modern State and its relationship to its space (territory). Methods (sometimes compelling and sometimes violent) and multiple procedures, the best known of which is 'expropriation', give concrete expression to this eminent right which we know extends itself to under the ground and to air space, forests and water sources, rivers and coasts, maritime territories and to recently extended territorial waters. Productive forces tend to the worldwide. Unfortunately, this tendency of productive forces – the latest worldwide experiences and of primary importance – has engendered 'supra' or 'multi' firms and companies which, as we know, tend to outclass States, and to use them to dominate and manage a territory to their profit.

When philosophy has explored worldliness, it has established significant propositions. When Heidegger utters '*Die Welt weltet*' (the world worlds [*le monde se mondifie*]),[4] this statement, which is close to a tautology, has great sense. He means to say that the worldwide conceives itself in and by itself and not by another thing (history, spirit, work, science, etc.). The world becomes world, becoming what virtually it was. It transforms itself by becoming worldwide. In it discovery and creation converge. It does not exist before it creates itself, and yet, it proclaimed itself, possible-impossible, through all the powers, technology, knowledge, art. This '*terminus ad quem*' has a consistence and an existence in its own right. Are we looking to the '*terminus a quo*', inaccessible and definitively lost, for the original? That is a mistake of the ancient philosophy. The secret, the code of being, is not discovered in the original, but in the possible, without omitting history. The whole process, history (of being in Heidegger) can and must be considered, but does not contain the world of the enigma. The possible and the impossible manifest themselves in the here and now as call or interpellation The worldwide cannot represent itself. The worldly represents itself: it is composed of representations (is conceived by representative thoughts), according to principles of identity, of difference, of non-contradictions, abstract principles. The being [*l'étant*] is represented, but not Being [*l'Être*]. The worldwide is born from cosmic duration; it is produced as world, 'by making luminous, making shine the dispensations taken by the being', it is the dispenser of being. Heidegger adds, along the lines of Heraclitus: 'the dispensation of being – a child that plays'. Man is engaged in this game and by this sets into motion: play is without why, but it is played and cannot but play. Only play remains, that which is the most elevated and the most profound. It is the One, the Unique.

Therefore the worldwide, the stake of this play [*enjeu de ce jeu*]⁵ in which being, no longer hiding itself, will unfold and spread.

In the same vein, K. Axelos defines or rather conceives the world as a 'limitless horizon'. The play of the world embraces and crushes games and rules, transgressions and calculations, significations and interpretations, all the truths and all the figures of error. The worldwide would not have, according to Axelos, more consistence than the real or the actual. The totality on the move or rather in progress has neither centre nor focus, nor source nor core: this non-centre, that is play which in this way plays at chasing a centre. He who is closest to a centre is at the same time he who is furthest from it, whether philosopher or scholar, lover or politician, magician or artist. All great thinkers think (and miss) the meaning of the totality of the world. Thus Nietzsche's thought has a centre: the death of God. But his voice says and repeats that there is no answer in the (modern) world to the *why*, as the world of non-total totality (the being inseparable from nothingness and death) has no bottom [*fond*]: is play. So that Nietzsche anticipates the crisis of the *future world* (of the possible). After Marx and Nietzsche the death of philosophy is long celebrated, institutionalized and ritualized. It no longer counts because it counts for too much, wanting itself to be competent and accountable. The philosopher no longer plays, no longer takes part in the game [*jeu*], while basic forces and their powers continue their game: language and thought, work and struggle, love and death, which leads the game, sometimes by their presence, sometimes by their absence – sometimes by the *said*, sometimes by the *done* (the Logos and Praxis). For us the *planetary* is the only figure accessible to the worldwide. Thus goes the world without truce, without end.⁶

Before the transition from philosophy to metaphilosophy, Marx had explored the worldwide by contributing a double proposition, one 'realist', the other theoretical. For Marx, in practical terms, the world first takes this form: *the worldwide market*. Marx had outlined history: he started the elaboration of the concept without finishing it. He distinguishes periods of the worldwide market: before capitalism and after capitalism. He knows that commodity and money markets go together but do not coincide, any more than with the labour market (of the labour force). The worldwide market, for Marx, already multiplied and differentiated, always presents itself according to a spatial configuration. The domination of a political power and centre (England in Marx's time), not without giving rise to often violent interactions and reactions, takes along and governs this configuration that governs the fluxes of goods and investments. Marx did not go to the end of this analysis, any more than that of the reintegration of the spatial (the ground and beneath ground, the earth and land rent) analysed in reality.

The world and the worldwide are also understood by Marx from the point of departure of philosophy, that is, from its overcoming. Philosophy makes itself world: it makes the world and the world is made through it. The world is produced to the exact measure whereby philosophy is realized, and realizing, becomes world. Philosophers have interpreted the world: now it must be changed; can this change be accomplished without philosophy?[7] No, because it consists in the practical realization of what philosophers have only thought of or represented: freedom, happiness, knowledge, joy. Who can realize philosophy by overcoming it, by realizing it in such a way that it becomes world? Who carries the becoming-world (the world in becoming and the becoming of the world)? *Total* revolution, which proclaims and executes the order of endings, the end of capitalism, of the bourgeoisie, of the State, the family and the nation, of work, of the separated individual, of the historical, of the economical, and of the political, etc. So, the working class, the carrier of this capacity, is *universal* as such and only as such.

In the course of the present work, we have proposed the theoretical discourse – a non-contradictory discourse on the contradictions of the modern world – which envisages the worldwide. By *becoming worldwide* [*en se mondialisant*] itself on the basis of the worldwide market, the State opens and closes the paths of worldliness [*mondialité*]. This therefore calls for the end of the State (that is, its withering away). This last image of historical time is also the first of worldwide space [*l'espace mondial-figure*] – an image which will fade and already is becoming blurred before other configurations. The world? It is the planetary, therefore *space* at one and the same time product and *work* [*oeuvre*]: an ensemble of places, and result of a creative and thus artistic activity, both conscious and unconscious. The worldwide does not define itself by Nature: nature opens onto the worldwide, but transformed into 'second nature', disturbing and poorly defined. The Earth, threatened by terricide,[8] as such the stake of a terrible game, is proposed as the beginning and end of the productive-creative activity. Before that of the galaxy, planetary space gives itself to the human species as theatre and scenario, field of the possible and sudden appearance of the unforeseen.

The State, this unforeseen which political thought could have and should have foreseen, which it glimpsed with Hegel without daring to extend it to the world, by reserving it for Europe and the elected nation – the State has nothing eternal about it. Already the absolute and perfect State, the nation-State according to Hegel and according to the French revolution, this State is moving away. It explodes, caught in contradictions, torn apart between what overwhelms it from the inside and from the outside. In this, the State relates to history and historicity and time. What will carry it away and already is sweeping it away? Worldliness. The State has not lost its link with the 'real', notably with the spatial. It runs the risk, precisely in this way, of becoming the instrument of multinational firms, or to collapse under their blows and manipulations. The least of these risks: to consolidate, enrich and become more oppressive and repressive. This State will not let itself wither away or be overcome without resistance. Which announces new events similar but without reproducing them to the older ones (fascism, Stalinism, anarchism, terrorism, etc.). Perhaps the worldwide would take form only in the course of a worldwide crisis? Or after it?

[...]

The questioning, which once again concerns the *possible* considered at one and the same time as founded on reality, and as perspective on the real, finds its answer in the trilogy: 'historicity–worldliness–spatiality'. The 'historicity–worldliness' conflict resolves itself in and by the production of worldwide space, the work of an historical time in which it is realized. The contradictions conveyed by historical time go through various fortunes; some worsen, others wane; new contradictions manifest themselves, overloading or neutralizing according to the conjuncture, the previous ones. It is through these obstacles, these risks, that the *new way* appears, that the present work has tried to open up. It is through these difficulties that new values are created, among which are those attached to space (*oeuvre* and product) which have been used here as illustration.

Let us include the following in the list of the experience of worldliness:

a) *The making worldly of Marxism* – as already noted with its numerous consequences. Certain 'Marxist' concepts tend towards the concrete universal; that of praxis, that of contradiction and conflict, etc. As can be witnessed in the work of Mao Tse-Tung. Which on the contrary does not exclude either the renewed use of certain concepts (surplus product or global surplus value, organic composition of capital, etc.) or the introduction of new concepts (including the everyday, difference, the urban, social space, the SMP), etc.[9]

b) *The worldwide market*, one and many, understood at its most complex. Which involves the worldwide division of productive labour, knowledge at the worldwide scale and information, space on a worldwide (planetary) scale, gold as supreme equivalent, the problem of transfers of surplus value and monetary exchanges, etc.

c) *The existence*, the growing power, the menacing action of *multinational firms* [*firmes mondiales*] manipulating currencies, resources, territories, the States themselves (national or multinational).

d) *The nature of the transformation of the world*, made up of various movements, including (itself characteristic of) the working-class.

e) *The failure of authoritarian and centralized planning* (USSR). A relative failure: it accelerates growth but by directing it (heavy manufacture, arms) and worsening internal inequalities (poorly developed zones, for example, agriculture). Which leads to an *inversion of the situation*. 'Socialism' and 'Marxism' change into their opposites; absolute domination of the State, ideology of the State, oppressive character of the State, etc.

This relative failure of the SMP with 'socialist' components corresponds to the relative failure of the SMP with 'capitalist' components. The latter functions by also promoting gigantism (enterprises, cities) and simultaneously by excluding from growth an increasing number of casualties. The failures of the two forms of the SMP correspond without however being confounded. It could be that the future of the State differs according to its modality of existence; that it degenerates here (without withering away in the Marxist-Leninist sense) and that it prospers there (without entering in the 'reign of liberty').

The failure of the SMP with 'socialist' components involves the failure of a society (a 'culture', a civilization) founded on labour and the valorization (ethical, aesthetical) of productive material (manual) work. The corresponding failure of the SMP with capitalist components involves the failure of a society founded on the formalism of art, discourse, etc.

f) *The making worldly of the State* as hierarchical morphology conveys with it *possibilities of rupture* rather than the stabilization of the whole. The worldwide experience includes that of rupture, collapse, deterioration, pulverization of State units (recent examples are Portugal, the State established by Salazar flying into pieces after the death of the Prince, Portuguese imperialism unable to sustain itself; or Chile).[10] It is one of the essential elements or moments of worldwide experience, which makes certain the impermanent nature of the State.

g) *The cultural revolution considered as political revolution*: assault from the 'grassroots' against hierarchical apparatuses (party, administrations, institutions) erected above society.

h) *Self-management* [autogestion] (along the lines of the Yugoslav experience) with its problematic: relations of self-managed units with the market and investments – extension of the self-management practice to the whole social space.

i) *The Spanish and Italian experience of the regions*, of active decentralization, not without risk of decomposition of the State which would make it vulnerable to imperial powers and multinational firms, without as such bringing about the rational withering away of the State and the double reabsorption of the State into civil society and of the political into the social. The region as substitute of the State is nonetheless an important stage in the global process.

Along this difficult road *difference*, category (concept), both theoretical and practical, that is to say, gathering together long-disunited practice and theory, makes its way.

j) *The experience of 1968 in France and elsewhere*: the State threatened by the extension of the movement from a vulnerable point: the occupation of its space by the working-class, etc.

k) Let's add here pell-mell disparate aspects often mentioned: pressure of becoming worldly [*mondialisation*] on each country and on each national State, risks of productivism transformed into absolute ideology, the break-up of spaces coming from history and of historical time, the relativity of borders, the decline of political parties, etc.

The various moments of the worldwide experience do not lie outside one another. They make a whole: the acquired assets of theory and practice can in the twentieth century open and cast light upon a path yet to be followed.

The outcome is that these times are not without challenges. These are challenging times! But what is being challenged? The products and creations of history. The challenge of the worldwide consists mostly in this, that the transformation of the world which produces the worldwide is accompanied by the most terrifying danger and terror. The planet enters its unitary existence and life at total risk. Which is not to say that destiny declares itself thus and that the final catastrophe is fatal.

Revolution presents itself as worldliness [*mondialité*] on the move: transformation with multiple aspects, dominated by peasant, national, state and political questions. Turning the world upside down also includes the overturning of this domination. Which leaves room for the combined action of the worldwide working-class and of theory reaching the concrete universal.

The theory explores the possible-impossible and declares that 'one must' (theoretical imperative and non-ethical) want the impossible to realize the possible.[11] Nothing closer to and nothing further from the possible. Utopia therefore takes on the character of urgency. *Urgent utopia* defines a style of thinking turned towards the possible in all areas. Which tends to redefine 'socialism' and 'communism' not by the state and the political, but by on the one hand a critique of the State and the political, and on the other, as production, appropriation and management of space. Neither the individual nor the group exist without an appropriated space (produced as such).

Conceptual thought explores ways, ventures on paths. It can precede practice, but cannot separate itself from it. Practice alone, freed from political obsession and released from State pressure, can effectively realize what promises to be the simultaneous use of concept and imagination (utopia). Theory opens the road, makes a new way; practice takes it, it *produces* the road and the space.

Paris, September 1976–May 1977

Preface to the New Edition
The Production of Space

(from *La Production de l'espace*, 3ᵉ édn (Paris: Anthropos, 1986), pp. i–xii; repr. in *La Production de l'espace*, 4ᵉ édn (Paris: Anthropos, 2000), pp. xvii–xxviii)

Ten or fifteen years ago, when this book was written, conceptions of space were muddled, paradoxical, mutually incompatible. With interplanetary rocket technology and the feats of the astronauts, space was undoubtedly 'in vogue': space of this and space of that – pictorial, sculptural, even musical space – but what the vast majority of people and the general public understood by the word 'Space' (with a capital), laden with new and unusual connotations, was only the distances of the cosmos. Traditionally, the word suggested little more than mathematics, (Euclidean) geometry and its theorems, and was thus an abstraction: a container without content. And in philosophy? Space was mostly treated with disdain, as one 'category' among others (an 'a priori', as the Kantians said: a way of organizing sensory phenomena). Sometimes it was loaded with all kinds of illusion and error: deflecting desire and action, the interiority of the 'self', thus psychological life towards the exterior and inert, dividing and divided (with and as language: Bergson). As for the disciplines that studied it, they parcelled it out amongst themselves, and space became fragmented according to simplified methodological premises: geographical, sociological, historical, etc. At best, space passed for an empty zone, a container indifferent to its content, but defined by certain unexpressed criteria: absolute, optico-geometrical, Euclidean-Cartesian-Newtonian. We may have been accepting 'spaces', but we were bringing them together in a concept whose scope was poorly defined. The poorly assimilated idea of *relativity* established itself on the margins of this concept, of representations and above all, of the everyday, in thrall to tradition (the three-dimensional, the separation of space and time, the metre and the clock, etc.).

Paradoxically, that is to say, in a (diabolical) unexpressed, unavowed, inexplicit contradiction, practice – within existing society and its mode of production – was going in a different direction from fragmentary representations and forms of knowledge. *Someone* (the politicians? No; it was more their collaborators and technocratic assistants, endowed with considerable power and authority), *someone* invented spatial planning; and in France, mainly; the project was to no less rationally fashion and model French space; by surrendering to the inevitable, it was seen (not without reason) to be developing a poor appearance and regrettable tendencies: desertified here and congested there, etc. In particular, the 'spontaneous' axis that goes from the Mediterranean to the northern coast, via the valleys of the Rhône, the Saône and the Seine, already posed problems. There was a project to build 'regional capitals [*métropoles d'équilibre*]' around Paris and in various regions. The official body responsible for regional development,[1] a powerful, centralized organization, lacked neither resources nor ambitions: to *produce* a harmonious national space – to bring a little order to 'wild' urban development, which answers only to the pursuit of profit.

Today nobody is unaware that this innovative planning initiative (which was consistent neither with input-output analysis nor state control over capital spending, i.e. planning by financial criteria) was wrecked, reduced to practically nothing by neo-liberalism and since clumsily put together again.

Hence a remarkable but nevertheless little noticed contradiction between theories of space and spatial practice. A contradiction concealed – one might say stifled – by the ideologies that threw into confusion debates on space, jumping from the cosmological to the human, from the macro to the micro, from functions to structures, without being thought out, conceptually or methodologically. The ideology of spatiality, which is very confused, collapsed into a single whole rational knowledge, effective but authoritarian planning and trite, commonplace representations.

Hence the effort to escape confusion by no longer considering (social) space and (social) time as facts of 'nature', modified to some degree, nor as simple facts of 'culture' – but as *products*. That brought about a change in the use and meaning of that word. The production of space (and time) did not see them as some kind of 'object' or 'thing', created by hand or machine, but as the principal features of *second nature*, as effects of the action of societies on 'first nature', on sensory data, matter and energy. Products? Yes, in a specific sense, particularly in a certain character of *globality* (not of totality) that they have, but which 'products' in the ordinary everyday sense (objects and things, merchandise) do not (even though the very space and time that are produced, but 'parcelled out', are exchanged, bought and sold, just like 'things' and objects)!

It should be noted in passing that even at that time (around 1970) *urban* questions were being raised with great clarity (too blindingly clear for many people, who preferred to avert their gaze). Official documents could neither regulate nor mask the new barbarism. Massive and 'uncontrolled', with no other strategy than to maximize profits, devoid of rationality or creative originality, construction and urban development, as they called it, were having noticeably disastrous effects – visible on all sides even then. Under the colours of 'modernity'. Even then!

How are we to maintain without new arguments the thesis (Graeco-Latin: our own, that of our civilization!) that the City, the Town, the Urban, are the centres, the privileged places, the cradles of thought and invention? The 'city–country' relationship was changing, at the world scale, with 'extremist' interpretations (the worldwide countryside versus the worldwide city!). How to think about the City (its widespread explosion-implosion, the 'modern Urban') without conceiving clearly the space it occupies, appropriates (or 'disappropriates')? It is impossible to think of the modern city and modern urban phenomena in terms of *oeuvres* (in the broad, powerful sense of a work of art [*oeuvre d'art*] that transforms its materials) without first conceiving of them as products. And this within a specific mode of production, which all at the same time fails, shows its extreme consequences, sometimes allows 'something else' to emerge, at least as expectation, demand, appeal. Of course, environmentalists had already raised awareness and stirred up public opinion: territory, environment, polluted air and water, nature – this 'raw material' – the material of the City, ravaged without scruple. What this environmental movement lacked was a general theory of the relationship between space and society – between the territorial, urban development, the architectural . . .

The conception of space as a social product did not develop without difficulties, in other words, without a problematic that was partly new and unforeseen.

As it did not denote a particular 'product' – a thing or an object – but a cluster of relationships, this concept required that the notions of *production* and *product*, and their relationships, be enlarged. As Hegel used to say, a concept only emerges when what it refers to is under threat and nearing its end – and its transformation. Space can no longer be conceived of as passive or empty, nor as having, like 'products', no other meaning than that of being exchanged and consumed and disappearing. As a product, interactively or retroactively, space intervenes in production itself: organization of productive work, transport, flow of raw materials and energy, product distribution networks. In its productive role, and as a producer, space (well or badly organized) becomes part of the relations of production and the forces of production. Thus the concept cannot be isolated or remain static. It becomes dialectical: product-producer, underpinning economic and social relations. Does it not also play a part in *reproduction*, reproduction of the productive apparatus, of enlarged reproduction, of relations which it realizes in practice, 'on the ground'?

Does not this idea become clear as soon as it is formulated, and does it not clarify many things? Does it not reach this obvious point, the realization 'on the ground', and thus in a social space that is *produced*, of the social relations of production and reproduction? Can they remain 'in the air', abstractions created by and for academic study? Furthermore, this way of theorizing enables us to understand (while remaining within the framework of the existing mode of production) the originality of the *project*, which is spatial planning. To understand it, but also to modify it, and complete it, as part of other claims and projects, but while taking into account its nature, and especially the fact that it is concerned with urbanization. And therefore to take up again.

A second and no lesser difficulty: in the strict Marxian tradition, social space could be seen as a superstructure, as outcome of forces of production and of structures, including property relations. Now space enters into the forces of production, the division of labour; it has a relation with property, that is clear – with forms of exchange, with institutions, culture, learning. It is bought and sold; it has exchange value and use value. Thus it is not located on this or that 'level' or 'plane', as defined in traditional hierarchies. The concept of (social) space, and space itself thus escape the classification 'base–structure–superstructure'. Like time? Perhaps. Like language? That remains to be seen. Should Marxist analysis and orientation be abandoned for as much? Invitations and suggestions that we do so came from all sides. And not only with reference to space. But could we not, on the contrary, go back to the sources and deepen our analysis by introducing new concepts and trying to find new, subtler approaches? Which is what this work attempts to do. It assumes that space appears, is formed, acts, sometimes on one of these levels, sometimes on another. Sometimes in the area of work and relations of domination (property), sometimes in the way superstructures (institutions) work. Unevenly, therefore, but everywhere. The production of space would not seem to be 'dominant' in the world of production, but would seem to bring together aspects of practice by coordinating them – by unifying them in precisely that, a practice.

And that is not all. Far from it. (Social) space may act in the world of production, as effect, cause and reason all at once, but it changes with this mode of production! That's easy to understand; it changes with 'societies', if you can put it like that. There is thus a *history of space* (as of time, of the body, of sexuality, etc.). A history yet to be written.

The concept of space links the mental and the cultural, the social and the historical. By reconstituting a complex process: *discovery* (of new or unknown spaces, of continents or of the cosmos) – *production* (of the spatial organization characteristic of each society) – *creation* (of *oeuvres*: landscape, the city with monumentality and décor). A process that is gradual, genetic (with a 'genesis'), but follows a logic: the general form of *simultaneity*; because every spatial mechanism rests on the juxtaposition in the intelligence and on the material assembly of elements from which we *produce* simultaneity.

However, the thing gets more complicated. Is there perhaps a connection – direct, immediate, immediately grasped and therefore transparent – between the mode of production (the society under consideration) and its space? No. There are discrepancies: ideologies are interpolated, illusions interposed. That is what this work began to elucidate. Thus with the invention of perspective in Tuscany in the thirteenth and fourteenth centuries. Not only in painting (the Sienese School) but first in practice, in production.[2] The countryside changes, it passes from the feudal domain to the sharecropping system; avenues of cypresses lead from small farms to the lord's residence, where a steward is installed, because the landowner lives in the city, where he is a banker, or an important merchant. The city changes, with implications for architecture: façade, alignment of buildings, horizon. This production of a new space – perspective – is not separate from an economic change: increases in production and exchange, the rise of a new class, importance of cities, etc. But what actually happened does not have the simplicity of a chain of cause and effect. Was this new space conceived, engendered, produced by and for princes? For rich merchants? By a compromise? Or by the city as such? Several points are still unclear. The history of space (like that of social time) is far from exhausted!

Another case in point, even more surprising and also referred to and poorly explained in this work: the *Bauhaus*, plus, Le Corbusier. We took the *Bauhaus* people – Gropius and his friends – for revolutionaries, in Germany, between 1920 and 1930; for Bolsheviks! Persecuted, they went to the United States.[3] There they emerged as *practitioners* (architects and planners) and even *theoreticians* of so-called modern space, the space of 'advanced' capitalism. They helped to construct it, to create it 'on the ground', through their works and their teaching. What a misfortune and sad fate for Le Corbusier! And again, subsequently, for those who saw large complexes and long, low-rise blocks as a habitat specific to the working-class. They neglected the concept of the *mode of production*, which also produced its space and so came to an end. Under the colours of modernity. The space produced by 'modernity' has specific characteristics: homogeneity–fragmentation–hierarchy. It tends towards the homogeneous for various reasons: manufacture of elements and materials (and corresponding demands on the part of those involved), methods of management and control, surveillance and communication. Homogeneity, but no plans or projects. False 'ensembles' – in fact, units. Because paradoxically (again) this homogeneous space is fragmented: lots and parcels. Reduced to crumbs! Which produced ghettos, units, clusters of detached houses [*groupes pavillonnaires*] and pseudo-schemes [*pseudo-ensembles*], poorly linked with their surroundings or with town centres. With a rigid hierarchy: residential areas, commercial areas, leisure areas, areas for the marginalized, etc. This space exerts a curious logic, which we mistakenly connect with computerization, and which hides 'real' relationships and conflicts behind its homogeneity. Furthermore, it seems that this law or model of space, with its logic (homogeneity–fragmentation–hierarchy) has acquired a broader scope and achieved a kind of generality, with analogous effects, in the domains of learning and culture, in the workings of the whole society.

Preface to the New Edition: The Production of Space 211

This work therefore attempted not only to describe the space we live in, and its origins, but to retrace the origins, through and by the space it produced, of present-day society. An ambition the title does not declare overtly. Let us resume this proposed plan, inherent to the approach: a 'retro' study of social space in its history and genesis – from the present going back towards this genesis – then return to the present, which allows us to glimpse into if not to foresee the future and what is possible. This approach leads on to local studies, on different scales, inserting them into the general analysis, the global theory. Its implications and logical overlappings are understood as such, but in the knowledge that this understanding does not exclude (far from it) conflicts, struggles and contradictions, nor, conversely, agreements, understandings, alliances. While the local, the regional, the national and the worldwide interweave and overlap, and this is incorporated into space, actual or virtual conflicts are neither absent nor eliminated. Implications and contradictions, in space as in other domains, have wider meaning now than when this book was written. Relations of implication do not prohibit opposing strategies, either in markets or in armed conflict. And so in space also.

There are analogous relations between the territorial, planning and the architectural: implications and conflicts. Which can only be grasped if we have understood the relationships 'logic–dialectic' and 'structure–conjuncture', which are presented and assumed here in a certain way and made fully explicit elsewhere.[4] These relationships, which are both abstract and concrete, come as a surprise in a philosophical and political 'culture' that puts this 'complexity' to one side and looks for it elsewhere.

Research on social space refers to a globality. It does not, let us repeat, exclude specific, defined research projects 'on the ground'. However, the danger inherent in 'one-off' studies, valued as such because they can be controlled, sometimes measured, is that it separates what is connected, and disconnects what is 'articulated'. It thus accepts or endorses fragmentation. Which leads to excessive practices of 'de-concentration' and decentralization, practices that break up spatial networks, links and relations, and therefore social space itself, by making production disappear! This avoids a host of questions – pedagogical, logical, political . . .

A central idea to which we must return before concluding: the mode of production organizes – *produces* – at the same time as certain kinds of social relations, its space (and its time). That is how it works. Supposing we were to ask, has 'socialism' created its space? If not, it is because the socialist mode of production does not yet exist in concrete form. The mode of production projects these relations on to the terrain, which reacts with them. Though there is no exact, previously assigned correspondence between social and spatial (or spatio-temporal) relations. We cannot say that from the start the capitalist mode of production, by inspiration or intelligence, 'ordained' its extension in space, which by now should cover the whole planet! First there was the use of existing space, for example, waterways (canals, rivers, seas), then roads, followed by the building of railways, then motorways and aerodromes. No means of spatial transport – on foot, on horseback, by bicycle, etc. – has entirely disappeared. Nevertheless, it is a new space that has been created in the twentieth century, on a world scale; its production has not ended but still continues. The new mode of production (the new society) appropriates, that is to say, adapts to its own ends, pre-existing space, whose patterns had been previously formed. Slow changes, penetrating a space that had already been consolidated, but sometimes brutally disrupting it (as in the case of the countryside and rural landscape in the twentieth century).

Undeniably the railways played a fundamental role in industrial capitalism and the organization of its national (and international) space. But at the same time, at an urban scale so did trams, underground railways, buses. Then on a worldwide scale: air transport. The previous organization disintegrates and the mode of production absorbs the results. A double process, visible for several decades in our towns and countryside, with the help of recent technology – but extending from the centres of cities to their distant outskirts.

The organization of centralized, concentrated space serves at one and the same time political power and material production, optimizing profit. Social classes stake a claim to it, and disguise themselves in it, in the hierarchy of occupied spaces.

However, a new space *tends* to develop, at the world scale, integrating and disintegrating the national and the local. A process full of contradictions, linked with the conflict between a division of labour on the planetary level, in the mode of capitalist production – and the effort to create another, more rational world order. This penetration of and into space has been as historically important as achieving hegemony through penetration of institutions. A crucial if not the ultimate point of this penetration: the militarization of space, not treated (and for good reason) here, but which completes the demonstration, on both the planetary and the cosmic scale.

This thesis, as that of a space that was both homogeneous and fragmented (like time!), provoked many objections ten or twelve years ago. How could a space obey common rules, constitute an 'object', and disintegrate, all at the same time?

It is not a question of contending that the recent and already famous theory of the *fractal object* (B. Mandelbrot) has a connection with the idea of fragmented space, which is put forward here.[5] However, we can point to both the quasi-simultaneity of the theories, and the fact that the physico-mathematical theory makes the socio-economic theory more accessible and more easily accepted. Physico-mathematical space contains voids and solids, hollows and projections; it maintains coherence although 'worked' by fragmentation. These theoretical endeavours are thus analogous.[6]

The relationship between this fragmented space and the multiple networks that work against fragmentation and re-establish, if not a rational unity, at least homogeneity, has still to be worked out. Could there not emerge, through and against hierarchization, here and there, in architectural or planning terms, 'some thing' that comes out of the existing mode of production, that is born from its contradictions by exposing them, and not by covering them with a veil?

A point of self-criticism: this book has not described in a direct, hard-hitting, even pamphleteering style the production of housing schemes, ghettos, isolates, false 'ensembles'. The project for creating a new space remains uncertain; several features of the draft outline may now be adjusted. The role of architecture as the *use* of space does not always emerge clearly.

Nevertheless, this book retains several focal points, and can be *reread* today using an approach that puts it to good use (as knowledge).

First phase or moment: the elements and the analysis that isolates them, the 'actors' of production, the profits made, etc.

Second phase: paradigmatic oppositions brought to light: public and private – exchange and use – official and personal – frontal and spontaneous – space and time . . .

Third phase: 'dialectization' of this static picture: power relations, alliances – the conflicts, social rhythms and phases produced in and by this space . . .

Such a reading should spare this work the twin charges of u-topia (a false construction, in the verbal vacuum) and a-topia (elimination of concrete space, leaving only the social vacuum).

Paris, 4 December 1985

Politics

Introduction

> I had no political ambitions and I always say that we must distinguish between the politician and the political thinker.[1]
>
> Henri Lefebvre, 1986

Lefebvre described his life as one of politico-philosophical engagement. An engagement which marked each of its moments and was a measure of himself. For Lefebvre, the lived is political. There is Lefebvre as young philosopher, as pre-war PCF militant, Lefebvre in the Resistance, Lefebvre researcher at the CNRS, Lefebvre separated from the PCF, Lefebvre as university professor, activist, pundit and mentor. And there is also 'Lefebvre after Lefebvre', bearer of the possible and of practical utopia in a world denuded of the political. There is no Lefebvre without politics.

These final selections make no attempt to illustrate what Lefebvre had to say on specific topics such as the State, the Party, etc., for politics was integral to everyday life. Indeed, it was the very claim to its reappropriation, and to separate out politics from everyday life was its very denial. Instead, these selections sketch moments of Lefebvre's lifelong preoccupation with understanding Marxism and himself as a Marxist. Moments in a meditation on the relation of the self to others, things and institutions which are always supported by the belief and possibility of a post-capitalist future. For Lefebvre, Marxism was no less than a way of life and a fight for life.

First published in 1936 and republished in 1999, *La Conscience mystifiée*, written with Norbert Guterman, is a foundation stone of Lefebvre's entire thought.[2] There the concept of political alienation is worked through, consciousness is given a status separate from proletarian consciousness, what is meant by a revolutionary critique is set out and a first mention of the notion of *moments* (as 'the innumerable incidents of becoming') is made.[3] There too is a first discussion of nationalism at a time of rising National Socialism. This first selection anticipates Lefebvre's *Le Nationalisme contre les nations* published in 1937 – the only critique in France of nationalism before the war.[4] A critique which will find later echoes in Lefebvre's analysis of the global and *mondialisation*. Both books also make clear Lefebvre's position of innovative criticism within the Party.

In this first of two passages from *La Conscience mystifiée*, 'Nation and Culture', Lefebvre and Guterman argue that the nation is overcome by historical and economic necessity and that Fascism, under the pretext of going back to the roots, is actually uniformization whereby national culture is destroyed. In the name of national culture, one must be an internationalist. In turn, in the second passage, 'Between yourself and you', Lefebvre and Guterman lay down their manifesto on consciousness: the reality of human consciousness as the movement of human things goes far beyond work to be productive, creative labour and this means transforming the present capitalist nature of labour. Revolution is only possible by recognizing first that we are of this world, are suffocating in it and then that we can work towards its transformation.

After he left the Communist Party and had become an established critical academic, Lefebvre was often interviewed by scholars and journalists and he himself published two politico-philosophical autobiographies, *La Somme et le reste* in 1958, two years after leaving the Party, and in 1975, *Le Temps des méprises* in the form of an extended interview.[5] A far more substantial text, *La Somme et le reste* resumes Lefebvre's adventures so far, the politics of his writings and publications and his position on philosophy, politics and history via, among others, Nietzsche, Lukács, Pascal, Descartes, Diderot and the Surrealists. Most significantly, he resumes the essence of his two most important endeavours: to restore and give meaning to the notion of 'movement' and '*dépassement*' (overcoming) and the philosophical project to focus on the explication of the concept of alienation, and from that, of moments and civilization.

Chapter IV of the Sixth Part of *La Somme et le reste*, 'Être Communiste', is an answer to a question Lefebvre poses to himself – 'how do you see yourself as Marxist and communist'?

By the mid-1980s Lefebvre was living in semi-retirement in his mother's house in Navarrenx and had formed around him somewhat Socratically, a group of young researchers and activists who became known as the *Groupe de Navarrenx*. They had gathered together to reflect on a new citizenship: global in scale, presupposing self-management (*autogestion*), new relations between individual, society and State, and resting on a notion of belonging whereby difference was not juxtaposed to citizenship. The penultimate selection included here is Lefebvre's Introduction to a collection of essays written by members of this group and published posthumously.[6] In his Introduction Lefebvre identifies the need to redefine citizenship in the face of '*mondialisation*', immigration and migration and new forms of belonging. The aim of this new contract of citizenship is to reanimate the dictatorship of the proletariat and without brutalities, the withering away of the State – a project first set out in 1936 in *La Conscience mystifiée*.

The final selection is again from the 1980s. It is taken from a monthly magazine also centred around members of the *Groupe de Navarrenx* and of which Lefebvre was both director and founder. The magazine, *M: Mensuel, Marxisme, Mouvement*, was short-lived (from May 1986 to October 1987), cheaply produced but had lively graphics (Lefebvre himself did the artwork for a Special Issue on *Autogestion*) and an impressive Support Committee (*comité de soutien*) which included recognizable names from amongst the French intellectual elite and a wide range of professions, including a large sprinkling of architects, researchers at the CNRS and psychotherapists. In his letter of resignation published in *M* in October 1987 (the magazine appears to have folded immediately afterwards), although Lefebvre expresses the opinion that his directorship was largely fictitious, he is succinct about the purpose of the project – the publication of a magazine for those seeking and waiting for a political reinvention. This would rest on three propositions: the right to difference, a redefinition of citizenship and self-management. Earlier in the year *M* had published an interview with Lefebvre in which he was to make his final politico-philosophical statement. It is included here.

Elizabeth Lebas

Nation and Culture

(from Norbert Guterman and Henri Lefebvre, *La Conscience mystifiée* (Paris: Syllepse, 1999 [1936]), pp. 81–91)

Over the past ten years, a couple of new and bizarre terms have enriched the political vocabulary of the West: 'national revolution'. Previously, the natural association of the word 'revolution' was with 'international', and the call for the workers of all nations to unite is one of the principles of Marxism. Since then, the fascists, and then the Nazis, have declared that the true revolution consists in subordinating all individual life to the nation-state, and it is not about liberating labour and workers, but above all, the 'nation'.

Applied to oppressed or colonized peoples, the words 'national revolution' have a very precise meaning. These peoples are exploited by foreign imperial powers; for them, to become independent nations, with their own State and army, represents real economic and cultural progress, and an almost immediate rise in their standard of living. A national revolution frees them all at once from the heavy tribute they have to pay to foreign masters.

It is quite different when Europe or the United States are involved. Here the issue becomes more complicated and obscure. In the case of Italy, Germany or Austria, we seem to be dealing with nations that were 'liberated' long ago. These nations have proclaimed themselves independent and sovereign States. How can it be that in those countries the national mystique be presented as a programme to be fought for? In a State with well-defended frontiers, what meaning could there be in a nationalism that has to assert itself through struggle?

Clearly, after the last war, some States found themselves bound and crushed by treaties that imposed payment of reparations, forbade the growth of armed forces, etc. To some extent, the constraints imposed by the Treaty of Versailles explain recent feelings of resentment. But not entirely. For nationalist mystique is also employed in the 'victorious' countries, even those under no kind of military threat. Wherever there is fascist opposition to liberal capitalism, it invokes 'national revolution', and in each case we find mobs who give enthusiastic support to that programme. This, then, calls for closer analysis.

Fascist theoreticians claim that the 'nation' is the timeless expression of an equally timeless human nature. To hear them talk, you would think there had always been 'nations', clearly separated one from another and based on racial, biological or at the very least, geographical features.

These assertions go against the most elementary truth. Without denying that a certain solidarity arises naturally in human communities, we have only to look, for example, at any European country in the fifteenth or sixteenth century to see that this feeling has never taken the form of nationalism. At the individual level, it is obvious that a 'nobleman' from any given country felt very much closer to a 'nobleman' from another than to a serf from his own, even if the latter spoke the same language. (It is the same today; a member of the British or American *grande bourgeoisie* has much more in common with his French counterpart than with a worker from his own country). In all aspects of everyday life – eating, playing, falling in love or marrying – his relations with a member of his own class will be much more comfortable and natural than with a member of his 'nation' who comes from another class. When a *grand bourgeois* travels, he hardly notices he has gone abroad, as his immediate environment, hotels, meals, etc., are practically identical to those at home. Fascist agents and 'international nationalists' know this very well! 'Nations' thus found it perfectly natural to unite when there was a marriage between their ruling families, and there was no 'national' spirit to oppose such unifications.

At that time, a country's unity did not lie in nationalism, but was expressed in the person of the King. The king, both the mystical and 'real' incarnation of his people, was first and foremost the owner of the land making up the kingdom, sharing and granting his property according to a set of laws and customs. The monarchy was an organization based on feudal ownership of land. Of course, the king often made alliances with the bourgeoisie, and made use of it, as it did of him. Royalty had used manipulation. But it was still based on feudal property relations, and could not go beyond the geographical and territorial unification of the country. For the king, the bourgeoisie was no more than a reserve of dangerous allies, and of money. Religious denominations, corporations, traditions and customs, tolls and taxes were the tools and frameworks of royal and aristocratic domination. To go from this to an organization based on production of goods and capital, a revolution was needed – and it was this revolution only which, through the need to replace the feudal body politic by a new one, created the nation in the modern sense of the word.

The nation was thus a revolutionary, progressive creation. Its separation from the royal person was a violent act, carried out in those countries (such as England and France) where it took a classically 'pure' form, with the guillotine or the axe. In France, the revolution of 1789 thus brought to completion the economic, legal and cultural unity of the country – a unity the monarchy was unable to achieve because it was tied to outdated institutions. Only this particular sum of characteristics – a common territory, language, culture, tradition and economic life – gives the formal idea of the Nation its specific content.

What, then, is the meaning of this impersonal personality, the Nation, substituted for the mystical personality of the king?

Under the *ancien régime*, the only ties were between individuals, between overlord and vassal, and the land belonged to the lord. The necessary connection between labour and means of production (the land) took the form of the *personal* relationship between serf and lord. The labourer is bound to the glebe and this dependency, this belonging, constitutes the basis of the feudal order. Feudal harvest dues, the earliest form of unpaid labour, were not exacted from the labouring class by laws of exchange, but directly and universally by personal threats or pressures (military service, the forced labour system, etc.) In that society, therefore, men of a single 'nation' are not linked together by the spiritual bonds of nationalism, but by direct, personal ties.

An abstract idea like that of the nation could therefore not appear under the *ancien régime*; only the person of the monarch evoked feelings of attachment, loyalty or honour. Countless historical instances show that throughout the Middle Ages there was never a case of 'national honour', but, on the contrary, we often see the feudal lords of one country finding no difficulty in serving the king of another.

National consciousness appears when the bourgeoisie starts to separate its interests from those of the king, and to see them as opposed. It can then envisage the general and free functioning constituted by the monarchy from which his fortune is made – exchange, trade and manufacture of goods – operating freely throughout a geographical domain constituted by the monarchy. It gradually conceives the idea that order might pass from the hereditary royal person, and be divided among public powers that would oversee the exercise of liberty and the automatic working of the economic laws that are the condition of that liberty.

As a result of the Revolution, the established order loses its direct and palpable character, and under the guise of liberty, deliberately distances itself from medieval custom, becomes divided in the abstract. The powers possessed by the king or delegated by him to others are replaced by remote laws and a Code of Law. Direct relationships and clearly perceptible inequalities are replaced by abstract legal equality between individuals and a new inequality of actual conditions that is not officially acknowledged. In other words, abstraction contains something very specific: the free operation of capitalist laws. Feudal constraints are broken, but the real mechanism of society is neither perceived nor expressed; on the contrary, it becomes enveloped in a series of legal fictions and political entities. The Nation is the geometrical place for all these abstractions at the same time as the establishment of an actual national community. The triumph of the national idea is the political expression of the triumph of the impersonal and international power of money, capitalist economic laws and the 'free' contracts substituted for the unique, concrete royal person.

At the 'beginning', that is, when the forces of production develop as a result of the advent of capitalism, the national idea is dynamic and revolutionary. Despite all its abstraction, it is infinitely superior to the mystique of kingship of divine origin. At the time of the French Revolution, the content of this idea, its reality, dominates its form to the point that nationalism presents itself as a universal doctrine, applicable to every country, that is, as *international*. In the context of a reactionary Europe, the patriotism of the Jacobins was an appeal to peoples against tyrants. The French Revolution was to give the signal for a whole series of national revolutions.

Nevertheless, as is the case with every bourgeois or capitalist phenomenon, the national idea is ambivalent from the outset. When it claimed to liberate its entire 'people', the bourgeoisie in fact only liberated itself. At the same time as it carried out the revolutionary work of unification, of breaking down feudal oppression, and creating the foundations for a wider community and culture, national identity and economic growth, the bourgeoisie established the class State and the exploitation of the proletariat. After some initial ups and downs, Thermidor and Napoleon clearly demonstrate the nature of that state. Patriotism, speculation and declamation were from the start, truly united.

In America, this link between the interests of the bourgeois merchant class and the national idea is quite obvious, almost conscious. It was in order to protect and liberate its economic interests that the United States constitutes an independent nation with the famous Declaration of Independence, which later inspired the Declaration of the Rights of Man. And we know that the Founding Fathers were merchants and speculators who emerged immensely richer from the war against England. The patriot George Washington was a great landowner who made his fortune by speculating in land. But the economic significance of nationhood is not always as apparent for French revolutionaries. There, from the beginning, nationalism appears in a mystified and idealist form. The Jacobins were bourgeois, national revolutionaries, but the thing was quite confused for them, expressed in grandiloquent language and imperial roman posturing. Many of them were not particularly insightful, it would seem – executive officers buffeted by events and pretty much groping in the dark, rather than great men. They did not clearly understand what they represented, nor the forces they were manipulating. Those who were corrupt were probably more intelligent than the hard-liners – Mirabeau and Barras smarter than Robespierre.[1] In fact, their successes are explained by the liberation of national bourgeoisies in all the countries they penetrated; Napoleon's conquests rested on the bourgeoisies of the countries he conquered, and where there was no sufficiently developed native bourgeoisie, Napoleon's military genius was unable to achieve very much, as in Spain and Russia. But the Jacobins themselves understood their project as a mission given to France by Reason: the liberation of the world. If this project brought with it fruitful operations and conquests, they were simply one more chapter in the glorious narratives of Reason and Nation.

For nationalisms, the honeymoon is soon over. The bourgeoisies of the different countries came into conflict; the need to protect domestic markets makes the idea of the nation lose its expansionary, universal character, and the different nationalisms become mutually exclusive. The birth of German nationalism is explained by the clash of French and British interests. Of course it is true that Fichte and the *Addresses to the German Nation*,[2] and the enthusiasm of Prussian youth,[3] and so forth, took their inspiration from the Absolute Spirit, God, Offended Honour and other benevolent demons. But objectively speaking, the success of the German national movement against Napoleon, a movement that would in fact hold back Germany's economic development for several decades, would have been inconceivable without British money.[4] Even then, we see the idea of the nation used as the sordid tool of foreign capital, in the same way as Austrian 'nationalism' is being used by Mussolini.[5]

One is not surprised when one sees that the history of the nineteenth century is the history of successful efforts by the forces of reaction to take over the principle of national revolutions. The policies of Napoleon III, Cavour[6] and Bismarck were the critical moment in this successful strategy. The weaknesses and doubts of bourgeois revolutionaries didn't count for very much.

At the time when capitalism is reaching maturity, and the increasingly powerful industries of individual nations begin looking outward towards imperial expansion (during the first, relatively 'peaceful' phase of the struggle for the global market), the idea of the nation is not greatly in evidence and 'national' sentiment seems curiously diminished. Of course, nationalism is used everywhere as a tool in the class struggle; capitalists in the different countries collude in preaching hatred among the workers – just as today, Schneider is in agreement with Krupp in stirring up hatred between the French and the Germans, and in backward countries, governments encourage anti-Semitism as a means of diverting the masses from revolution, and so on.[7] At this point, the only 'sincere' form of nationalism is found in the petty bourgeoisie and its ideologues. It is a clearly reactionary movement, linked with a clumsy defence against domination by big capital, a political expression of the danger of 'proletarianization' that is an increasingly visible threat to the petty-bourgeoisie. We are already dealing here with a nationalism that is small-minded indeed in comparison with the revolutionary teaching of the Montagnards.[8] This current of feeling becomes the receptacle for a sense of great spiritual powerlessness, the most commonly accepted justification for moral and material poverty. Spiritual eunuchs without the slightest gift for real creativity fall back on nationalist themes! And every poor wretch thinks he is redeemed by the fact that Goethe 'also' was a German, or Britannia rules the waves! It was a clear prefiguration of modern Aryanism, which lets every German idiot think he is infinitely more fortunate and important than Einstein, because Einstein's Jewish. When you have really nothing left to be proud of, you can always glory in being German, Jewish or Persian. Naturally, all these inanities found ideological expression of the most exalted kind – but what shameful thing has not been justified in the name of some high-flown mystique? In France, this rather desperate petty bourgeois movement is reflected in literary attempts to revive the Republican-Jacobin mystique (Péguy is the purest, most sincere of these nationalists) through 'Barrès-ism', through the chauvinist tendency that goes back to the Dreyfus affair, etc.[9] But all these ideologies are extremely isolated, and limited in their effects; 'big' capital has little time for them. Nationalism had so little 'popular' support in 1914 that not one of the great powers invoked it to justify its participation in the war. Germany fought because it was 'economically encircled', the *Entente* wanted to see justice and liberty triumph.[10] Even the most 'national' of all demands, the recovery of Alsace-Lorraine, was presented as simply a question of justice.[11]

The principle of nationalities does not reappear as a political force until the end of the war, to justify the imperialist manoeuvring of the Treaty of Versailles. So even then it was a huge piece of idealist deception; nations are dismembered in the name of national liberty, and Europe was Balkanized into unviable little 'nations', theoretically independent but actually in thrall to monopolies and finance capital. In every one of these small States created by the treaty, nationalism immediately takes a rabid and oppressive form; in Poland, Romania and Yugoslavia, astonished idealists see a wave of savage terror unleashed against suffering minorities: Jews, Hungarians, Ukrainians, Croats and Macedonians. The only content of this modern nationalism is oppression of the weakest; as a dynamic, liberating theory it has reached the stage of total degeneration.

Today, the Nation has been *left behind* by historical and economic realities. The forces of production cannot continue to develop if the political framework of the nation is retained. Even the petty bourgeoisie can no longer escape poverty and proletarianization except by helping the proletariat to abolish itself as a class, liberate labour and organize the economy on a global basis.

How is it, then, that today we are seeing a resurgence of nationalist ideas?

This fact, too, is explained by the capitalist development of the economy. As the global market shrinks, the imperial powers are forced increasingly to turn towards intensified exploitation of their domestic markets; monopolies can now only grow stronger by crushing small capitalists, and by ruthlessly eliminating free competition. In these operations, finance capital is now using the ideology of nationalism developed by the petty bourgeoisie, which it also needs as a force to use against the revolutionary proletariat. The nation is now the 'home base' for the dominance of the bourgeoisie, the framework in which it acts, the focus of its violence. The apparatus of the nation-state is a wonderful tool, currently used by the monopolies. However, these monopolies are not necessarily national; the region in which capital is invested and is productive may coincide with nation-states, but not the form that capital takes, i.e. money, which is well and truly international. A large stake in

Italy's state railways, for example, is held by American capital. Finance capital dominates and extends beyond the limits of the nation (not entirely: within finance capital there are competing enterprises that are English, French or American, but each has branches in the other countries). To achieve domination, international capital uses national structures, and the nation-state masks the domination of international capital. It acts and manoeuvres behind these forms, held before the eyes of the oppressed. Within the nation-state, finance capital allies itself with the national bourgeoisie, which it needs in order to act locally and to repress or divert discontent. Inside nations sometimes its strategy is to 'divide and rule', and to provoke conflict and rivalry among the discontented, and sometimes it is to promote the idea of a supposed national 'community', as with the Hitlerians; not only does it set nation against nation, but when necessary it cobbles together utterly 'genuine' nationalisms, as Austrian or Manchurian nationalism. Finance capital, incarnated into monopolies, supports a section of the national bourgeoisie, while at the same time it may sacrifice another section – property owners or small firms – in order to reduce discontent and appear sympathetic towards socialism. It hardly matters by whom or by what a figure like Hitler believed himself to be inspired. Among people of little education, economic necessity, the obscure, hidden force that rules bourgeois society, can take the name Jesus, or Wotan, or the Race. In fact, and events bear this out, the inspiration for Nazi ideology came from Thyssen and the representatives of a financial system that by its very nature is international and anonymous. Thyssen, Krupp, Schneider-Creusot, I. G. Farben, etc., are Hitler's advisers or direct auxiliaries.[12] Dollfuss has put Austria into the hands of Mussolini.

In capitalist countries today, nationalism is but a tool for domination by the monopolies. 'National revolution' is now neither revolutionary nor national. It expresses the manipulations of finance capital and its stranglehold over a nation. It represents nothing but the subservice of that nation to monopoly capitalism, which is international! Nationalist propaganda is a way of betraying the real nation – the real substance of the idea – just as spiritualism is a betrayal of the spirit and rationalism a betrayal of reason.

The economic absurdity of autarky and the material disasters of chauvinist extremism are so obvious that theorists of the Nation usually chose to justify their ideas using arguments of a spiritual kind. People try to excuse oppression and the diminution of real life by invoking national culture and the need to preserve picturesque traditions.

In its initial phase, precisely because it expressed genuine development of the forces of production, nationalism was a powerful cultural stimulant. Unification of dispersed and economically isolated communities, use of national languages instead of medieval Latin, and the global horizons opened by economic expansion liberated enormous cultural forces. The rise of the bourgeoisie coincided with an immense flowering of art, philosophy, science and literature. However, we should not forget that the products of this culture are only of value to the extent that they are *universal*. Even from a French national point of view, there is a big difference between a figure like Montaigne and one such as Diderot or Barrès.[13]

It should be noted here that culturally speaking, the bourgeoisie has never distinguished between the various elements of its national culture. In the nationalist church, Madame de Pompadour and Descartes, Louis XIV and Racine[14] are all on the same level, and have equal status within the precious heritage that is venerated and taught in school.

Today's fascisms go further. Under the pretence of going back to their 'roots' they are destroying universal elements and promoting the local and the accidental. Nationalism and national culture are now in total contradiction! To be convinced of this one need only recall the cultural 'achievements' of a Hitler or Mussolini. Fascism rejects Goethe and Heine and reverts to Odin;[15] it destroys both the rationalism and the romanticism that have always accompanied national cultures, and have been an integral part of those cultures. But the 'genius of France' surely consists of something more than some dubious Gallic revivalism. To throw out Montaigne, Voltaire and Diderot, and then dress up in white robes to go gathering mistletoe would indeed be a crime against French culture!

Fascism is perpetrating this crime. It returns to survivals from the remotest past, in order to re-establish medieval ties of personal dependency. And despite their political differences, all forms of fascism, as if by chance, adopt more or less the same kind of mysticism, using barbarous language and different terminology. It is imperialist fascism that leads to uniformity! Only international revolution is capable of freeing cultures from national frameworks that have become oppressive. It has never been a question of imposing on nations an ideology that is 'proletarian' in a cold or rigid sense. That image of cultural revolution is a mere caricature. Cultures are used, squandered, distorted and finally destroyed by the politics of the bourgeoisie and its continuation as fascism. The Russian experience proves once and for all that proletarian revolution makes cultures truly national by extending them to the masses and opening up access to spiritual life for yesterday's oppressed classes. Peaceful coexistence among peoples united in one global economy will liberate new cultural forces that are at present diverted into maintaining exclusivity, and it will give the spirit of each people full scope to express itself spontaneously. Revolution will deliver national cultures from reactionary putrefaction. Naturally, it introduces new elements, an *international* (i.e. universal) *content*, to culture in a national form. These elements consist especially of the kind of dialectical thinking that is incomparably flexible and whose method is to *integrate*. Through revolution, each national culture is able to flower and increase for its own sake, while at the same time being linked together in the universal. And they will thus become liberated aspects of the human experience, moments within a single whole. Culture will be both national and international: international content in a national form.

We therefore have to be internationalists in the name of national culture.

Fascism is a general and multi-faceted process of mystification; it makes improper use of the forms, structures and moments of reality. It uses them against the historical movement by preventing their being surpassed, to the benefit of society in its capitalist form.

And this is why it rants about national revolution, because the nation was, *at a certain moment*, a revolutionary creation …

In Germany, the bourgeois revolution did not have the pure, classical character of 'our' 1789. It started outside the country; Napoleon arrived, shaking up feudalism and setting off the process of unification. The revolution of 1848 failed, and every further step towards national unity was to the advantage only of Prussia and Prussian militarism. Feudalism left a much more extensive legacy in Germany than in France, and it made cosy alliances with industrial and finance capital. The revolution of 1919 was a proletarian revolution manqué – and a delayed bourgeois revolution. Weimar, that travesty, left power in the hands of country landowners and investment bankers. And Germany was not even unified!

Today, that unfinished process of national unity serves the interests of German capitalism and its manoeuvrings. The Third Reich brings the nation to completion. Of Hitler's twenty-five points – and despite the delays that can be ascribed to the Prussian opposition – this is just about the only one on which he has been true to his word.[16]

This gives Hitlerism the appearance of a certain dynamism and effectiveness. The Nation did not yet exist; the period now ending was only one of a gradual growth of consciousness. The Nation is about to begin, the Nation is coming into being, the German fascists declare, and write; the Third Reich, powerful and magnificent, is on the march!

And this is how the *opposite* of a 'national revolution' once again saves the Nation's face and recovers its old revolutionary prestige. And this 140 years after 1789 – when it involves the mere *consolidation of an existing state of affairs*, and the unification of violence!

An absurd situation, you say? Evidence of a 'stupid' mentality? A lie? No, much more like the use of a form that conceals the opposite of its former content: Mystification.

In every bourgeois nation there are two nations, said Lenin. It is perfectly legitimate to set the real nation of the working masses in opposition to the 'International' of fascist parasites and their mystifying nationalism, the enemy of the true nation.

Between Yourself and You

(from Norbert Guterman and Henri Lefebvre, *La Conscience mystifiée* (Paris: Syllepse, 1999 [1936]), pp. 145–6)

In the preceding pages we have tried to describe the consciousness men have of themselves, their relationships, their unity – the consciousness they have spontaneously, in the capitalist world, of what it is to be human. And the result is certainly paradoxical; there is nothing more unstable, more contradictory, more elusive, than that consciousness.

What was elevated into an absolute value has now become weak, immeasurably fugitive and defeatist. Always driven beyond itself. Always hiding something else. Even the anxious immobility of total scepticism no longer offers a refuge; everything, including that refusal to think that is scepticism, is revealed as suspect thinking – a form of unconsciousness!

When one examines them, problems, with their words, seem to disappear. Ideologies undergo a ghostly transformation, as if the eye has magical powers and kills what it wishes to surprise: life itself. Where we thought we saw solid outlines, we find a bit of mist – and something else behind it, something else, ad infinitum. The ideologies that appear to be most solid and affirmative, those that insist most strongly on human nobility and invincibility (religion, fascism) are revealed as the most deceitful, the most ignoble. Nothing is more frankly self-seeking than gratuitous lyricism, nothing more impure than purity, nothing more corrupt than 'free' detachment, nothing uglier than 'beauty', nothing more base than nobility ...

That's how everything's suspect. You emerge from a lie and fall into a deeper lie. In desperation, you give up on the universal, and the human, you announce that all men are mutually hostile and you search for possession of yourselves in isolation. But even that is impossible. You find yourself with a phantom that can no more be grasped than the surroundings you are fleeing. You are riven by internal contradictions that tear you apart, separate you from each other, devour you. There is no more solitude.

Is there, then, no way out? Is the only solution to stay there, passively, like a recumbent animal – because to retreat in himself has proved impossible; man cannot evade his consciousness without ceasing to be human, and a fascism that proclaims the abolition of knowledge and ideas is very much a conscious trick. Purely and simply silence the desire for truth that is a fertile source of pain? But these underlying contradictions will rend you nonetheless, and distress will find a way to enter beneath your conscious will.

No, the solution is not to give up thought, or to remain passive. Because, though conscience may prove a liar, this is not entirely so, since it also emerges that it is lying. Consciousness thus contains the potential to overcome itself. When consciousness is understood as a lie it even then declares a truth through that very lie. Taken in itself, separate and sovereign, consciousness is a lie; truth, then, is only possible in a consciousness that has surpassed that consciousness, which has re-established its relationship with all that is not consciousness, with the material world. The reality of human consciousness is the movement of human affairs. It is not the idea of man which is the truth of man, but exactly the opposite.

For the reality of the human world is not this or that self-image that it has constructed in any given period, but creative, productive work – not work in an abstract sense, but in all its historical and social determinations. A real solution is thus only possible through the transformation of work – of its present forms. That is the revolutionary communist solution, the solution of dialectical materialism.

Therefore, dialectical materialism, does not appear as a revelation, or a form of grace. It provides its own birthright; it is no more than the continuation of human effort, a method of conquest conceived in struggle itself. In the middle of this world, Revolution appears as the reality that rescues and watches over all that remains of the real. It is solution not because it combines or rearranges existing terms, but because it transforms them – both things and human beings. It is invoked by them – but as their own renewal. Not only does it usher in a new world, but it explains this one. Such is its independence of spirit vis-à-vis all other doctrines. It involves us in active overcoming, and thus, when we act, we immediately become more real and more true.

Any other 'solution' is an attitude, one of ultimate mystification to which we are painfully driven by the mystifying and mystified environment. It leaves us – escapism, scepticism, solitude and idealism – right in the heart of this world.

The only avenue capable of making us a man, or even a 'spirit', in the dialectical sense of the word, is that of overcoming. He who surmounts is a man.

We can only truly escape from this world by first acknowledging that we are in it and that we are suffocating, and then by working practically for its transformation.

Being a Communist[1]

(from *La Somme et le reste* (Paris: Méridiens Klincksieck, 1989 [1959]), pp. 683–92)

I can already hear the chorus of imprecations and objections, the first from 'adversaries' and the second from friends and ex-comrades.

'How, with your present attitude and state of mind, can you claim to be a Marxist and a communist? You were a member of the French Communist Party for 30 years, and an active grassroots militant. There is a remarkable inconsistency there, or at least a strange kind of misunderstanding, which you have been in no hurry to clear up. You must have suffered greatly, or have kept yourself hidden away, or admitted that you compromised many of your principles.' That is what one lot will say. The others will declare, 'He's a bit mad. He's neither a Marxist nor a communist. He never understood anything. He misled the Party by removing half his mind and half his life out of the Party's control, and from its action and discipline. Now, unmasked by those who are most vigilant, and removing his mask himself, he shows himself for what he has always been. He was never a true member of the Party. Exclusion? One would have expected that logical term to have come up long ago, had it not been for the Party's patience, its attention to individual cases, its efforts to help the comrades ...'

My response is that in my opinion (and I am the one most closely involved) there was no real misunderstanding, and no duplicity. Those who use that sort of language have never understood anything about contradictions, living or lived – that is, about dialectics.

First of all, we have to be in agreement about the words '*being* a Marxist, *being* a communist'. I contend that ontology, preserved and systematized within so-called Marxism, has literally contaminated these words. We have understood Marxism and communism ontologically (*being*) instead of presenting them, like Marx, in movement and as becoming. We have focused on the mode of being and an ontological participation in the future, the actual reality of the communist. What is meant by 'communist man', in 1940, in 1950? What demagoguery, or what a production! What mystification! I know of no communist man other than in a communist society, about which I can say nothing, because it does not yet exist. I maintain that the ontological idea has spread to the conception of the party and the State. Marxism has been turned into a metaphysics of the party and the State, elevated into absolutes that demand unconditional allegiance. The term 'being', transferred from its speculative substance onto the State and the Party, has taken on new vigour. These entities demand unconditional recognition and loyalty. More than that. Marxism, imprisoned within categories it had critiqued and dismantled, has itself become a system, an entity; and in another retrograde move, we have sanctified and socialized that entity. To 'be' a Marxist and a communist is thus to be part of a sacred, sanctified entity.

To summarize a diffuse argument, I admit that if we mean by the words 'being a communist' a kind of substantive quality or ontological essence that is supposed to turn on the spot the Marxist or the communist, into a changed man, different from others, freed from their contradictions and participating in truth as in the future, I am not, nor have I ever been, a good or true communist. (I would ask readers, and anyone who responds to this, not to pick this sentence out or to quote it out of context.) I believe that this claim has led to the creation of a category of impossible, unacceptable and insufferable people; they *are* those who already hold power over a third of the globe. They *are* the bearers of historic verities, the 'new men', contemporaries of the future, men already living in the society to come, without contradictions, communists through and through, free from the problems of real people within the social praxis of mid-twentieth-century France, of bourgeois society. Heroes? Men of solutions and not of problems? Perhaps. Time does its work, and changes the hero into something else, changes the man without problems into a problem without humanity. For my part, I have been, and am, of my time – as fully and painfully, as humbly and proudly as possible. I want to 'take on' all contradictions, to the last drop. It is my belief that the person who leaps above the times, his time, and believes he is already 'communist man', is most mistaken. And first of all, that makes no sense. With the passing of time, this vaunted condition of 'exception' must surely turn into its opposite: discipline into spinelessness, freedom into dogma, dedication into careerism. In my view, that is the imminent punishment (and the reward) for an attitude that on the theoretical level can only be described as idealist: superfluity, a parasitic excrescence on the tree of knowledge and the tree of life.

If 'being a communist' is understood as implying unlimited loyalty to a man or men (yesterday, Stalin; tomorrow, who knows?), to a country (yesterday or today, the USSR), to a nation, a political institution (the Communist Party, the State, etc.), my answer is this: I am not, I have never been and I never will be a communist. Because I accept no absolute, nothing 'unconditioned'. And I never have accepted it, because I believe that the dialectic upsets all absolutes, all 'unconditioned' and that is its *principle*. Only the truth has an unconditional and absolute right: that it is always relative. I have never, and I will never give up freedom of thought, a freedom, by the way, that is conditional and limited by acceptance of disciplines and decisions. That it is not easy to resolve these contradictions, and that I have not always come out of it very well, is one thing. That we have to retain both sides of the contradiction, in order to resolve it, is another, very definite idea. In this case, the philosopher's conscience sees to it that both sides of the contradiction are preserved, to avoid a bad solution, one that is worse than all others: unilaterality, which liberates the particulars from the problem, and allows individual critical thought to escape in one direction, and discipline in action, in the other.

I declare here that we must once again relativize and 'de-absolutize' everything related to politics, the State, the Party. Marx defined communism in terms of movement – not of 'being' – and as a movement towards a specific, clearly stated goal. I am not interested in a definition that makes nothing of this goal. *To be* a socialist or a communist is in essence to desire a specific step with defined limits in space and time: the end of private ownership of the means of production. This commits us to studying, accepting and desiring the practical measures that will make possible this abolition as well as the consequences for the economy and a social practice thus made rational and coherent (more rational, more coherent).

Abolition of private ownership of the means of production is not arbitrarily ordained. It has historical, economic and political conditions. It is not enough – not nearly enough – to imagine and conceive of private ownership as being replaced, in order for it to be replaced in fact. That abolition, as a project, springs from (dialectical) analysis of social development, and its contradictions. Such an analysis gives us some sense of the possibility of a society based on the multiplication of needs, and of ways of satisfying them, in such a way that *in time*, a certain number of words will either lose their meaning or acquire an entirely different one: democracy, freedom, justice, law, and perhaps philosophy, truth, etc …

'Being a communist' means desiring the advent of that society, with the greatest possible economy of time and effort and the least harm and violence; it therefore means being informed and perceptive about the present social and political situation from the perspective of what is to come, and of *movement* towards it, and seeking to direct that movement towards the future without ignoring the lessons of the past. It thus means knowing that historical development is not judged only in terms of the past or the existing state of affairs, but of what is possible. It also means knowing that we cannot simply leap into that future, that we cannot simply skip certain stages in that movement, that the process presents contradictions (some of them profound) and that we have to choose those we can resolve, and distinguish them from those for which we as yet have no solution.

Several questions arise at this point. Among those who want to forge ahead, some want to stop at a particular stage, and bring movement to a stop there. Thus, there are democrats who do not claim to be socialists, even though democracy tends towards socialism and only the abolition of private ownership of the means of production can bring about democracy. Others say they are socialists, and like to think they are, but not communists. It is clear that we are dealing here with questions that are badly posed, totally muddled, containing an element of the absurd. The difference between socialism and communism cannot and should not appear until socialism is achieved, since for communists, communism follows socialism, which is an essential stage. From which we may conclude that the division between socialists and communists (the right and left wings of the movement) springs from historical and political contingencies and has nothing necessary about it. Communists must have made some serious mistakes for communism to have become separated from and opposed to socialism and democracy. Which in no way absolves democrats and socialists! Is this division, therefore, an absurdity? Yes, and what's more, it is a fundamental, characteristic absurdity, which explains the feelings of ambiguity and absurdity that affect so many hearts and minds. What measures leading towards communism could be proposed (in principle) by communists, but ought to be opposed by socialists? We need to go beyond the situation, theoretically. However, this situation is a historical fact. We are emerging from a period in which it was systematically exploited. We are still there. Stalin played on the opposition of right and left, alternately taking rightist and leftist positions, beating off his enemies, now those on the left, now those on the right, muddying the waters and calling rightists leftists and vice versa. He is not the only one to have played on division. Is it an absurd one, resulting more from political tactics and strategy than from historical necessity? Not entirely, to the degree that democrats and socialists represent social groups and classes who wish to have an impact on the pace and methods of the movement, and to be part of it, rather than see themselves done away with, or face that risk. We've met this problem before, the problem (or one of them) of the left. The solution is obvious; those who represent the most active, most revolutionary elements, must keep in mind the others, and their interests and demands, without thereby allowing them to halt the movement.

If we define communism not as a being or a 'state' (the pun is intentional) but as movement, and in movement, *towards* a possible future, established as such, then I lay claim to being an excellent communist. The Party is then defined as the free association of those who align themselves with this future, and its achievement in the shortest possible time, with the least possible harm. On every current issue, communists adopt the solution that is oriented towards the future. They accordingly accept rational discipline in the sphere of political activity. A broad and clear definition; it does not claim that the Communist Party as such is the only social force leading towards socialism, or the only political force capable of bringing socialism about. It only says that the Party brings together those who openly and expressly, in the name of Marxist understanding, wish to see capitalist society overtaken by socialism, and socialism overtaken by communism. There will be objections (and they are unavoidable) that these views do not realistically take into account the social and political forces present in the world. We can refute this objection by saying that these very real and firmly established forces put us in an impasse from which a way out should, if possible, be found.

It is worth recalling here how broadly Marx, Engels and Lenin understood historical movement. In their eyes, those tending towards anarchism were not wrong to hate constraint, authority, politics and the State. They were wrong to try to leap over the transitional phase in which there were good reasons for imposing discipline and uncomfortable restrictions on freedom. For Marx and Engels, 'being a communist' was thus to defer the demands of the individual into the future, and to locate them in what was to come, and in possible developments. The irony is that the 'communists', have, like the anarchists, leaped in a single bound into a future in which discipline would be absolute, the State would rule alone, unchecked, authority would meet with no obstacle and the individual would sacrifice himself entirely to society. They identified themselves – humbly – with that future. 'To be a communist' was thus 'to be' the opposite of what communism is, the reign of liberty.

The theory that has become current and officially accepted in France, according to which discipline and 'loyalty to the party' should come before knowledge and understanding, is simply ridiculous. It enables us to show how far theory has degenerated. It is the philosophical and ontological expression of the 'being' of the Party machine. According to it, you do not come to the Party via knowledge, but to knowledge via the Party. This theory, which makes the formation of Marxism and the Party incomprehensible, draws implacably logical conclusions from Party philosophy. If the Party *is* a philosophical system, you have to begin by belonging to it in order to have access to that system, which is itself the key to knowledge. Unconditional devotion becomes the condition for knowledge. The starting point is materialist ontology conceived not as a confirmation of common sense, but as a political position. A logical connection is established between materialist ontology and political theory (dictatorship of the proletariat, the role of the Party). The one cannot be accepted without the other. This monolithic system has no meaning except where it is supported by State power. There are people (not only worker-militants but also students and intellectuals) who come to believe they are great thinkers because they loudly declare that a glass or a table exists outside themselves. They come to believe you have to 'be a communist' to believe it. By way of political philosophy you arrive at a stupefying party subjectivism. This, paradoxically, is how materialist ontology and idealist ontology become identical, as outmoded varieties of philosophy. Materialist ontology, systematized philosophy, turns into an idealism with a materialist terminology, and in a subjectivism for political purposes, all because ontology, system and philosophy have been overtaken and left behind. Philosophical materialism turns into idealism. Another consequence of the philosophical illusion, even more prevalent, though less often expressed: the Communist Party and the communist, as such, are said to be above contradictions. Purified, and they dominate them. Instead of the 'problem man' of the bourgeoisie, we have 'solution man', flawless without problems. Collectively and individually, 'being' a communist would seem to be precisely that quality, that essence. Such a theory has nothing to do with dialectics. It is political metaphysics, an extreme form of political alienation, linked to philosophy and ontology. The idea of a practical solution of contradictions is confused with the very different thesis according to which the force capable of resolving contradictions escapes them and acts from outside and above them in order to resolve them.

If we put the political party above society, above the masses and above its members, like something free of contradictions – on the analogy of the absolute State, and omitting Marxist critique of the State and politics – we inevitably reach the point where we put a man, a political apparatus and a police force above the Party. This dialectical process is directly linked with the politicization of philosophy, with political ontology and the political claim to occupy a place 'within the positivity of the entity'. It is the internal dialectic of political absolutism and alienation.

The Party is not an absolute. The philosophical (metaphysical) concept of the Party was only an ideological tool, making use of Marxism disguised as a system. The Party will wither away like the State, like politics, like systematized philosophy (materialist or idealist), giving way to forces and forms of social life for which – if it fulfils its function – it will have opened a way, as opposed to containing or creating them. That the Party is not an absolute has consequences. The mere fact of 'being' does not make it a programme. Taking power cannot be its only programme. It needs a programme.

Nor does democracy, any more than the Party, represent an end in itself, another political absolute, because there is no other political absolute, but only a form of political alienation, in political struggle, through the illusion of an absolute. There is no need to have second thoughts about democracy, an essential tool and mediator, the central demand of the day in all domains, and the 'value' that today is crucial without being able to claim to be absolute.

In a situation as confused as this, so marked by aspects of the deterioration of practice and the degeneration of theory, the philosopher gains freedom of action. To invert the proposition: *the philosopher once again declares himself such, in order to regain his freedom of action and thought* and to say what he must say, including on philosophy. It is his duty to help redefine the goals, interests and elements of action and theory. He has to harry with questions those who offer ready-made answers: 'What is socialism? What was it for Marx? What will it be for us? What is the precise significance of the Chinese communes or Soviet decentralization? Do they affect us, or not? What is democracy? What is happiness? What is materialism? What is idealism? What is dialectics? What is practice?'

It is clear, too clear, that *if* history had followed the straight path indicated by Marx – *if* the proletariat of a major industrial country had achieved its revolution and had assimilated thought and knowledge – *if* existing socialism was really the blossoming of humanism and democracy – *if* somewhere the State was withering away, together with politics as such – *if* there had been no Stalin and no Hungary[2] – *if* there was a revolutionary party with a clear programme rationally asserting itself – *if* there was no political Machiavellianism, etc. all problems would now be addressed differently, including the problem of philosophy and the philosopher.

The attitude of the communist 'being' has as its mirror image the 'antibeing'. Anti-communism, like the 'communist being', or even more so, is to some extent made up of mythology. The 'antis' have for reasons of class, economic and political reasons for stabilizing society in its present form, for holding back future change. They thus form the party of immobility. To these disputable, but real and not mythical arguments are superimposed reasons given by communists themselves, in particular by Stalinist practice and ideology. The politics of immobilism then disappear as such, and turn into meta-politics. The anticommunist *is* anticommunist; that is how he defines himself. How can someone define himself so strongly as being against something that does not exist? The 'anti' never asks himself this question. Political terminology helps him, since every day the newspapers and the politicians chatter away about 'communist States', and communism allows itself to be presented as something real and achieved. In opposition to this existent entity, which is aggressively but at the same time badly defined, 'immobilism' has the opportunity to accumulate acquired meanings ('values', morality, liberty). It thus becomes doubly embedded in being. To the men of becoming who thought well to justify themselves through ontology, and 'being', are opposed men who have sounder reasons for justifying themselves through 'being' because in fact they wish to maintain the existing state of affairs. The 'communist' and the 'anti' thus stand face to face, philosophically and politically, frozen like two abstract qualities or two essences. Movement, becoming, transcendence and the possible then lose their meaning. The 'communist being' and the 'anti being' mask the next step, socialism. We are witnessing nothing other than the collapse of two breeds of political animals. In this struggle and for an advanced country like France, the antis are closer to their truth, what exists and immobilism Communists, revolutionaries, by defining themselves at the level of being, put themselves on the enemy's territory. They are in the here-and-now, facing the legal owner of the here-and-now. They have no programme, because they 'are' to such an extreme degree. In the battle thus drawn, it is almost impossible for them to gain the upper hand. It would require exceptionally favourable circumstances for a problem so badly posed to be resolved to their advantage. The dilemma encircles us in absurdity. How are we to crack it?

From the Social Pact to the Contract of Citizenship

(from *Du Contrat de citoyenneté* (Paris: Syllepse, 1990), pp. 17–37)

Marxism: Inventory and Balance Sheet

The undeniable social power of information science has as its converse and inverse the ideological power of the media. All the more so since ideology, which never declares itself as such, but as self-evident truth, now parades as pure information. So let us not be afraid to repeat yet again some propositions that would be agreed upon if ideology (of information) did not come into the picture. In a little over a century, Marx seems to have died three times: physically, politically and philosophically. It is futile to consign Marx's work to the archives, to scholarship, or to history, like some old philosophy or ideology that is receding into the past. It is not so much a question of Karl Marx as an historical figure as of the concepts he helped establish. Now concepts lead a hard life, to put it facetiously. Concepts do not fade away like mere operations; once the fashion – the ideology of the media – has passed, they re-emerge intact. Do we believe that the notions of time, space or energy are eclipsed? To be faded out is not to disappear, but a phase. Sometimes even an enrichment. Furthermore, it is absurd and pointless to think of Marx's work as a system that is both intangible and true. These two illusions face to face sustain one another. The same goes for Newton, and Einstein; in order to go further and make progress, we have to go by way of them; an attitude of pure rejection sterilizes theory and practice, but nor can we think of the work of Marx (and Engels) as a rock, a foundation, even if it is dubbed epistemology! Their work only has meaning when it confronts events and actions in the so-called modern world. This involves critique and further elaboration, even transformation. That approach avoids from the start some blunders and misunderstandings, for example, understanding and interpreting everything in relation to intellectuals and their social role – or taking technology as an absolute, out of context, etc.

The ephemeral reputations of those who set themselves the task of 'cleaning up' Marxism have something to teach us. Propelled onto the political scene by the media, they come and go. We learn what we suspected:

a good publicity campaign begins with the declaration, 'this is not a publicity campaign, it is a set of truths, it is the 'very truth'.

Any attempt to take stock (of the inheritance) and to see where we stand (in terms of progress made) needs to point to the philosophical 'drift' of Marxist thinking and thinking in general. When the first questions asked are, 'But where does philosophy stand? Where is it going? Does it still exist? Isn't it moribund? Isn't it reduced to its history, to a form of psychology, sociology or anthropology?', we turn Marx and his thinking into a philosophical system (dialectical materialism, in a word, the official, institutional 'diamat').[1] Thus, all works since Heraclitus turn into 'systems' whose histories are written, whose legacies are described, and which are compared with others, so that every philosophy becomes an (abstract) 'object'. Intentionally? Spontaneously? In both cases, this drift mirrors the tendency of systems, their wish to halt, to paralyse everything. From fear of what could happen if stability does not rule. But philosophical systems have all in fact exploded, scattering their pieces far and wide, whether created by the philosophers themselves or constructed by commentators. Including the one attributed to Marx, or that of his predecessor Hegel, whose good bits Marx was able to use. 'Great' philosophers simply float along on aphorisms, mottoes: 'Know thyself', 'Cogito ergo sum', etc.

More-or-less-dialectical materialism has split along two opposed lines. On the one hand, materialist philosophy emphasizes the 'real', the outside world, work, physical nature and activities that modify it; it moves towards a kind of political positivism. On the other hand, philosophy moves towards radical critique, pure negativism, according to which to assert materiality is to sound the death knell of thought. For example, Adorno believes that the great moment of history has been missed. It will not come again. Time thus enters a state of pure negativity. This systematization within the negative, which takes it to the absolute, loses its way in 'critical critique', autocritique and hetero-critique. It offers nothing, but only proclaims the end of everything: philosophy, knowledge, political action. On the one hand, dogmatism (institutional Marxism) sadly lacks a critical dimension, but on the other, hypercriticism runs up a blind alley. This expresses a general, universal situation: either stagnation or catastrophe. Which means we now have to discover and open up not a 'third way', but a way!

The break-up of Marxism has already been declared many times: with no effect among either 'friends' or 'foes'. A fact that demonstrates both the fecundity of Marx's work and the difficulties and transformations of the modern world. And also the need to bring together in a new whole, outside the old systems, its dispersed elements, gains and conquests, the old and the new. Using critical perspectives, not dogmatic assertions. So is it a question of following Marx's trail and, so to speak, taking the exact same path? No, it is a matter of using him as a starting-point and inventing something new. Of returning to the process of becoming and opening up a future.

What we might call 'philosophical drift [*dérive philosophique*]' has influenced Marx and Marxists, not only by paralysing them and preventing movement, but also by concealing gaps and fractures. To such a degree that we continued to hold forth about (for or against) Marxism, when that entity was no more than a fiction. And we noticed neither the break-up, nor the fecundity (through dispersal), nor the new problems (the impact of new concepts), nor the gains and the legacy. Today that legacy can be divided (using signs that are later than Marx, but useful) into categories, themes and problems. If we accept that classification, at least as a working hypothesis, we can create a sort of table summarizing the state of Marxism, without too many words, and, on beyond [...],[2] a significant part of the ideological situation within modernity.

Categories

These are concepts. From the Marxist perspective, there is a dilemma and a choice: either theoretical concepts – or empiricism and the irrational, scepticism. Concepts join up to form a theory. You can develop them, reveal their connections, even add to them; they have a solidity, without which they would come under a different heading. Production of things and (social) relationships comes first, with its complement, reproduction (of objects and subjects), which is often overlooked. Reproduction is never identical, unless it is programmed to be so. It also creates differences and evolution (history consists of identical reproductions and of differences reaching the point of contradiction). Other concepts: capital, capitalism, the organic composition of capital, surplus value, concentration of capital. To this list can be added categories and concepts developed after Marx's time: the urban (the fragmented city) – the worldwide – the everyday, the repetitive and the differential, the struggle against time within time itself, the ends in becoming (the end of wage-earning, capital, the State, classes, history, philosophy, etc.).

Themes

Themes have not attained the precision and certainty of concepts. As developed by Marx (and Engels) they pervade their work without reaching a conclusion or a final form. So they are perpetuated. Take alienation, a Hegelian theme transformed by Marx; it is no longer the loss of an essence but an obstacle on the path of the possible. Or again, take merchandise and exchange, the world of merchandise and the world market – take ideologies – and the dialectic itself, conflicts and contradictions, as realities and as a procedure of discovery (NB: Many people would like to consign these themes to oblivion, rather than continue to use them; they want novelty, at any price!).

The Problematic

Trivialization and misuse of the word 'problem' have made it intolerable. There is no alternative in our language for the slightly pedantic word 'problematic'.

The problematic is therefore vast. With time, questions proliferate and answers become scarce – acceptable or credible answers, at least. Where to begin? With philosophy? With economics? With 'the political' or 'politics'?

Mastery of social phenomena raises many of these questions. There have been failed attempts. Marx attributed to the working-class (organized, assimilating theory and transcending itself by abolishing classes) the ability to gain rational control over the economic, the social and the political. In fact, the State almost everywhere tries to play this role. How are we to organize the economy? By a plan? By a programme? By a project, and if so, what project? Does history have a direction, a meaning? Or does the role of chance and randomness make the future unpredictable? Which has the upper hand, identity (homogeneity on a universal scale) or difference, to the point of conflict? Stagnation or catastrophe? How are we to interpret the resurgence of religious faiths? Or the automation of productive work? Does 'actually existing' socialism have any connection with Marx's concepts, and if so, what? How are we to understand the general bureaucratization of modern societies and the elevation of the nation-state to the world scale, and of multinational firms? The growth and fragmentation of cities? Lastly, and always, what about philosophy, its place in our culture, its practical scope?

This gaping problematic, which is part of the legacy, forces us to speak of a critical state and not simply a crisis of Marxism, modernity and the modern world. Bankruptcy? Annihilation? No, we need not rush to those hasty conclusions. But definitely an enormous theoretical and practical task. It means a revival of thinking and action under the sign of Marx and not that of the State, or technology. But is it not a sense of the difficulties of Leninism (which people still see as all of a piece with Marxism) missing from this picture – theories of imperialism, the peasant question, science, and so on? Leninism is in decline. Imperialism has changed its method, i.e. its strategy. The theory of knowledge has been modified, since the technological revolution did not come via socialism. The peasant question has shifted; food production is now a prime consideration, since we do not eat steel or computers. And we have to feed billions of people, a planetary problem.

The Jacobin Legacy

Marx's clarion call for total revolution – an appeal that received only partial responses and is now partly eclipsed – ought not to mean that the French Revolution is forgotten. What remains of it? For a time, it seemed close to revolution in the Marxian sense; its predecessor, in harmony with it. Then divergences and distances became more marked. Has the Enlightenment disappeared, leaving us in darkness and (Marxism apart) threatening us with obscurantism? What place are we to give to the legacy of Rousseau and Condorcet?[3] To the Jacobin legacy? Stimulus or obstacle? Is French society trapped between the two traditions of Jacobinism and Bonapartism? How can it be freed? In the name of Jacobinism and sometimes of Marx, we have made a distinction between patriotism (genuine national feeling) and chauvinism. In fact, fusion and confusion have been at work. The stimulus can become an obstacle, given events and political situations that demonstrate a kind of 'State fetishism' (to talk like Marx) which is unequally distributed but on a world scale. In fact, this fetishism is accepted in both the Jacobin and the Marxist camp, although not without certain divergences on the exercise of power. Some think it able to work miracles, notably to solve all economico-socio-political problems. Others restrict its scope. All, or nearly all, make an abstraction of the creative involvement of the people, the rank-and-file, even the working-class (a class sometimes fetishised, sometimes despised). In that context, polemics between democracy and authoritarianism, which should have been resolved long ago, start afresh: between the strong State and direct democracy, between the idea of global consensus and the project of self-management on different scales, from the firm to the society. All of which would seem to release the Jacobin heritage from the liens encumbering it.

The Other Founding Figures

Might we find suggestions and pointers in some not inconsiderable thinkers such as Max Weber, Rosa Luxemburg, or Trotsky? We thought they had been consigned to 'history', but in fact they live on. From Weber we get the theory of a rationality that evolves in the City (the town) and because of it. He also put forward an idea that is hardly compatible with Marxism and 'class' in the Marxian sense: the idea of the 'political class'. It turns out that the facts match Weber's notion, to the extent that politics has become a career.

From Rosa Luxemburg comes the fruitful opposition of the centre and the periphery, which revitalizes analysis of imperial policy. From Trotsky come critiques of Stalinism (receding along with their 'subject' but still valid). There is no space here to examine these contributions, or others, in detail. This is not the heart of the matter; that lies in our malaise, our need for and expectation of a coherent project that answers the above questions, and others, deploys concepts, adds to our core of knowledge, and creatively seeks the possible (the future) without redundant philosophical or technological speculation. In a word, what we need is a politics.

On a Recent Case

This was an affair involving politics and the law; the events took place in Spain and had considerable repercussions, although the case is in danger of being completely forgotten and not leading to what we hoped for: a major political trial, a tragi-comic drama in the style of Aristophanes or Shakespeare.

On 21 July 1986, a Madrid judge published the grounds for a decision he had pronounced a month previously, involving a complaint lodged by a Catalan, the songwriter Lluís Llach, in February 1986. The European organization *Droit et raison d'Etat* supported the complaint, against the Spanish Socialist Party (then in power) and its General Secretary, the Prime Minister.[4] The reason for the complaint was breach of contract. The election manifesto of the PSOE represented a contract with the electorate. But its promises were not kept, and there was therefore a breach of contract. Judge Don Jesús Ernesto Peces y Morales ruled in effect that there is a contractual relationship between citizens and political parties, who are then responsible for the fulfilment (or not) of their promises. The judge thus called for the introduction of a general political contract, enshrining in law the citizen's right to participate actively in political and civil society. By the same token, the judgement gave citizens the right to go to law if they believe they have been injured by whatever party is in power. People will say it was a 'political manoeuvre against the PSOE'. That was not proven, and it is not important. Nor is the way the affair ended; it tends towards the extension of democracy through a contract of citizenship, a contract that needs to be spelled out and formulated in detail. The idea of a New Citizenship and the proposal for a contract of citizenship are thus no longer abstractions. They have entered the realm of the practical by an unexpected route: the courts – the fight in the name of justice against misuse of language, and against rhetoric and demagogy. And this is in a democracy that is still new and uncertain, and it has international implications. The political contract, sooner or later, will replace the 'social contract'; it will replace politics, everyday politics. Its form and scope have still to be decided.

Put plainly, politicians have come to think only in terms of power relations ruling out thought, even – or especially – political thought, whose existence they dispute or deny. They try to catch out those who defend the relative autonomy (there is no absolute independence vis-à-vis conditions or circumstances) of thought, knowledge and theory. These politicians, moreover, swing between dogmatic satisfaction and terror of a vacuum. The implicit or sometimes explicit dilemma, 'either ... or' distorts questions and brings things to a stop: 'either with us – or against us'.

When in our writing we affirm the truth of the proposition, 'between the State and the market there is nothing', we pose a false dilemma, because between the two there is already the bureaucracy; tomorrow there may be self-management [*autogestion*]. It is a matter of concepts and propositions, not of positions. If one side accepts such or such a proposition, that is fine. If not, too bad for those who propose it. What needs to be renewed is not one or other party; is it not rather (in this country and elsewhere) thought, consciousness, political life? And what's more, it is only too true that 'politology' and political science do not have much in common with political activity.

Did Machiavelli, Hobbes or Rousseau make a career of politics? No, no more than did Hegel. Were they politicians? It all depends what you mean by the word. Rousseau says it right at the beginning of *The Social Contract*.[5] Politicians get all the dirty work, but also the honours, the profits, the glory. They come with power. Those who theorize politics are left outside, even when they try to get in (Machiavelli). It is as though the subject could only be conceived of or understood by not being inside it, trapped by a particular 'experience', that of power and violence (see *Le Mémorial de Sainte-Hélène*).[6] Is that not the case with Marx? However, the most remarkable case of all is that of Rousseau, who tried to live according to what was 'natural' and who wrote the 'social contract', initiating a line of theoretical (philosophical and political) enquiry that continued through Hegel and Marx. No work (apart from the *Manifesto of the Communist Party*) has had that sort of political influence.

Jean-Jacques Rousseau and the Social Contract

Rousseau bases society on a 'general will', which is not reducible to the sum of individual wills. In the 'general will', each member of society is both sovereign and 'subject'; he is nothing, can do nothing except through all the others (Book II, Chapter VII). This sovereignty is the source of the law, legislative and executive power, government and the judiciary. 'The essence of the body politic lies in harmony between obedience and liberty, and in that the words *subject* and *sovereign* are identical correlates, whose meaning is summed up in the single word *citizen* (Book III, Chapter XIII).

Politics, government and the State are included in Rousseau's thesis, but as consequences, secondary effects of the social pact. It is as if a society's constitution was the result of a meeting, an assembly of all those who make it up.

Much has been written on these ideas. Did Rousseau see the pact that is the basis of society and of harmony among its members as an historical fact or a fiction, a 'real' event, an abstraction expressed in naturalistic language, or a collective act of men forcing and extending nature, and thus moral? These disputes are no longer of great interest, but the response is clear: the social pact and the general will are concepts, that is, concrete abstractions, with a content: the members of a society must accept it and accept one another as such, otherwise they disappear: criminals, émigrés, vagrants, etc. Using language and ideas that are no longer Rousseau's, we could say that human societies that have not subscribed to this pact have disappeared; those that have, have protected their weakest members, the sick, women, children, the aged, as virtual or actual members of a community. It is the same with the so-called higher animals. As far as human associations are concerned, the content of Rousseau's concept is civil society, which is not subject to any authority – religious, military, feudal or political – that might legitimate it and give it legality. Its laws and customs derive only from itself. This notion of 'civil society' appears in Hegel and Marx, though modified, even transformed. It persists as a concept and an ethical and political 'ideal', while history itself moves away from it after the Revolution and the Empire, with wars and the unexpected rise of the State. In short, we exist within this social pact, even when its effects become distant. And yet we are no longer within it today. The full history of the concept (civil society) and the actual conditions that corresponded with it, while following their own course, would be long and difficult to establish, if we were to take the full context into account. The idea and the social reality that was its content were fought against and muddied by disputes, but were still a force throughout that history. Does the fact of calling oneself 'French' or 'German' not imply acceptance, and despite Marx, an implicit pact? The influence of Britain, which we agree is substantial, needs to be re-examined not only as an example of (to some extent) liberal democracy but as an historic compromise between dominant classes (the bourgeoisie and the aristocracy) that was successful only there. Why? Several obscure areas remain. Inter alia, we would need to look at the activity of freemasons, and at notions of 'civilization' and 'civility' (notions permeated by ideology but which also correspond with a practice that does indeed include a pact, though not one formulated as such). And we should also look at the contradictions of the French Revolution: action by the people, but with state control and militarization (Jacobinism followed by Bonapartism). These last points have not been clarified. Nor has Marx's relationship with Rousseau. If the general will were to succeed in formulating itself and taking action, would it not make the State redundant? But according to Marx, this 'will' is neither formed nor formulated. Because there are classes! The working-class cannot, should not, give its consent to existing society. At the same time, Marx's objective is not in conflict with Rousseau's: to strengthen civil society to the point that it absorbs the State and politics. The best historians in the age of the French Revolution and the Empire had great respect and admiration for the events they reclaimed in order to balance partisan distortions of a religious or military origin. It is not easy to expose the contradictions, for the lack of a dialectical concept of time. Similarly, 'Marxists' have demonstrated only to a very limited extent the contradictions in both Marx and the political consequences of 'Marxism', from the lifetimes of its founders, Lenin in particular, onwards. The distances between theory and practice, conceptions and actions, promises and achievements, were seen as inevitable features of political history; serious students of politics left the field to the men of power and the party machine, to members of the 'political class', some of whom set themselves up as political thinkers, justified by theory. Separation between theory and practice was thus accompanied by increasing confusion, which was not cleared up by the media, either in words or images. What were the roots of this situation? To understand it, we have to go back in time.

Declarations (Humanity and Citizenship)

The first Declaration of Rights was promulgated in Virginia in 1776. The French Declaration dates from August 1789; it came close on the heels of the fall of the Bastille, but its historical origins are in the immense work of the Enlightenment. Popular uprising and philosophy played equal parts; the notions of 'civil society' and of 'man', not as a member of a given society but of the human race, two different but mutually supportive ideas, had the same status in the proclamation of the Rights of Man. Their demands and affirmations have the same source and involve the same outrage against tyranny, despotism, arbitrary rule and the violation of Liberty. The fact that this last idea – which makes positive demands, and provokes action – is unclear was not apparent in 1789. The relationship between nature and reason was a fruitful theme for German philosophers from Kant to Hegel, and they put enormous effort into studying the political revolution in France. For French philosophers, and politicians, there was no problem; reason is based on nature and if nature has to bow to the demands of reason it is so that both can attain Liberty on an equal basis. Jean-Jacques Rousseau had opened up the question; he foresaw the issue: of history in general, the history of accepted institutions and tolerated forms of oppression, and, therefore, of the alienation of liberty. Condorcet similarly underlined the limits of the fundamental Declaration of 1789, especially where women were concerned, but he saw no problem in the relationship between law and nature; human rights are natural rights.[7] Because of the importance of philosophers and philosophy, it is 'man' who comes under the spotlight, who is the focus of attention: man in general, as subject and object of universal reason. 'Man'? This had the extraordinary consequence, which we can now call illogical, that women were not taken into account; they were excluded from the human race, from reason and nature, and from society. But nor did the people's voice, its 'will', understood as specific, not general, as with Rousseau, figure any more prominently. To be a 'man' you had to be a property-owner, though that was not a sufficient condition. 'Man' did not mean democracy, in spite of the familiar association 'Liberty–Equality–Fraternity'. Nevertheless, that abstraction did not remain abstract, because it was connected with theoretical and practical reason, with knowledge, the organization of social life and burgeoning industry. Despite their original limitations, the Rights of Man were in time further defined, becoming more complex and inspiring intense struggles. They were extended to include specific gains made in the course of those struggles, which included class struggles but also rivalry and conflicts between peoples. Rights become diversified and turn into practices as they are contested. The right to property does not, of course, disappear but it ceases to define what it is to be 'human'. It allows the introduction of the right to schooling and education, to health, to work, and even to retirement for the individual after productive work ceases. But above all, rights are extended to women, children, habitat, etc.

Would not a serious error on the part of the Marxist tendency be to have underestimated and even ignored both human rights and the universal struggle for those rights, the struggle to make them broader and deeper? Because of their 'bourgeois' origins? Probably, but that did not stop Marxists claiming allegiance to the French Revolution. By limiting the aims of the class struggle, that attitude did not avoid splits and setbacks in the (revolutionary, Marxist) working-class movement. It has not been accompanied by analysis and development of the concept of citizenship, which has everywhere been ignored.

If man is defined in terms of the human race, rationality and society in general, citizenship is defined by membership of a specific society, and thus by nation and nationality. This includes something different from and over and above the social contract.

During this century, innumerable texts and speeches have been devoted to national questions. Few works have been inspired by Marx or Marxism, given the importance of internationalism and the scornful rejection (already by Marx) of the nation and the nation-state. We should recognize the importance of Stalin's text, *Marxism and the National Question*, published in 1913.[8] What happened to this text, which perhaps gave a foretaste of Stalinism, with the break-up of the Third International in 1943?[9] Like it or not, this text marked a turning-point. It was hugely famous, and is unjustly forgotten today. Not only did it help to launch Stalin's career, it also introduced the concept of the nation into Marxism, with great force. It does not explain the relationship between classes and nations; rejecting a common destiny, it points towards acceptance by the working-class of the fact of being a nation. So what happened?

Many events and developments. Were they connected? Certainly. Rationally, according to a 'reason in history'?[10] No! Some are known about and to some extent understood: crises, wars, treaties. Others are poorly understood, among them the unexpected rise of the State and the nation (in place of the 'class', or of rational universalism and internationalism), with its trail of ideologies: nationalism, chauvinism, 'actually existing' socialism, etc. Thus the international comes to an end during a period when the universal is advancing, from commerce to culture. The only world powers are:

companies, the Church and (modernized) imperialism. Although defeated militarily, has not racist and fascist nationalism changed the (previously expected) course of history? Is anyone responsible for this 'modern' situation which is more paradoxical than it first appears? It is hard to deny the responsibility of Marx and Marxism; if only because Stalinism involves the fusion and confusion of knowledge with State-political power. Yes, Marx hoped to unite what reached him as separated: theory and practice. What Hegel had attempted, but in a way that was contestable and contested. Taking up Rousseau's strand of political thought, Hegel left behind a theory of the State: the 'State of right', bringing with it 'consensus', general acceptance, the consolidation of State power, the deployment of rationality in the process of evolution, from Nature to the Idea. It is a theory that appears abstract, and remote from practice, but also powerful and coherent. We now realize that, a hundred and fifty years later. By trying to go back to this concept, by making it dialectical, by introducing class struggle but seeing politics as the application of theory, Marx was preparing the ground for fusion and confusion between knowledge and power, between what is real and politico-dogmatic assertion, between effective action and official ideology. And this was later to be effected in his name, though in an unforeseen way.

In fact there was the influence of one insidious interpretation ineffectually resisted by Marx on his thinking: the vision of Ferdinand Lassalle, the historical (though often misunderstood) founder of State socialism, and therefore a congenital enemy of 'Marxist' thought, since he remained a Hegelian without making a critique of Hegel's legacy.[11] Presented and adopted despite the texts, this version of 'Marxism' led to the formation, legitimated by 'science' and reason, of the state mode of production, the triad of 'knowledge–power–possession'. In the name of Marx! And this when Marx himself had predicted it all: the power of critical knowledge, total revolution, the rapid transformation and disappearance of the State and the withering away of the nation during the transformation as well as the withering of the nation before the international become the 'human race'. History has been influenced as much, if not more, by the falsification of Marxism as by Marx's thinking. It is true that since then, it has been shown that falsifications are an integral part of the fertility of great doctrines of thought. It is still the case that the history of modernity has not only not followed the predicted and expected path, but that it also shows how difficult it is to control the economy, to set a political course, and to make society function rationally other than by and for technology. Would history be absurd? No. If (philosophical) reason is not at work in becoming, nonetheless everything that happens has reasons which are later recognized: reasons and not determinism, a linear chain of causes.

Over two centuries the rights of man have slowly worked their way into the thinking of the age. While the rights of the citizen have been left in limbo. Why is that surprising? From the first declarations they appeared defined: the right to move freely within one's own (national) boundaries; the right to freedom of opinion (freedom of thought, except where it involves a crime or nuisance, these being left to the authorities to define as they please) and the right to the vote (representation). This has significant consequences for institutions and constitutions. With citizens' rights just as with human rights, in Goethe's famous words, a new world has begun.[12] The right to representation, proclaimed in a revolutionary way, was won through reforms. In France they are still being argued over two hundred years later (proportional representation? majority vote?). Representative democracy swings between direct democracy, which it never achieves, and authoritarian democracy, towards which it always leans, after an 'excess' of liberty. In order to make up for the vagueness in the idea of 'belonging', we define it poorly: sometimes by birth, sometimes by residence, but when the party machines entrench themselves, at every level, from the village to the nation, it has meaning only in and through the nation or the nation-state.

The role of representative democracy, as the representation of the various interests within a population (strata, or classes and fractions of classes), as an historic compromise, in the formation of States on the world scale, cannot be ignored; is it not the most rational aspect of 'modernity'? It goes with a multifaceted cultural transformation.

Throughout the history of the so-called 'modern' world (the word often referring only to one of its aspects, technology), the gap between human rights and citizens' rights has widened. The first are implemented, become diverse, give rise to international conferences, to epic, titanic, sometimes tragi-comic struggles. And what of the others, the rights of the citizen? Frozen, reduced to the minimum for survival, to their initial definition, which seems to be final. There are some we do not talk about any more: the right to rebel against injustice. For the world has changed, albeit not in the hoped for or expected direction, and has become ... worldwide. Links of dependence and interdependence are multiplying. Two realities, in particular, demand that we redefine citizenship: the continent, that is, Europe, and emigrant and immigrant movements of population. Interdependence takes the contradictory form of dependence–independence. Becoming worldly takes the contradictory form of identity (belonging) and of difference, expressed in rivalries and quarrels, understandings and misunderstandings. The economy takes the form of wastefulness and destruction. Technology –information science in general – also takes a contradictory form: communication and transparency; opacity and secrets. Most attempts at analysis omit one or other of these dimensions and contradictions, overestimating this dimension, obscuring that contradiction.

Belonging can no longer simply be defined by family and name (birth) or by place (residence). It has multiplied, and we all 'belong' to our family, to a village or a town, a region, a trade or occupation, a country (homeland, nation and nationality), a State, a continent (in our case, Europe), and to one or more cultures, etc. If we visualize this question in all its breadth, we realize that it is as ethical and philosophical as political. It is this last aspect that we examine here, but in all its dimensions.

The more we study it, the more we see that this situation is complex and murky. The relationship between members of a society, and thus a nation and a State, with that State and nation needs to be redefined. This relationship, i.e. citizenship, stipulates some specific conditions, which go beyond acquired rights of representation. To stipulate rights is first to negotiate them and then to embody them in a contract. While Rousseau explicitly distinguishes between politics and the social contract (see Book III, Chapter XIII), seeing it as a mere circumstantial effect of the general will, the 'modern' formulation of citizenship has to take the form of a contact. Between whom and whom? Between the State and the citizen. And this diminishes (to the point of eventually removing it) the distance between the State, the government, established power, on the one hand, and the citizens – civil society – on the other. Enshrining the relationship in a contract does not give the State greater weight. A political formulation of the relationship, on the contrary, reduces the tendency towards autonomy of the realm of the political and the State, their exteriority vis-à-vis civil society and its sovereign authority. The contradiction that goes to the heart of the political, above 'politics', offers the way to a solution. Which becomes part of a social project that is clearly much larger, because it has to include the field of the economy, the domestic market, industry and food production, the fate of companies, relations with the world market and the multinationals, etc.

The new rights of the citizen, tied in to the demands of everyday life in the modern world, should have been the subject of a detailed declaration at the time of the bicentenary of the French Revolution, which would then not have been reduced to pomp and circumstance, but would have served as the basis for a new beginning.

The New Rights of the Citizen

Traditional humanism declared, against religion, the unicity of the human being, rejecting separation between flesh and spirit, the individual and the social. Taking its inspiration from this humanism, the French Revolution tried to bring about this unity through the Declaration of the Rights of Man and the Citizen. However, the human being as such, in the broadest terms, an abstraction made concrete by certain specific traits, belonged to the human race. As a citizen, the same human being was a member of a specific society (France), part of a network of social practices, by virtue of which he had many obligations. He is in his society, which is itself plural, with its communities of family, work, habitat (village or town, region). This is enough to show the complexity of a concept and a situation that appear to be simple. Citizenship, a source of obligations (paying taxes, declaring ownership of one's property, doing military service, etc.) has from the beginning offered almost nothing in return but the right to vote, that is, to elect a representative, whose subsequent actions will to a greater or lesser degree be under the voters' control.

The condition of citizen nevertheless involves other rights, and for 200 years we have seen them appearing and disappearing, asserting or diluting themselves, depending on the degree of political democracy the nation has achieved, or relinquished.

The right to information
This already exists, in a reduced form that makes it absurd. We all have the right not just to read newspapers and books, but to publish them. Economic conditions reduce the scope of this right to freedom of opinion and expression. But the most serious questions come from elsewhere: we can drown information in an abundance of information, and then there are secrets: State secrets, 'secret services', technical secrets, etc. Secrecy spreads with information. It has been said over and over again that disinformation follows the advance of information like its shadow. However, it would be both utopian and unfeasible to propose, either in principle or as an ethical ideal, the suppression of all secrets. Personal (inner, private, etc.) life is rightly protected from intrusions and indiscretions. Nevertheless, the law must prohibit prosecution of those who reveal a secret – journalists, writers, even pamphleteers. Are there limits to the right to information? Yes, but set as far away as possible, and only out of due respect for individuals. But the most controversial area involves **databanks:** what they collect and keep, and access to the information contained in them. What is the status of databanks? Who is recording whom? Who is reporting, on what? Who can use this knowledge, and what is it for? In the United States, everything is 'free', but access to databanks costs a lot. So their status must be settled contractually, with reference to citizens' rights.

The right to free expression
A citizen may not, and cannot, remain silent about things that concern him, even if they concern him only indirectly. And that means a great deal; all matters in society concern all its members. Hence the right to discussion, to talk, to writing. The fact that this may involve abuses and the intent to cause harm cannot prevent the right being exercised; intentions to cause harm sink and disappear if they do not point to a real danger. However, the law should provide for difficult cases and problems; it is indisputable that information science has its own casuistry.

The right to culture
This goes well beyond setting up museums or the obligation on children to go to school. It involves the right to enjoy art and to explore the world. Here again, this takes place in second-hand or adulterated forms: tourism, shows, spectacles of various kinds. A right of this sort first declares itself abstractly. It, too, covers a wide terrain, and will occupy a long period of time. It connotes a horizon and a path, rather than steps taken along it, which have to be seen in context: from basic literacy to high art.

The right to identity within difference (and equality)
Difficulties mount up. A 'propositional' text should emerge from working collectively with those involved. On the one hand, it is clear that we cannot treat as vagrants 'without hearth or home' neither the human beings hired to work and be productive in a country, nor their children and families. On the other hand, 'integration', as we call it, cannot come about automatically, as a pure formality. And what does integration consist of? Integration into what? A reality that is crumbling away, or an ideal state that is growing shadowy? Nationality and citizenship always have content, and are not just formal! We thus need to provide for very flexible clauses: stipulated degrees and levels of citizenship. In such a way that every 'foreigner' can preserve his identity – keep it, without setting it in stone – and become aware of his difference without suffering isolation or hostility. Isn't that what happens, in fact (in the best circumstances at least)? A contract would turn these facts into rights. Those becoming 'citizens' would enjoy the same right, in a state of equality that takes account of all differences: of ethnicity, age, sex, culture, etc. In every case and every situation, identity is established, practically and theoretically, in equality and awareness of differences, an awareness that is part of all cultures.

The right to self-management
Self-management is defined as knowledge of and control (at the limit) by a group – a company, a locality, an area or a region – over the conditions governing its existence and its survival through change. Through self-management, these social groups are able to influence their own reality. The right to self-management, like the right to representation, can be proclaimed as a citizen's right, with the ways in which it is applied being spelled out later. Action and initiative by the rank-and-file are always desirable. But have we to wait until the practice is working before espousing the principle? The growth of democracy goes like this: either democracy declines – or the right to self-management is brought into the definition of citizenship. There is no need to show here that local councils or firms are moving in that direction, incompletely, and sometimes subverting it. The right to self-management involves the right to democratic control of the economy, and therefore of companies, including national or nationalized companies, i.e. those up to

now under some degree of state control. So far, we have not discovered the practical formula for democratic control of that kind, or even looked for it.

The right to the city
The right to urban life, with all its services and advantages, has been discussed at length elsewhere.[13] With its implications and consequences, which are still not firmly attached to the new citizenship. The link between 'being a city-dweller' and citizenship is inevitable in societies that are becoming urbanized.

The right to services
This is perhaps the most important, and yet the most implicit of rights, the one that brings the citizen out of isolation and gives meaning to all his obligations. He has the right to use services, first of all, public services: street-cleaning, refuse disposal, transport, etc. The right to transport, even though it is not stipulated or codified, exists as such. The citizen not only has the right to travel without difficulty, but also to find a mode of transport: by rail, road, plane or car, etc. This right to public services does not always have to be formulated. That is not always true in the case of non-public services. But practical rules still implicitly govern them. A shopkeeper does not normally refuse to sell the (solvent!) customer what he wants. Here we move from a practice that is enshrined in law, stipulated, established, to social practice: to ordinary everyday life, governed by tacit agreements that are stronger than laws and create civil society (commercial society, based on profit, etc.). Are these agreements part of citizenship? Yes and no. A foreign visitor will have the same rights as a local citizen as long as he has money. This is not to say that an individual who is known and recognized as a member of the local community does not have some advantages: he is better received, given credit, etc. In this way, citizenship shows up, but without legal or juridical force, in habitual behaviour, that is to say, in the everyday.

The New Contract

A number of rights have been highlighted in this work. Most of them have either been formally set out, or anticipated in social practice. The whole ensemble remains to be organized and put into effect. That could take an entire age. The political contract thus put forward will form no more than a starting-point for initiatives, ideas, even interpretations. It is not a dogmatic text. What is important is that around this idea – stipulated, contractual citizenship – a renewal of political life should take place, a movement with historical roots – revolution, Marxism, production and productive work – but which transcends ideologies, so that new forces could come into action, uniting and exerting pressure on the established order. This would complete, democratically, the abandoned project of the dictatorship of the proletariat. Avoiding brutality, it would cause the political State to wither away (a paradox for the politicians). It does, in fact, demand a paradox: creative discovery. Thus, neither absolute negativism and its corollaries: pessimism, nihilism and despair, nor positivism: realism that blocks the horizon. Neither stagnation nor catastrophe.

Some Questions About Asking Questions

(from *M: Marxisme, Mensuel, Mouvement*, 7 (Janvier 1987), p. 54)

People are probably expecting that the topic here is going to be 'Marxism', and that I shall answer the question that is so often asked: 'Where is Marxism going today?', What does Marxism have to say on this problem or that: the state of the world, threats, secrets of States and peoples, the fine arts, technology, etc. Now, I have nothing to say about Marxism, or in the name of Marxism, unless it is that after several decades, this word (which is still in current, official use) no longer means very much, always assuming it once had a precise meaning. I shall come back to this. Meanwhile, I shall say briefly what 'being a Marxist' means to me today. Some of the themes and arguments I shall put forward look rather subjective; on the other hand, some are objective and general in scope. First of all, an anecdote. I recently had a fairly long text to be typed. I write badly. I gave the manuscript of this book to a girl, a literature student, who wanted to earn a little money during the vacation. When she returned the text and the copy, I noticed that 20 or 30 times she had written 'diabolical' for 'dialectical'. By accident? Perhaps, to start with. Out of mischievousness, I'm sure, as she went on. At all events, a meaningful accident or mischief. I learned later that this girl was a devout practising Catholic. Today, 'being a Marxist' is to accept that many people will take one for a creature of the devil, a monster, a demon. In fact, it is a tool for enlightenment. It uncovers, it brings to light, it destroys, or begins to destroy, what it drags out of the shadows, out of the world of secrets. You will object: 'What weight does the fact of being a Marxist carry today, what with Star Wars, and nuclear and conventional weapons? To be a Marxist is to embrace an ideology . . .' And I'll say, No! It is not a question of repeating ideologically what we believe Marx presented scientifically over a century ago! Nor of reproducing tired old controversies. It is not just a matter of using a method, the dialectic, refined through two and a half thousand years of usage, since Heraclitus! And it is not just a question of employing one or two concepts that are taken as granted: alienation, surplus value, exploitation, etc. More than that, and above all, it is to innovate, to explore the world and the worldwide, to suggest, in short, to invent! Thought does not capitulate; perhaps a few thinking heads are worth a whole lot of nuclear warheads. Is that a paradox? Yes, but it is the sense of several thousand years of philosophy and knowledge.

Going a little further, I would say that 'being a Marxist' today is at one and the same time a certain way of *thinking*, a way of *living* (and behaving) and a way of *being*. From this point of view, the political position is not seen as fundamental or essential. It is a product, and is not posed as a principle. Theoretical thinking regains primacy.

a) The way of thinking does not reject logic. On the contrary, it 'thinks through' logic (the logical),[1] that is, coherence, in speech, knowledge and action, and makes them part of a wider conception. Thought uncovers those conflicts and contradictions that ideologies – coherently, because all strategies have their logic – conceal. In such a way that conflicts and contradictions no longer present themselves as such but *represent* themselves (which enables 'mutation', 'dialogue', etc. to be substituted for conflicts).

And 'Marxism'? It become an historical fiction and a political ideology. For a long time we believed in a 'system', and thus a closed, complete, perfect whole. What a mistake! In Marx's own day, there were conflicts and contradictions in and around him: State control, or opposition to it; Marx and Lassalle (historically more effective!). These conflicts give Marxism its fertility and brilliance, its permanent 'crisis' and the reason for its spread worldwide. The tree of 'Marxism' has its historical roots, a strong trunk and many branches, some of which are dry and dead. There are Chinese, Yugoslav, Russian, American and German forms of 'Marxism'. There are names and works: Ernst Bloch,[2] Adorno, Gramsci.

A question that strikes me as central today: the relationship between logic (the logical), and logics – the dialectic. I insist on it. There is general, formal logic, with its mathematical continuations and applications, which extends as far as computing and machine languages. There are also plural logics, including those of strategies, with their coherences and secrets, covered up by ideologies. And then there is dialectical thinking as a method and procedure of discovery, more penetrating than any other method of analysis or empirical observation. Neither its relations nor its usage are simple. Think about the principle, 'The theory of contradictions is not contradictory!' What is more, secrets have means, not only ideological ones, of resisting discovery. It took centuries for thinking using pertinent (structural) opposites to free itself from myths and Manichean ideologies: God and the Devil, Good and Evil. It also took a long time for the triadic understanding of Becoming to free itself from its theological and metaphysical straitjacket (the Trinity, the Three Periods of History, etc.). And to reach its dialectical formulation with Hegel (thesis, antithesis, synthesis) and with Marx (peasantry, bourgeoisie, proletariat, etc.).

Ideology substitutes representations (which have consequences) for the contradictions and conflicts that do not, in fact, disappear, but which, stifled, unobserved, poison 'real' life and condemn it to unease and unrest. From this perspective, work is understood as the human being's relationship with the world, not as a constraint that oppresses some of us. We have to understand violence, peace, the nation, the worldwide, in the same way.

b) So 'being a Marxist' today is to my mind to take a *critical distance* vis-à-vis facts and events, 'real' actions, without being left in the shadow-land of ambiguity. Among others, the relationship between consciousness and the 'material' body, which is so poorly understood and which is gradually falling into place, is revealed. The same goes for (manual, productive) work, without reducing social activities to work. The relationship with 'others' is now defined in terms of conflicts between *realization* (of the individual and the group) and *alienation* – but also in terms of conflicts between relationships of power and of alliance. 'To be a Marxist' is to live in this society, without letting oneself get caught by its seductions or its traps. It is also to discover innumerable secrets, and to 'bring them out' of their variously dark boxes.

c) Lastly, 'being a Marxist' is not to quote or invoke Marx or any other writer on every occasion. It is a way of *being*. It is to understand the mutual ambivalence of life and death. In their intense struggle, to act so that life wins (in the 'nuclear' stakes, for example). This means holding out a hand to the psychoanalysts, on one condition: that they do not put the emphasis, when it comes to the 'death wish', on the 'death instinct' and the 'work of mourning'. The work of the negative is enough for the dialectician. There are always numerous opposing possibilities, and thus possible choices, points of view and options. No determinism nor ready-made meanings of 'history', which marks a break with the tradition that turns Marxism into an ideology.

Notes

INTRODUCTION

1 He was born on 16 June 1901 and died in the night of 28/29 June 1991. For an obituary, see Michael Kelly, 'Henri Lefebvre, 1901–1991' in *Radical Philosophy*, 60 (Spring 1992), pp. 62–3. For a more general sketch of his life in English see David Harvey, 'Afterword' in *The Production of Space*, tr. Donald Nicholson-Smith (Oxford: Blackwell, 1991), pp. 425–32.
2 As Michel Trébitsch relates in *La Revue des Revues*, 3 (Printemps 1987), p. 6, in the sixth and last issue of *Philosophies* (5/6 [March 1925]) Lefebvre puts forward, influenced by the emergent 'surrealist revolution', a theory of 'total action' in which revolution appears as access to totality. Lefebvre had published a number of short pieces in earlier issues of this journal.
3 *Eléments de rythmanalyse: Introduction à la connaissance des rythmes* (Paris: Syllepse, 1992).
4 *Dialectical Materialism*, tr. John Sturrock (London: Jonathan Cape, 1968); *The Sociology of Marx*, tr. Norbert Guterman (Harmondsworth: Penguin, 1968); *The Explosion: Marxism and the French Upheaval*, tr. Alfred Ehrenfeld (New York: Modern Reader, 1969); *Everyday Life in the Modern World*, tr. Sacha Rabnovitch (Harmondsworth: Allen Lane, 1971; new edn, London: Continuum, 2000).
5 *The Survival of Capitalism*, tr. Frank Bryant (London: Allison & Busby, 1976). This is a translation of the Introduction and Chapters I, II, III, VII and XI of *La Survie du capitalisme* (Paris: Anthropos, 1973; 2e édn, 2002).
6 *The Production of Space*, in August 1991; *Critique of Everyday Life*, tr. John Moore (London: Verso, [October] 1991).
7 *Introduction to Modernity*, tr. John Moore (London: Verso, 1995); *Writings on Cities*, tr. and ed. Eleonore Kofman and Elizabeth Lebas (Oxford: Blackwell, 1996).
8 *Critique of Everyday Life, Volume Two*, tr. John Moore (London: Verso, 2002); *Critique of Everyday Life, Volume Three*, tr. John Moore (London: Verso, forthcoming); *The Urban Revolution* (Minneapolis: University of Minnesota Press, forthcoming); *Rhythmanalysis: Space, Time and Everyday Life*, tr. Stuart Elden and Gerald Moore (London: Continuum, forthcoming).
9 The term *engagé*, the first of many French terms to be encountered in this book, means more than 'activist'. Used in France to denote an all-embracing political commitment (usually on the Left), it does not have the connotation of multiple community actions and 'activities' of Anglo-Saxon societies.
10 Two coauthors are represented here: Norbert Guterman, an early colleague of Lefebvre's who later moved to New York and worked as a translator, and Catherine Régulier, who was Lefebvre's last wife. The selection 'From the Social Pact to the Contract of Citizenship', comes from *Du Contrat de citoyenneté* (Paris: Syllepse, 1990), which was a collaborative venture between Lefebvre and the 'Groupe de Navarrenx', although the texts were individually signed.
11 *Rabelais* (Paris: Les Éditions Français Réunis, 1955; 2e édn, Paris: Anthropos, 2001); *Alfred de Musset: Dramaturge* (Paris: L'Arche, 1955; 2e édn, 1970); *Descartes* (Paris:

Éditions Hier et Aujourd'hui, 1947); *Pascal* (Paris: Nagel, 1949), Tome Premier; *Pascal* (Paris: Nagel, 1954), Tome Deux.
12 See Rémi Hess, *Henri Lefebvre et l'aventure du siècle* (Paris: A.M. Métailié, 1988), pp. 131–8.
13 *Méthodologie des sciences: Inédit* (Paris: Anthropos, 2002).
14 For an examination of this in a little more detail, see Stuart Elden, 'Through the Eyes of the Fantastic: Lefebvre, Rabelais and Intellectual History', *Historical Materialism*, 10: 4 (December 2002), pp. 51–73.
15 *Rabelais*, 2ᵉ édn, for example, pp. 56–9.
16 *Descartes*, pp. 144–7, 187–243; *Pascal*, Tome Deux, *passim*.
17 For example, *Le Temps des méprises* (Paris: Stock, 1975), a somewhat bad-tempered book-length interview of Lefebvre, was published as the first of a series on 'great thinkers'.
18 See Didier Eribon (ed.), *L'Infréquentable Michel Foucault: Renouveaux de la pensée critique* (Paris: Epel, 2001).
19 Hess, *Henri Lefebvre*.
20 Perusal of a special issue of *Yale French Studies*, 73 (1987), on 'Everyday Life', eds. Alice Kaplan and Kristin Ross, and a special issue of *Parallax*, 2 (1996), also entitled 'Everyday Life', both explicitly indebted to Lefebvre, demonstrate quite different uses of Lefebvre's thought, their romanticism associated perhaps more with urban nostalgia than with the man himself.
21 The first colloquium, entitled 'Quand urbain et mondialisation révolutionnent le mode de production capitaliste, quels possibles?', which the editors attended, was held on 25/6 November 2000 at the Salle Espaces Marx in Paris. The second colloquium, also organized by Rémi Hess and the group associated around the Syllepse and Anthropos re-editions among others, to celebrate the centenary of Lefebvre's birth ('Colloque Centenaire Henri Lefebvre'), was held on 26/7 June 2001 at Université Paris 8 at St Denis. In the meantime, regular meetings at the Espaces Marx take place and an internet newsletter is in operation.
22 Eleonore Kofman and Elizabeth Lebas, 'Recovery and Reappropriation in Lefebvre and Constant' in Jonathan Hughes and Simon Sadler (eds.), *Non-Plan: Essays on Freedom Participation and Change in Modern Architecture and Urbanism* (Oxford: Architectural Press, 2000), pp. 80–89.
23 Stuart Elden, *Mapping the Present: Heidegger, Foucault and the Project of a Spatial History* (London: Continuum, 2001).
24 Stuart Elden, *Henri Lefebvre* (London: Continuum, forthcoming); 'Politics, Philosophy, Geography: Henri Lefebvre in Anglo-American Scholarship', *Antipode: A Radical Journal of Geography*, 33: 5 (November 2001), pp. 809–25; 'Through the Eyes of the Fantastic'; 'Between Marx and Heidegger: Politics, Philosophy and Lefebvre's *Production of Space*', *Antipode: A Radical Journal of Geography*, forthcoming, 34: 1 (January 2004).
25 Whilst a number of sources have been consulted in providing this information, *Chambers Biographical Dictionary*, ed. Melanie Parry, 6th edn (Edinburgh: Chambers, 1997), has proved invaluable.

MARXISM AND PHILOSOPHY

Introduction

1 See *La Présence et l'absence* (Paris: Castermann, 1980), p. 143; 'Triads and Dyads', below, p. 50.
2 Jean-Paul Sartre, *Critique de la raison dialectique précédé de questions de méthode, Tome I: Théorie des ensembles pratiques* (Paris: Gallimard, 1960), p. 50; *Search for a Method*, tr. Hazel E. Barnes (New York: Vintage, 1963), p. 51.

Retrospections

1 [Editors' note: The café frequented by Sartre and de Beauvoir, amongst others.]
2 M. André Breton has falsified history in his '2ᵉ Manifeste du Surréalisme'. The money lost did not belong to the Communist Party. What's more, Politzer and Lefebvre counted for nothing in the business; they opposed it as soon as they knew – too late. And Politzer caused the Party to get involved. 'A' was expelled. It was too brutal a measure, inspired by a latent workerism. The sanction was lifted a few years later, at the instigation of Maurice Thorez, who was always entirely understanding.
3 [Editors' note: The doctrine that knowledge depends on an act of faith.]
4 See *Action*, 29 December 1944.
5 [Editors' note: André Gide (1869–1951), French novelist, best known for his novels *The Immoralist* and *Strait is the Gate*.]
6 [Editors' note: Jean Cocteau (1889–1963), French writer and artist.]
7 [Editors' note: Lafcadio is a character in Gide's *The Vatican Cellars*. In a famous scene he pushes Amédée Fleurissoire from a train, as simply a 'gratuitous act'.]
8 See *Etoiles*, 12 February 1946.
9 [Editors' note: These are effectively Kant's questions in his *Logic* – What can I know? What must I do? What may I hope for? – except that the question of the possibility of knowledge becomes one of existence.]
10 [Editors' note: An allusion to Sartre's trilogy *The Roads to Freedom*.]
11 [Editors' note: Albert Camus, *The Myth of Sisyphus*, tr. Justin O'Brien (Harmondsworth: Penguin, 1975), p. 11.]
12 See *L'Etre et le néant*, pp. 46ff.; p. 234; pp. 291ff., etc. [Editors' note: Lefebvre is using the original edition: *L'Etre et le néant: Essai d'ontologie phénoménologique* (Paris: Gallimard, 1943); tr. Hazel E. Barnes as *Being and Nothingness: An Essay on Phenomenological Ontology* (London: Routledge, 1958), pp. 5, 185, 235ff.]
13 *L'Etre et le néant*, p. 142 [*Being and Nothingness*, p. 98].
14 See p. 717 and the whole of the conclusion. [*Being and Nothingness*, pp. 622–3, 617–28].
15 Merleau-Ponty, *Les Temps Modernes*, no. 2, p. 345.

Prolegomenas

1 [Editors' note: Friedrich Engels, *Origins of the Family, Private Property and the State: In the Light of the Researches of Lewis H. Morgan* (London: Lawrence & Wishart, 1972), p. 96. Lefebvre references the Bottigelli translation; which omits to mention that Engels provides a reference to Morgan's work. See Lewis H. Morgan, *Ancient Society, or Researches in the Lines of Human Progress from Savagery, through Barbarism to Civilisation* (New York: World Publishing Company, 1963), p. 444.]
2 [Editors' note: Jean Rameau (1683–1764), French composer, author of the influential *Treatise on Harmony*.]
3 [Editors' note: Étienne Bonnot de Condillac (1715–80), French philosopher, author of *Essay on the Origin of Human Knowledge*, and contributor to Diderot's *Encyclopaedia*.]
4 [Editors' note: Charles Fourier (1772–1837), French socialist. See *Actualité de Fourier: Colloque d'Arcs et Senans*, sous la direction de Henri Lefebvre (Paris: Anthropos, 1975).]
5 [Editors' note: This is akin to the notion of a cyborg – a human in a symbiotic relation with a machine. It is Lefebvre's term for technocrats, explored most fully in *Vers le cybernanthrope: Contre les technocrates* (Paris: Denöel/Gonthier, 1971).]

Marxian Thought and Sociology

1 See *Capital*, vol. I, bk I, ch. 1, sec. 4, [Editors' note: 'The Fetishism of the Commodity and Its Secret'.]

Beyond Structuralism

1 François Wahl, *Qu'est-ce que le structuralisme?* Seuil, 1968, pp. 390–1.
2 [Editors' note: 'Sur une interprétation du marxisme', 'Forme, fonction, structure dans «Le capital»', and 'Les paradoxes d'Althusser' in *Au-delà du structuralisme* (Paris: Anthropos, 1971). These three pieces, but not the whole of this book, are reprinted in *L'Idéologie structuralisme* (Paris: Anthropos, 1975).]

Hegel, Marx, Nietzsche

1 [Editors' note: Arthur Rimbaud (1854–91), French writer, known for poems such as *Illuminations* and *A Season in Hell*.]
2 [Editors' note: See H. Lefebvre, *La Fin de l'histoire* (Paris: Éditions de Minuit, 1971; new edn, Paris: Anthropos, 2001).]
3 See *La Fin de l'histoire*, but also H. Lefebvre, *Nietzsche* (Paris: Éditions sociales internationales, 1939), in which, even before the war, he rejected the political accusations made against Nietzsche, by Georg Lukács in particular.
4 [Editors' note: Friedrich Karl von Savigny (1779–1861), professor of law at Marburg, and Prussian jurist. He suggested that laws derived from the spirit of the people, and is best known for his books on Roman Law.]
5 [Editors' note: The Comte de Saint-Simon (1760–1825) and Charles Fourier (1772–1837) were two French socialists, influential to and criticized by Marx for their utopian ideas.]
6 [Editors' note: Ferdinand Lassalle (1825–64) was a German revolutionary in 1848, when he met Marx, but later established the Universal German Working Men's Association, which later became the Social Democratic Party, and campaigned for Universal Suffrage. His ideas and legacy were criticized by Marx in the *Critique of the Gotha Programme*.]
7 [Editors' note: Wilhelm Reich (1897–1957), Austrian psychoanalyst, author of *The Function of the Orgasm* (1927) and *The Mass Psychology of Fascism* (1933); Georges Bataille (1897–1962), French author and philosopher, known for works such as *The Accursed Share* (1949) and *On Nietzsche* (1945).]
8 [Editors' note: Cornelius Jansen (1585–1638), Dutch Roman Catholic theologian. François, Sixth Duc de La Rochefoucauld (1613–80), French writer and member of Louis XIV's court. He challenged Cardinal Richelieu's power, and is best known as a writer for his *Reflections*.]
9 [Editors' note: Friedrich Nietzsche, *Thus Spoke Zarathustra*, Book III, 'On Old and New Tablets 2', tr. Walter Kaufmann, in *The Portable Nietzsche* (Harmondsworth: Penguin, 1954), p. 309.]
10 See G. R. Hocke's remarks in *Labyrinthe de l'art fantastique*, p. 189. [Editors' note: Gustave René Hocke, *Labyrinthe de l'art fantastique: Les racines du surréalisme* (Paris: Denoël/Gonthier, 1967).]
11 One star of major importance is missing from the constellation: Clausewitz. As a political strategist, he belongs to a different study and a radical critique of politics as

such. The same goes for Lenin and Mao. What is Leninism today, if it, too, is subjected to critical analysis? A diversion of Marxism towards undeveloped, mainly agricultural societies, which has profound causes and grave consequences. Mao's prodigious political activity has not led to theoretical advances of the same order, despite his texts on contradiction, practice, etc. There is nothing more irritating and deadening than fetishization, of a work or of a person.

N.B.: The person writing these words in the autumn of 1973 declares himself pro-Chinese, and therefore strategically 'Maoist'. (To be continued.)

[Editors' note: Karl von Clausewitz (1780–1831) was a Prussian soldier and author of *On War* (1883).]

Triads and Dyads

1 [Editors' note: A reference to the poem of Angelus Silesius (1624–1677), whose first two lines are 'A rose is without why/it blooms because it blooms'.]
2 [Editors' note: Antonin Artaud (1896–1948), French surrealist, creator of the Theatre of Cruelty. He was declared insane and spent the last years of his life in an asylum.]
3 [Editors' note: Friedrich Nietzsche, *The Gay Science*, tr. Walter Kaufmann (New York: Vintage, 1974), pp. 273–4. This is the passage where Nietzsche first outlines the idea of the eternal return of the same.]

Twelve Theses on Logic and Dialectic

1 [Editors' note: This is the famous 'All Cretans are liars, said the Cretan'. Whether this was said by Epimenides is debatable.]
2 [Editors' note: Kurt Gödel (1906–78), Austrian-born US mathematician, published a proof which showed that all formal systems of arithmetic must rest on elements which cannot be proved or disproved within the system. The paradoxes of set theory probably refers to [Bertrand] Russell's paradox. This paradox arises when we consider the set of all sets that are not members of themselves – i.e. the set of all dogs is not itself a dog. Is that set a member of itself or not?]
3 [Editors' note: And untranslatable. Lefebvre is punning on empire, empiricism, and *l'emprise*, ascendancy.]

State

1 [Editors' note: *Macbeth*, V. v. 27.]

THE CRITIQUE OF EVERYDAY LIFE

Introduction

1 Georges Labica, *Colloque Pensée d'Henri Lefebvre* (Paris: Espace Marx, 25–6 November 2000).
2 [Editors' note: The Centre National de Recherche Scientifique (CNRS) is the French national central research body. It is funded by the State and its research employees are de facto civil servants.]

3 Henri Lefebvre, *Critique de la vie quotidienne III: De la modernité au modernisme (Pour une métaphilosophie du quotidien)* (Paris: L'Arche, 1981).

Mystification: Notes for a Critique of Everyday Life

1 [Editors' note: Henri Bergson (1859–1941) philosopher; Paul Valéry (1871–1945) poet and writer; Marcel Proust (1871–1922), author of *À la recherche du temps perdu* [*In Search of Lost Time*].]
2 [Editors' note: Georges Duhamel (1884–1966), novelist and poet; Clément Vautel (1876–1954), writer and critic.]
3 [Editors' note: Julien Benda (1867–1956), best known for his book *La Traison des clercs* [*The Treason of Intellectuals*], published in 1927, but also for his critiques of Bergson.
4 [Editors' note: Stéphane Mallarmé (1842–98), French poet and Symbolist.]
5 [Editors' note: 'Par la vieille Sorbonne' – literally, 'by the old Sorbonne'.]
6 [Editors' note: Arthur Rimbaud, 'Mauvais Sang', in *Oeuvres* (Paris: Éditions Garnier Frères, 1960), p. 215; 'Bad Blood' in *Complete Works*, tr. Paul Schmidt (New York: Harper & Row, 1975), p. 193.]
7 [Editors' note: Charles Rist was the coauthor with Charles Gide of *History of Economic Doctrines: From the time of the Physiocrats to the Present Day* (1909) and the author of *Essais sur quelques problèmes économiques et monétaires* [*Essays on Some Economic and Monetary Problems*] (1933). Jacques Rueff (1896–1978) was the financial adviser to the French Embassy in London (1930–1936), and author of *Sur une théorie de l'inflation* [*A Theory of Inflation*] (1925) and *Théorie des phénomènes monétaires* [*Theory of Monetary Phenomena*] (1927). John Maynard Keynes (1883–1946) was an English economist, whose major work *General Theory of Employment, Interest and Money* (1936) was published after this article was written. Lefebvre and Guterman are probably referring to his *A Treatise on Money* (1930).]
8 [Editors' note: This is a translation of the French which Lefebvre provides. A standard English version, from the New International Bible, is 'For what I do is not the good I want to do; no, the evil I do not want to do – this I keep on doing' (Romans 7:19).]
9 [Editors' note: Caliban is the slave in Shakespeare's *The Tempest*.]
10 [Editors' note: The Culture, or Cultural, Philosophers, who attempted to overcome an outdated sense of culture. The term was coined around 1900 to describe Georg Simmel (1858–1918); later exponents would include some elements of the Frankfurt school and early structuralism.]
11 [Editors' note: Georges Duhamel (see n. 2 above) pursued his critique of mechanized civilization in works such as *La Possession du monde* [*The Possession of the World*] (1919), and *Scènes de la vie future* [*Scènes from the life of the future*] (1930).]
12 [Editors' note: Emmanuel Berl (1892–1976), was a writer and journalist, author of *Mort de la pensée bourgeoisie* [*Death of Bourgeois Thought*] (1929) and *Mort de la morale bourgeoisie* [*Death of Bourgeois Morality*] (1930). He was later a speech writer for Philippe Pétain in the Vichy years. Marianne is the Republican symbol of France, dating from the Revolution – it is also the name of a magazine. Berl ran *Marianne* in the 1930s.]
13 [Editors' note: Jean Guéhenno (1890–1978), was a novelist and critic.]
14 [Editors' note: Pierre Drieu-la-Rochelle (1893–1945) was a French writer and fascist theorist.]
15 [Editors' note: We have been unable to locate the source of this quotation. See note 12 above on Emmanuel Berl.]
16 [Editors' note: Arthur, Comte de Gobineau (1816–82) was a French diplomat and author of *The Inequality of Human Races* (1853–5). Gottfried Feder (1883–1941) was

an early member of the Nazi party, on the anti-capitalist wing. After the 1934 'Night of the Long Knives' he resigned from the government and worked as a University lecturer. Arthur Moeller van der Bruck (1876–1925) wrote a book called *Das Dritte Reich* [*The Third Reich*] (1923). Alfred Fried (1864–1921) was an Austrian pacifist who protested against the Versailles treaty after winning the Nobel peace prize.]

17 [Editors' note: It is not clear whether this was ever done in article form. The best place to look is Norbert Guterman and Henri Lefebvre, *La Conscience mystifiée* (Paris: Syllepse, 1999 [1936]).]

18 *Histoire des doctrines economiques*, ed. Costes, VIII, p. 164. Other passages: *Capital*, vol. I, pp. 57–58; *Histoire des doctrines economiques*, ed. Costes, VIII, pp. 126, 128, 154, etc.; *Deutsche ideologie, passim*; *Gesamtausgabe*, Abt. I, vol. 3, pp. 81–94; Crit. écon. pol., ed. Giard, p. 53, etc. [Editors' note: Lefebvre and Guterman use such old editions of Marx that these are very difficult to trace. Our best bet is the following. The quote is probably from *Theories of Surplus Value*, Part III, tr. Jack Cohen and S. W. Ryazanskaya (London: Lawrence & Wishart, 1972), Addenda. The other passages cited are: *Capital: A Critique of Political Economy, Volume I*, tr. Ben Fowkes (Harmondsworth: Penguin, 1976), pp. 165–6; *Theories of Surplus Value*, Part III, Addenda; Marx and Engels, *The German Ideology*, ed. C. J. Arthur (London: Lawrence & Wishart, 1970); 'Estranged [or Alienated] Labour' in *Early Writings*, tr. Rodney Livingstone and Gregor Benton (Harmondsworth: Penguin, 1975), pp. 322–34; *A Contribution to the Critique of Political Economy*, tr. S. W. Ryazanskaya (London: Lawrence & Wishart, 1971), p. 49. The *Gesamtausgabe* referenced is an old (and unfinished) collected works of Marx (*Historisch-kritische Gesamtausgabe*, Frankfurt am., Main, Berlin, etc.: Marx-Engels-Instituts Moskau, 11 Volumes, 1927–32), not the more recent *Marx-Engels Gesamtausgabe* (Berlin: Akademie Verlag [MEGA]).]

Elucidations

1 [Editors' note: The notion of *dérive*, in the sense of a drift through urban space, was much used by the Situationists. Lefebvre was closely linked to them until a break in the early 1960s. See 'Henri Lefebvre on the Situationist International', interview conducted and translated by Kristin Ross, *October*, 79 (1983).]

2 [Editors' note: See Karl Marx, 'The Eighteenth Brumaire of Louis Napoleon' in *Surveys from Exile: Political Writings Volume 2*, tr. David Fernbach (Harmondsworth: Penguin, 1973) p. 146.]

3 [Editors' note: Although this notion is regularly attributed to Marx, closer formulations are actually found in Engels. Marx suggests that '*the political state disappears* [untergehe] in a true democracy' ('Critique of Hegel's Doctrine of the State', in *Early Writings*, tr. Rodney Livingstone and Gregor Benton (Harmondsworth: Penguin, 1975), p. 88 [*Marx Engels Gesamtausgabe*, Band I. 2, 32]); Engels that 'the state is not "abolished", it withers away' (*Socialism: Utopian and Scientific*; Peking: Foreign Languages Press, 1975, p. 94). This work of Engels is excerpted from his *Herr Eugen Duhring's Revolution in Science* (popularly known as *Anti-Duhring*). Although the passage appears in the *Marx Engels Werke*, Band 20, p. 262; it is replaced in MEGA I. 27, p. 445, with 'Die freie Gesellschaft kann keinen "Staat" zwischen sich und ihren Mitgliedern brauchen oder dulden [The free society will not need or permit a "state" between itself and its members].' The notion is developed at some length in V. I. Lenin, *The State and Revolution: The Marxist Theory of the State and the Tasks of the Proletariat in the Revolution* (Moscow: Progress Publishers, 1965), pp. 18–24, 79–80.]

4 We know that the Yugoslavs, with many difficulties and twists and turns, are retaining the Marxist model. [Editors' note: Tito's Yugoslavia broke from Cominform and the

USSR in 1948, and pursued a more decentralised form of communism with a strong emphasis on worker's self-management – a term Lefebvre discusses as *autogestion*.]

The Social Text

1 [Editors' note: The notion of spectacle was also central to Situationist writings. See, above all, Guy Debord, *The Society of the Spectacle*, tr. Donald Nicolson-Smith (Zone Books: New York, 1994).]
2 Problems of semiology, general semantics, 'semantemes' and partial systems of social signs will be dealt with under 'models of communication'.

The End of Modernity?

1 [Editors' note: Georg Lukács (1885–1971), Hungarian Marxist, is best known for his *History and Class Consciousness* (1923) and *The Destruction of Reason* (1954). The more relevant references here are *Goethe and His Age* (1947) and *Balzac und die französische Realismus* [*Balzac and French Realism*] (1952).]
2 [Editors' note: Theodor Adorno (1903–69), German theorist and member of the Frankfurt School, wrote widely on modern art. See, for example, *Aesthetic Theory*, tr. C. Lenhardt (London: Routledge & Kegan Paul, 1984), and for a broader theoretical work, *Negative Dialectics*, tr. E. B. Ashton (London: Routledge, 1973).]
3 [Editors' note: Charles Baudelaire (1821–67), French poet, best known for *Les Fleurs du mal*; Samuel Beckett (1906–89), Irish writer who lived mainly in France, wrote plays such as *Waiting for Godot* and *Endgame*.]
4 [Editors' note: The original French is '*aboli bibelot d'inanité sonore*', a quote from one of Mallarmé's sonnets. See Stéphane Mallarmé, *The Poems*, bilingual edn, tr. Keith Bosley (Harmondsworth: Penguin, 1977), p. 171.]

On Vulgarity

1 [Editors' note: Robert Schumann (1810–56), German composer who concluded his work *Carnaval* with the 'March of the League of David [*Davidsbündler*] against the Philistines'. In his *Neue Zeitschrift für Musik* [*New Journal for Music*], Schumann had led a cast of characters called the Davidsbündler against the music of Rossini, Liszt and Wagner.]
2 [Editors' note: There is no easy way to resolve this pun – the French is '*malaise à mal-être*'.]
3 [Editors' note: In his *What is to be done? Burning Questions of Our Movement* (London: Lawrence & Wishart, 1944), p. 40, Lenin quotes a long passage from Karl Kautsky (from *Neue Zeit*, 1901–2, XX, I, no. 3, p. 79): 'the vehicles of science are not the proletariat but the *bourgeois intelligentsia* [K. K.'s italics]; it was in the minds of some members of this stratum that modern socialism originated, and it was they who communicated it to the more intellectually developed proletarians who, in their turn, introduced it into the proletarian class struggle where conditions allow that to be done. Thus it is something introduced into the proletarian class struggle from without (*von Aussen Hineingetragenes*), and not something that arose within it spontaneously (*urwüchsig*)'. The interpolations in the text are Lenin's.]
4 [Editors' note: A 'class in itself' is a group of people that share common interests in terms of their relation to capital. A 'class for itself' is aware of this. This is a distinction taken from Hegel's *Science of Logic* and applied to class. See Karl Marx, *The Poverty of Philosophy: Answer to the 'Philosophy of Poverty' by M. Proudhon* (Moscow: Progress Publishers, 1975), pp. 159–60: 'Economic conditions had first transformed the mass of the people of the

Myths in Everyday Life

1 [Editors' note: Elizabeth Taylor (1932–), who was on her fourth marriage at the time.]
2 [Editors' note: A reference to the closing words of Goethe's *Faust*, Part Two: 'the eternal feminine draws us on [*Das Ewig-Weibliche/Zieht uns hinan*]'.]
3 [Roland Barthes, *Mythologies*, tr. Annette Lavers (London: Vintage, 1972).]
4 [Norbert Guterman and Henri Lefebvre, *La Conscience mystifiée* (Paris: Syllepse, 1999 [1936]).]
5 [Editors' note: The diachronic – historical, analysis of change through time – and the synchronic – atemporal, analysis at a single moment – were particularly important in structuralism, which privileged the latter.]
6 [Editors' note: See Sigmund Freud, *Introductory Lectures on Psycho-Analysis*, Standard Edition vol. XV, ed. James Strachey (London: The Hogarth Press, 1961), pp. 159–60.]
7 [Editors' note: Who this reference is to is unclear. It is probably to Alfred Memmi (1920–), a Tunisian writer on colonialism. He is best known for his novel *Pillar of Salt* (1955), and the psychological study *The Colonizer and the Colonized* (1957).]

THE COUNTRY AND THE CITY

Introduction

1 *La Vallée de Campan: Étude de sociologie rurale* (Paris: PUF, 1963).
2 Rémi Hess, 'Présentation de la troisième édition' in *Du Rural à l'urbain*, 3e édn (Paris: Anthropos, 2001), p. xxii.
3 *Du Rural à l'urbain*, 3e édn (Paris: Anthropos, 2001).
4 *Du Rural à l'urbain*, p. 10.
5 See 'Preface to the New Edition: The Production of Space' in this volume, pp. 325–37.
6 See especially, Jean-Paul Sartre, *Critique de la raison dialectique précédé de Questions de méthode, Tome I: Théorie des ensembles pratiques* (Paris: Gallimard, 1960), p. 50; *Search for a Method*, tr. Hazel E. Barnes (New York: Vintage, 1963), p. 51.
7 Hess, 'Présentation de la troisième édition', p. xxi.
8 *Du Rural à l'urbain*, p. 14.
9 See 'The Bureaucratic Society of Controlled Consumption' in *Everyday Life in the Modern World*, tr. Sacha Rabinovitch, 2nd revd edn (London: Continuum, 2000).
10. [Editors' note: The Institut de Sociologie Urbaine was one of the first French urban research institutes supported by the Ministère de l'Equipement in the early 1960s following the establishment of a national system of planning regulations. Lefebvre became its first director.]
11 This is discussed in the Introduction to *Le Droit à la ville* on p. 35.
12 See 'From the Social Pact to the Contract of Citizenship' in this volume, pp. 379–404; 'Right to the City' in *Writings on Cities*, tr and ed. Eleonore Kofman and Elizabeth Lebas (Oxford: Blackwell, 1996).
13 'Vue de la fenêtre', *Éléments de rythmanalyse: Introduction à la connaissance des rythmes* (Paris: Éditions Syllepse, 1992); Catherine Régulier and Henri Lefebvre, 'Essai de

rythmanalyse des villes méditerranéennes', *Espace Temps*, 33 (1980), pp. 17–19. Both pieces appeared in *Writings on Cities*.
14   See David Harvey's remarks in his *Social Justice and the City* (Blackwell: Oxford, 1988 [1973]), pp. 302–14.

Perspectives on Rural Sociology

1   'Problèmes de Sociologie rurale, La Communauté paysanne et ses problèmes historico-sociologiques', *Cahiers Internationaux de Sociologie*, VI (1949), pp. 78–100 [Editors' note: reprinted in *Du Rural à l'urbain*, 3e édn (Paris: Anthropos, 2001), pp. 21–40.]
2   [Editors' note: This remark, found in the Preface to the *Phenomenology of Spirit*, para. 31, is misquoted by Lefebvre. The original German is 'das Bekannte ist darum weil es bekannt ist nicht erkannt'. A. V. Miller (G. W. F. Hegel, *Phenomenology of Spirit*: Oxford: Oxford University Press, 1977, p. 18) translates this as 'Quite generally, the familiar, just because it is familiar is not cognitively understood.' Lefebvre similarly misquotes this (in the German this time) in *Critique of Everyday Life Volume I: Introduction*, tr. John Moore (London: Verso, 1991), p. 15.]
3   See, in particular, recent works by Daniel Guérin and the novels of Steinbeck, Caldwell and others. [Editors' note: Daniel Guérin (1904–98) was an anarchist Marxist. The work Lefebvre is referring to is probably *Ou va le peuple americain? (Where are the American People Going?*; Paris: Julliard, 1950). John Steinbeck (1902–68) and Erskine Caldwell (1903–87) were both US novelists: Steinbeck is particularly known for *The Grapes of Wrath* (1939); Caldwell for *Tobacco Road* (1932).]
4   By members of the School of human geography.
5   [Editors' note: A kind of digging fork with two prongs, particularly used in the Basque region.]
6   [Editors' note: *Kolkhoz* – a collective farm – and *sovkhoz* – a state farm, were the two types of farm established in the USSR in 1917, becoming widespread from 1929 on. Collective farms were less subject to state control, made their own decisions on profits, but were obliged to meet quotas; state farms were owned by the state and workers were paid a salary: they became more and more common over time.]
7   [Editors' note: Jean Chombart de Lauwe (1909–2001) was a writer on agricultural issues. Lefebvre is possibly referring to *Recensements de l'agriculture* (Paris: n.p., 1949), or *La structure agricole de la France* (Paris: P. Dupont, 1946).]
8   [Editors' note: This is likely to be a reference to Carl C. Taylor *et. al.*, *Rural Life in the United States* (New York: A. A. Knopf, 1949).]
9   Lowry Nelson, *Rural Sociology* ([New York:] American Book Co., 1948), pp. 323–74.
10 [Thomas] Lynn Smith, *The Sociology of Rural Life* ([New York:] Harper Brothers, 1947), pp. 87ff.
11 Even in the USA, a rural 'history' would seem to be indispensable, especially in the South, where, as in Europe, one finds traces of feudalism, and share-cropping (a semi-feudal tenure system), coexisting with the continuation and consequences of slavery.
    I would point once again to Paul Landis's book *Rural Life in Process* [2nd edn; New York: McGraw-Hill Book Co., 1948]. He is one of the few writers to have studied the American rural experience in *evolution* and to have given a (somewhat) critical account of the actual situation of American country-people.
12 Marc Bloch, *Les caractères originaux de l'histoire rurale française* ([Paris:] A. Colin, 1952); [editors' note: tr. Janet Sondheimer, *French Rural History: An Essay on Its Basic Characteristics* (London: Routledge & Kegan Paul, 1978). Bloch (1886–1944) was a historian, a cofounder of the *Annales d'histoire économique et sociale* journal.]

268   Notes

13 In order to explain the facts, Bloch hesitated between a technological theory (role of the plough) and the invocation of collective mentality (communitarian or individualistic outlook). Since then, some sociologists have become fond of setting up a contrast between the 'natural' world and the technological or 'machine-based' world, which seems to me just as spurious.
14 [Editors' note: *Latifundia* were large farms constructed from a number of smaller ones. They were originally set up in Rome after Hannibal's invasion. The term was revived in the colonization of the new world, and is used today in Italy, Spain and Latin America to describe large estates – often with absentee landlords.]
15 The first 50 pages of the recently translated book by Lord Ernle, *L'Histoire rurale de l'Angleterre* ([Paris:] Gallimard, 1952). [Editors' note: Original version: Rowland, Baron Ernle, *The Land and its People: Chapters in Rural Life and History* (London: Hutchinson & Co., 1925).]
    Cf. Denise Paulme's book, *L'Organisation sociale des Dogons* [Paris: Université de Paris, Institut de Droit Comparé, 1940], and countless studies (not yet fully systematized) in various countries and languages.
16 [Editors' note: This is doubtless a reference to the *Manuel de sociologie rurale* whose manuscript was stolen from a car and consequently never published. See Rémi Hess, 'Présentation de la troisième édition' in *Du Rural à l'urbain*, 3e édn (Paris: Anthropos, 2001), p. xxii.]

Preface to the Study of the Habitat of the 'Pavillon'

1 [Editors' note: A *Pavillon* is a small detached house or bungalow. Because Lefebvre uses the term so regularly, and occasionally in adjectival forms, we have often left it untranslated or included the French in brackets.]
2 [Editors' note: There are some very slight changes to the footnotes in the 2nd edition of *L'Habitat pavillonnaire* (Paris: Éditions du CRU, 1971), which we have included here.]
3 [Editors' note: Le Corbusier (1887–1965) was a French architect and writer on architecture and art.]
4 [Editors' note: Gaston Bachelard, *The Poetics of Space*, tr. Maria Jolas (Boston: Beacon, 1969).]
5 [Editors' note: The French is 'la terre est l'habiter de l'homme, cet "être" exceptionnel parmi les "êtres" (les "étants"), comme son langage est la Demeure de l'Etre absolu'. *Habiter* is the standard French translation of Heidegger's *wohnen* – the standard English translation is 'to dwell'. *L'habiter* and *la habitation*, which are both possible translations of *das Wohnen*, presents more problems, as there is a distinction between the generalized place of dwelling (the earth) and a particular place of dwelling (sometimes the German *die Wohnung* is used, for which the usual French translation is *le logement*). As far as possible they have here been rendered as 'dwelling' and 'the dwelling' or 'dwelling place' to accord with standard English translations. This fails to take into account the use of *la Demeure* by Lefebvre, which we have marked in the text, but seems preferable to alternatives.]
6 [Editors' note: Friedrich Hölderlin, 'In lovely blueness …', *Selected Verse*, German-English edn, tr. Michael Hamburger (Harmondsworth: Penguin, 1961), pp. 245–6.]
7 *Essais et conférences* [tr. André Préau; Paris: Gallimard, 1958], pp. 170ff., 'Bâtir, habiter, penser'; pp. 224ff., 'L'homme habite en poète'. [Editors' note: These texts originally appear in Heidegger's *Vorträge und Aufsätze* (Pfullingen: Günther Neske, Vierte Auflage, 1978), as 'Bauen Wohnen Denken' and '… dichterisch wohnet der Mensch …'; translated by Albert Hofstader as 'Building Dwelling Thinking' and 'Poetically Man

Dwells' in *Poetry, Language, Thought* (New York: Harper & Row, 1971). The quote – for which Lefebvre gives no exact reference – is in the second text: *Vorträge und Aufsätze*, p. 183; *Essais et conferences*, p. 227; *Poetry, Language, Thought*, p. 215.]
8 [Editors' note: Now that Lefebvre is moving on beyond Heidegger, *l'habiter* is rendered as 'habitat', *la habitation* as 'habitation', and *la demeure* as 'dwelling'.]
9 [Editors' note: It is possible this is a reference to Heidegger's ski cabin at Todtnauberg, which was known as *die Hütte*.]
10 On the semantic field, see H. Lefebvre, 'Introduction à la psycho-sociologie de la vie quotidienne' in *Encyclopédie de la psychologie*, éd. Nathan, pp. 102ff.; also, *Critique de la vie quotidienne I*, pp. 278–315. See also the work of Roland Barthes, notably *Essais critiques* [Paris: Éditions du Seuil, 1964], pp. 155ff. [Editors' note: The full reference for source of the first piece is *Encyclopédie de la psychologie*, ed. D. Huisman (Paris: Éditions Fernand Nathan, 1961), pp. 102–7. It is reprinted in *Du Rural à l'urbain*, 3e édn (Paris: Anthropos, 2001), pp. 89–108. The other Lefebvre reference is actually to the *Critique de la vie quotidienne II: Fondements d'une sociologie de la quotidienneté* (Paris: L'Arche, 1961), pp. 278–314. A part of this chapter is translated as 'The Social Text' in the Critique of Everyday Life section of the current volume, pp. 88–92. For Barthes's piece in English, see *Critical Essays*, tr. Richard Howard (Evanston: Northwestern University Press, 1972), pp. 151–61.]
11 Cf. [Maxime Rodinson] *Islam et capitalisme*, [Paris: Le Seuil, 1966], p. 202 [tr. Brian Pearce (Harmondsworth: Penguin, 1977), p. 192].
12 [Jacques Berque], *La Ville, Entretiens sur les sociétés musulmanes* (Publications E.P.H.E.), pp. 58ff.
13 [Guy Palmade, 'Les attitudes des Français en matière de logement',] 1961, 90 p., mimeo; see pp. 71–2. See also, 'Logement et vie familiale', Centre d'étude des groupes sociaux, 1966, bibliographical appendix, pp. 105–7.
14 On presence-absence, see Michel Foucault's book *Les Mots et les choses* [Paris: Gallimard, 1966], and notably the analysis of Vélasquez's painting '*Las Meninas*', pp. 20–31 [*The Order of Things* (London: Routledge, 1970), pp. 4–16]. We have also drawn on the work of Roland Barthes, Jean Baudrillard, Henri Raymond, etc.

Levels and Dimensions

1 [Editors' note: An allusion to Arthur Schopenhauer's *Die Welt als Wille und Vorstellung*, whose French title is *Le Monde comme volonté et comme representation*.]
2 [Editors' note: Wiltold Gombrowicz (1904–69), Polish writer, known for his short stories, *A Recollection of Adolescence* (1933) and the novel *Pornography* (1960).]
3 This grid was constructed and tested on the highly unusual urban space of Kyoto, Japan, where the architecture and town planning services were kind enough to provide the author with useful information on history, land-holdings, demography, etc. In the course of an all too short visit to Japan (about two months), he attempted (in a first, rough version, obviously) to make a study of its urban and architectural space, on the basis of western analytical categories. The possibilities of such a study, involving on the one hand knowledge of ideograms and the associated time-space, and on the other, familiarity with the Asiatic mode of production and of China, etc., were no more than glimpsed. It is about an historic space, pre-capitalist and pre-industrial, but highly complex.

The work announced here and devoted to analysis of space (or, rather, time-space) will treat:

a) the principle of interaction, interpenetration and *superimposition* of spaces (journeys),
b) the concepts of *multifunctionality* and the *transfunctional*,

c) the dialectic of centrality,
d) the contradictions of space,
e) the concept of the *production* of space of (time-space) etc.

Following this series of links (moving from the abstract to the concrete, from the logistical to a dialectical exploration of the contradictions of space, will we be able to speak of an epistemology of town planning? Perhaps, but with reservations. The creation of supposedly definitive 'cores' or 'centres' of knowledge is never without dangers. Rational solidity and 'purity' lead to a curious form of segregation, on the level of theory itself.

4   See A[natole] Kopp, *Ville et révolution* ([Paris:] Éditions Anthropos, 1968). [Editors' note: tr. Thomas E. Burton, *Town and Revolution: Soviet Architecture and Town Planning 1917–1935* (London: Thames & Hudson, 1970).]
5   [Editors' note: Lorraine is a region of France bordering on Germany; Dunkirk is a port on the English Channel; Mauritania was a French colony until 1960; Moureux is a town in the French Pyrenees, founded in 1958 and heavily reliant on natural gas. Lefebvre discusses Moureux in detail in 'Notes on the New Town (April 1960)' in *Introduction to Modernity: Twelve Preludes*, tr. John Moore (London: Verso, 1995).]
6   [Editors' note: Yona Friedman (1923–), Hungarian architect, author of *L'Architecture Mobile* [Mobile Architecture] (1957) where the occupier and not the building is mobile.]
7   [Editors' note: Walter Gropius (1883–1969) was an architect and founder of the Bauhaus school, who moved from Germany when the Nazis came to power. He became a Harvard Professor.]
8   [Editors' note: Friedman was also the creator of the notion of a 'spatial city', where planning is in three dimensions, with cities built over unusable land or existing cities.]
9   Texts taken from the Manifesto of 1919, the catalogue and the Bauhaus review (no. 4, 1928), collected for the Bauhaus exhibition at the Musée d'Art moderne, Paris, 1969. [Editors' note: Hans Meyer (1889–1954) was a Swiss architect, who drew criticism for his Communist views. The texts can be found in *Bauhaus 1919–1928*, eds. Herbert Bayer, Walter Gropius and Ise Gropius (New York: Museum of Modern Art, 1938).]
10 [Editors' note: See Karl Marx, 'Postface to the Second Edition', *Capital: A Critique of Political Economy Volume I*, tr. Ben Fowkes (Harmondsworth: Penguin, 1976), p. 103, where he suggests that with Hegel the dialectic 'is standing on its head. It must be inverted, in order to discover the rational kernel within the mystical shell'.]
11 [Editors' note: Ivan Petrovich Pavlov (1849–1936), Russian physiologist, best known for the salivating dog experiments, showing what he called conditioned reflexes.]
12 These remarks are directed at Roger Garaudy and his 'Marxist humanism' as well as Louis Althusser (*Pour Marx*) and Lucien Sève (*Marxisme et théorie de la personnalité*), etc. It is especially curious to trace in Marxist (so-called Marxist) thought the consequences of the 'philosophizing' attitude, the efforts to maintain and sustain it, to preserve its abstraction as the *private property* of an apparatus, (which thus maintains the private property of ideas). [Editors' note: Roger Garaudy (1914–) was a leading theorist for the PCF. He later converted to Islam and has more recently written works which challenge accepted views of the Holocaust. Althusser's book *Pour Marx* (Paris: François Maspero, 1965), is translated by Ben Brewster as *For Marx* (London: NLB, 1969). Sève's *Marxisme et théorie de la personnalité* (Paris: Éditions Sociales, 1969), is translated by David Pavett, *Marxism and the Theory of Human Personality* (London: Lawrence & Wishart, 1975).]

Is not to study social relations without taking into consideration places (occupied by these relations) and (material) morphology, pure *idealism*? The attitude of these philosophers who call themselves materialists can only be explained by the ideological power of the apparatus. [Editors' note: Althusser's essay 'Ideology and Ideological State Apparatuses' first appeared the same year, 1970, in *La Pensée*.]

The Other Parises

1 [Editors' note: A reference to Jean-Jacques Rousseau, *Rêveries du promeneur solitaire* (*Reveries of the Solitary Walker*) (1778).]
2 [Editors' note: These give the east, west, north and south limits of the area.]
3 [Editors' note: The *Palais de Justice* is on the Île de la Cité in the middle of the Seine.]
4 [Editors' note: The Marais – literally the 'marsh' – on the right bank of the Seine, was uninhabitable until drained in the thirteenth century.]
5 [Editors' note: The Louvre is on the right bank; the ministerial district directly opposite over the river.]
6 [Editors' note: Apart from les Invalides, a hospital built for injured soldiers, and the Champ-de-Mars these are on the right bank.]
7 [Editors' note: Both these roads head north-east from Île de la Cité.]
8 [Editors' note: The rue du Faubourg Saint-Antoine runs between Place de la Bastille and Place de la Nation on the right bank, on the east side of the city. In the fifteenth century the King exempted craftsmen in this area from corporate control. Montmartre is to the north, Belleville to the north-east. Georges, Baron Haussmann (1809–91), was Prefect of the Seine under Napoleon III, and rebuilt much of Paris. His broad streets were partly designed for troops and artillery, and he built barracks in strategic places to control the working classes. He constructed the Parc des Buttes-Chaumont in the area of Belleville.]
9 [Editors' note: Les Halles – previously a working-class quarter and market area – was extensively rebuilt in the 1970s and 1980s. Lefebvre wrote this piece right at the beginning of this redevelopment. La Défense – named after the 1870 defence of Paris – is another area which has undergone substantial development: much of it, including *La Grande Arche*, long after Lefebvre wrote this piece.]
10 [Editors' note: Rue des Archives runs from the Hôtel de Ville through the Marais.]
11 [Editors' note: Rue d'Assas runs past the Jardin du Luxembourg gardens and the University of Paris V.]
12 [Editors' note: Rue Monsieur is just south of les Invalides.]
13 [Editors' note: Also known as the 'Maison de Verre' [House of Glass], the house of Dr Dalsace (a gynaecologist), was designed by Pierre Chareau (1883–1950) in the Internationalist Style. The rue Saint-Guillaume is near St Germaine de Prés on the edge of university district.]
14 [Editors' note: This is in an area filled with ministries, south of the Assemblée Nationale.]
15 [Editors' note: Belleville and Couronnes are on line two, in the north east of the city.]

HISTORY, TIME AND SPACE

Introduction

1 Friedrich Nietzsche, *Thus Spoke Zarathustra*, tr. Walter Kaufmann in *The Portable Nietzsche* (Harmondsworth: Penguin, 1954); Martin Heidegger, *Nietzsche*, tr. David Farrell Krell, Frank Capuzzi and Joan Stambaugh (San Francisco: HarperCollins, 4 vols., 1991 [1961]), esp. vol. II.
2 Rob Shields, *Lefebvre, Love and Struggle: Spatial Dialectics* (London: Routledge, 1999).
3 *Hegel, Marx, Nietzsche ou le royamme des ombres* (Paris: Castermann, 1975); see above, pp. 61–76.
4 Daniel Bell, *The End of Ideology: On the Exhaustion of Political Ideas in the Fifties* (Illinois: Free Press of Glencoe, 1960).

5 Francis Fukuyama, 'The End of History?', *The National Interest, Summer 1989; The End of History and the Last Man* (Harmondsworth: Penguin, 1992).
 6 *L'Irruption de Nanterre au sommet* (Paris: Éditions Syllepse, 1998 [1968]); translated by Alfred Ehrenfeld as *The Explosion: Marxism and the French Upheaval* (New York: Modern Reader, 1969).
 7 Kristin Ross, *The Emergence of Social Space: Rimbaud and the Paris Commune* (Minneapolis: University of Minnesota Press, 1988).
 8 *Critique de la vie quotidienne*, vol. II (Paris: L'Arche, 1961), p. 20, in which in the context of a discussion of everyday life and feminine reality, Lefebvre brings up the concept of ambiguity and the persistence of cyclical time, of cosmic and biological origins, at the heart of the linear time of technology.
 9 Henri Lefebvre and Catherine Régulier, *La Revolution n'est plus ce qu'elle était* (Hallier: Éditions Libres, 1978).
 10 *Rhythmanalysis: Space, Time and Everyday Life*, tr. Stuart Elden and Gerald Moore (London: Continuum, forthcoming).

The Inventory

 1 [Editors' note: Mouvement Républicain Populaire – French Christian-Democratic party between 1944 and 1968.]
 2 [Editors' note: Bertolt Brecht (1898–1956), German playwright. The reference is probably to his *The Caucasian Chalk Circle* (1948).]
 3 [Editors' note: Boris Pasternak (1890–1960), Russian novelist. The reference is to the banning of his *Dr Zhivago* (1957), and his expulsion from the Soviet Writers' Union.]
 4 [Editors' note: Henri-Frédéric Amiel (1821–81) was a writer and critic, best known for his *Journal Intime* (1883). We have been unable to find out whether he made such a comment.]
 5 [Editors' note: An *aliéné* is someone who is alienated, but also a mental patient.]

Time and History

 1 [Editors' note: A reference to Hegel, *Lectures on the Philosophy of World History* (*Vorlesungen über die Philosophie der Weltgeschichte*).]
 2 [Editors' note: Karl Marx, 'Critique of the Gotha Programme' in *The First International and After: Political Writings Volume 3*, ed. David Fernbach (Harmondsworth: Penguin, 1974), esp. sec. IV, pp. 354–8.]
 3 [Editors' note: The Blessed Isles appear in Nietzsche's *Thus Spoke Zarathustra*.]
 4 [Editors' note: *Le Nationalisme contre les nations* (Paris: Éditions Sociales Internationales, 1937; 2ᵉ édn, Paris: Méridiens Klincksieck, 1988) was an early book of Lefebvre's.]
 5 [Editors' note: The first moon landing, 20 July 1969, was around the time Lefebvre wrote this book, first published in 1970.]
 6 [Editors' note: This word, much used by Nietzsche (and later Heidegger) is usually translated as 'to overcome' or 'to surmount'.]
 7 [Editors' note: This word, much used by Hegel and Marx, has a range of meanings, including 'to lift up', 'to preserve' and 'to cancel'. It is sometimes translated as 'to supercede' or 'to sublate', and is intended to capture dialectical transformation.]
 8 [Editors' note: See the footnote to 'Critique of Everyday Life', above, p. 264.]
 9 See 'The Critique of the Gotha Programme'.

The Style of the Commune

1 [Editors' note: Whilst we are translating fête by 'festival' this is not completely satisfactory. Lefebvre uses the term in a number of places, notably his work on everyday life, on Rabelais, here on the Commune, and later in *Right to the City*, and his analysis of May 1968. The *fête* is the antithesis of commodity value and its products and the compliment of creativity and the '*oeuvre*', and is therefore related to the project of recovery and reappropriation of the everyday, of space and of the city. Alternatives to 'festival' – themselves not perfect either – would be 'festivities' or 'feast'. The word *fête* has braided together formal and informal elements. It is both party and commemoration, often spontaneous and revolutionary.]
2 [Editors' note: 18 March 1871 was the day Adolpe Thiers, President of the Third Republic, sent troops to Montmartre to retake cannons that had been kept there. A crowd resisted and murdered two generals which led to the evacuation of the city by the government and their troops. It is looked at as the beginning of the Commune.]
3 Let us say immediately that we are well aware of the role of Versailles in the blazes of Bloody Week. [Editors' note: Bloody Week (*la Semaine sanglante*) – 21–27 May 1871 – is the name given to the retaking of Paris by the government in exile in Versailles.]
4 [Editors' note: This is more likely a reference to Wilhelm Liebknecht (1826–1900), German revolutionary and correspondent of Marx, than to Karl Liebknecht (1871–1919), his son, who, along with Rosa Luxemburg led the 1919 'Spartacus Uprising' in Berlin, during which he was killed. The source of the quotation is unknown.]

The Rhythmanalytical Project

1 [Editors' note: Henri Lefebvre, *Éléments de rythmanalyse: Introduction à la connaissance de rythmes* (Paris: Éditions Syllepse, 1992); *Rhythmanalysis: Space, Time and Everyday Life*, tr. Stuart Elden and Gerald Moore (London: Continuum, forthcoming).]
2 [Editors' note: In Hegel's philosophy, logic, the conceptual, is mental and internal. Nature is physical and external. Spirit, *Geist*, which is their unity, has overcome these dualities, and is therefore both mental and physical, internal and external.]
3 [Editors' note: The standard source for Protagoras's statement is Plato, *Theaetetus*, tr. Robin A. H. Waterfield (Harmondsworth: Penguin, 1987), 152a.]

The Worldwide Experience

1 [Editors' note: Lefebvre's usage of these terms presents serious problems for a translator. In our contemporary parlance, it is tempting to resort to the language of global, globality and globalization. However, these are words of recent coinage in English, and Lefebvre himself carefully distinguished between his use of *global* and *mondial*. Accordingly, we have tried to render words with the root of '*monde*' with variations on the English 'world'. Where there might be confusion we have included the French in brackets.]
2 See the book by A. Mattelart already mentioned and the 'Radio-Alice' collective, Bologna, 1976. [Editors' note: Armand Mattelart, *Multinationales et systèmes de communications* (Paris: Anthropos, 1976); translated by Michael Chanan as *Multinational Corporations and the Control of Culture: The Ideological Apparatuses of Imperialism* (Brighton: Harvester Press, 1979); Collective A/Traverso, *Alice è il diavolo: sulla strada di Majakovskij: testi per una pratica di comunicazione sovversiva* (Milano: L'Erba Voglio, 1976); translated by Danièle Guillerm and G. Marco Montesano as *Radio Alice, radio libre*, preface by Félix

Guattari (Paris: Jean-Pierre Delarge, 1977). Radio Alice was a pirate radio station set up to challenge the state and capitalism. It broadcast a mix of music, left-wing and other radical news, and phone-ins. It was raided by the police and the organizers imprisoned. A manifesto appears as 'Radio Alice-Free Radio', tr. Richard Gardner and Sybil Walker in Sylvère Lotringer and Christian Marazzi (eds.) *Italy: Autonomia* (New York: Semiotext(e), 1980), vol. III, no. 3, pp. 133–4.]
3 [Editors' note: The right to use and profit from property belonging to another.]
4 [Editors' note: 'Welt *ist* nie, sondern *weltet*' – 'world never *is*, but *worlds*'. See 'Vom Wesen des Grundes' in *Wegmarken* (Frankfurt am Main: Vittorio Klostermann, 1967), p. 60; 'On the Essence of Ground', tr. William McNeill in *Pathmarks* (Cambridge: Cambridge University Press, 1998), p. 126.]
5 See *Le Principe de raison* [tr. André Preau (Paris: Gallimard, 1962)], last pages. [Editors' note: *Der Satz vom Grund* (Pfullingen: Günther Neske, 1957), pp. 186–8; *The Principle of Reason*, tr. Reginald Lilly (Bloomington: Indiana University Press, 1991), pp. 111–13. The quotes are from pp. 187–8/113 (something of a loose paraphrase for the first). The French *disposition*, which has been translated as 'dispensation', is a very limited translation of the German *Geschick*, which is related to *Geschichte*, history, and might be better rendered in English as 'destiny' or 'sending'. The Heraclitus fragment is number 52, translated by Jonathan Barnes as 'Eternity is a child at play, playing draughts: the kingdom is a child's', *Early Greek Philosophy* (Harmondsworth: Penguin, 1987), p. 102.]
6 See K[onstas] Axelos, *Le Jeu du monde* ([Paris:] Editions de Minuit, 1965).
7 [Editors' note: 'The philosophers have only *interpreted* the world, in various ways; the point is to *change* it' – Karl Marx, 'Theses on Feuerbach' in *The German Ideology*, ed. C. J. Arthur (London: Lawrence & Wishart, 1970), p. 123.]
8 [Editors' note: *Terricide* is Lefebvre's term for the death of the earth.]
9 [Editors' note: SMP [MPE] is an abbreviation of State Mode of Production (*le Mode de Production Étatique*). Lefebvre discusses this in *De l'État-3: Le mode de production étatique* (Paris: Collection 10/18, Union Générale d'Éditions, 1977); and 'Comments on a New State Form', tr. Victoria Johnson and Neil Brenner, *Antipode*, 33: 5 (November 2001), pp. 769–82. The SMP is a notion designed to understand the state's taking control of production, as a critique of Stalinism and state socialism, fascism with its economic and political plans, but also social liberalism with attempts at some redistribution without addressing the underlying issues (i.e. the state appropriation of the result of exploitation).]
10 [Editors' note: António Salazar (1889–1970) was Portuguese dictator until 1968. When he died the dictatorship swiftly collapsed, with elections in 1976. The 'Prince' is presumably an allusion to Machiavelli's book. The Chilean government of Salvador Allende was overthrown in 1973 by the army led by General Augusto Pinochet. Pinochet declared an 'authoritarian democracy' in 1976.]
11 [Editors' note: 'Politics means slow, strong drilling through hard boards, with a combination of passion and a sense of judgement. It is of course entirely correct, and a fact confirmed by all historical experience, that what is possible would never have been achieved if, in this world, people had not repeatedly reached for the impossible.' Max Weber, 'The Profession and Vocation of Politics' in *Political Writings*, ed. Peter Lassman and Ronald Speirs (Cambridge: Cambridge University Press, 1994).]

Preface to the New Edition

1 [Editors' note: While Lefebvre refers to the Délégation à l'Aménagement du térritoire et des regions, this is actually a reference to the Délégation à l'Aménagement du Térritoire et à l'action Régionale, which was set up in 1963.]

2 [Editors' note: The Sienese School was a school of Italian painting between the thirteenth and fifteenth centuries, producing late Gothic religious art. Although some of its artists utilized perspective, the invention of perspective is more commonly associated with the Florentine school.]
3 [Editors' note: See p. 268, n. 3 and p. 270 n. 7 in 'The Country and the City' on Le Corbusier and Gropius.]
4 See *Logique formelle, logique dialectique*, 3ᵉ édn ([Paris:] Messidor, 1981). [Editors' note: Most bibliographies – and the book itself – says the date was 1982 rather than 1981.]
5 Benoit Mandelbrot (1924–), mathematician, probably best known for his *Fractal Geometry of Nature* (1982).]
6 See *La Recherche,* November 1985, pp. 1313ff.; and also Paul Virilio's *L'Espace éclaté.* [Editors' note: Estelle Asseo, 'Le rayonnement des pulsars', *La Recherche*, 171 (Novembre 1985), pp. 1314–23. Virilio's book is not listed in bibliographies of his work, and is likely to be a reference to *L'Espace critique* (Paris: Christian Bourgeois, 1984).]

POLITICS

Introduction

1 Michel Trebitsch, 'Le Renouveau philosophique avorté des années trente. Entretien avec Henri Lefebvre', *Europe*, édition spéciale, 'Arts et litérature', 683 (1986), pp. 29–41, esp. p. 37.
2 Norbert Guterman and Henri Lefebvre, *La Conscience mystifiée* (Paris: Syllepse, 1999 [1936]).
3 Guterman and Lefebvre, *La Conscience mystifiée*, p. 36.
4 Henri Lefebvre, *Le Nationalisme contre les nations.* (Paris: Éditions Sociales Internationales, 1937); see also his *Hitler au pouvoir: Bilan de cinq années de fascisme en Allemagne* (Paris: Bureau d'Éditions, 1938).
5 Henri Lefebvre, *Le Temps des méprises* (Paris: Stock, 1975).
6 Henri Lefebvre et le Groupe de Navarrenx, *Du Contrat de citoyenneté* (Paris: Syllepse, 1990).

Nation and Culture

1 [Editors' note: Honoré, Comte de Mirabeau (1749–91) was a member of the National Assembly, and was elected its president in January 1791, but died later that year. Paul, Comte de Barras (1755–1829) was principally responsible for the overthrow of Robespierre, became a member of the Directory and virtual dictator of the Republic. He was overthrown by Napoleon, a one time friend.]
2 [Editors' note: Johann Gottlieb Fichte (1762–1814) was a philosopher, a friend and disciple of Kant. He is best known for his *Science of Knowledge*, *Science of Rights*, and *Science of Ethics*. His *Addresses to the German Nation* were an attempt to resist Napoleon's dominance of Europe.]
3 [Editors' note: This could be a reference to 'Young Germany' – a semi-revolutionary nationalist movement.]
4 'Under the rule of Napoleon, the German bourgeoisie pursued to an even greater degree their petty trade and their great illusions. The German bourgeois, who cursed Napoleon for compelling them to drink chicory and for disturbing their peace with military billeting and recruiting of conscripts, reserved all their moral indignation for Napoleon and all their admiration for England; yet Napoleon rendered them the greatest services by

cleaning out Germany's Augean stables and re-establishing civilized means of communication, whereas the English only waited for the opportunity to exploit them unabashed. In the same petty-bourgeois spirit the German princes imagined they were fighting for the principle of legitimism and against revolution, whereas they were only the paid mercenaries of the English bourgeoisie. In the middle of these universal illusions it was quite in the order of things that the professions [*die Stände*] privileged to cherish illusions – ideologists, school-masters, students, members of the virtuous associations [*die Tugendbündler*] – should talk big and give a suitable high-flown expression to the universal mood of mystification [*Phantasterei*] and indifference', Marx and Engels, *Die Deutsche Ideologie*, Gesamtausgabe, 1, 5, pp. 177–8 [Editors' note: Marx and Engels, *The German Ideology*, ed. C. J. Arthur (London: Lawrence & Wishart, 1970), pp. 99–100. Whilst I generally have followed the translation used by Arthur, some changes have been made to bring it closer to the points Lefebvre is emphasizing. Interpolations in the quotation are Lefebvre's own. *Die Tugendbündler*, 'League of Virtue', was a patriotic secret society.]

5 [Editors' note: When Engelbert Dollfuss (1892–1934) become Chancellor of Austria in 1932, he attempted to preserve Austrian independence from an *Anschluß* with Germany because of his opposition to National Socialism. He was supported by the Italians under Mussolini, and moved toward a version of fascism. Dollfuss was assassinated by the Nazis in 1934, who finally seized Austria in 1938.]

6 [Editors' note: Camillo di Cavour (1810–61) was the Prime Minister of Piedmont-Sardinia in the 1850s and early 1860s. He resisted Garibaldi's attempts to turn Southern Italy into a Republic and assisted Victor Emmanuel II in becoming the first king of a unified Italy.]

7 [Editors' note: Eugene Schneider was president of the French Schneider-Creusot Company, which made armaments across Europe, and was a supporter of Hitler. Gustav Krupp (1870–1950) was the head of the Krupp industrial empire until 1943. He armed the German Reich in World War I and was a financial supporter of Hitler. He was central to Germany's rearmament in the 1930s.]

8 [Editors' note: The Montagnards were a political group during the French Revolution. They were closely associated with Robespierre.]

9 [Editors' note: Charles Pierre Péguy (1873–1914) was a writer, a Catholic, socialist and nationalist. Maurice Barrès (1862–1923) was a writer and nationalist politician.]

10 [Editors' note: The *Entente Cordiale* (friendly understanding) was an agreement between Britain and France, originally concerned with interests in North Africa.]

11 [Editors' note: Alsace-Lorraine, region in North East France, conquered by Germany in 1871, and returned in 1919 at the Treaty of Versailles.]

12 [Editors' note: With the exception of Schneider-Creusot, these are all German industrialists or companies. On Schneider-Creusot and Krupp see note 7 above. Fritz Thyssen (1873–1951) was the head of the Thyssen iron and steel company; I. G. Farben was a chemical and dye works.]

13 [Editors' note: Michel de Montaigne (1533–92), is best known for his *Essays*. Denis Diderot (1713–84) was a writer and playwright, and responsible for the *Encyclopaedia*. Lefebvre wrote a study of him: *Diderot* (Paris: Editions Hier et Aujourd'hui, 1949, 2e édn, *Diderot ou les Affirmations fondamentales du matérialisme*, Paris: L'Arche, 1983). Maurice Barrès (1862–1923) was a writer and nationalist politician.]

14 [Editors' note: Jeanne Pompadour (1721–64) was ennobled by Louis XV, and influenced his policy. Jean Racine (1639–99) was a dramatist and poet.]

15 [Editors' note: Heinrich Heine (1797–1856) was a German writer who lived in France, and attempted to improve relations between the two countries.]

16 [Editors' note: The Twenty-Five Points were the original political manifesto of the NSDAP, announced by Hitler on 24 February 1920. The first point called for a union of all Germans, based on the principle of self-determination, to form a Greater Germany.]

Being a Communist

1 [Editors' note: The title of this section is 'Etre Communiste'. As a verb, *être* can mean both 'to be' and 'being', and can also be a noun, *un être*, 'a being'. Lefebvre plays with these meanings throughout.]
2 [Editors' note: A reference to the Soviet overthrow of the reforming government of Imre Nagy in 1956.]

From the Social Pact to the Contract of Citizenship

1 [Editors' note: Dialectical materialism, particularly in its Stalinist form.]
2 [Editors' note: A word is missing from the French text at this point.]
3 [Editors' note: Marie, Marquis de Condorcet (1743–94) was a mathematician and politician. He became President of the Assembly in 1794, but is perhaps best known for his mathematical work, which is sometimes used to support Rousseau's idea of the General Will.]
4 [Editors' note: The Prime Minister was Felipe Gonzalez; the Spanish Socialist Party is abbreviated as PSOE in what follows. On this affair, see Olivier Russbach, *La déraison d'État* (Paris: Éditions La Decouverte, 1987).]
5 [Editors' note: 'I shall be asked if I am a prince or legislator, to write on politics. I answer that I am neither, and that is why I do so. If I were a prince or a legislator, I should not waste my time in saying what wants doing; I should do it, or hold my peace.' Jean-Jacques Rousseau, *The Social Contract* in *The Social Contract and the Discourses*, tr. G. D. H. Cole (London: Dent, 1973), p. 165.]
6 [Editors' note: *Le Mémorial de Sainte-Hélène* was written by Count Emmanuel de Las Cases (1766–1842) in 1823, and commemorates Napoleon's last years on the Island of St. Helena.]
7 See Crampe Carnabet, *Condorcet*, PUF, 1986, p. 39.
8 [Editors' note: Josef Stalin, 'Marxism and the National Question' in *Works* (Moscow: Foreign Languages Publishing House, 1954), vol. 2, pp. 300–81.]
9 [Editors' note: Lenin established the Third International, on the model of the first and second, in 1919. It aimed to promote communism on the world stage. Stalin dissolved it in 1943, claiming that it was not possible to coordinate internationally. This was the doctrine of socialism in one country, as opposed to Trotsky's idea of world revolution.]
10 [Editors' note: A reference to Hegel's teleological view of history – the introduction to his *Philosophy of World History* is sometimes called 'Reason in History'.]
11 [Editors' note: See 'Marxism and Philosophy', above, p. 261, n. 6.]
12 [Editors' note: The idea of a 'new world' appears regularly in *Wilhelm Meister's Apprenticeship*, for example 'Shakespeare's plays had opened a whole new world', bk IV, ch. I (*Goethe's Collected Works*, vol. 9; New York: Suhrkamp, 1989, p. 121).]
13 [Editors' note: See *Le Droit à la ville* (Paris: Éditions Anthropos, 1968); tr. 'Right to the City' in *Writings on Cities*, tr. and ed. by Eleonore Kofman and Elizabeth Lebas (Oxford: Blackwell, 1996).]

Some Questions About Asking Questions

1 [Editors' note: The French is '*le (la) logique*' – a formulation on the lines of politics and the political.]
2 [Editors' note: Ernst Bloch (1885–1977) is best known for *The Principle of Hope*, tr. by Neville Plaice, Stephen Plaice and Paul Knight (Oxford: Basil Blackwell, 3 vols., 1986).]

Index

absence 55
  and pathology 56
  and presence 51–6, 132
  representation 53
abstract, the 94
abstractions 58
Adorno, T. 93, 94, 239
adulthood 138–9
  myth of 105–6
advertising 105
agrarian capitalism 112–13, 118
agrarian civilization (or regime),
    France 115–16
agrarian reform 112
agricultural development 119
alienation 14, 75, 82–3, 218, 240
  and cities 143
  and de-alienation 84, 181
  and the theory of moments 175–6
Althusser, Louis 39
  criticism of 38
anarchism 10, 235
appropriation 130–31, 181–2
  and cities 130
  of space 131–2
archaic and modern, in agriculture 112–13
archaic systems 23
architecture 142
Au-delà de structuralisme 4, 37–41
Les Autres Paris 110
Avant Poste 69
  'Notes for a Critique of Everyday life'
    71–83
Axelos, K. 201

Bachelard, Gaston 122
balance 52
Barthes, Roland 102, 133
Bauhaus 210
Becoming 16, 17, 18, 19–21, 65, 66, 178
Being 18, 19, 49, 200
  and communism 237
Being and Nothingness, Sartre 11
Bell, Daniel, *The End of Ideology* 163

belonging 249–50
Berque, Jacques 127
binary approach 65–6
Bloch, Mark 115
blockage 52
bourgeois revolutionaries 77–8
bourgeois thought 71
  unity of 72–5
bourgeois values 75–7
bourgeoisie 222, 223
  decline 93

Cahiers Internationaux de Sociologie
  XIV 111–20
  XXXIII 100
Camus, A., *The Myth of Sisyphus* 10–11
capital 31–2, 76
Capital, Marx 17
  form, function and structure in 38–9
capitalism 6, 8, 9, 31, 77–8, 82–3, 180,
    222, 224
  and agriculture 118
catastrophe hypothesis 184
centrality 146
centralized planning, failure 203–4
chance 54
change 34
childhood 105, 138
choice, and existentialism 8–9, 11
Chombart de Lauwe, J. 113
cities 89–90, 110, 122, 128–9, 137–8,
    143–4, 208
  and alienation 143
  and appropriation 130
  arguments against 143
  right to 253
citizen, new rights of 250–51
'civil society' 42, 245
civilization 171, 172
  and Nietzsche 44
class 9, 26, 35, 73–4, 157, 185, 242
  in the countryside 120
'class logics' 136
colonization 114

Communications, 41   190
communications model   88
communism   180, 231–7
  and being   237
  defined   234
  in France   235
  and Marxism   231–3, 236
competitive capitalism   32–3
La Conscience mystifiée   69, 102, 217, 220–28, 229–30
consciousness   80, 86, 197, 229–30
  Sartre on   11–12
consumer society   106
content   52
continuity, and rural life   116
creative capacity   22–3
Critique de la vie quotidienne (Critique of Everyday Life)   69–70
  II   88–92, 164
  III   93–5, 96–9
Critique of Dialectical Reason   109
Critique of the Gotha Programme, Marx   46, 180
culture   171, 207
  and Nation   220–28
  right to   252
CUMA (French agricultural equipment cooperatives)   113
cycles   192–3
cynicism   6

databases   251
De l'Etat   164, 199–205
de-alienation, and alienation   84, 181
Déclaration des droits de l'Esprit   6
Declaration of Rights   246
declarations   246–50
democracy   249
Depression   78
desire   48
detached houses   129, 130
deviations   85
dialectic   57
Dialectical Materialism   3, 4, 14–21
dialectical materialism   12, 230
dialectical thinking   57, 58
dialectics   4
Dialectics of Nature, Engels   17–18
differences   179
distinction   96
divergence   179
diversity   74
division of labour   26

Dollfuss   226
domination   130
Le Droit à la ville   110, 151
Du Contract de citoyenneté   238–254
Du Rural à l'urbain   109
Duhamel, G.   72
dwelling   122, 139
dyads   50

Eiffel Tower   152
Elle   101
The Emergence of Social Space, Ross   164
The End of Ideology, Bell   163
Engels, F., *Dialectics of Nature*   17–18
ephemeral, the   147
escapism   10
Espaces et Sociétés   110, 151–9
Europe
  agriculture   114
  ruptures, dissolutions and destructions   24–5
events   178–9
everyday, definition   100
everyday life   69–70
  myths in   100–106
  and rhythms   190–93
existence   11, 16
existentialism   4
  and choice   8–9, 11
  and faith   8–9
existentialist movement   6
existentialist philosophers   7–8
experience, worldwide   199–205

facades   155–6
factories   92
faith, and existentialism   8–9
family   104–5
  Engels on   22
  Marx on   36
Fascism   217–18, 220, 227–8
fetishism, in Marx's work   82–3
feudalism   118
fideism   8
La Fin de l'histoire   163, 177–87
'for itself' concept   12
forces of production   225, 226
form   171
  in *Capital*   38–9
forms
  large constituted   23–4
  systems and structures, unequal development   22–7

Fourier, C. 27, 46
fractal object theory 212
fragmented space 212–13
France
　agrarian civilization (or regime) 115–16
　communism in 235
　revolution 221–3
freedom, existentialist conceptions 9, 11
freedom of expression, rights to 251
French Declaration 246
French Revolution 245
　and Marxism 241–2, 247
Freud, S. 3, 47–8, 97, 98, 102
Friedman, Y. 145, 147
Fukuyama, F. 163
function, in *Capital* 38–9

games 167–8
The Gay Science, Nietzsche 56
The German Ideology, Marx 32
German National Socialism, and Nietzsche 46–7
Germany 228
　nationalism 224
Gide, A. 9
global level 136, 137, 141
globalization 164
Greece 23–4
Gropius, W.A. 148, 210
Groupe de Navarrenx 218
Guterman, Norbert 102, 217

'habitat' 121
L'Habitat pavillonnaire 121–35
habitation 123–5, 126, 127, 128, 138, 139, 141, 142
happiness 94
Harvey, David 110
Haumont, Nicole 131, 132
Hegel, G. W. F. 3–4, 14, 20–21, 186, 192, 248
　and the negative 93–4
　and State 44, 45
Hegel, Marx, Nietzsche 4, 42–9
Hegelianism 15–16, 42, 43
Heidegger, Martin 3, 4, 49, 122, 163, 182, 200
Heraclitus 57, 239
'historical materialism' 32, 33, 34
history 85, 181, 184–5
　Marx on 33–4
　meaning of 182–3

and sociology 115
　worldwide ('Weltgeschichte') 179–80
homogenization 179, 185, 186
houses 122
housing 109–10, 122–3
housing estates 129, 130, 133
human development, history 26–7
human nature, meaning of 166
humanism 14

identity 59
identity within difference, right to 252
ideologies 72
ideology 39, 40, 259–60
　of the *pavillon* 133–4
'in itself' concept 12
industrialization 145, 179, 182
information 238
　rights to 251
information theory 88–9
innocence 80, 82
Institut de Sociologie Urbaine 123
institutional space 137
interviews 127–8
irreducibles 29–30

The Jewish Question, Marx 46
justice 168–9, 172

Knopf, A. A., *Rural Life in the USA* 113–14
knowledge 19, 54, 71, 99
　materialist theory of 72
Kopp, A. 110

Labica, G. 69
landscape 89
language 125–6, 127, 226
large constituted forms 23–4
Lassalle, Ferdinand 248
Lebenswelt ('the lived' or 'lifeworld') concept 69
Lefebvre, Henri
　at CNRS 109
　as historian 164
　and Marxism 217
　and politics 217
　as a sociologist 69
　as taxi driver 7
Lefebvre, Love and Struggle, Shields 163
Lenin, V. I. 3, 228
L'Etre et le néant, Sartre 12
levels and dimensions 136–50

L'Existentialisme 4, 6–13
Liebknecht, W. 189
Llach, Lluís 243
logic 57–8, 259
  and capitalist production 60
logical empiricism 60
logical form (identity) 59
logics 136, 140
Logique formelle, Logique dialectique 4, 57–60
love 76, 77, 101, 102, 139, 167, 171, 175
Lukács, G. 93, 94
Luxembourg, Rosa 242

M: *Mensuel, Marxisme, Mouvement* 218–19, 258–60
Machiavelli 244
Mallarmé, S. 73
Mandelbrot, B. 212
Le Manifeste de 'Philosophies' 4
Manuel de sociologie rurale 109
Mao Tse-Tung 3, 203
Marx, K. 3, 85, 201
  as an economist 31
  Capital 17, 31, 32, 35, 36, 40
  Critique of the Gotha Programme 46, 180
  The German Ideology 32
  on history 33–4
  The Jewish Question! 46
  Lefebvre on 31–41
  Manuscript 14
  and society 44
  sociological interpretation 34–5
  and Stalinism 45–6
  use of totality 35
  works of 14
Marxism 40, 42, 78, 97, 98, 149, 203, 209, 245, 248, 258–60
  and communism 231–3, 236
  concepts 240
  and the French Revolution 241–2, 247
  inventory and balance sheet 238–54
  and Lefebvre 217
  the problematic in 241
  themes 240
Marxism and the National Question 247
materialism 14, 15
materialist theory of knowledge 72
Memmi, A. 102
mental illness 54
Merleau-Ponty, M., *Les Temps Modernes* 12

Métaphilosophie 4
Métaphilosophie: Polégomènes 23–30
metaphilosophy 49
metaphysics 71
  critiques of 56
Meyer, Hans 148
middle-classes 96
mimesis 28–9
Mind 21
mixed level 137–8, 141, 143
mobility 145, 146–7
mode of production 210
modern and archaic, in agriculture 112–13
modern art 93
modernity 93–5, 210, 249
moments 170, 172–3, 174–5, 217, 218
moments theory 173
  and alienation 175
monuments 152–3
Mougin, H., on Sartre 9
multinational firms 203
mysticism, critiques of 56
mystification 81–3
myth of adulthood 105–6
The Myth of Sisyphus, Camus 10–11
myths
  in everyday life 100–106
  functions 102–3

nation 217–18
  and culture 220–28
nation-states 42, 63
national consciousness 222
'national revolution' 220
nationalism 221, 225–6
  Germany 224
  USA 223
'naturality' 133
nature 17, 18, 207
  and reason 246
  and society 172
Nazis 46–7, 226
needs 109–110, 121
negative 93, 183
neo-dirigism 137
neo-liberalism 137
new formations 25
new rights of citizens 250–51
Nietzsche, F.W. 3, 4, 180, 186, 201
  and civilization 44
  The Gay Science 56
  and German National Socialism 46–7
  Thus Spoke Zarathustra 163

Nietzscheanism 42–3
Norbert, G. (Mesnil) 7

object, and subject 54–5
order 74
Other, the 51–2, 53, 59, 81

Palmade, Guy 129
paradoxes 60
Paris 7, 110, 151–9
 of business, commerce and production 154–5
 history 155–6, 158
 of knowledge (Latin quarter) 153
 political 153–4
 underground 157, 158
 of wealth and power 156–7
 working class neighbourhoods 157
Paris Commune 46, 164, 178, 179, 188–9
Parti Communiste Française 3
pathology, and absence 56
pavillon, ideology of 133
peasant 'culture' 120
peasants 111, 117–18, 119
perpetuity hypothesis 184
perspective 209–10
philosophy 201–2, 239
play 166–8, 175, 200–201
poetry 169–70
poiesis 22, 27–8
political alienation 217
political power 62, 63
 and the state 61–2
politics, and Lefebvre 217
la politique (the political), and le politique (politics) 4, 61
positive hypothesis 184
praxis 20, 34, 39–40, 150, 171, 172
 definitions 25–7
presence 52, 53
 and absence 51–6, 132
La Présence et l'absence 4, 50–56
private level 138
private life, and public life 84, 86, 100
problematic, in Marxism 241
La Proclamation de la commune 164, 188–9
production 240
The Production of Space 109, 110, 165, 206–13
'proletarinization' 224
Protagoras 197

psychoanalysis 28, 47–9, 97, 102, 182
public life, and private life 84, 86, 100

questionnaires 127

rational planning 130
Raymond, Marie-Geneviève 135
re-creation 168
reality 18, 96, 97, 192
reason, and nature 246
recession 94
regions, Spanish and Italian experience 204
Regulier, Catherine 164
relativity 20
reproduction 208, 240
rest 168
Le Retour de la dialectique 4, 61–4, 65–6
revolution 98, 189, 202, 204, 205, 218, 220
 France 221
 worldwide 199
La Revolution n'est plus ce qu'elle était 164
La Révolution urbaine 110, 136
La Revue Marxiste 7
rhythm, defining 193–8
Rhythmanalysis 69, 164
rhythmanalytical hypothesis 195–6
rhythmanalytical project 190–98
rhythms, and everyday life 190–93
right to
 city 253
 culture 252
 freedom of expression 251
 identity within difference 252
 information 251
 self management 252–3
 services 253
rights 248–9
Rights of Man 247
Rimbaud, A. 74
risk 54
rituals 102, 172
The Roads to Freedom, Sartre 11
Rodinson, Maxime 125
Rome 24
Ross, Kristin, *The Emergence of Social Space* 164
Rousseau, J.-J. 244–6, 246
 and the social contract 244–6
ruptures, dissolutions and destructions, Europe 24–5

rural life
  complexity 112–13
  and continuity 116
Rural life in the USA, Knopf 113–14
rural sociology 109, 111–20
  methods 116–17
  USA 113–14

Saint-Simon, Comte de 46
same 54
  and other 59
Sartre, J.-P. 4
  Being and Nothingness 11
  on consciousness 11–12
  Lefebvre on 12–13
  L'Etre et le néant 12
  Mougin on 9
  The Roads to Freedom 11
scale 197
scientism 39
'Seen from the Window' 110
self-management 204, 218
  right to 252–3
services, right to 253
sexuality 97, 139
sharecropping 117
Shields, Rob, *Lefebvre, Love and Struggle* 163
signals 88
signs 88
sincerity, a critique 79–81
slavery 118
social contract 250
'social mystery' 17
social relations 140, 192
social space 209, 211
social text 88–92
social time 190–91
society
  and Marx 44
  and nature 172
sociology 33–4, 173
  and history 115
  Lefebvre's use of term 69
The Sociology of Marx 3, 4, 31–41
solitude 77
La Somme et le reste 163, 218, 231–7
space 56, 140
  concept of 209
  conceptions 206
  as a social product 207–8
Spanish Socialist Party, case against 243

spatial planning 207
spatiality 163
Stalin, J. 234
  Marxism and the National Question 247
Stalinism, and Marx 45–6
state 61–4, 136, 137, 200, 202–3, 204
  and Hegel 44, 45
  history of 62–4
  and political power 61–2
  war and violence 62–3
  withering away of 86
streets 90–92
structuralism 4, 37–8
structure, in *Capital* 38–9
subject, and object 54–5
'suburbanites' 134
superstitions 102
symbolism 102
symbols 88
Systematics 38

technological alienation 27–8
technology 94, 102, 113, 150, 249
temporality 174
Le Temps des méprises 218
Les Temps Modernes, Merleau-Ponty 12
Third Term 20
time 56, 65, 133, 138, 163, 190
  concept of 177–8
  measurement 191, 193
  use of 191
totality 18, 71
  Marx's use of 35, 36
town planning 121, 147
towns 114
transcending 16–17, 20
transformation 203
transition period 180–81
transitional systems 23
transport 212
triadic (ternary) analysis 66
triads 4, 50–51, 58
Trotsky, L. 242
trust 79

u-topia 186–7
unitary approach 65
universal interdependence 18
upside-down world theory 149
urban phenomena 136–50, 140
  dimensions of 140
urban reform 142

urban space   140
  grid   141
urbanization   109, 144
USA
  colonization   114
  nationalism   223
  rural sociology   113–14
Utopia   86, 132, 133

Vallée de Campan   109
values   76–7, 178–9
Vautel, Clément   72, 73
villages   89, 117, 119, 144
vulgarity   96–9

waves   195, 197
Weber, Max   242
will-to-power   52–3
women   103–4
working class   98, 203
world, concept of   26
worldliness   200, 203–5
worldwide, concept   199–200
worldwide experience   199–205
worldwide history ('Weltgeschichte')   179–80
worldwide markets   201, 203
worldwide revolution   199